MERLEAU-PONTY
AND THE FOUNDATION OF
AN EXISTENTIAL POLITICS

STUDIES IN MORAL, POLITICAL,
AND LEGAL PHILOSOPHY

General Editor: Marshall Cohen

MERLEAU-PONTY AND THE FOUNDATION OF AN EXISTENTIAL POLITICS

Kerry H. Whiteside

PRINCETON UNIVERSITY PRESS
PRINCETON, NEW JERSEY

Published by Princeton University Press, 41 William Street,
Princeton, New Jersey 08540
In the United Kingdom: Princeton University Press, Guildford, Surrey

This book has been composed in Linotron Palatino

Clothbound editions of Princeton University Press books
are printed on acid-free paper, and binding materials are
chosen for strength and durability. Paperbacks, although satisfactory
for personal collections, are not usually suitable for library rebinding

Printed in the United States of America by Princeton University Press,
Princeton, New Jersey

Library of Congress Cataloging-in-Publication Data

Whiteside, Kerry H., 1953–
Merleau-Ponty and the foundation of an existential politics / Kerry H. Whiteside.
p. cm. — (Studies in moral, political, and legal philosophy)
Bibliography: p.   Includes index.
ISBN 0–691–07781–9 (alk. paper) ISBN 0–691–02288–7 (pbk.)
1. Merleau-Ponty, Maurice, 1908–1961—Views on political science.
I. Title. II. Series.
JC261.M47W48 1988   320'.01—dc19   88-12653

CONTENTS

ACKNOWLEDGMENTS

It is a pleasure to acknowledge those whose support made this book possible. Several organizations financially underwrote my research. The Princeton University Committee for European Studies funded two months of exploratory research in France, while another ten months was supported by grants from the Social Science Research Council, the Fulbright-Hays Program, and the French-American Foundation. Princeton University's Charlotte Elizabeth Proctor Fellowship allowed me to write up the first version of this work without the distractions of penury. Franklin and Marshall College granted me a leave that enabled me to revise my manuscript.

In conversation and correspondence, many in France kindly shared their remembrances of Merleau-Ponty with me. Their names are found throughout my work. Thanks also go to the Phonothèque of the ORTF, the Director of the ENS, and the Service des Archives de l'Université de Paris for permission to consult archival materials under their control. I am especially grateful to Mme Susanne Merleau-Ponty. By allowing me to examine her husband's unpublished papers and by helping me to transcribe his often difficult script, she contributed immeasurably to my understanding of the philosopher's work. The gracious welcome she gave a foreign scholar remains among my fondest recollections of a year in Paris.

Professors Sheldon Wolin, Arno Mayer, and Claude Lefort read my work as it evolved and probed and commented on it. Each brought political acumen and interpretive penetration to bear upon my ideas. Comments from Bernard Yack, Scott Warren, James Schmidt, and Peter Caws led me to sharpen many critical points. The typographical assistance of Rose Musser has been invaluable throughout the preparation of this book. Finally, for providing the moral support necessary for writing this book, I have my parents and my wife, Julie Nelson, to thank. To say that this work would have been impossible without the contribution of all of these people is to confirm Merleau-Ponty's own view that whatever truth we have arises in a dialogue that touches every facet of our lives.

ABBREVIATIONS AND SOURCES

References to Merleau-Ponty's most frequently cited works are given in parentheses in the text according to the following system of notation.

AD = *Les aventures de la dialectique;* tr. = *The Adventures of the Dialectic*

BP = *Bulletin de Psychologie: Merleau-Ponty à la Sorbonne*

EP = *Éloge de la philosophie;* tr. = *In Praise of Philosophy*

HT = *Humanisme et terreur;* tr. = *Humanism and Terror*

IN = *Inédits, 1940–1950**

OE = *L'oeil et l'esprit;* tr. *The Eye and the Mind*

PM = *La prose du monde;* tr. = *The Prose of the World*

PP = *La phénoménologie de la perception;* tr. = *The Phenomenology of Perception*

RC = *Résumé de cours, Collège de France;* tr. = *Themes from the Lectures*

S = *Signes;* tr. = *Signs*

SC = *La structure du comportement;* tr. = *The Structure of Behavior*

SNS = *Sens et non-sens;* tr. = *Sense and Non-Sense*

VI = *Le visible et l'invisible;* tr. = *The Visible and the Invisible*

Page numbers immediately follow the abbreviation. Full citations for these works, as well as for the rest of Merleau-Ponty's writings and interviews, are given in the Bibliography. I am responsible for all translations of Merleau-Ponty's works, both published and unpublished.

* *Inédits* refers to Merleau-Ponty's personal, unpublished lecture and reading notes from the 1940s. With the gracious help of Mme Susanne Merleau-Ponty I transcribed these notes and bound them into a volume of 238 pages. I have included the table of contents of this volume in the Bibliography. Any quotation from these materials must, by stipulation of Mme. Merleau-Ponty, indicate that these notes were not intended for publication.

MERLEAU-PONTY
AND THE FOUNDATION OF
AN EXISTENTIAL POLITICS

INTRODUCTION

In his first essay published after the liberation of France, Maurice Merleau-Ponty described with chagrin the facile reasoning with which he had once discounted political affairs. "Before the war," he wrote, "politics seemed to us *unthinkable* because it is a statistical treatment of men, and it makes no sense, we thought, to treat these singular beings . . . as if they were a collection of substitutable objects" (SNS 255, tr. 145, emphasis added). Six years of destruction, foreign occupation, and resistance had shown how vital it was to overcome such naïveté. Making politics "thinkable" was the most urgent problem facing postwar philosophy.

Merleau-Ponty's response to that problem is the focus of this study. I examine his appraisal of the conditions under which an existential theory can make sense of political life, serve as the ground for political choices, and orient political actions.

Better known as a philosopher of perception than as a political theorist,[1] Merleau-Ponty was nonetheless never far from political controversy. Born in 1908, he was part of a generation that twice endured the trauma of total war. It was to combat habits of thought conducive to war that he joined Jean-Paul Sartre in founding *Les Temps Modernes*, a journal dedicated to political commitment. From 1945 to 1950 he worked out his political ideas in articles on topics as diverse as the relation of Marxism and existentialism, the Moscow trials, Machiavelli's views on violence, and the Marshall Plan. His disappointment in the conduct of Communist states made him increasingly critical of revolutionary politics in the 1950s. Still influenced by Hegel and Marx, however, he participated in efforts to establish a "new liberalism" that would leave room for state intervention in a capitalist economy. His tragically premature death in 1961—he was only fifty-three years old—cut short a meditation on the relation of philosophy and politics that, had it been completed, might well have attenuated attacks

---

[1] Maurice de Gandillac lauds him as "the virtually unchallenged teacher of an entire generation" of French philosophy students in "In Memoriam—Maurice Merleau-Ponty," p. 103, while A. J. Ayer regards him as "the best French exponent" of phenomenology. See *Philosophy in the Twentieth Century*, p. 216.

3

on the philosophical tradition that have been in vogue in France in recent decades.[2]

Yet in spite of this extensive record of theoretical engagement, considerable obstacles face any interpreter who proposes to regard Merleau-Ponty's writings as an important contribution to political theory. At one time the supposition that the Soviet Union might be on the road to establishing the first entirely nonviolent society in history was absolutely central to his views. Revelations about the Gulag, periodic invasions of border countries, and repression in Poland have long since discredited such ideas. In fact, Merleau-Ponty ultimately renounced his attitude of "Marxism in waiting," leaving the interpreter with the difficult task of taking seriously ideas that their author eventually saw as misguided. Moreover, more recent Marxists like Louis Althusser have found Merleau-Ponty's earlier brand of humanistic revolutionary theory to be misguided,[3] while non-Marxists like Michel Foucault have at times simply relegated him to a bygone era of French intellectual debate.[4] One can easily grant that Merleau-Ponty belongs in any historical treatment of postwar French political thought. But can one maintain that his existential political writings still merit serious consideration for their *theoretical* importance?

If we refuse to take all our cues from the changes in philosophical fashion on Paris's Left Bank, the answer is clearly yes. For there is an intriguing and profound problematic animating Merleau-Ponty's political writings that his critics have virtually ignored—at the risk, I would argue, of crippling their own theoretical endeavors. It concerns the issue of a thinkable politics.

What would it mean to make politics thinkable? When, in another essay, he charges that "the weakness of democratic thought is that it is less a politics than a morality" (SNS 180, tr. 103), we hear echoes of a familiar admonition. It is an admonition addressed to those who do not usually think politically—moralists, economists, technocrats, academics—warning them to pay particular attention to various constraints imposed on action by the requirement of assuring the support of people who wield power. "Thinking politically" means downplaying moral principles, technical expertise, or known truths in the interest of maintaining political support.

[2] Lefort, "Penser les rapports de l'homme avec l'Etre," p. 20.
[3] *Pour Marx*, pp. 227–238.
[4] Poster, *Foucault, Marxism, and History*, p. 5

But a closer look at his first postwar reflections reveals that a thinkable politics implies much more than that. As Merleau-Ponty recalls his views from "before the war"—a time when he was already well schooled in the works of men like Descartes and Kant— he expresses a belated realization that some philosophical assumptions do not allow us to conceive of collective life in a way that thinking about politics demands. The complaint is epistemological. When he speaks of a "statistical treatment of man," moreover, he introduces an activistic perspective. There is a hint here that the problem concerns not just the adequacy of certain intellectual tools for grasping political phenomena theoretically, but also the relation of those tools to practice. He suggests that an inability adequately to conceive political phenomena inhibits or misdirects political action. And finally, his mention of treating individuals as "substitutable objects" brings in a moral point of view. Something *of value* is lost when a mode of analysis treats human beings as if they were things. If politics concerns the processes by which community is created, authority constituted, values distributed, violence controlled, and collective choices made, then Merleau-Ponty is arguing that the very existence of politics as a region of human experience *puts special demands on thought itself*. Simply put, truly political thinking presupposes a particular philosophical foundation. An existential politics must rest upon a philosophy of man and action that will allow us to *understand* the perplexing vicissitudes of political life, to *evaluate* the alternatives it presents, and to *act* so as to advance humanistic values. Meeting these three demands simultaneously is the primary goal of Merleau-Ponty's political theory.

Three general arguments sustain my interpretation. First, Merleau-Ponty raises a subtle theoretical problem: the most widely accepted conceptions of human action and consciousness simply *do not connect up* to even the most rudimentary facts about political existence. Such rudimentary facts include the recognition that in politics people disagree; that politics involves choices; that political systems often exercise violence against individuals. Of course, other theories freely discuss these issues. But Merleau-Ponty shows that they cannot do so in a way consistent with their theories of mind. He demonstrates that the ability even to conceive of such features of political life becomes problematic if any of three theories of human existence—idealism, empiricism, or Sartrean existentialism—is considered foundational. To say that Merleau-Ponty is concerned with the foundation of a politics is to maintain that he attempts to stake out a philosophical position with a conception of consciousness adequate to the comprehension of political phenomena.

The second level of my argument is that, in order to ground a political theory, Merleau-Ponty deliberately engages in a systematic transformation of the works of other existential thinkers. He reworks existential as opposed to empiricist or idealist thought because he believes that existentialism offers the most nearly correct, if still imperfect, formulation of the nature of human knowledge and action. While sympathetic to existential attacks on scientific objectivism, he criticizes his colleagues for masking the relative continuity and rigidity of social structures by characterizing human subjectivity primarily in terms of freedom, choice, and creativity. True political thinking, he argues, must adjust itself in relation to social structures in order to improve its chances of successful action. Existentialism can be a suitable foundation for political theory only if it adopts a philosophy that, like Merleau-Ponty's phenomenology, understands the conditioned character of social meaning.

At a third level I examine what is political in the very way that Merleau-Ponty writes and disseminates his theory. His activity as a political editor who deliberately draws others into debate is *part of* his theory. His journalistic dialogues with existentialists, liberals, and communists *are* an existential politics insofar as they show him doing what his theory says politics is about: bringing out presuppositions, dealing with persons "en situation," challenging competing views, developing values.

These three lines of interpretation converge toward my main objective, to comprehend Merleau-Ponty's political writings as the expression of a single problematic. This book is therefore not just a survey of his political views, nor a study of their historical roots and influence.[5] The organization of this work is more thematic

---

[5] The existing studies of Merleau-Ponty's political theory are of two types. Some, like Barry Cooper's *Merleau-Ponty and Marxism: From Terror to Reform* and Sonia Kruks's *The Political Philosophy of Merleau-Ponty*, review the development of his political ideas. However, for historical detail and careful drawing of connections between philosophy and politics, Albert Rabil, Jr.'s *Merleau-Ponty: Existentialist of the Social World* remains the best of this genre. Other works situate his political theory in relation to larger themes. For James Miller, in *History and Human Existence: From Marx to Merleau-Ponty*, Merleau-Ponty's phenomenological interpretation and later critique of Marx culminates a discussion of the place of subjective agency in Marxism. Mark Poster's *Existential Marxism in Postwar France* places Merleau-Ponty at the center of the intellectual ferment in which postwar existentialism developed. In

than temporal because I believe Merleau-Ponty's unifying project, summed up in the phrase "the foundation of an existential politics," is revealed through a specific sequence of topics leading from phenomenology to political theory.

This sequence proceeds as follows. In his phenomenological investigation of the nature of consciousness, Merleau-Ponty concludes that the body synthesizes meaning in a way that cannot be described through traditional categories of subject and object. The environment cannot "objectively" determine the behavior of living beings because their interaction with their environment establishes what it will be for them. He calls characteristic patterns of such interaction "structures" or "Gestalten." The structures of human behavior differ from those of other animals insofar as man is not locked into a narrowly restricted set of interactions. Our ability to shift perspectives and to use symbols endows us with freedom.

Freedom is laden with political significance. Positively, it is the foundation of mankind's cultural and material progress. Human consciousness completes itself by assimilating and building upon the achievements of its predecessors. We are, as Merleau-Ponty says, in a "dialogue" with every human creation that we perceive. Negatively, freedom is the foundation of the human form of violence. Our very ability to shift perspectives enables us to view other creative subjects as mere objects suitable for exploitation. Economic motives loom large in this objectification of others. A tendency toward domination constantly endangers communal life.

Through politics the community attempts to control violence so that it can secure its cultural acquisitions. But not every sort of thinking permits those who engage in politics to calculate responses to conflict or to prepare for the mass assertions of will that violently transform societies. Successful political action requires a mode of thought that, at a minimum, grasps the unique nature of human freedom and violence. At a higher level political thinking becomes a philosophy of history, since successful action requires grasping the probable direction of cultural development. Political thinking reaches its most ambitious form in Marxism (with some Leninist emendations), for Marx develops a philosophy of history

---

Perception, Expression, and History, John O'Neill contends that there is political activity in the phenomenologist's readings of the social world. Thomas Langan, in *Merleau-Ponty's Critique of Reason,* stresses the relation between truth and practice in post-Kantian philosophy. Scott Warren's *The Emergence of Dialectical Theory* sympathetically treats Merleau-Ponty's work as a dialectical alternative to positivist and Straussian political inquiry.

that not only embraces the cultural evolution of all societies, but ties this evolution to an ultimate resolution of the problem of violence. In this way, the issues in Merleau-Ponty's political writings comprise a systematically interrelated set of ideas.

Although this is not primarily a study of the evolution of Merleau-Ponty's political beliefs, no interpretation claiming fidelity to his thought can be silent about his changes and self-criticisms through time. Chapter 1 discusses how he gradually constructed the problematic of an existential politics in the years before 1944, while the ideas outlined above, set out in Chapters 2 through 5, describe his political theory from about 1944 to 1950. Chapters 6 and 7 look at the ways he used this theory in a corrective dialogue with liberal and communist contemporaries. With his confidence in Marxism shaken by the outbreak of the Korean War and no longer convinced that his phenomenology gave a satisfactory account of the transition from perception to culture, he began in the early 1950s to develop a new political theory combining Saussure's methods and Weber's pessimistic liberalism. Chapters 8 and 9 show that this new theory yielded some telling criticisms of his former views and a fascinating analysis of revolutionary politics. Nonetheless, I conclude that his later work, while standing by the general requirements that he had placed on political thinking in the 1940s, adopted assumptions that ultimately defeat political thinking in practice.

In my opening remarks I intimated that Merleau-Ponty's political theory contains lessons of enduring value. I know of no better way to demonstrate that claim than by showing how his work opens fresh perspectives on theorists whose works are widely esteemed today. My concluding chapter therefore compares Merleau-Ponty's ideas with those of Michael Walzer, John Rawls, and Michel Foucault. My purpose here is not to reveal the degree to which Merleau-Ponty anticipates contemporary views, but to evaluate the ideas of others in light of his problematic—and his in light of theirs.

Reconstructing this problematic in a way that reveals its thematic unity is an interpretive project that, at a time when interpretive issues have come to the fore in political theory, cannot be taken for granted. Consequently a few remarks on two unusual aspects of my approach are advisable at the start. First, I used a variety of sources that have never before been consulted by students of Merleau-Ponty's thought. Included are tape recordings made by the French radio and television agency in the 1940s and

1950s and Merleau-Ponty's personal reading and lecture notes from the 1940s.[6] Even if such sources reconfirm his published views, as they almost always do, they must be used with caution. Products of a mind at work cannot be equated with a philosopher's finished statements. Still, they help the interpreter to distinguish between views held with certainty and with doubt. They also identify better than ever before his sources and his targets. Similar benefits were gained in interviews with a number of Merleau-Ponty's colleagues. Their recollections were particularly important in helping me to correct errors in Sartre's "Merleau-Ponty vivant," an essay that almost every investigator of Merleau-Ponty's thought has used uncritically.[7] Furthermore, I have tapped a number of seemingly ephemeral sources like Merleau-Ponty's uncollected editorials and newspaper interviews. In these I have sometimes found the most revealing formulations of his goals precisely because they record occasions when he put a hold on detailed philosophical argument so that he could explain his theory to the uninitiated. All of these sources, with their unique emphases, repetitions, and concrete references, have affected my reading of Merleau-Ponty's published works.

Second, a special interpretive approach supported my investigation. This approach starts with the observation, best defended by Sheldon Wolin, that there is such a thing as a politics of theory.[8] To have a politics means to think and act according to a plan that integrates a series of choices so as to make them serve the good of a community as a whole. The case for a politics *of theory* begins with the realization that even once theorists have set the manifest content of their writings, they still must resolve numerous questions concerning audience and form. Who is to be convinced and who needs to be refuted: intellectuals, the "average voter," workers? Ideas about who has the most power and whose convictions have the best chance of serving the entire community are likely to influence theorists' choices. Political theorists, after all, often write out of an urgent sense that the community must *do* something to

---

[6] For a detailed summary of these sources, see the Bibliography.

[7] This essay was originally published in the October 1961 issue of *Les Temps Modernes*, which was dedicated to Merleau-Ponty. An earlier version of Sartre's essay has recently become available. See Sartre, "Merleau-Ponty [1]," trans. Hamrick, pp. 128–154. However, this essay is no more accurate in its biographical detail than the first published version.

[8] Wolin, "Max Weber: Legitimation, Method, and the Politics of Theory," 401–424.

protect or to create right order and so are not indifferent to the practical effects of their writings. They design their writings to "alter the accepted ways of viewing politics," to draw the reader "out of one way of looking at politics in order to attract him toward another and different way."[9] After the theorist targets an audience, questions about style and rhetoric follow. What vocabulary should be used: academic or popular, metaphorical or starkly realistic? What examples will be most effective: ones that are narrowly nationalistic, broadly historical, or imaginatively abstract? How should arguments be constructed: as deductive propositions, as poetic appeals, as dialogues?

If such rhetorical decisions are controlled in a philosophical framework and if the guiding purpose of this framework is the actual furtherance of a public good, then it is appropriate to say that a theory has a politics. The theory itself becomes, in Wolin's words, "a model for a new form of politics, not only in the manifest sense of presenting a new political vision, but in the exemplary sense of showing how political action should be conducted extra-murally."[10] Its communicative techniques act out a politically motivated conception of whose attention it is vital to attract, who has power, and what imagery or argument will actually cut into the dense mass of prevailing opinion. Thus the theorist's practical intentions make available to the interpreter an additional level of meaning about the nature and the norms of political life.

The objectives of an interpretation attentive to the politics of theory differ from those of two other genres with which it might easily, but misleadingly, be confused. Unlike an intellectual historian, I use history without attempting to relate texts to "previous expressions in the same branch of cultural activity," or to connect "the content of the intellectual object to what is appearing in other branches . . . of a culture at the same time."[11] Guiding my interpretive practice is a first-order concern with Merleau-Ponty's meaning and philosophical acuteness, not his historical significance. However, since the politics of his theory appears only in the particular performative relationship between his writings and his targets' beliefs, I have had to undertake a program of historical contextualization to establish the identity, works, and reputations of his interlocutors. Only after such contextualization does one

[9] Wolin, "Political Theory and Political Commentary," in *Political Theory and Political Education*, ed. Richter, p. 192.
[10] Wolin, "Max Weber: Legitimation, Method, and the Politics of Theory," p. 404.
[11] Schorske, *Fin de Siècle Vienna*, pp. xxi–xxii.

perceive the oblique references in his vocabulary and become attuned to rhetorical strategies aimed at critics of different backgrounds.

Unlike a comparative textual analyst, I do more than examine and evaluate Merleau-Ponty's ideas vis-à-vis those of other thinkers.[12] My interpretation seeks out not just commonalities and differences, but a strategic design linking those features in a single pattern. Being open to that design requires one temporarily to defer asking whether Merleau-Ponty rightly understood others. Otherwise one misses the possibility that many of his "inaccuracies" are part of an argument deliberately patterned to persuade. Yet I do not exempt him from all criticism. An interpretation that *reduced* writing to rhetorical strategies and therefore refused all judgments about its truth would also not reach the politics of theory. Having a politics of theory means that through his rhetoric the theorist gives form to his vision of a better, even a truer, politics. And truth claims are appropriately subject to critical scrutiny.

The substantive yield of my search for a politics of theory is found in my reconstructions of Merleau-Ponty's dialogues with his contemporaries. These seemingly dated exchanges are *performances* of his phenomenological concept of communication. They show how the activity of founding an existential politics invokes a new sense of foundations and how it actually structures its own discourse according to perceptual premises. They are the philosopher's engagement in the process of constituting truth. The practice of dialogue, in other words, unites Merleau-Ponty's concepts of polemical strategy, political thinking, and philosophical foundations.

"Foundation" is the crucial term here. Because it describes both the philosophical ground of an area of inquiry and an activity of founding, it summarizes Merleau-Ponty's complex project succinctly. His founding activity is journalistic. In his writings he tries to settle the values of an existential politics, to propound them, and through phenomenologically structured debates, to have them accepted by a specific audience. In a more strictly philosophical sense "foundation" resonates with overtones of Kant's notion

---

[12] Archard's *Marxism and Existentialism* exemplifies the strictly comparative genre. He points to differences between Merleau-Ponty and Sartre while refusing to judge whether either represents the more authentic existentialism. Evaluative comparisons are more important in Whitford's *Merleau-Ponty's Critique of Sartre's Philosophy* and in Schmidt's lucid analysis of Merleau-Ponty's misreadings of Husserl and Saussure in *Maurice Merleau-Ponty: Between Phenomenology and Structuralism*.

of *Grundlegung*. Phenomenology translates Kantian conditions of possibility of a subject's experience into conditions of reality of a group's knowledge and action. This double sense of foundation thus suggests the precise complementarity of the two most important dimensions of Merleau-Ponty's work. His *activity* of founding seeks to revise others' political ideas when they rely on *philosophical* foundations that make their thought unsuitable for political engagement. At stake in both aspects of his foundationalism is how to think politically once one understands that human activity creates the very standards that regulate communal life. That is a problem whose significance is undiminished by the decline of proletarian internationalism, or by the eclipse of totalizing philosophies of history, or even by the pretensions of philosophies announcing the demise of the subject.

O N E

FIRST ESSAYS:
THE INTERSECTION OF
PHILOSOPHY AND POLITICS

Between 1925 and 1945 French philosophy underwent far-reaching changes in style, in the canon of authors it studied, in the subject matter it deemed worthy of attention. Merleau-Ponty's primary thesis for his *doctorat d'État* included, for example, a chapter on "The Body as a Sexed Being." His adviser, Émile Bréhier, a philosopher of apparently traditional sensibilities, was taken aback. Bréhier asked him if he could make this chapter a trifle more discreet; Merleau-Ponty promised that this suggestion would receive the thoughtful consideration it deserved. A week later he announced his decision: Alas, he could not change a single word.[1] Even fig leaves would have to drop before the phenomenological credo "to the things themselves."

The point, of course, is not that Merleau-Ponty launched his university career with a reputation for joining obstinacy to immodesty, but that he had an uncompromising sense of the unity of his philosophical project. A discussion of sexuality is an intrinsic part of a study of how meaning, knowledge, communication, and action are rooted, not in rational reflection, but in "pre-reflective" modes of apprehension—in the perceptual faculties of the body and in the absorption of culture.

A philosophical discussion of sexuality was not, however, Merleau-Ponty's last surprise for his Cartesian readers, for appended to that same chapter was a lengthy footnote outlining "the existential interpretation of dialectical materialism" (PP 199–202, 528, tr. 170–173). In it he develops a startling juxtaposition. Just as sexual motivations suffuse individual conduct without determining it, he argues, so economic motivations favor but do not determine choices made by groups. Economic conditions, not just rational

[1] Interview with Jacques Merleau-Ponty, April 3, 1981.

13

judgments, incline people to defend the status quo or to revolt against it. In Merleau-Ponty's phenomenology, as in Hegel's, rationality is something "more comprehensive than understanding"; it is inseparable from sexuality, culture, and history (SNS 110, tr. 63).

A review of Merleau-Ponty's early career sets the stage for an understanding of his political theory in three ways. First, through it one witnesses a confrontation of two generations of philosophers over the sort of knowledge that can count as the foundation of reason. The contours of Merleau-Ponty's later philosophy stand out as if in relief when viewed against the French intellectualist tradition. Second, his biography from 1925 to 1944 shows him putting into place a unified philosophical problematic that links problems in the theories of perception, value, history, and politics. Third, this historical investigation identifies the members of a philosophical and political cohort with whom Merleau-Ponty was in dialogue throughout his life.

Philosophy and Orthodoxy

By 1925, when he was seventeen years old, Merleau-Ponty had already heard his philosophical calling, and even then he was steeped in a distinctively French philosophical tradition. It is a measure of the depth of this tradition that the questions on the oral part of his *baccalauréat* examination prefigured the work of his entire life. One question, on "the nature of external perception," asked for his views on the paradoxes of the perceiving subject. The other, on "the idea of God in the works of Descartes," tested his comprehension of the philosopher he would be reading at the moment of his death.[2] His superb responses to those questions and the top prize in philosophy that he won at the Lycée Louis le Grand in 1926 gained him entry to the most elite school for the study of philosophy in France, the École Normale Supérieure (ENS). Elite and—as the center of academic philosophy—orthodox. To study philosophy at the ENS was to study a particular canon of texts, to master a well-defined style of thought, to develop certain expectations about the fundamental nature of philosophy itself.

Orthodoxy in the 1920s and 1930s meant doing philosophy with

---

[2] Archives Nationales de France, Les Fonds de l'École Normale Supérieure, AJ 16 3917.

tools forged in the workshops of Descartes and Kant. Since Merleau-Ponty sometimes refers to these two thinkers almost interchangeably, it is important to see their relationship, particularly as understood by the man who was his teacher and who incarnated the spirit of philosophy at the ENS before World War II, Léon Brunschvicg. "Brunschvicg passed on to us," Merleau-Ponty explains, "the idealist heritage. . . . This philosophy consisted largely in a reflexive effort. . . . His philosophy sought to grasp either external perception or scientific constructions as the result of mental activity."[3] It was above all to Descartes that Brunschvicg owed his belief in the primacy of rational consciousness in the constitution of knowledge.

Merleau-Ponty recounts the lessons that a reflexive philosopher like Brunschvicg draws from Descartes' *Meditations*. His explanation is worth quoting at length because Descartes' reflection is in an important sense the point of origin for the entire problematic of an existential politics.

> I say that I see a piece of wax. But what precisely is that wax? Certainly it is not the whitish color, nor the flowery odor that it may still have retained, nor that softness that my finger feels, nor that dull sound it makes when I drop it. None of that is constitutive of the wax, since it can lose all of these qualities without ceasing to exist—for example, if I melt it and it is transformed into a colorless liquid, with no appreciable odor, and that no longer resists my finger. I say nonetheless that the same wax is still there. How can we understand that? What remains in spite of the change of state is only a fragment of matter without qualities and, at the extreme, a certain power to take up space and to receive different forms—the occupied space or the received form not being in the least determined. There is the real and permanent kernel of the wax. Now it is obvious that that reality of the wax does not reveal itself to the senses alone because these only offer me objects of a determined size and form. The true wax, therefore, is not seen by the eyes. One can only conceive it through intelligence. (IN 195)

Descartes's famous cogito, which stands for the reflexive effort of intelligence, thus takes credit for determining what something

[3] "La philosophie de l'existence," p. 309.

really is. What *is* is what is *known*. That is the first principle of Brunschvicgean idealism.[4]

Three centuries of scientific advance since Descartes taught Brunschvicg that mind seldom comes by its most important knowledge in the philosopher's study. Brunschvicg regards science as the primary agent of the progress of reason. Science dissolves myths and discovers the hidden order of nature. Yet how can one reconcile faith in contemporary science with Cartesianism? The professed epistemology of science has typically been empiricism, not idealism. Are the achievements of science not due to its careful attention to sense experience and disregard of philosophers' claims to a priori knowledge? Does science not assume, moreover, that the universe is composed of objects whose relations are causally determined, and does this assumption not preclude in the final analysis the notion of a subject who freely reflects on objects to discover their essence? Does science not emphasize *what is*, not *what is known*?

For Brunschvicg, Kant performs the service of reconciling science and the Cartesian subject.[5] According to Kant causality is an a priori category of the understanding. The human mind synthesizes experience; it gives form to experience in order to make it intelligible. Causality is among the concepts of the understanding that make objective experience possible. Thus deterministic laws do not exclude the subject; they give proof of a subject *for whom* laws and objects exist. However, for Brunschvicg there can be no fixed categories of the understanding, but only the progress of reasonable minds in history through scientific analysis and reflection. Mind, especially using the scientific method, moves knowledge onto vaster planes and assimilates it in increasingly pure symbolic forms. Precisely because of their distance from error-ridden human perception, these forms make knowledge more exact, secure, and rationally comprehensible. Louis Lavelle explains that for Brunschvicg, the ideal in this progress is to look "at the world with reason and not with the senses."[6]

Although hardly a political philosopher, Brunschvicg does trace out certain affinities between his metaphysics and a Kantian version of liberal politics. Analyzing the Socratic dialogues, Brunschvicg observes that "ideas of family, of the city are born . . .

---

[4] Descombes, *Modern French Philosophy*, p. 19.

[5] Bréhier, *Transformation de la philosophie française*, p. 11.

[6] Lavelle, *La philosophie française entre les deux guerres*, p. 188.

before our very eyes from the intellectual effort by which the individual, instead of considering his action from an egocentric point of view, . . . sees himself bound to his fellow citizens by a system of reciprocal, but not interchangeable relations." The foundation of such a system, he says, is a "norm of justice."[7] Just as the scientist knows his personal perspective on the universe to be incomplete and distorted, yet "neutralizes [these] distortions by means of an operation of intellectual coordination that takes into account simultaneously all centers of reference," so the moral actor neutralizes the distortions of self-interest by taking the broadest possible perspective on community life. He thereby generates universal norms of behavior. Essentially, politics incorporates reason in the form of law, as known rules applied without prejudice to all members of the community.[8] Justice is the harmony of universal norms of morality and institutional practices; it is made possible by an agreement between the freely willing self and all other rational beings. In this view, politics and morality are predicated upon the common rationality of human beings, a rationality that makes possible the union of their wills. Summarizing Brunschvicg's view, one student of his thought concludes that "politics is nothing other than the application of a morality of liberty on the social level."[9]

The philosophical groundwork of these political values was embedded even in the program of study in philosophy at the ENS. There was a virtual canon of texts that subtly reinforced intellectualist idealism and, by its omissions, discouraged alternative perspectives. In their exercises in textual explication, students were most frequently questioned on Descartes, Kant, and Spinoza or, among the ancients, on Plato and Cicero—all defenders of the universality of reason. Hegel and Marx, not to mention Kierkegaard and Nietzsche, were notably absent from the list of authors used between 1920 and 1930.[10] A philosophy student might have read at least a few of Marx's post-1848 works, but Brunschvicg's attitude toward Hegel and Marx was unlikely to inspire serious study. He opposed them for their fabrication of systems that made history seem so orderly that contingency was ignored, for their failure to follow true science, and for a relativism that denied that

[7] *Le progrès de la conscience dans la philosophie occidentale*, pp. 720–721.

[8] Brunschvicg, "Les fonctions de la raison," p. 127.

[9] Deschoux, *La philosophie de Léon Brunschvicg*, pp. 149–151.

[10] Archives Nationales, Les Fonds de l'ENS, *Diplômes d'études supérieures pour la philosophie*: Université de Paris, 1906–1938, AJ 16 4954.

universal norms could be formulated to regulate human conduct across nations, classes, and epochs.[11] The philosophy of history, according to Brunschvicg, was the "particular weakness of the nineteenth century." So when his students wrote their first, short thesis, they chose one of the canonical philosophers. Raymond Aron studied Kant, Simone de Beauvoir Leibniz, and Merleau-Ponty wrote an essay on Plotinus.[12] For the more definitive work of a doctoral dissertation, students obeyed Brunschvicg's intellectual priorities and selected a scientific problem for philosophical scrutiny. Merleau-Ponty chose topics in psychology and perception.

Idealism and Nationalism

As a student at the ENS from 1926 to 1930, Merleau-Ponty was philosophically even more idealist than was characteristic of the regnant idealism. He was a thorough-going rationalist, once recalling his early taste for Octave Hamelin—a Catholic idealist whom Brunschvicg himself criticized as overly abstract. Merleau-Ponty knew Simone de Beauvoir well in these years, but was suspicious of her more wide-ranging interests. He disapproved of the way she confounded the literature of Proust with philosophy.[13] He had no taste for speculations that did not remain within the boundaries of the philosophical tradition.

Traditionalism describes the inheritance of social and moral ideas that he brought with him to the ENS. His father, who died in 1913, had been an officer in a colonial artillery division. His mother was a devout Catholic. Acquaintances characterize his attitudes in his student years as "bien pensant" and nationalist.[14] At the ENS Merleau-Ponty was known as a "tala"—one who goes to mass.[15] His evident religious inclinations were so disagreeable to the young atheist Jean-Paul Sartre that close personal relations

[11] Brunschvicg, "Histoire et philosophie," p. 308.

[12] Archives Nationales, *Diplômes d'études supérieures*, 1927 and 1929, AJ 16 4954.

[13] *L'École Normale Supérieure: Simone de Beauvoir et Sartre*, Merleau-Ponty interviewed by Georges Charbonnier, RTF, 1959; Beauvoir, *Mémoires d'une jeune fille rangée*, p. 347.

[14] Interviews with Claude Lefort, April 2, 1981; Jacques Merleau-Ponty, April 3, 1981; Mme Susanne Merleau-Ponty, April 13, 1981.

[15] The term "tala" comes from the expression "ceux qui vont à la messe" (those who go to mass).

never developed between them in their school days, even though only one year separated them in their study of philosophy.[16]

Merleau-Ponty's religious traditionalism no doubt brought him into contact with political conservatives. He once remarked to Claude Lefort that he had "brushed with" Charles Maurras's political group, Action Française. He probably meant that, in the Maurrassian revival at the ENS in the late 1920s, he was familiar with and shared some of the nationalist and religious views of this right-wing group. One of his closest friends was Maurice de Gandillac, who was deeply interested in Maurras at the time.[17] Merleau-Ponty may have attended some of the meetings of the Circle of Thomist Studies held by Jacques Maritain who, up until 1926, had had open sympathies for Action Française.[18] These associations shed new light on a passage that Merleau-Ponty wrote in his mid-thirties.

> Men of thirty-five are all the more aware of [the problem of the French intellectual right] because at some moment it was theirs in one way or another. Around 1930 Action Française enjoyed such credit among students as is unimaginable to the young people of today. . . . There was a healthy reaction against the Kantian illusions of democracy in the Maurrassism of 1900. . . . The weakness of democratic thinking is that it is less political than moral, since it poses no problem of social structure and considers the conditions for the exercise of justice to be given with humanity. In opposition to that particular moralism, we all rallied to realism. (SNS 179–180, tr. 102–103)

Maurrassian realism, he suggests, is at odds with intellectualist ethics and politics. Maurras contends that democracy, because it is grounded in individual reason and interest, willingly sacrifices the strength of the nation to the abstract question of the fate of a single man—as French liberals had done during the Dreyfus affair. He argues for the primacy of the citizen's duties to the social system. Such duties secure the continued existence of traditional institutions like the monarchy, the Church, and local authorities. These make justice possible and are the backbone of French civilization.[19]

In this context it comes as less of a surprise to learn that Mer-

---

[16] Sartre says his early relations with Merleau-Ponty at the ENS were "very bad." See "Merleau-Ponty [1]," p. 129.

[17] Interview with Maurice de Gandillac, February 18, 1981.

[18] Maritain, *Carnet de notes*, p. 218.

[19] Curtis, *Three against the Third Republic*, pp. 68–72, 77, 87–88, 94, 169, 234.

leau-Ponty, in a speech bidding farewell to his first philosophy students at the Lycée Beauvais in 1932, edifies his listeners with a lesson on the "essence" of France. He repays a debt to Brunschvicg by stating that respect for human dignity and a commitment to clear and communicable ideas define French civilization. But the young philosopher's conservatism makes him distrust the idea of progress. He warns his students against the excesses of German philosophy—its taste for the obscure "Dionysiac torrent of life," its pessimism and desire for ceaseless change. With all the sobriety befitting a fashioner of impressionable minds, he concludes with a *mise en garde* against revolutionary movements: "Let us be inclined to understand other peoples and let our intelligence be flexible and benevolent. But let it be without illusion, and let us . . . oppose with a decided 'no' any violent attempt to drag us toward what one calls a 'new age,' toward an absurd and inhuman economy, toward unawareness and impulse."[20] The social traditionalism evident in these words must have stood in some tension with the highly individualistic, progress-oriented philosophy he was taught at the ENS. National community is an historical product, not the creation of abstract reason.

In early 1929 he fulfilled a student teaching requirement at the Lycée Janson-de-Sailly, under the direction of Gustave Rodrigues. Rodrigues, an atheist and president of the League of the Rights of Man, impressed Merleau-Ponty by his "extraordinary moral character." The young Catholic perceived that "an atheist resembles other men."[21] But more important, it was through Rodrigues's teaching that Merleau-Ponty recognized that idealism could not adequately account for our relations with other people. It was unclear how one mind could know another if the grounds of certainty were located wholly within the subject's inner reflections.[22] By 1945 Merleau-Ponty would assert that a theory of politics—and politics is relations with others par excellence—presupposes the resolution of this fundamental problem.

At the periphery of his field of philosophic apprehension must have been the growing interest in German philosophy among the French in the late 1920s. In 1927 the first student theses on Hegel

---

[20] "Discours d'usage," p. 28. I am grateful to Mme Merleau-Ponty for having brought this, the earliest of her husband's publications, to my attention.

[21] *La vocation du philosophe*, Merleau-Ponty interviewed by Georges Charbonnier, RTF, 1959.

[22] Ibid. He mentions Rodrigues's *Le problème de l'action* (Paris: Félix Alcan, 1909) as a particularly important source of questions on this subject.

and Husserl joined the steady trickle of works on Marx undertaken by ENS students; in 1936, when Merleau-Ponty was back at the ENS as a sort of tutor, four theses were written on Hegel, two on phenomenology.[23] Meanwhile, in 1929 Husserl had lectured on "The Introduction to Transcendental Phenomenology" at the Sorbonne and Jean Wahl published *Le malheur de la conscience dans la philosophie de Hegel (The Unhappy Consciousness in Hegel's Philosophy)*. From 1928 to 1930, Georges Gurvitch gave a course at the Sorbonne on the philosophy of Heidegger, Scheler, Husserl, and others in the phenomenological movement.[24] Merleau-Ponty may have warned his students against Germanic philosophy in 1932. Nonetheless, at that very moment at the Lycée Beauvais, he was learning German in order to read this philosophy firsthand.[25] His access to developments in German philosophy and psychology would shape his entire career, giving him a new way to think about the relation of mind to meaning.

The Philosophical Transition

Merleau-Ponty's interest in problems of meaning drew him into the complex ferment of French and German philosophy known as the "philosophy of existence." In 1933 Sartre succeeded Raymond Aron at the French Institute in Berlin, discovering for himself the works of Husserl, Heidegger, Scheler. Upon his return to Paris he spread their works to others, including Merleau-Ponty.[26] Even before this, however, Merleau-Ponty had been attracted to German psychology, which figured prominently in his proposal for his doctoral thesis on "The Nature of Perception." By 1933 he was prepared to see in *Gestalttheorie* a means to refute French intellectualist philosophy. "Perception is not an intellectual operation," he wrote; "the [intellectual] 'form' is present in sensible knowledge itself."[27]

Of substantial importance in helping him link psychological research and phenomenology was his friendship with Aron Gurwitsch, a student of both Husserl and the Gestalt theorists Gelb

[23] Archives Nationales, Les Fonds de l'ENS, AJ 16 4954.

[24] Roberto Salvadori reviews these developments in detail in *Hegel in Francia: Filosofia nella cultura francese del novecento* (Bari: De Donato, 1974).

[25] Gandillac, "In Memoriam," p. 104.

[26] Merleau-Ponty, "La philosophie de l'existence," p. 315.

[27] Merleau-Ponty, "Projet de travail sur la nature de la perception," in Geraets, *Vers une nouvelle philosophie transcendentale*, p. 9.

and Goldstein.[28] It is to Gurwitsch that Merleau-Ponty owes one of his most basic insights into the nature of meaning. "For *Gestaltpsychologie*," he explains, "an object does not gain relief by its 'signification' . . . , but rather because in our perception it has a special structure—the structure of the 'figure on a ground.' "[29] Perceptual experience varies according to a relationship between a figure and a larger field, and not as a direct, point-by-point function of sense data.

Significantly, Merleau-Ponty first met Gurwitsch at the home of Gabriel Marcel, France's indigenous philosopher of existence. Marcel's *Metaphysical Journal* (1927) and *Being and Having* (1935) inform Merleau-Ponty's thought about meaning through their critique of nineteenth-century psychology. Implicitly following Descartes' mind-body distinction, such psychology attempts to explain all perception in terms of disparate qualities given by sensations.[30] Marcel objects that our experience of our own bodies does not accord with this picture. Our bodies are our means of access to all that exists, and as such, the condition of our ability to have knowledge of the world. "Incarnation [is] the central given of metaphysics."[31] What is the very foundation of reflection cannot be merely another object.

This account of the body threw new light on Merleau-Ponty's central concern with the knowledge of other minds. In a review of Marcel's *Being and Having*, he cites Descartes' remark that when he looks from his window to see people in the street below, they might as well be mannequins driven by springs for all that direct perception tells him about them. Descartes concludes that mind knows that these are actually men only by assembling the fragmentary sense data it receives; it must *judge* the meaning of its sensations. But this, Merleau-Ponty protests, is to "take as a model for the perception of others an unfocused attention in which . . . I do not perceive men, but human forms that seem vaguely to move." Cartesians err in assuming that things human

[28] Lester E. Embree, ed., "Biographical Sketch of Aron Gurwitsch," in *Life-World and Consciousness*, pp. xix, xxvi. Merleau-Ponty also attended Gurwitsch's course between 1934 and 1939. See A. Métraux, rev. of *Vers une nouvelle philosophie transcendentale*, by T. Geraets, in *Archives de Philosophie* 38:1 (January–March 1975), p. 163.

[29] Merleau-Ponty, "La nature de la perception," in Geraets, *Vers une nouvelle philosophie transcendentale*, p. 193.

[30] Merleau-Ponty, rev. of *Être et avoir*, p. 99.

[31] Marcel, *Being and Having*, pp. 11–12, 84–87

are properly understood from a detached, spectatorlike attitude that sees all that is external to the mind as objects. They open a chasm between the subject and all that is outside him. The chasm must then be crossed with heavy philosophical bridgework—theories of judgment and the like. The Cartesian cogito faces the constant danger that its judgment will collapse, cutting it off from the world and others. What intrigues Merleau-Ponty in Marcel's notion of the *corps propre* (the body as the ground of knowledge) is the assertion that this rift need never have been opened.[32] Others are not at first alien to me and then accepted after a process of conscious evaluation; I am from the start familiar with and open to them. To adopt the theme of the corps propre is to accept a theory of mind that makes the idea of community comprehensible.

Marcel, a reader of Scheler and Heidegger, was versed in at least the rudiments of phenomenology. In the same review Merleau-Ponty emphasizes this "new type of knowledge" and gives it compact definition. "Phenomenology, to the extent that it will not allow itself to allude to *things* behind the actual or virtual object of our thought . . . confers immediately an undeniable value on the established distinctions between the 'contents of thought.' In this sense, Marcel can adopt a 'phenomenological' or 'transcendental' point of view.' "[33] The sine qua non of phenomenology—and this Merleau-Ponty retains even as he criticizes Marcel and looks to the more rigorous approach of Edmund Husserl—is the idea that what is *immediately* given to perception is the primary material on which all intellection is built. Phenomenology refuses to accede to Kant's assertion that phenomena are merely manifestations of a "noumenal" reality that is never perceived. Perceptual phenomena cannot be conceived as secondary products of an unknowable natural substratum.

Merleau-Ponty began reading Husserl's published works in the mid-1930s. A thorough account of Merleau-Ponty's complex and often critical relationship with Husserl's phenomenology cannot be undertaken in a study of existential political thinking.[34] But two aspects of Husserl's philosophy are essential to understanding Merleau-Ponty's later approach to political problems and so deserve mention here.

First, Husserlian phenomenology equates the apprehension of

[32] Rev. of *Être et avoir*, p. 99.

[33] Ibid., p. 102.

[34] See Geraets, *Vers une nouvelle philosophie transcendentale*; Waelhens, *Une philosophie de l'ambiguïté*, and Schmidt, *Maurice Merleau-Ponty*, chaps. 2 and 3.

phenomena with the comprehension of meaning. Merleau-Ponty writes that "for Husserl, [the truth of consciousness] can be reached only if one abandons . . . the realism of common knowledge and of all the sciences, for a transcendental attitude where all things are resolved into significations."[35] Not the causes of which scientists speak, but meanings define the subject's original perceptual relation to objects. To grasp Husserl's point at the simplest level, one need only reflect that no account of a causal chain relating a tree, light waves, a subject's retina, and neural impulses could ever make one understand what it was like to see a tree. A physiological psychologist may explain the perception of a "tree," but that explanation cannot supplant the original perception because, without the perception itself, there is nothing to explain. Phenomena are irreducible to their scientific explanations. To explore meaning one must abandon the assumptions of realism and its explanatory principle of causal determination.

The concept of the "life-world" is the second of Merleau-Ponty's major Husserlian acquisitions relevant to political theory. In the spring of 1939 he travelled to Louvain, Belgium, to be one of the first scholars to consult Husserl's late, unpublished works, including *The Crisis of the European Sciences and Transcendental Phenomenology*.[36] In Husserl's early philosophy, any question of the factual genesis of meaning is laid aside in order to examine the internal logic of the processes of signification. Such an examination might be accomplished by any reflecting subject who could "bracket" the peculiarities of his or her circumstances (e.g., class position, employment, national milieu) in order to describe the "essences" of objects. Husserl's late philosophy marks a radical departure from this Cartesian approach. It looks to the historical origin and cultural constitution of meaning.[37] The subject lives in a life-world of preconstituted meanings—the very meanings "bracketed out" in his early work. Even after the most stringent reflection, there remains a residue of meanings that can be understood only through an investigation of their evolution. The life-world is a horizon for all philosophical, scientific, and cultural questions. It is a concept that reorients Husserl's investigations—and Merleau-Ponty's—in the direction of a philosophy of history (SNS 239, tr. 135).

[35] Rev. of *L'Imagination*, pp. 759–760.

[36] Van Breda, "Maurice Merleau-Ponty et les Archives-Husserl à Louvain," pp. 410–430.

[37] Waelhens, "De la phénoménologie à l'existentialisme," in *Le choix, le monde, l'existence*, pp. 42–49.

The Political Transition

It is clear that Merleau-Ponty's political no less than his philosophical assumptions underwent profound changes in the 1930s. Still Catholic in 1934, he was "carried to the left . . . by the requirements of his faith" (SNS 305, tr. 172). He sympathized with a protest initiated by the journal *Esprit* against the violent repression of Austrian workers by the "Social Christian" regime of Engelbert Dollfuss.[38] He once recounted that a Dominican priest told him at this time that Catholics might condemn Dollfuss, but only qua citizens, not qua Catholics. From the Catholic point of view, the priest suggested, "the established power" was merely exercising its police function.[39] Merleau-Ponty replied that "this justified the workers' opinion of Catholics: regarding the social question, they can't be counted on all the way" (SNS 306, tr. 173). More congenial to his evolving political sensibilities would be the intellectual climate of the journal *Esprit*, which combined Christian inspiration, a "leftish" political tendency, and a philosophical orientation favoring the emergent philosophy of existence.

The historical record on Merleau-Ponty's affiliation with *Esprit* is rather bare. From January 1935 to February 1936 he tried to establish a local "Amis d'*Esprit*" group in Chartres, where he was teaching at the local lycée. He attended the *Esprit* congress in 1936. His political drift to the left is evidenced by the signature he added, along with many from the *Esprit* group, to a petition protesting the bombing of Guernica.[40]

That petition was directly in the line of the politics of *Esprit*, even though many in the French Catholic community sympathized more with Franco's rebellion than with the victims of Guernica. The journal, founded in 1932 by Emmanuel Mounier, had among its goals the dissociation of the Christian order from the powers of money and the politics of the Right.[41] To do this, Mounier argued, requires anchoring politics in a revised scheme of values—values favoring the free spiritual development of the person. Christians cannot be satisfied with holding to pure values; their task is to advance the "incarnation" of values in the institutional

[38] Geraets, *Vers une nouvelle philosophie transcendentale*, pp. 24–25.

[39] The priest was probably R. P. Maydieu, the man who solicited Merleau-Ponty's articles for *La Vie Intellectuelle* and was later a prominent figure in the Resistance.

[40] *La Croix*, May 8, 1937, cited in René Rémond, *Les catholiques dans la France des années trente*, p. 183.

[41] Rauch, *Politics and Belief in Contemporary France*, pp. 62, 74.

setting of the community. Mounier concludes that achieving a political order with a "personalist" ethic requires the "engagement" of the individual. Engagement signifies a refusal to equate political quiescence with innocence; it requires a deliberate choice to abolish social injustices.[42] But in spite of the apparently activist bent of his thought, Mounier was reticent about political action. Especially before the war, his references to "revolution" implied something closer to spiritual regeneration than to violent uprising.[43]

At the time of his affiliation with *Esprit*, Merleau-Ponty apparently agreed. On June 4, 1935, Inspector General Parodi reported on the following lesson that Merleau-Ponty gave to his pupils at Chartres. "According to Gandhi, if nonviolence were cowardice, violence would be preferable. [But] the professor, relying upon a passage from Alain, shows how violence, being only weakness and psychological disturbance, may be at times a practical necessity, but cannot have any moral justification."[44] Only after accepting "history" as a central concept of his philosophy would Merleau-Ponty give an ethical defense of certain violent "engagements" in politics.

Mounier once shared credit for developing the idea of engagement with Max Scheler,[45] whose work *Ressentiment* Merleau-Ponty reviewed in 1935. The question of the relation of individual to institution and of value to reality is at the center of Merleau-Ponty's concerns. Scheler's major work, *Formalism in Ethics*, gives a new twist to the phenomenological program. Where "mainstream" phenomenology argues that intentional acts reveal the signification of the sensible world, Scheler feels that there is also an intentionality of emotional life, giving access to value essences such as the good, the bad, the beautiful, the noble. The contents of these essences cannot be known by ordinary sense perception; they have to be seen through a *Wesenschau* (intuition of essences) unique to a being that can know values. Values are prior to will and exist independently of it. Scheler opposes Kant, whose ethics is purely formal, a theory of objective values that give precise content to moral life.

In his review Merleau-Ponty endorses this theory of value—and

---

[42] Schalk, *The Spectrum of Political Engagement*, p. 25.

[43] Rauch, *Politics and Belief*, pp. 80–82.

[44] Rapport de M. l'Inspecteur Général Parodi sur Merleau-Ponty, Professeur de Philosophie, Carnot, June 4, 1935, Dossier de Merleau-Ponty, Service des Archives de l'Université de Paris.

[45] Mounier, *Le personnalisme*, p. 164.

its implications for social organization. According to Nietzsche's radical critique of Christian values, the Christian who accepts suffering and turns the other cheek when provoked proves only his impotence. Christian values are born of weakness, hate, resentment. They enshrine as "good" what the weak can do and deny the value of things beyond their limited power. Scheler and Merleau-Ponty object that Nietzsche treats values as mere epiphenomena. He *reduces* the phenomenon of value to the status of a biologically rooted will to power. Nietzsche's reductionism evidences "an empiricist prejudice."[46]

But if values are not grounded in life, what is their source? Merleau-Ponty replies that this question is not fundamental. "The first task of reflection is to . . . accomplish a description of consciousness without giving sensible existence priority." In that case, values have an equal status with biological facts. They are irreducible "because they are apprehended with a certainty which, from the phenomenological viewpoint, is a final argument."[47] Thus it is phenomenology that allows him to assert that "the realization of the highest values—the essence of the moral act—is a form of participation or complete perception and not the heroic affirmation of an empty form."[48] In this early article Merleau-Ponty finds in Scheler a phenomenological justification for the possibility of specifically Christian values.

Georges Gurvitch, in his Sorbonne lectures (attended by Merleau-Ponty), pointed to a political danger in Scheler's theory of value. He maintains that Scheler's certainties about moral objectivity could underwrite an authoritarian politics. Scheler's theory implies that those who *know* what is ethical might have the exclusive *right* to govern. This theory, Gurvitch cautions, could justify a Christian community of "hierarchical personalism."[49] Merleau-Ponty contests this interpretation, while admitting that he draws Scheler's thought "to the left." It is not moral certainty but the idea that spiritual values are merely affective states (he has in mind here Luther's "justification by faith alone," where salvation is sought in strictly personal terms) that makes collective life problematic. At least historically, this seems to be the philosophy associated with authoritarianism.[50] The advantage of Scheler's vision

[46] Merleau-Ponty, "Christianisme et ressentiment," p. 288.
[47] Ibid., p. 290.
[48] Ibid., p. 291.
[49] Gurvitch, *Les tendances actuelles de la philosophie allemande*, pp. 88 and 117ff.
[50] Merleau-Ponty, "Christianisme et Ressentiment," p. 297.

of Christianity, in Merleau-Ponty's view, is that it is "transcend-ent"—nonpolitical in formulation and therefore suitable to sit in judgment upon all varieties of temporal politics. In fact, rather than regard the powers that be with stolid passivity, "Christianity must make those who live by it more demanding, . . . more aware in sociopolitical matters."[51] Merleau-Ponty does reproach Scheler, however, for being too politically withdrawn, too disposed to a "Christian pacifism." Scheler is right to emphasize Christian inten-tions, but "it is nonetheless the characteristic feature of Christian-ity to admit that there are acts that affect the 'spiritual person,' even when he has stayed on the sidelines—a link between what we do and what we are worth. In this sense Christianity, in all its purity, 'fights against' ['milite contre'] murder, just as it fights to tear the poor away from their poverty."[52] In the mid-1930s Mer-leau-Ponty was taking his religion in the direction of leftist political activism.

But around 1936 he broke entirely, if discreetly, with his faith.[53] This break negated many of the specifics of his defense of Scheler while retaining the essential. Ethical norms, he would continue to believe, elude a philosophy of voluntaristic affirmation or Kantian formalism, while they are accessible to phenomenological obser-vation. His later phenomenology, however, will discover the reg-ulative ideals of political judgment not through a Wesenschau, but through a perception of history.

The philosophy of history, along with phenomenology, was the formidable intellectual engine used to batter the edifice of French academic philosophy in the 1930s. Alexandre Kojève and Jean Hyppolite were especially important in propounding new inter-pretations of Hegel's *Phenomenology of Mind.* Kojève lectured on the *Phenomenology* at the École Pratique des Hautes Études be-tween 1933 and 1939. Merleau-Ponty, back in Paris from 1935 to 1939, was one of Kojève's most assiduous auditors. He even led

[51] Ibid., p. 298.

[52] Ibid., p. 304.

[53] There is some controversy concerning how long Merleau-Ponty maintained his religious beliefs. Sartre seems to say that Merleau-Ponty lost his faith around 1928; Geraets rightly points out that Merleau-Ponty defends a Christian point of view in 1935. Compare Sartre, "Merleau-Ponty vivant," p. 315, and Geraets, *Vers une nou-velle philosophie transcendentale,* p. 17. Both may be right. Apparently Merleau-Ponty had by 1926 already renounced his faith, only to readopt it when he visited the Benedictine abbey at Solesnes with Maurice de Gandillac around 1926. By 1936, he had quit the Church once more. Personal letter from Gandillac, July 12, 1979. See also Beauvoir, *Mémoires d'une jeune fille rangée,* p. 376.

his own students over from the ENS to initiate them to Hegel.[54] Jean Hyppolite was one of his acquaintances from his own student days at the ENS; during the war their friendship became steadfast.[55] In the mid-1930's Hyppolite had begun the interpretive articles on Hegel that culminated in his thesis, *Genesis and Structure of Hegel's Phenomenology of Mind*.

Three broad interpretive options in Kojève's and Hyppolite's works attracted Merleau-Ponty. The first was to read Hegel seriously as a philosopher rather than as an artifact to be dusted off only by historians. Alexandre Koyré, who lectured on Hegel at the EPHE before Kojève, said that although one could marvel at Hegel's thought, one could not follow it.[56] Kojève and Hyppolite contradicted that assertion. They carefully interrogated Hegel's reasoning, his transitions, the nature of his claims. The rigor of their inquiries established that Hegel was a philosopher of reason—with the crucial caveat that Hegelian reason was historical and dialectical, not reflective.

Second, both interpreted Hegel in essentially humanistic and atheistic as opposed to theological terms. Kojève bluntly, Hyppolite with some reservations, maintained that the Hegelian tale of the odyssey of *Geist* concerned the spiritual and material development of mankind. Every episode of the *Phenomenology* had its concrete expression in historical events, particular philosophical systems, human struggles toward freedom and knowledge. Whatever its origins in youthful theological speculations, the Absolute in the *Phenomenology* of 1807 was not God, but man's self-transcending freedom. Especially for Kojève—who had left Russia in 1920 but whose admiration for Stalin was high in the 1930s—Hegel resembled Marx, with his stress on the transformative power of labor and on the struggle of the slave toward freedom.[57]

The third interpretive option was an emphasis on history as the medium of human community. Merleau-Ponty, explaining the formative elements of existentialism, recalls that the very notion of history raises the troubling question of the Other. "What both attracts and scandalizes philosophers in history is precisely man's

---

[54] Interview with Jean-Toussaint Desanti, April 8, 1981. In 1938 Merleau-Ponty was teaching a course on "La notion de l'expérience" ("The Notion of Experience") at the ENS. Archives Nationales, Les Fonds de l'ENS, 61 AJ 264.

[55] Hyppolite, "Notices: Maurice Merleau-Ponty," p. 54.

[56] Koyré, "Hegel à Iena," in *Études d'histoire de la pensée philosophique*, p. 135.

[57] See Kojève, "Hegel, Marx, et le Christianisme," pp. 339–366; and Heckman, "Hyppolite and the Hegel Revival in France," p. 133.

condition when . . . he is considered facing others. . . . We are then no longer dealing with juxtaposed individuals, but with a sort of human tissue. . . . From the moment when philosophy begins to become interested in human history in general . . . something has changed."[58] What changed was attitudes toward Brunschvicgean idealism. The Cartesian cogito attains to truth by the rigorous questioning of its own sensations and beliefs. Kojève and Hyppolite's Hegel challenges this conception by demonstrating that truth is reached not in solitary reflection, but through historical action. Man realizes truth in a necessarily temporal process, by risking private certainties in public ventures and by seeing them there as others see them—external, "objectified." The public character of knowledge is neither incidental to its truth nor the product of a universal structure of the human mind. The power of subjective visions to gain public recognition *constitutes* truth. In this view, each certainty can be only a provisional step in the expansion of knowledge toward the furthest horizons, because each will eventually be contested in the name of alternative visions.

Marxism, War, and Political Action

Coincident with the Hegelian revival and the maturation of existential thought, a new reading of Marx was taking place. The French came to focus on the works Marx wrote before 1848. Merleau-Ponty probably began his acquaintance with Marxism in the context of a series of seminars organized by *Esprit* in 1935.[59] Marcel Moré's lectures on "Karl Marx's Years of Apprenticeship," which commented on Marx's *1844 Manuscripts*, first made Marx accessible to a convinced phenomenologist by teaching him that Marx's seeming positivism was simply a polemical tactic used to combat idealism.[60] Probably even more important for Merleau-Ponty's political development was the Marxism that he absorbed from philosophy students at the ENS in the 1930s. Anti-Fascist political sentiments prompted respect for Marx's analysis of the decline of capitalism; Husserlian phenomenology called the positivist tendencies of Marx's metaphysics into question. Perceiving the con-

---

[58] "La philosophie de l'existence," pp. 314–315.

[59] Interview with Maurice de Gandillac, May 18, 1981.

[60] Compare SNS 227, tr. 128 and Marcel Moré, "La pensée de Marx et nous," *Esprit* (January 1, 1936), p. 561. Moré's other articles on "Les années d'apprentissage de Karl Marx," appeared in *Esprit*, in June 1934 and April, June, September, and October 1935.

flict, students were in search of a new synthesis. Merleau-Ponty's colleague at the ENS in the 1930s (and later his most persistent detractor in the Communist party), Jean-Toussaint Desanti, recalled that around 1934 "all fundamental truth had, for us, been suspended." Marxism was simply a "philosophical attitude," something offered up for research; "it was necessary to found it."[61] The newly translated early works, showing Marx's Hegelian inspiration, his interest in the individual, and his concerns about alienation, were particularly suitable for conceiving of a more existential foundation for radical political theory. But even if widely proposed, no one in France essayed in published form a systematic encounter of Marxism and phenomenology in the 1930s.[62]

Merleau-Ponty was exposed to more diverse brands of Marxism than even these connections would suggest. One of his closest friends at the ENS was François Cuzin, a brilliant student in philosophy and a courageous member of the Communist party in the late 1930s.[63] Although he and Merleau-Ponty undoubtedly talked politics, no trace of their exchange remains.[64] In 1939, on the invitation of Sartre's Communist friend Paul Nizan, Merleau-Ponty visited the vacation home of Laurent Casanova, who was the personal secretary of Maurice Thorez and later the Communist party chief of cultural affairs (S 42, tr. 31).[65] And then, also before the war, Merleau-Ponty knew David Rousset. At the time Rousset was a devoted Trotskyist, a combatant in the Spanish civil war, and a founding member of the Fourth International in France.[66] There is ample evidence to suggest that Merleau-Ponty could not have been innocent of Marxism in the 1930s, none to prove him a decided Marxist.[67]

[61] Desanti, "Sur les intellectuels et le communisme," pp. 96–97.

[62] In Germany, such an encounter began with Herbert Marcuse's "Beiträge zu einer Phänomenologie der historischen Materialismus," *Philosophische Hefte* 1 (July 1928), pp. 45–68. But I have found no evidence that Marcuse's work attracted any attention in France in the 1930s. See Piccone, "Phenomenological Marxism," p. 6.

[63] Interviews with Simone Debout-Oleszkiewicz, February 28, 1981 and Jacques Merleau-Ponty, April 3, 1981.

[64] In *Humanism and Terror* Merleau-Ponty anonymously eulogizes two Communist students killed in the Resistance—Cuzin and Yvonne Picard—by saying that, in contrast to the Communists of 1946, "one could talk with them" (HT 37, tr. xlvi).

[65] Susanne Merleau-Ponty remembers that her husband came away much impressed from his meeting with Casanova. Interview, June 8, 1981.

[66] *Revue des Conférences Françaises en Orient* (1946), p. 446; Beauvoir, *La force de choses*, I, p. 205.

[67] Sartre wrote that "from a number of conversations that we had later, I had a feeling that [Merleau-Ponty] had been closer to Marxism before 1939 than he ever

The Trotskyist connection is significant. Not only was Rousset directly affiliated with the Fourth International, but Cuzin also turned toward Trotskyism when he quit the Communist party in 1939. Claude Lefort recalls that it was on Merleau-Ponty's personal suggestion in 1941 that he first read Trotsky's works. In the late 1940s Merleau-Ponty would distinguish between Stalinist and Trotskyist communism—the latter bearing a striking resemblance to his own political views (BP 288). Trotsky stood for a non-Stalinist interpretation of Marx, a careful reading of the combination of opportunistic and democratic strands in Lenin's writings, and an ambivalent evaluation of the USSR.[68] The Russian Revolution, according to Trotsky's analysis, had laid the economic base of socialism, but had also degenerated into a hierarchical, bureaucratic state. One would not expect an intellectual attracted by Trotsky to accept uncritically the Communists' views of their action or of the evolution of Soviet society.

Less systematic but all the more striking in emotional power was a third quasi-Marxist current that fed into Merleau-Ponty's developing political convictions—Malraux's writings on revolutionary struggles, *Les conquérants (The Conquerors)* (1928), *La condition humaine (Man's Fate)* (1933), and *L'espoir (Man's Hope)* (1937). Malraux depicts revolution as a spontaneous movement of the masses, a lived experience with the force of millions of wills behind it. A participant in the Spanish civil war, he saw the Communist party ambivalently, as the only force with sufficient organization to lead the people to victory and yet also as a power whose tactics often negated the very goals of justice and individual dignity for which it fought. Significantly, when in the 1940s Merleau-Ponty traces the genealogy of French existentialism in order to prove its Gallic pedigree, he passes from Descartes to Pascal to Malraux. Malraux's novels on revolution are existential, he maintains, in that they admit the dilemma of the individual facing death and portray action proceeding from will, not causes (IN 17–20).

Although Merleau-Ponty's political leanings undoubtedly shifted to the left in the 1930s, they did not translate into activ-

---

was afterwards." See "Merleau-Ponty vivant," p. 315. In interviews with Merleau-Ponty's widow and with his ENS students from before the war—Pierre Kaufmann, J. T. Desanti, Monette Keim (Martinet)—I found none who would confirm Sartre's opinion. Furthermore, Merleau-Ponty himself, in his various autobiographical reflections, never mentions this prewar Marxism.

[68] Interviews with Claude Lefort, January 12, 1981 and April 2, 1981.

ism.[69] In this he was like Sartre and Simone de Beauvoir, who before the war were unconvinced of the need, appropriateness, or inevitability of their own direct political involvement.[70] Personal philosophical projects displaced concern over political events in this troubled decade. It was not until the time of the Munich conference that Merleau-Ponty began to take an active interest in political affairs.[71] By then war was only months away.

He was called to active duty in August 1939 and served as a second lieutenant in an infantry division in the "phony war" of the winter of 1939–1940. After France's rapid defeat the army was demobilized, and he returned to Paris in September 1940. There he immediately joined friends at the ENS in a unit of "résistance de la première heure." They called themselves "Sous la botte" (Beneath the Boot). Merleau-Ponty helped them print up and distribute resistance tracts.[72] A slightly more significant group formed in the spring of 1941, after Sartre returned from prison camp. The apolitical metaphysician of the 1930s was suddenly a staunch moralist, an advocate of political engagement.[73] He set about organizing, with Merleau-Ponty's help (and from this moment dates a relationship of close collaboration for over ten years), a resistance network called "Socialisme et liberté." Their goal was to establish a political order that would reconcile the socialist economy with individual liberty. "Socialisme et liberté" absorbed "Sous la botte," and extended its membership to include many of those who later would constitute the editorial board of *Les Temps Modernes*.[74] This group embraced Marxists and non-Marxists; editorial tasks were divided between them. Unfortunately, no traces of the group's papers have ever been found.[75] Even today, however, participants recall that Merleau-Ponty soon showed his penchant for political

[69] Interviews with Jacques Merleau-Ponty, April 3, 1981; Colette Audry, June 27, 1979; Monette Martinet (Keim), May 22, 1981; Susanne Merleau-Ponty, April 13, 1981; Jean-Toussaint Desanti, April 8, 1981.

[70] Burnier, *Choice of Action*, pp. 3–7.

[71] Beauvoir, *The Prime of Life*, pp. 267–268; interview with Susanne Merleau-Ponty, June 8, 1981.

[72] Their ranks included François Cuzin, Simone Debout, Jean-Toussaint and Dominique Desanti, and Jacques Merleau-Ponty. Interview with Simone Debout-Oleszkiewicz, February 28, 1981; Dominique Desanti, "Le Sartre que je connaîs," *Jeune Afrique* 2058 (November 8, 1964), p. 27.

[73] Beauvoir, *The Prime of Life*, p. 342.

[74] The most complete account of both groups is in Cohen-Solal's *Sartre*, p. 224–244.

[75] Whiteside, "The Merleau-Ponty Bibliography," p. 196.

reflection. He wrote up the paper's manifesto, conceived a plan for a new constitution ("Trotskyist" in orientation, says Simone Debout), and circulated a long paper on political themes to members of the group.[76] But with the help of a rumor started by Communists reporting that Sartre was an agent provocateur, the group broke up around the end of 1941.

With those brief lessons in political impotence behind them, those who stayed in Paris marked time and chose resistance activities more suited to their everyday roles. Sartre wrote for underground newspapers, furiously composed *Being and Nothingness*, and produced a play, *The Flies*, whose theme was the urgency of free resistance against a foreign invader. The Vichy press carefully ignored Sartre's political intentions and evaluated the work in purely aesthetic terms. Merleau-Ponty then reviewed Sartre's play, stressing that the "naïve spectator" would "perceive" its real message.[77] Optimistically overstating the political power of phenomenology, he implied that perception preserves a domain of truth in the face of propaganda. As a professor of philosophy at the Lycée Carnot, and in opposition to the offical curriculum, he introduced his students (among them Claude Lefort) to the thought of Karl Marx.[78] In one lesson he sought "to refute the objection that any reflection on morality only ends up by making us break with what is immediate and with life and by uselessly delaying action."[79] Moral reflection, he argued, is consistent with political activism. It was a lesson he continued to put into practice. During the liberation of Paris he joined an armed street patrol;[80] earlier he was among the professors who belonged to the Front National Universitaire, probably to distribute resistance literature in the lycée.[81] He also deepened his theoretical understanding of

[76] Personal interviews with Simone Debout-Oleszkiewicz, February 28, 1981; Dominique Desanti, April 8, 1981; Jean Pouillon, July 20, 1979. Mme Desanti was the group's typist. She recalls that Merleau-Ponty's tract was probably some fifty or sixty pages long.

[77] Rev. of *Les mouches*, p. 516.

[78] Interview with Claude Lefort, January 12, 1981.

[79] Rapport de M. l'Inspecteur Général Davy, May 30, 1941, Dossier de Maurice Merleau-Ponty, Service des Archives de l'Université de Paris. Merleau-Ponty could risk such a lesson because he knew Davy, a friend of Sartre, worked for the Resistance from within the Vichy administration. See Beauvoir, *The Prime of Life*, p. 382.

[80] Interview with Susanne Merleau-Ponty, April 13, 1981.

[81] Lablénie, *Aspect de la Résistance*, p. 47; 58 *récits de la Résistance universitaire* (Paris: Les Publications de l'Association des Anciens Combattants de la Résistance de l'Éducation Nationale, 1948), pp. 5, 28, 95.

political issues during the war by reading Lenin, Marx, and Trotsky.[82] But he had to await the Liberation of France to publicize his radical political views. He did so as part of an intellectual movement that he helped to form.

Existentialism

By 1945 "existentialism" had become the most significant intellectual phenomenon of the postwar years in France. Sartre's *Being and Nothingness*, which had been published and ignored in 1943, suddenly became the center of public controversy. Newspapers wrote of existential cafés, existential jazz, and existential suicides. In the fall Sartre gave his famous lecture on existentialism and humanism. Simone de Beauvoir's *The Blood of Others* and Merleau-Ponty's *Phenomenology* appeared. These three philosophers formed the editorial core of a new journal, *Les Temps Modernes*, which was viewed at the time as the more-or-less "official organ" of existentialism.[83] The poet Boris Vian wrote anagrams from the names of the "café philosophers": Pontbeaumerle de Savoirtre, Pontartre de Merlebeauvy, Merloir de Beauvartre.[84] Vian captured an important truth. Merleau-Ponty is so closely associated with his existentialist colleagues that to separate his name from theirs would risk seriously distorting his work of the 1940s. It would obscure his unifying intention to propagate and *transform* "existentialism."

Notwithstanding Sartre's greater notoriety as the dean of existentialism, it is arguable that Merleau-Ponty worked more to spread, defend, and extend existentialism than any of his colleagues. He was the main point of contact between the existential movement and a larger public. As editor in chief of *Les Temps Modernes* he sat in the front office to receive the inquiries of young enthusiasts and hostile critics.[85] More sociable than Sartre (who detested social gatherings), Merleau-Ponty established the contacts that brought many authors to write for the journal. He gave the journal much of its tone through his frequent political com-

[82] *Humanisme et terreur*, Merleau-Ponty interviewed by Georges Charbonnier, RTF, 1959. This is the only time he ever identified, however vaguely, the timing and sources of his political education.

[83] Robert Kantus, "L'actualité littéraire," *L'Age d'Or* 1 (1947), p. 138; cf. Yves Lévy, "Les revues," *Paru* 13 (December 1945), p. 101; G. Mavester, "Revue de revues," *Masses: Socialisme et Liberté* 1 (1946), p. 29

[84] "Chronique du menteur," *Les Temps Modernes* 21 (June 1947), pp. 1717–1720.

[85] *Les Temps Modernes*, Merleau-Ponty interviewed by Georges Charbonnier, RTF, 1959.

mentary and by writing most of the anonymous introductory material for articles.[86]

As a professor at the Université de Lyon (1945–1949) and then at the Sorbonne (1949–1952), he was not, of course, the champion of a single philosophy. But neither did his courses on the philosophy of history or on the linguistics of Saussure ignore the existential perspective.[87] Hundreds of students emerged from his courses knowing that the early Hegel was not guilty of system building and that Saussure's insights could be applied to a philosophy of history. On the public lecture circuit he was an indefatigable proponent of existentialism. He delivered talks on "The French Tradition of Existentialism," "Political and Social Aspects of Existentialism," "Marxism and Existentialism." He set forth his views before French audiences at the Institut d'Études Politiques, the Collège Philosophique, and the Société Lyonnaise de Philosophie.[88] He took his existentialist message to Brussels and Geneva in 1946, to Sweden and Norway in 1947, and to Mexico, the United States, and Italy in 1949. Moreover, when other intellectuals like Raymond Aron or Emmanuel Mounier gave lectures on existentialism, Merleau-Ponty was there to challenge and correct them. He was also the existentialists' most direct contact with the French Communist party and, for a couple of years after the war, managed to sway a few Party intellectuals—notably Pierre Hervé and Jean-Toussaint Desanti—in favor of some aspects of existentialism.[89]

Most telling of all, his published works demonstrate that giving form to an "existential" movement was of the greatest importance to him. *The Structure of Behavior* and *The Phenomenology of Perception* invoke the term in numerous and crucial arguments. His most well-known political work, *Humanism and Terror*, ends with a meditation on the nature of "existentialism." In *Sense and Non-Sense*,

[86] Interviews with Jean Pouillon, July 20, 1979 and May 29, 1981.

[87] Robinet lists Merleau-Ponty's courses in *Merleau-Ponty: Sa vie, son oeuvre*, pp. 72–78.

[88] Unfortunately, Merleau-Ponty's notes contain no trace of several lectures he is known to have given in the 1940s: "Les problèmes pratiques dans la perspective de l'existence" (see *Études Philosophiques* [January–March 1947], p. 77); "De l'intérieur à l'extérieur: La liberté" (see *Études Philosophiques* [July–December 1947], p. 309); "L'homme et l'objet" (see J.-L. Dumas, "Les conférences," *La Nef* 5:45 [August 1948], pp. 150–151); and "Descartes, Kant, et la philosophie contemporaine" (see *Le Figaro Littéraire*), May 7, 1949, p. 5).

[89] Sartre, "Merleau-Ponty vivant," pp. 311 and 328.

essays like "Hegel's Existentialism" and "The Battle over Existentialism" are entirely devoted to the defense of existentialism against its detractors and misinterpreters.

Knowing that Merleau-Ponty intended his works of the 1940s to be seen as "existentialist" crucially affects one's understanding of them. Without this knowledge it would be tempting simply to take note of his differences with other existentialists and conclude that he offered an alternative philosophy. But by laying claim to this publicly known title—not even insisting on some minor verbal distinction between his thought and "existentialism"—Merleau-Ponty tells his readers that he is not seeking to establish a different philosophy.[90] He is offering a *superior* expression of the *same position* that others have already tried to stake out.

At the heart of his project is the belief that his theory is superior particularly in accounting for the political dimension of existence. He thinks that a wide range of "existentializing" thinkers, including Marcel, Aron, Sartre, Beauvoir, Mounier, Malraux, Scheler, and Heidegger, have gone wrong when it comes to thinking politically. They misformulate their own existential insights in ways that either deprive their theories of political relevance or lead to tragically mistaken political commitments. He then modulates and reformulates their positions to explain how a theory can be both existential and political.

It is therefore important at the start to grasp what defines an existential perspective. "Existence" in this context refers above all to *human* existence. Among all things, according to the existentialists, there is one that can never be defined by a set of fixed qualities, laws, or concepts. That being is man. In Sartre's terms, man is a "nothingness," a being with no given essence. Man's freedom allows him to escape all determinism and create something new. To the claims of positive science to describe human behavior in terms of causal laws, existentialism replies that only an undetermined being can discover a law; against Hegelian idealism which reduces the individual to a mere "moment" in the development of truth, existentialism reaffirms the truth of the individual's experience.

Thus existentialism opposes both modern science and most forms of rationalism. It argues that they are like in supposing that

---

[90] For the negative reaction of some thinkers to this label, see Spiegelberg, *The Phenomenological Movement*, pp. 408–409.

the growth of knowledge depends upon a distancing of the knower from individual experience. The great achievements of science depended upon a turning away from the anthropomorphizing tendencies of common sense and toward causal explanations of events. Carried to its logical conclusion, scientific reductionism sees even human perceptions and emotions as *things* whose motions can in principle be explained as a function of certain antecedent conditions. Rationalist philosophies, in spite of their emphasis on the role of consciousness in organizing experience, similarly devalue perception. Descartes does so, for instance, when he examines the piece of wax. Not the ensemble of the qualities given to immediate perception but only those knowable to consciousness are essential to the wax. By tradition, "there are . . . only two meanings of the word 'exist': something exists as a thing or something exists as a consciousness" (PP 231, tr. 198).

Yet there is a third and more fundamental meaning of existence. "Existence in its modern sense," says Merleau-Ponty, is "the movement by which man . . . engages himself in a physical and social situation that becomes his point of view on the world" (SNS 125, tr. 72). All inquiry starts from particular circumstances—a place, a particular sort of lighting, personal interests and emotions, culturally transmitted predispositions—that direct the knower toward certain beliefs and conclusions. Existentialists assert that the subject is not just a thinker, but is an "initiator of action and a center of feeling" in the whole range of his existing.[91] They deny that any human being, whether scientist or philosopher, ever stands above the individuating conditions of knowledge. Existential engagement is "the sole means of gaining access [to the world], of knowing, and doing something" (SNS 125, tr. 72).

No metaphysical determinism underlies the existential notion of conditioned knowledge—quite the contrary. "Existence is undetermined," contends Merleau-Ponty, "inasmuch as it is the very operation by which what had no meaning takes on meaning" (PP 197, tr. 169). According to the existentialists, we do not passively receive sense data or suffer the blows of social forces. Human subjectivity chooses, selects, forms, and evaluates the objects of its attention. In phenomenological terms consciousness is always "intentional." No outside force can simply act on human conscious-

---

[91] Macquarrie, *Existentialism*, p. 2.

ness because we must first *choose* to focus effort or awareness upon events and give them meaning.

We are therefore self-creating in the sense that, as beings without a given essence, we determine what we shall be by the very choices we make. No god or nature or *Weltgeist* decides what we shall do with our freedom. Existential freedom has, however, a troubling ethical corollary. Deprived of "destiny," we also lose any transcendent court of appeal for our decisions. The values by which people are judged are themselves human creations. And because we are free nothing—not even our own previous choices—can bind us. Human existence is a constant process of self-transcendence, of going beyond each limit that we encounter. Human existence must be described temporally since it has no eternal essence.

If all experience is individuated, developing, grounded in existence, what ensures that the beliefs and values of different people are compatible? As Sartre might say, absolutely nothing. Two important consequences follow from the contingency of existence. The first is the rejection of any view of rationality implying that there is some sort of "natural affinity" between human reason and the structure of the cosmos. There is no reality independent of our cognitive and practical activities that is in principle knowable in the same way to all reasoning beings. It is a short step from the rejection of any metaphysical guarantee of human agreement to the second consequence: conflict is a recurring problem in human coexistence.

What this very general exposition has not explained is how these existential themes are to be formulated philosophically. What is the nature of this third mode of existence? Can it be described without dualistic categories (for example, subject and object, mind and body) inherited from the tradition of Western philosophy? Can there be degrees of freedom? When existentialists claim that "man" creates his values, are they referring to each individual or to some larger group? If a group, what binds its members together? If there is conflict, are there conditions that could mitigate it?

Merleau-Ponty adumbrates his own answers to these questions in the first article he wrote for *Les Temps Modernes*. In many ways the best introduction to his political thought, "The War Has Taken Place" combines a reflection upon the lessons of the Occupation with an announcement of most of the themes of an existential politics.

In contrast with the self-congratulatory tone of the memoirs of so many résistants, Merleau-Ponty's is remarkably somber. He has little to say about heroism or about the solidarity resistance created among participants. Indeed, he cautions that the Resistance was unrepresentative as political experience. Taking the Resistance as the model of political action would, "by making us believe that politics is a relationship of man to man or consciousness to consciousness, foster our illusions of 1939 and mask the truth that the Occupation taught us . . . , that is, the incredible power of history" (SNS 267, tr. 151). Not the glorious moment of Liberation but the pain and humiliation of living in a defeated country are most pregnant with significance for political understanding.

Merleau-Ponty portrays the war as a process of Hegelian *Bildung*. It was an *educative* experience that moved men closer to universality and self-consciousness by forcing them to encounter and surmount problems. The war precipitated a collision between the Cartesian consciousness and modes of thought and action that it could not assimilate. "History" is what finally disabused the French of "that optimistic philosophy that reduced human society to a sum of consciousness always ready for peace and happiness" (SNS 246, tr. 139). Merleau-Ponty agrees with Hegel in saying that deeply rooted assumptions are not overturned by philosophical questioning. War is the sort of harsh experience that awakens consciousness to new truths.[92]

At least three meanings of "history" can be isolated in Merleau-Ponty's essay, and each contrasts to Cartesian presuppositions. History implies, first, the existence of cultural groups as fundamental entities. It is irrelevant to the Cartesian thinker that the individual has national roots or religious ties or a social position. But the lesson of war was that "in coexistence, each of us presents himself to others on a ground of historicity that he did not choose; he conducts himself vis-à-vis others as an 'Aryan,' a 'Jew,' a 'Frenchman,' a 'German' " (SNS 254, tr. 144). During the war it became vitally important to discard the belief that social roles were only incidental variations on a rational essence shared by all men. To avoid giving implicit support to the invader, the French had to refuse all extraneous relations with Germans. The latter, mean-

[92] Meyer, "Maurice Merleau-Ponty und das Schicksal des französischen Existenzialismus," pp. 136–137.

while, distinguished between Aryan and Jew, collaborator and resister.[93] Social polarization in the war situation highlighted disturbing truths that could have been learned earlier: there are
"masters and slaves in peacetime society" and "each consciousness . . . becomes fixed and generalized beneath the gaze of a
stranger" (SNS 250–251, tr. 142). Others tear the individual away
from autonomous reflection and impose their judgments on him.
Social differentiation is at the heart of conflict, and history is the
record of its numerous forms.

Second, history stands for the ways that the effects of action extend through time. Too often these effects escape the notice of the
isolated thinker. In a philosophy of universal reason right action is
identical with action undertaken for good motives. Responsibility
follows from the goals sought, not the consequences produced.
But the Occupation could not tolerate so simple a morality. "We
were led to assume and to consider as our own not only our intentions . . . , but also the consequences of those acts in the outside
world" (SNS 256, tr. 145). To be attentive to "history" is to take
responsibility for evaluating one's actions in light of their subsequent impact on the welfare of others.

History implies, third, that there are social currents that sweep
the individual along and that can at best be channeled, but not
definitively controlled. Merleau-Ponty's essay, "The War Has
Taken Place," plays upon the title of Jean Giraudoux's 1935 drama,
La guerre de Troie n'aura pas lieu (The Trojan War Will Not Take Place).
Giraudoux shows how obscure hatreds and long-established customs push ineluctably toward war, frustrating the efforts of the
most resolute peacemaker. That we inherit social roles means that
we are more often unconscious carriers than willing initiators of
historical action. It is a Cartesian illusion, Merleau-Ponty warns, to
believe that "free acts might . . . shatter all external determinisms
with a single blow" (SNS 246, tr. 139–140). "History" demands a
way of thinking that finds "a middle ground between the volun-
tary action of some and the passive obedience of others" (SNS 253,
tr. 143).

Since political action is embedded in history in this threefold
sense, a political theory cannot simply be welded onto the existing
structure of philosophical discourse. The way of thinking it presupposes is fundamentally incompatible with Cartesian ortho-

[93] King, "Philosophy and Experience: French Intellectuals in the Second World
War," p. 199.

doxy. History demands a tough-minded realism in political thought. It requires that one plan action while accepting limited options and moral compromise. Theory must henceforth take account of social roles, the violence of collective relations, and the consequences of action. The project of founding an existential politics entails reconceiving politics from the ground up: from a general theory of the nature of meaning, to its application in social relations, to a philosophy of history, and finally, to the design of a political program.

T W O

PHENOMENOLOGY AS
A PROLEGOMENON TO
POLITICAL THEORY

In the mid-1930s the quality of results on the *agrégation* examination at the ENS had declined noticeably in relation to previous years. A meeting was called to discuss the problem, and Merleau-Ponty, then a tutor for candidates for the exam, gave an acute diagnosis. The variability in results was due, he maintained, to a shift in the focus and breadth of philosophical interests among the students. After explaining their almost unanimous rejection of empiricism, he described the direction of their research—in terms that applied equally well to his own. "Once the mind's activity in constructing the sciences has been made evident, they [the students] are not immediately persuaded that the entirety of man is there nor even what is essential to him. They seek to determine philosophically his total activity, by an analysis that is still transcendental, but extended to objects of experience that are not those of exact science: the phenomenon of art, the phenomenon of other people, the phenomenon of history."[1] He recommended adjustments in the teaching program—a little less Kant and inductive psychology, a little more room for "Hegel and his posterity: Marx, Nietzsche, or even Husserl." Philosophy needed a new impetus from the "concrete" problems of "aesthetics, philosophy of law, and politics."[2] Somehow, areas of human experience whose ingredients included strong measures of the irrational and the transitory had to be brought under the aegis of philosophy. The result would be a decidedly post-Cartesian interpretation of rationality.

By July 1945, when he defended *The Structure of Behavior* and *The Phenomenology of Perception* for his doctorat d'État, Merleau-Ponty had laid the groundwork for such views. With concepts like the

[1] "L'agrégation de philosophie," p. 131.
[2] Ibid., p. 132.

corps propre (body-subject), the perception of structures, and phenomenal objectivity, he elaborates an overarching transcendental theory of reason whose foundational character commands its application in all domains of thought and action—including political theory.

Although hardly political on their face, the principal themes of Merleau-Ponty's phenomenology furnish the materials he will use to make politics thinkable. He will argue that powerful political movements begin in people's lived experience of economic change, such that understanding power itself depends on grasping the meaning of social conditions. He will contend that massive historical structures condition the evolution of popular movements and that the effectiveness of political leadership depends on the leaders' ability to perceive these structures accurately. Moreover, he will trace the defects of liberal moralism, communist opportunism, Cold War Manicheism, and existential voluntarism to a metaphysical dualism that his phenomenology strives to overcome. Since this dualism originates with Descartes, a brief rehearsal of some familiar themes from the *Discourse on Method* is useful in raising the problems that drive Merleau-Ponty's ideas about political thinking.

The Cartesian Legacy: Subjects and Objects

The fourth part of the *Discourse* lays out the essence of Descartes' project. To secure reason against sceptical attacks, Descartes announces the necessity of putting human knowledge on "solid foundations." Only a proposition that resists all doubt will suffice, and he claims to find one: I think, therefore I am. He then accepts the existence of the thinking subject, the cogito, as "the first principle" of his philosophy.[3] Importantly, this "I" whose existence has been established is purely a thinking substance. What is external to thought is of an entirely different order. Descartes' meditations on the piece of wax are part of an attempt to determine what is essential to this external order. He learns, first, that the essence of things in the physical world is the ability to occupy space and eventually concludes that all extended substances move according to fixed natural laws of cause and effect. But he emphasizes, second, that the discovery of this essence comes not through perception, but through a conception of matter derived by intellection.

---

[3] Descartes, *Oeuvres philosophiques*, vol. 1, p. 603.

Therefore the thinking soul is in no way part of this material order.[4] Descartes' strict division of what exists into mind and matter is, in Merleau-Ponty's view, the origin of the metaphysical dualism that has bedevilled so much modern philosophy.

In particular, Cartesian dualism leads to vexing questions concerning the nature of the body. On the one hand, the body is merely one more thing in the physical world. It is an essentially mechanical system composed of matter.[5] On the other hand, it is the home of a mind that directs its action. Yet how can an immaterial cogito move a mass of tendons, bone, and blood? For that matter, how can my stomach (mere matter) tell me (the thinking substance) that I am hungry? Few have been convinced by Descartes' theory that soul and body mix in the pineal gland. But to reject some such hypothesis is to leave philosophy in the embarrassing position of having made unintelligible how there can be any relationship between the two entirely different types of substance that it knows are joined.

One way out of this impasse is to show that the two substances are really one and hence that no difficult questions of relationship arise. But which substance is truly fundamental, matter or mind? Descartes' dualism opens up two seemingly antithetical approaches to a monist ontology.

The empiricist solution is to reduce mind to a natural phenomenon.[6] Mental phenomena are interpreted not as acts of consciousness, but as effects of the interactions of elementary, nonmental causes in the natural environment. Mind is essentially reactive; it registers external forces. The empiricist allows no reference to the subject's intentional ability to aim at its environment. Phenomena like intentions and values are ruled out of explanations because they suggest that behavior is forward-looking and thus not merely the consequence of prior conditions. With regard to perception, this means that the complex phenomena of visual sensation are to be explained as a function of discrete stimuli acting invariably upon separate neural elements. One important corollary of this understanding of perception is the "constancy hypothesis," which

---

[4] Ibid., p. 631.

[5] Ibid., p. 628.

[6] Merleau-Ponty is less than rigorous in using philosophical labels. Where many would insist on distinguishing "empiricism," "positivism," "realism," "materialism," and "objective thought," he uses all of these terms to describe the position presently under consideration. He names the contrary position "idealism," "intellectualism," "rationalism," and "criticist thought."

predicts that a subject's sensations will conform to precise stimuli in a constant way (PP 14, tr. 78).[7] Repeatedly stimulating the same neural element produces the same sensory experience each time, regardless of what happens in other elements. The entire stimulus-response model of behavior is an elaboration of empiricist metaphysical assumptions and corresponds quite well to Descartes' view of the human body as a machine.

But Descartes can also be called as the primary witness against this reductive understanding of human consciousness. If reflection discovers matter and its causal relations, if it formulates the criteria by which we decide what is real, then it must have absolute priority over matter. Jacques Havet lucidly summarizes the Brunschvicgean idealist position: "The existence of the objects of knowledge is entirely relative to the truth of the judgment attesting to them; the judgment precedes the terms which it brings together. . . . The truth of a particular judgment is recognized by the mind through reflection."[8] Thus an idealist like Brunschvicg reduces not soul to body, but body to soul. Matter can only be understood as a *representation* interior to the mind of a thinking subject. According to such a philosophy, perception is only a confused idea to which conscious attention (on the model of Descartes' reflection on the piece of wax) finally brings order and clarity. Illusions and hallucinations are merely failures of judgment.[9] Perception is simply a primitive stage of the constituting consciousness before it has become aware of itself.

For Merleau-Ponty, both monisms born of Descartes' dualism are philosophically deficient. Yet they are still useful from a phenomenological point of view, for it is through a critique of these highly intellectualized accounts of perception that he makes the most credible case for returning to lived, "originary" *sens* (meaning).[10] He argues that what is truly foundational in human understanding is neither particular sense data nor ideal definitions of

[7] See Gurwitsch, "Quelques aspects et quelques développements de la psychologie de la forme," pp. 413–471.

[8] "French Philosophical Tradition between the Two World Wars," in *Philosophic Thought in France and the United States*, ed. Farber, p. 15.

[9] See Waelhens, *Une philosophie de l'ambiguïté*, pp. 85–86.

[10] Caillois, rev. of *Une philosophie de l'ambiguïté*, by Waelhens, p. 285. I will frequently leave sens, a technical term in Merleau-Ponty's philosophy, untranslated. Because it signifies both "meaning" and "direction," no single English word can render his philosophical point, which is that there is a continuity between meaning in its most primitive manifestation as directionality and in its most developed manifestation as intention and symbol (PP 491, tr. 428).

entities and the laws holding between them, but rather structures that make it possible for sense data and definitions to have meaning.

The nature of his critique is perhaps best approached through one of his examples. Consider the possible alternative accounts that might be given of a subject's perception of a cube. The empiricist explains the subject's impression according to a causal model in which the brain records retinal images, that are themselves the product of the stimulation of certain nerve cells by the energy of light. Merleau-Ponty points out, however, that since at most three sides of the object are visible at one time, the subject should speak only of a precise impression of three sides. This implies that a causal theory of perception could never account for "the cube" without invoking some act of synthesis tying together the various perspectives that alone are given in perception. Yet synthesis is a mental act that empiricism cannot allow in its explanations. To the idealist, only acts of perspectiveless "intellectual coordination" give effective knowledge. The three sides seen by the subject are merely a defective anticipation of a cube in its geometric definition (SC 230, tr. 213). Immediate perception is just a psychological curiosity of no special philosophical significance. In a sense, the scientist reduces the assertion "X sees a cube" to "X sees three sides," and the cube disappears from consideration. The idealist reduces the perception to mere appearance—what X sees *is* a cube—and the three sides disappear.

Only phenomenology gives an account of the fundamental layer of experience called "perception." The phenomenologist says "X sees three sides of a cube." It is in the nature of our perceptual relationship to things, contends Merleau-Ponty, that we see them through successive profiles (SC 201–202, tr. 187). Perception is inherently incomplete. It is not, for all that, inherently uncertain. A phenomenological description grants that X sees only three sides, but also asserts that various factors "announce" the completion of the figure. Differences in the way light falls on each of the three sides and that particular regularity of deformation that we call perspective lead us to expect that the figure forms a whole, the cube (PP 20, tr. 13). A profile refers beyond itself to the structure of the whole. Profiles have a sens. It is appropriate to refer to "meaning" here (if only "nascent" or "imminent") because the functions of reference, demarcation, and differentiation, which we normally ascribe to precise, conceptual definition, are already prefigured in our spontaneous perception. Perception involves the general comprehension of phenomena as wholes before explicit intellectual effort is expended to understand them.

This wholeness is identical neither with the wholes constructed from the empiricist's discrete impressions nor with the ideal wholes of intellectual synthesis. In perception, the character of wholeness is something given to the senses. It is *lived* rather than known (SC 182, tr. 165). It depends, Merleau-Ponty maintains, on a preideational structure of the objects of perception, a structure that draws our attention and that our senses and ideas then explore. Only phenomenology starts from a present in which things are partially given in order to anticipate a future perception in which the form of objects is more perfectly (but never completely) manifest.

This emphasis on wholeness means that sens applies not to isolated things, but always to things in a "field of perceptions" (PP 10, tr. 4). The crucial discovery of Gestalt psychology was that the subject perceives structures rather than isolated sense data or stimuli. Even in the most primitive relations of differentiation, where a simple figure (e.g., a gray dot) appears against a ground (e.g., a white backdrop), there is a phenomenon of sens. The dot could not appear against a uniformly gray field, and hence "the gray dot" implicitly refers beyond the "thing itself" to the ground that makes it manifest. The dot cannot even be described without reference to the conditions under which it appears (as the constancy hypothesis presupposes) because its color does not exist independently of the perceptual field. The "same" gray dot *appears* darker or lighter as it is set against a grayish or black background (SC 89, tr. 80). The experimental data that Merleau-Ponty musters in *The Structure of Behavior* show that the experience of what is perceived (the "phenomenon" in its technical sense) varies according to the structure in which it is inserted. The subject registers structural changes without the intervention of such intellectual operations as comparison, measurement, or analysis. When Merleau-Ponty says that "a form is a perceived ensemble" (SC 155, tr. 143), he means that *what* we perceive in the most immediate sense are forms—structures of nascent sens. The relationship of figure and ground is the simplest example of a "structure"—a system wherein, if one part is changed, all other parts are modified, and conversely, the system as a whole can be changed while maintaining a constant relation among the parts (SC 50, tr. 47). If one asks how it is possible for there to be meaning, the preliminary answer is that objects of perception are ordered in structures that, rather than expressing meaning, "literally make meaning emerge from themselves," as Merleau-Ponty's student François Cuzin put it.[11]

The Perceiving Subject

Or rather, they make meaning emerge from themselves, provided that a suitable perceiver is present to grasp the Gestalt. Sens requires that perceiver and perceived be coordinated such that they form a single system. One shortcoming of stimulus-response psychology is its assumption that an environment can be described independently of the organism that experiences it. Gestalt experimentation shows that the organism must be prefitted with an assemblage of capacities allowing it to respond to particular sorts of stimulation. Sens is not something that an object has or that a subject gives. It emerges only at the intersection of forms that solicit an organism's attention and a preconscious bodily capacity to explore them.

Closely paralleling Scheler's account of the emergence of human spirit in *Man's Place in Nature*, Merleau-Ponty creates a classification of the sophistication of animal responses to problem situations.[12] He ranks them along a scale that measures increasing autonomy from the environment. At one end of the scale animal behavior is locked into restricted modes by vital needs and an instinctual apparatus. Even at this level structural cues are needed to elicit reactions, but responses are unchanged by failure, as when a toad repeatedly tries to bite an earthworm from which it is separated by a glass partition (SC 114, tr. 104). Higher-level animals see similarities between situations and make adjustments, provided that all the elements that they need for their action are immediately present in a certain structural configuration. For example, a monkey will draw a piece of fruit to within its reach by means of a branch—but only if the branch is placed near the fruit so as to suggest such a use (SC 124, tr. 114). The other end of the scale is reserved for symbolic human conduct. What attracts the attention of the human subject need not be restricted to a configuration actually present. The subject can imaginatively construct a context without reference to the immediate surroundings. Human beings are the most free-perceiving animals because they *create* problems by setting objectives and devising solutions.

[11] Rev. of *La structure du comportement*, by Merleau-Ponty, p. 460.
[12] See Scheler, *Man's Place in Nature*, trans. Meyerhoff, pp. 37–48.

At all levels of complexity the behavior of living beings refuses to fit neatly into Cartesian categories. Relations between organism and environment are "dialectical" rather than causal (SC 161, tr. 149). A cause represents a constant antecedent to a particular result; the cause remains unaffected by the result. Merleau-Ponty's dialectics show how the supposed "results" described in stimulus-response psychology are in fact conditioned by the animal's peculiar attunement to meanings in particular settings. The monkey's "intention" to use a branch as a way of bringing food closer, for example, only arises in an experimental situation of a particular structure. There is not an object with the precise meaning "branch" and then various ways of relating to it, but a structure of relations in which intention and meaning are intertwined. Merleau-Ponty speaks in Hegelian terms of a "being-for-the-animal" or of "a characteristic milieu for the species" to express just such a relational quality of perception (SC 136, tr. 125).

To explain the characteristic milieu for the human species, Merleau-Ponty elaborates on Marcel's notion of the corps propre. The corps propre is the body conceived as the metaphysical condition of our ability to have knowledge of the world. Things exist for us by virtue of the bonds our bodies establish with the environment. In Marcel's terms the body "participates" in the world.[13] Merleau-Ponty's phenomenology describes the genesis of meaning in the ways that the body, in its primordial contact with the world—prior to acts of intellectual reflection—joins in the constitution of perceptual phenomena. Our bodies are oriented to articulate our environment. When we stand outside at night and see a light in a home, the interior lighting gives everything a yellow and artificial cast. Once inside our senses quickly adjust so that all the colors appear in their normal hue. Our orientation toward space is similar. Fitted with inverting lenses, we at first see the environment upside down. Yet in a short while the world rights itself. These adjustments are intimately related to the body's practice, to its orientation toward *action* on certain planes, and in lighting that reveals detail and differentiation. We cannot speak of a world of objects "out there" because objects appear only by virtue of the ways that the body actively organizes its perceptual field (PP 97, tr. 82). The corps propre is, as William Hamrick says, a "knowing-body."[14]

[13] Straus and Machado, "Gabriel Marcel's Notion of Incarnate Being," in *The Philosophy of Gabriel Marcel*, eds. Schilpp and Hahn, p. 131.

[14] "Whitehead and Merleau-Ponty: Some Moral Implications," pp. 236–237.

The superior problem-solving ability of the human species implies that the form-giving syntheses of the natural body are only the beginning of our capacity to develop sens. Although I must defer a full treatment of the social development of meaning, it is important to understand at this point that originary meaning instigates the movement by which the body accumulates structures in experience, action, and learning. Just as the body gives us a sense of space and light that opens us to practical activity in the world and makes it seem "natural," so it incorporates the results of additional practical activity and makes our installation in a much more complex world of social meaning similarly effortless. The corps propre learns to perceive new visual patterns through new works of art and architecture; it develops a sense of harmony by listening repeatedly to certain configurations of notes; it alters its sense of motion through new modes of travel. In each case our bodies take up a structure, elaborate it, and, without invoking intellectual analysis, present it to us as something with coherence and significance. The subject is thus "inseparable from the world, but from a world that he projects himself" (PP 419, tr. 365). For Merleau-Ponty, the human essence consists in this ability of the corps propre to engage in a "dialogue" with its environment. Dialogue transcends each original situation at the same time that it deposits a deep "sediment" of meanings. These meanings furnish a comprehensive background against which explicit acts of intellection can appear.

Since neither empiricist nor idealist theories account for the "lived world" in which meaning arises, neither is foundational, and both become mired in insoluble paradoxes. If empiricism were consistent, perception would present only a kaleidoscopic field of constantly changing impressions that varied as a direct function of the movement of external stimuli. Perception would not even present objects, for objects have continuity and wholeness. Moreover, empiricism refuses to acknowledge how human subjects free themselves from rigid causal determination by viewing elements of their surroundings as symbols, and it ignores teleologies that alone explain the themes in a subject's behavior. Idealism hardly fares better. By reducing matter to mind, it rids the world of its opaqueness (PP v, tr. xi). It has difficulty explaining why I experience my perceptions "passively," not as the result of my conscious activity (SC 232, tr. 215). Idealists do not see that meaning arises in structures that limit the mind's ability to alter it (SC 233, tr. 216). Idealism makes me seem like an agent in full conscious control of all that I do, whereas most of the time my body spontaneously inserts me in a world of meaning and I act most of the time out of habit.

What is most unexpected in Merleau-Ponty's critique of empiricism and idealism is his demonstration that their errors stem from the same intellectual prejudice—a belief in the myth of the absolute object and in its correlate, the absolute subject. Empiricism depends on an ability to define elementary objects, to inventory their attributes independently of circumstance and of the peculiarities of any given perceiver. This allows it to characterize perception as a direct function of the action of those objects on the perceiver. But even the scientist's knowing is a mental state, and if mental states are simply the effects of antecedent conditions, knowing is no different from any other determined reaction. It is not knowing at all. Empiricism is saved from total incoherency only by smuggling an observing subject into its "objective world." Through analysis the scientist discovers that perception is the result of interactions between immutable objects. Yet absolute objects can only be conceived by absolute, subjective observers who claim to synthesize all points of view on an object (SNS 162, tr. 93). If observers always have a particular point of view, however, then "perception as [the empiricist] lives it puts the lie to everything he says of perception in general" (PP 240, tr. 207). To the extent that empiricism is driven to posit the existence of subjects who escape causal determination and know something, it fails to characterize the foundations of its own knowledge.

Idealism speaks of an immaterial subject who defines, judges, and intends apart from all external determinations. It therefore seems utterly dissimilar to empiricism. But the idealist (at least the Brunschvicgean) does not assert the primacy of reason in order to contest the validity of science. Brunschvicg knows that mind progresses only through experience and that science, since it systematically explores the world and discovers the laws of its functioning, is the greatest agent of progress. The idealist's point is just that science is grounded in certain a priori capabilities of consciousness. Nonetheless, an idealism that does not contest the scientist's methods is entirely parasitic on scientific objectivism. Thus empiricism and idealism are alike in a crucial respect–both "express the prejudice of a universe in itself that is perfectly explicit" (PP 51, tr. 36). Both suppose an unsituated observing subject, a spectatorial consciousness that is above all the phenomena that it surveys, and both support the idea of a fully constituted object.

Their inconsistencies reveal their failure to surmount Cartesian dualism.

Crucial to Merleau-Ponty's philosophy, on the other hand, is the claim that the phenomenological account of the genesis of meaning resolves the most troublesome problems in post-Cartesian philosophy. It locates a "primordial layer" of meaning that is "anterior to the ideas of subject and object" (PP 254, tr. 219). Radical reflection discovers a level of experience at which no dualism operates because neither subject nor object has yet taken form. If he is right, the mind-body dualism is not an inherent feature of the relationship of consciousness to the world. It is the fallacious conclusion of intellectual systems like empiricism and idealism that, following Descartes, postulate absolute subjects and absolute objects. By arguing that the "sole way for a thing to act on a mind is to offer it a meaning" (SC 215, tr. 199), Merleau-Ponty's phenomenology does not allow dualism to arise. Matter itself is ordered in signification-producing structures and mind is a structure-apprehending substance (SC 215, 220, tr. 199, 204). The form is an irreducible mixture of the subjective and objective.

A danger of such dialectics is that, by insisting on the interdependency of two terms, it can obscure how either term has an identity distinct enough to support investigation. When Merleau-Ponty speaks of a hierarchy of structures, he gives the first example of how his philosophy accounts for the individuation of phenomena. "There is the body as mass of chemical components in interaction, the body as dialectic of living being and its biological milieu, and the body as dialectic of the social subject and his group. . . . Each of these degrees is soul with respect to the preceding one, body with respect to the following one" (SC 227, tr. 210). The distinctive identity of different existents depends on the degree of their formalization. A body is not just a set of chemical reactions; it is matter organized into a whole that accomplishes particular functions. But in spite of physiological similarities, all human bodies do not behave identically. Individuated behavior must be understood in the context of a more inclusive organizing principle—the body's culture and social group. In a structural theory of sens, the full "truth" of a lower form is revealed only when it is included in the organizing principle of the higher-order dialectics.[15]

[15] Cooper, "Hegelian Elements in Merleau-Ponty's *La structure du comportement*," p. 418.

This account of the dialectics of meaning converges with the Hegelian concept of "Gestalt," that is, "the concept before it has become self-consciousness" (SC 227, tr. 210). Inherent bodily capacities and a larger social context pattern our behavior in ways usually unknown to us. The meaning of our actions transcends our conscious projects because we carry preconscious intentions towards a world (our "a prioris") and because our action takes place in larger context that modifies its meaning. Yet the very fact that behavior obtains meaning from a higher organizing principle opens the possibility that the preconscious meaning of conduct can become available to us. The "in itself" can become "for itself" if the larger structure is made manifest.

Phenomenal Objectivity

Can a philosophy that concentrates on the subject's internal experience of phenomena, on the perspectival relativity of perception, and on the structural dependency of meaning give an account of objectivity? Can it explain how different subjects have similar perceptions? Merleau-Ponty's theory of the corps propre seems to leave open the possibility that the experiences of each individual might be incommensurable with those of every other individual. An invidious subjectivism would then threaten existential theory. One of the great strengths of his philosophy, however, stems from his awareness of and response to this threat. He knows that if his theory is to have any credibility vis-à-vis the dominant scientific understandings of man, and if his subsequent application of phenomenology in social and historical analyses is to compel assent in the public arena, he must explain how it accounts for the public character of knowledge. He formulates a new concept of "objectivity," one that is internal to phenomenal experience.[16]

Phenomenological objectivity depends first on the agreement of perspectives. Already in 1936, when Gabriel Marcel chose to "exist" rather than to "live," Merleau-Ponty objected that this procedure was too private, too intuitive: "it lacks an *obligatory* force."[17] Merleau-Ponty maintains that in phenomenal experience, existing things have "a certain structure"; they present "partial aspects

---

[16] Although "objectivity" is often associated with the spectatorial attitude that Merleau-Ponty criticizes, it is his chosen term. See PP 346, tr. 300 and "Le primat de la perception et ses conséquences philosophiques," p. 132, tr. 24.

[17] Rev. of *Être et avoir*, p. 107.

that are sensed as such; each side is an invitation to go further."[18] A multiplicity of views supports rather than undermines our impression of coherent objects because perspectives are mutually confirming. "They present a world" (SC 236, tr. 219). It is true that this world sometimes fools us with illusions and misimpressions. But that only means that there are situational requirements for adequate perception. There is usually an optimal relationship of the corps propre to the phenomenon, one that permits it "to offer me a spectacle that is as varied and as clearly articulated as possible" (PP 289, tr. 250). When the phenomenon is too close or too far away, when the scene is too brightly lit or too dim, when the angle of vision is uncommon, my body may be unable to elaborate the spectacle in its habitual way and therefore mistake its sens. Objectivity presupposes an effort to search out an optimal position from which to explore the convergence of perspectives.

Second, Merleau-Ponty's theory explains the constancy of experience through the concept of a hierarchy of structures. It is true that an isolated element can usually support a number of interpretations. Perhaps this gray-colored plate that I perceive is in fact a gray-colored plate, perhaps it is a white plate darkened by shadow. But when an observer grasps the relation of meaning that ties together a body and its entourage, the significance of any given perception becomes relatively determinate. The true color of the plate becomes known when I investigate the structure in which it appears (i.e., the relation between the plate and lighting, the background on which it rests, etc.). Thus, the move from viewing an element in isolation to seeing it as part of a more comprehensive structure serves to specify its sens (SC 96, tr. 87).

Third, Merleau-Ponty uses the concept of an "a priori of the species" to indicate that members of a single species perceive certain forms in a like manner. "As Gestalttheorie has shown, there are for me preferred forms that are also preferred for all other persons" (PP 502–503, tr. 440). There are perceptual judgments that are natural—for example, my intuitive understanding of how to use my arm (PP 96, tr. 81), the feeling that the mountain I see is large compared with my body (PP 502, tr. 440). These bodily intentions define the general contours of the environment for human beings as a species. In virtue of the similarity of our bodies, there is a core of species-meanings that form the ground of our power to create and bestow meaning in general.

[18] Ibid., pp. 108–109.

Does this theory of phenomenological objectivity succeed? That is, has Merleau-Ponty accounted for the solidity and intersubjectivity of experience without making reference to things-in-themselves or to universal categories of the understanding? Although suggestive, none of the three components of objectivity is entirely satisfactory. The problem is that to the extent that he remains internal to subjective experience, he fails to explain intersubjectivity adequately, and to the extent he does explain intersubjectivity, he approaches the standard empiricist solution.

According to the first component, partial perspectives converge toward a perception of coherent objects. This fact, however, gives no assurance that the perspectives of *different* persons converge toward the *same* objects. It is conceivable that two people facing a cube will agree that there is a single object there, but will disagree as to what it is. This would be a particular problem if each were incapable of moving to the other's standpoint. In visual perception this problem is usually surmountable. But when the "situation" includes social conditions like economic position and religion, it may be practically impossible for subjects to trade viewpoints. In a phenomenology that stresses the sedimentation of contingent experience, *my* conviction that "there is a world" never assures that *we* all perceive the same world. So the notion of convergent perspectives is insufficient to ground intersubjective social knowledge.

Merleau-Ponty could reply that the concept of species-meanings bridges the gap between the self and others. While this move may explain the intersubjective consistency of primitive perception of colors or shapes, it too falters as soon as the corps propre assimilates more complex experience. The uniqueness of different persons' funds of originary meaning would foster divergent experiences of phenomena. Any intersubjective agreement about experience would be purely contingent. That is a very weak interpretation of objectivity and gives few clues as to how we might resolve disputes about the nature of very complex phenomena like works of art or political systems.

Moreover, to the extent that the second and third components do explain the interpersonal consistency of experience, they are questionably phenomenological. The problem is that embedded in Merleau-Ponty's early phenomenology are tacit references to an apprehending consciousness that exists independently of the phenomena it observes and to phenomena whose wholeness is self-contained. This problem is worth exploring in detail because unfortunately it later finds its way into Merleau-Ponty's characterization of the knowledge of Marx, Lenin, and Trotsky.

The corps propre, it will be recalled, gives us originary meaning. The subject's experience changes as a function of the structure of the perceptual field. The perceiving subject, however, is unaware of the structural dependency of experience because he is absorbed in the structure. Someone else must map out perceptual gestalten. The attempt to describe structures of originary meaning constantly exposes the phenomenologist to the temptation to stand outside of the body, so to speak, in order better to perceive its interaction with its environment.

Merleau-Ponty does not consistently refuse that temptation. One grasps structural sens, he argues, when one understands the gestalt that produces the *sens originaire* ("originary" sens).[19] This means that the structural dependency of the subject's experience is discovered by *an observer who is himself external to that experience.* The achievements of Gestalt psychology flowed from the work of experimental scientists who manipulated structural settings in order to learn about the changes they produced in their subjects' experience. They examined the gestalt before them as they would an object; they claimed to discover universal characteristics of human perception. Although Merleau-Ponty faults Gestalt psychologists for recurring to causal models of explanation, he never expects them to interpret *their own relationship* to the experimental setting as one internal to a larger structure. An unsituated, spectatorial point of view insinuates itself into his phenomenology.

This objectivism is particularly pronounced when he introduces

---

[19] My analysis of the two levels of meaning—originary and structural—owes much to Theodore Geraets. He argues that in the 1930s Merleau-Ponty was as yet unsure of his theory of meaning, sometimes seeing sens from an external perspective as a structure, sometimes implying its origin in lived experience. After a closer study of Husserl, he opted for a theory of lived meaning in *The Phenomenology of Perception*. See *Vers une nouvelle philosophie transcendentale*, pp. 66–68, 101–102, 144, and 177ff. I differ with Geraets however both interpretively and critically. I believe Merleau-Ponty maintained both perspectives on sens well into the 1940s. In numerous passages of the *Phenomenology*, it is clear that he believes that structural and originary meaning are the external and internal aspects of the same phenomenon. What the observer sees as a change in structure, the subject experiences as a change in sens originaire. (PP 20, 29, 61, 70–71, 369, tr. 13, 24, 49, 57, 319). This is not markedly different from his view in *The Structure of Behavior*. My critical point is that in both works Merleau-Ponty does not consistently stress that the perceiver of structures, *while perceiving those structures*, must himself be within another structure that he cannot perceive. Instead, he refers to these observations as if they were simply objective knowledge in the conventional sense.

the concepts of function and equilibrium into his phenomenology. At one point he describes a structure in the following way: "[It is] . . . an ensemble of forces in a state of equilibrium or constant change. . . . No law can be formulated for each part taken separately. . . . Each vector is determined in size and direction by all the others. Each local change in a form will be translated by a redistribution of forces that keeps their relationship constant" (SC 147–148, tr. 137). An equilibrium is an end point of a system of interrelated forces. The spherical shape of a soap bubble, for example, is the equilibrium solution to the problem represented by the contrary tendencies, on the one hand, of external air pressure to reduce the bubble to a single point and, on the other hand, of the enclosed air to realize the maximum volume possible (SC 158–159, tr. 146). The system is "oriented"; it contains a relation of meaning insofar as what is given (the parts) are by their configuration an implicit reference to something beyond them. If the equilibrium point of a system can be identified, then when the system is observed to be in disequilibrium, local changes that seem to be different in kind (e.g., a "distention" at two poles of the bubble and a "constriction" in the middle) can be shown to have equivalent meaning. Both are functional contributions to a particular result (the formation of a spherical structure) that will be achieved at a later time.

Merleau-Ponty describes the behavior of living beings similarly, except to note that in vital systems behavior is adaptive. What an organism seeks is not a static condition, but a range of behavior favorable to a particular way of "being in the world." Behavior is not the result of a simple interaction of predefined forces; the living organism works to maintain an equilibrium with its environment.[20] For instance, an animal will strive by various means to maintain itself upright; where one body part is damaged, another may assume the same function. Merleau-Ponty's point is that the coherency of vital behavior is to be grasped not in static laws, but through the animal's characteristic way of dealing with its environment—what he sometimes calls an "a priori of the species" (SC 139, tr. 129).

On the one hand, he uses such examples to show that an environment is not objective in the empiricist's sense. The animal's experience depends on how its structures of behavior interact with a structured environment. On the other hand, his conclusions still

[20] Muniz de Rezende, "Le point de départ chez Merleau-Ponty," p. 469.

clearly depend on interpreting the gestalt as something that realizes itself spontaneously in front of an observer. The equilibria in
the physical and vital systems are not equilibria between phenomena and the scientist's corps propre; they are attributes of self-contained systems that the scientist observes. Once again Merleau-
Ponty's phenomenological conclusions rely on an observational
objectivity that is close to empiricism.

Close but not identical—the great merit of his approach is that it
imposes tasks upon the observer that are quite different from analysis, hypothesis forming and testing, and causal explanation. The
objective of a phenomenological description is "understanding."
To understand something is to grasp the norms that comprise the
structure in which it exists, "it is to unite the ensemble of known
facts by their signification, to discover in all of them a general attitude toward certain categories of objects" (SC 17, tr. 19). Phenomenological description chooses and assembles facts, shows
their interconnections, explores their continuities, and elaborates
their meanings. It does not penetrate an illusionistic surface, it
pursues latitude and detail in observation so that it can map out
structures. Where the observer's baggage of acquired meanings
obscures authentic structures, phenomenology tries to identify
these acquired meanings and hold them in suspense. In the introduction to *The Phenomenology of Perception*, Merleau-Ponty defines
his goal and reveals its philosophical parentage: "Whether it is a
question of a perceived thing, of an historical event, or of a doctrine, to 'understand' is to recover the total intention . . .—the
unique way of existing that is expressed in all the properties . . .
of the glass or the piece of wax, in all the events of a revolution.
. . . In each civilization, it is a question of rediscovering the Idea
in the Hegelian sense" (PP xiii, tr. xviii). A successful phenomenological description identifies structures of meanings that others
recognize as "true" because they really do explain the coherency
of phenomena.

Foundations and Transcendental Philosophy

How does this phenomenological program inform Merleau-Ponty's political work? A claim that there was a deductive relationship
between the two would be far too strong. A theory of originary
meanings could presumably accommodate equally either a conservative theory of traditional society or a program of revolutionary
change. Yet to say that the relationship between Merleau-Ponty's

phenomenology and his political theory is merely analogical or that he simply translates historical materialism into a "new vocabulary" reduces the connection to the level of rhetoric or idiosyncracy.[21] It would be truer to the boldness of his philosophical project, I think, to regard his phenomenology as a transcendental theory of human understanding applying across experiential realms, necessarily encompassing the political in its sweep.

A transcendental theory focuses on the mental activities involved in the organization of experience into rationally comprehensible patterns. Kant accomplished his "Copernican Revolution" in philosophy with the transcendental argument that, in order to be known, objects must conform to special requirements of human understanding. Transcendental inquiry establishes that reason supplies synthetic categories that unify sense data and make experience intelligible. The transcendental is that which makes it possible for the world to be "given"; it is the "foundation" of our knowledge of the world.

The a priori that Merleau-Ponty posits, however, totally reconstructs the Kantian project. In the forward to the *Phenomenology*, he explains that a priori conceptions in previous philosophies have wrongly presupposed the rationality of the world. Phenomenology differs markedly in this regard. "For the first time, the philosopher's meditation is sufficiently self-conscious to avoid realizing its results in the world, in front of it. The philosopher tries to think through the world, other people, and himself, and to conceive their relations. . . . The phenonomenological world is not something that makes explicit a preexisting being, but is the foundation of being" (PP xv, tr. xx). In a revealing formulation Merleau-Ponty contrasts Kantian "conditions of possibility" with the "conditions of reality" sought in the new transcendental (PP 501, tr. 439). Conditions of reality are not universal, preexperiential categories of the mind. They are the accretion of meanings layered in human consciousness by its perceptual contact with the world. The structures of human understanding arise in our communication with the surrounding environment and with other people. The sense of space, sexual inclinations, even social position are invested with meanings that are "unthought." The "true transcendental" is in "the natural and social world" (PP 418, tr. 364). An existential philosophy founds meaning not in a universal subject, but in concrete,

[21] See respectively Miller, *History and Human Existence*, p. 207; and Invitto, *Merleau-Ponty politico: L'eresia programmatica*, p. 14.

individuated, "real" conditions of perception (PP 24, tr. 17). Like Kantian categories, however, these conditions of reality serve as the presuppositions of our explicit attitudes toward the world—including scientific and philosophical ones. Merleau-Ponty's insistence that "perception . . . is the background from which *all* acts stand out" (PP v, tr. xi, emphasis added) means that the commitment that he makes to phenomenology in his first works must function as a prolegomenon to the understanding of all experience. Historical and political phenomena too must have perceptual foundations.

Recently all talk of "foundations" has become philosophically suspect in a way that may rob Merleau-Ponty's enterprise of its credibility regardless of its concrete positions. Richard Rorty in particular has mounted perhaps the most powerful attack on any philosophy that claims to be "foundational in respect to the rest of culture . . . because it understands the foundations of knowledge."[22] Rorty maintains that foundational claims are always self-deceptive products of particular language games that obtain in particular cultures at particular times. Such games are composed of historical accidents that arbitrarily conflate philosophical questions (like those concerning minds and bodies). Yet even once philosophy's confusions are dissipated, what is left is no final epistemic authority, but instead a project of "edification" without foundations. "Edifying philosophers . . . keep space open for the sense of wonder" rather than pretend to adjudicate between competing epistemological doctrines.[23] I cannot attempt to assess the persuasiveness of Rorty's conception of philosophy here (although the sorts of arguments he makes will receive some attention in the final chapter when I compare Foucault and Merleau-Ponty). But to the extent that Merleau-Ponty's political theory is foundationalist, it is important to ask whether Rorty's attack fatally injures the existentialist's project.

Certain of Merleau-Ponty's formulations do indeed partake of a philosophical tradition that concerns itself with accurate representation. While his notion of the corps propre excludes any image of mind "mirroring" nature (since consciousness both forms the situation and is solicited by it), he does maintain that prereflective life is the absolute origin of meaning. Reflective consciousness is then "founded" on structures "borrowed" from the body's natural

---

[22] *Philosophy and the Mirror of Nature*, p. 3.
[23] Ibid., p. 370.

life (PP 225, tr. 193). The body's dialogue with the world writes a sort of primitive text that establishes a paradigmatic syntax and a treasury of metaphors from which all subsequent knowledge draws inspiration. Merleau-Ponty's complaint against empiricism and idealism is that, like languages composed entirely of technical jargon, they are unable to translate the rich poetry of primordial meaning. In a sense they do not really reflect man's relationship with the world, but instead cloud the mirror with a fog of categories unknown to perceptual life. So Merleau-Ponty is asserting for phenomenology the right to disqualify some epistemologies.

He does not seek, however, to devise "a permanent neutral matrix for all inquiry and all history."[24] In fact, he declares the impossibility of doing so. To understand Merleau-Ponty's special sense of "foundations," we must relate the term's etymology to his characteristic manner of establishing a phenomenological argument. "Any conceivable being," he contends, appears only "on the ground [fond] of this world" (PP 255, cf. 418–419, tr. 221, 364–365). He extends Gestalttheorie's observations on the importance of the figure-background distinction (figure et fond) to perceptual experience in all cognitive domains. Typically, his argument starts from an attempt to grasp the "background"—the ensemble of prereflexive meanings—that some type of thought or action habitually presupposes. He then reveals this background as the precondition of the experience in a triple sense. (a) It provides a differentiating factor that makes the perception empirically possible. (This dot cannot exist without a background.) (b) It is the philosophical presupposition that makes the entire phenomenon conceivable. (No "figure" is imaginable without some "background.") (c) It is what gives the phenomenon its distinctive character. (The color of the background affects the perceived color of the figure.)

The founding-founded relationship works, it must be stressed, in "two directions": "The founding term—the unreflected . . . perception—is primary in the sense that the founded presents itself as a more determinate or explicit form of the founding, which prevents the founding from ever reabsorbing the founded, and yet the founding is not primary in the empiricist sense and the founded is not simply derived since it is through the founded that the founding manifests itself" (PP 451, tr. 394). The activity of the philosopher engaged in a radical reflection on his prereflective life illustrates this complex relationship perfectly. His prereflective life

[24] Ibid., p. 179.

is founding since it makes possible the very phenomenon of meaning that he uses in his reflection. But in its turn, reflection is a sublimation and development of originary meaning. It is founded by, but not reducible to, primitive sens. And yet reflection can turn inward to reflect back upon originary meaning, bringing aspects of it to light and, as in Merleau-Ponty's case, using it to argue for a certain conception of philosophy. The dialectical reciprocity of this process means, however, that it is never complete; consciousness pushes at its own limits.[25] Elucidating backgrounds is an endless enterprise, since one background can only be made apparent by placing it on another which, for the time of that particular investigation, goes unexamined. The theme of "ambiguity" that has been so often associated with Merleau-Ponty's philosophy finds its justification in the inherent incompletion of meaning that results from viewing the dialectical relationship of body and world as the ground of all conceptually precise polarities.[26]

Indeed, Merleau-Ponty's notion of foundations joins with Rorty's conception of philosophy at numerous points. Both believe that philosophy yields no incontestable knowledge. For neither does philosophy challenge the validity of knowledge in other domains of culture, but instead proposes to enrich culture by pointing out undetected meanings and unpursued possibilities. Both see philosophy as a dialogue with contemporaries and predecessors rather than as a form of absolute knowledge that supersedes earlier understandings. When Merleau-Ponty writes of "that Reason . . . that [is] capable of respecting the variety and singularity of individual psyches, of civilizations, of methods of thought, and of the contingency of history" (SNS 110, tr. 63), he is not far from Rorty, who sees philosophical systems as the product of contingent historical circumstances in various domains of culture (e.g., literature and religion).

They do, however, differ in a crucial respect: Merleau-Ponty believes that historical accidents accumulate and form a structure that is the very advent of rationality. Even if reason is never complete and its continuation never guaranteed, generally it does *prog-*

---

[25] See Madison, *The Phenomenology of Merleau-Ponty*, pp. 160–161, and Langan, *Merleau-Ponty's Critique of Reason*, p. 15.

[26] Ferdinand Alquié was the first to highlight this theme in his seminal article, "Une philosophie de l'ambiguïté: L'existentialisme de Maurice Merleau-Ponty," esp. p. 68. Alquié, a Cartesian critic of Merleau-Ponty, was also his classmate at the Lycée Louis le Grand. Alquié, "In Memoriam," *Cahiers du Sud* 48:362–363 (September–November 1961), p. 153.

ress. Philosophy is the "realization of a truth" (PP xv, tr. xx). In contrast, Rorty's denial of the "commensurability" of ideas accepted in different eras forbids any speculation about a progressive evolution of reason.[27] Rorty's views—as he acknowledges—resemble Sartre's in such respects.[28] But that may only be to say that Rorty is vulnerable to the same criticism that Merleau-Ponty makes of his existentialist colleague's ontology. Both may have adopted modes of thought that overrule the very categories needed to make political life comprehensible. We turn then to Merleau-Ponty's first allusion to the political shortcomings of Sartrean philosophy in his existential account of freedom.

Existential Freedom

Sartre's interpretation of freedom reached a general public through his play, *The Flies,* in mid-1943. Using the allegory of Orestes' assassination of the tyrant Aegisthus, Sartre urged the French to forget recrimination over their defeat in war and to engage themselves for the sake of freedom. In the play Orestes discovers through his acts of political murder that he—not the gods, not fate—is the author of all his action. He tells the oppressed people of Argos that "each man must invent his own path." He even accepts the paradoxical implication that his claims to freedom mean he "will have to praise the freedom of the prisoner loaded down with chains at the bottom of his cell and of the crucified slave," because he is asserting that external conditions are never so constraining as to make free action impossible.[29] That Sartre would apply this analysis directly to political affairs was apparent in his first public exchange with the Communists. Just as Orestes was free to live under tyranny or could become truly free through political action he argued, so "the proletariat is free because it can always choose to accept its condition with resignation or revolt against it."[30]

Sartre laid out the theoretical foundations of his conception of freedom in *Being and Nothingness* in 1943, two years before Merleau-Ponty completed his *Phenomenology.* Undoubtedly the two men believed the goals of their philosophies to be largely the same. Sartre wrote that when he and Merleau-Ponty met again

[27] *Philosophy and the Mirror of Nature,* pp. 316–317.
[28] Ibid., p. 376.
[29] *Huis clos, suivi de Les mouches,* pp. 174–175.
[30] "À propos de l'existentialisme," p. 11.

during the war (having rarely seen each other since their days at the ENS), "the essential words were said—phenomenology, existence; we discovered our true concern."[31] Their common project involved much more than a few words. Before Merleau-Ponty, Sartre had publicly staked out positions on most of the issues discussed in this chapter. Sartre sought to describe the nature of a situated consciousness and criticized Husserl for "enclos[ing] himself in the cogito."[32] He denied the "translucidity" of consciousness, insisting that there is a "nonthetic," prereflective cogito that is the precondition of the Cartesian cogito.[33] Although he did not take up the role of the body in the constitution of knowledge until about one-third of the way through his massive tome, he did say that our bodies are our point of view on the world, and he made use of the Gestaltists' figure-ground relationship.[34] The disagreement between Merleau-Ponty and Sartre rarely concerns their conclusions. In question is a theory of consciousness that is consistent with those conclusions and that can inform political thought.

Sartre grounds his concept of freedom in Descartes' methodical doubt. It is an unchallengeable accomplishment of the Cartesian tradition, he believes, that "at the start there can be no truth other than this one: I think, therefore I am."[35] This "absolute truth" of the primacy of consciousness leads him to posit the duality between the in-itself and the for-itself. Being-in-itself is that being that simply is. It has no will and no consciousness of itself. It exists in the mode of the object, since it can neither initiate action nor reflect. It can only *be*. Being-for-itself is the human mode of existence revealed by the cogito. In stark contradistinction to complete, opaque being-in-itself is the "nothingness" that is man, a consciousness that aims at things but is free of their determination. It knows that it exists. Because experience must exist for man, he may choose not to accept what is presented to him. He can "negate" things as they are and make them to be otherwise. Man's ability to reflect on his own existence, his ability to become aware of the meaning of his action, amounts to an irreducible difference in the nature of his existence from that of things.

It might seem that this dualism must end in the assertion of the free subject's ability to impose meanings arbitrarily on the world.

[31] "Merleau-Ponty vivant," p. 307.
[32] *L'être et le néant*, p. 115.
[33] Ibid., p. 20.
[34] Ibid., pp. 270, 394, 380. See Whitford, *Merleau-Ponty's Critique*, p. 35.
[35] *L'existentialisme est un humanisme*, p. 64; cf. *L'être et le néant*, p. 83.

Sartre vigorously denies that this is the case. He relies on the theme of the situation to lend some stability to the concept of human existence. Freedom, he says, is always engaged in relation to a resistant world. A short man cannot "make himself" tall, he cannot make it so that the mountain ahead ceases to exist. One's body, past, position, and death are a set of "givens" that comprise one's situation, and the situation limits one's freedom.[36] However, Sartre emphasizes, it is always up to man to choose the meaning that the situation will have "for him." He cannot wish away the mountain ahead, but he is free to consider it as an obstacle to be avoided or a challenge to be surmounted.[37]

In the culminating chapter of *The Phenomenology of Perception*, Merleau-Ponty develops a different existential analysis of freedom that he *later* (in 1949) explicitly admitted had been written "against Sartre" (IN 153). I stress the timing of this admission because in the first years after the war, Merleau-Ponty covered over his differences with his existentialist colleagues and especially his differences with Sartre. Sartrean ideas appear in his works under the label of "idealism," or "Cartesianism," or simply anonymously. Often he made it seem that he and Sartre were in complete agreement, when in fact he was subtly altering Sartre's reasoning. Where their disagreements could not be so easily interpreted away, he made Sartre's position into a partial truth in a more extended argument. Merleau-Ponty engaged in a transformative defense of existentialism.

To ignore this rhetorical strategy would be to miss something important in his theory, for his argumentative design is an index of his political sensibility. He writes in view of a *public* that he wants to convince and of a fledgling *movement* that he wants to advance. If he mutes his criticism of other existentialists, it is because he has the political sense that direct attack might alienate his colleagues and confuse their growing following. Far better to reshape the public perception of existentialism by recuperating what is most valid in its conclusions than to provoke another division among its adherents. Better yet to move the primary theoreticians of existentialism toward his own views by convincing them that their reasoning does not support the very conclusions they want to establish. It is in this context that we should read Merleau-Pon-

---

[36] Sartre, *L'être et le néant*, p. 570.
[37] Ibid., p. 569.

ty's argument that Sartre's concepts of freedom and the situation are unable to explain the nature of constraints on human behavior.

Sartre had already shown, Merleau-Ponty agrees, that "it is inconceivable that I should be free in certain of my actions and determined in others; what sense could be made of an idling liberty that gives free play determinism?" (PP 496–497, tr. 434–435). Sartre knew that in using the concept of causation, the observer makes an a priori commitment to deterministic explanation. If an unexpected reaction follows from some conjunction of events, the observer assumes not that the action was undetermined, but simply that he has not yet identified all the operative causes. Freedom and causality do not mix easily. The Cartesian starting point allows Sartre to assert the priority of self-awareness and, hence, freedom in all acts of knowing, thus countering causal theories of perception. But ironically, just as positing the concept of causation ends by making the world seem comprehensively determined, so Sartre's interpretation of being-for-itself makes the subject seem comprehensively free. His insistence on our ability to interpret the situation (e.g., to decide what the meaning of the mountain will be for me) at first sounds like the plausible claim that interpretation works a narrow range of variations on a given object. But in fact, Sartre cannot make any sense of the concept of a "given" object. What is "the mountain" in his explanation of a situation? If it has no meaning prior to its involvement in my projects and if it can affect me only through its meaning, how can it influence me at all? If I am absolutely free to set the value of a situation, there is, in effect, no situation. Nor is there any reason to expect that others with different projects will ever agree with me in their interpretations of the situation. In fact, to the extent that I change my projects, there is no reason to expect that I will understand even my own prior experience. Sartre lacks an adequate concept of phenomenal objectivity. Brute facticity continually slips away into nothingness.

Significantly, Merleau-Ponty immediately picks up on the political implications of Sartre's metaphysics. He objects that Sartre makes liberty into an ontological condition, a "state of nature" from which man never emerges. If a slave is equally free in chains or in revolt, then "one cannot say that there is any *free action* since free action, in order to be discernible, must appear against a background of life that was not free or was less so" (PP 499, tr. 437). Freedom is understood only in relation to alternative situations where action is blocked. Liberty exists in a field; "it must have favored possibilities or realities that tend to maintain themselves in being" (PP 500, cf. 518, tr. 438, 435). We develop our sense of what is free from the experience of situations that resist our attempts to make them conform to our will. In a Sartrean world the concept of freedom would never arise, because a being-for-itself would meet no abiding realities that resisted its projects. A new theory of freedom is needed that both appropriates the truth of Sartre's insight that human behavior is free and modifies its reasoning to give a better account of how behavior is situationally limited. What is needed—as Merleau-Ponty observes in an article defending Sartre against Catholic and Communist critics—is a theory that can "make allowances for freedom . . . without giving it everything." Merleau-Ponty does not reject *Being and Nothingness*. He calls for a "sequel" that will develop a "theory of passivity" (SNS 133, tr. 77).

Passivity is a problem for any phenomenology. Why is it, if we encounter the world only through our intentions, that we experience phenomena as being beyond our intentional control? Why is it that we cannot reshape the meaning of the world as easily as we stipulate the meaning of new symbols? Most ways of characterizing passivity presuppose some form of philosophical realism. Realists argue that we cannot see simply what we intend to see because what we see is a function of what is out there to be seen. Objects in our environment impose their reality on our senses. But for the existentialists' intending consciousness, objects are always mediated by meaning. How can a meaning impose itself on a mind?

The Figure of Freedom, the Ground of Passivity

Merleau-Ponty explains passivity by pointing to a key property of the body-subject: it elaborates meaning by placing different perceptions in the relation of figure and ground. His mention of "a background [fond] of life" alludes to how the body spontaneously accumulates habits, practices, and goals in ways that become so deeply entrenched that they seem "natural." This sedimentation creates the field of meanings on which free action appears. Freedom consists not in an unrestricted capacity to define meaning, but in an ability to modulate meanings by transforming elements of the sedimented field of perception. Our freedom comes from our ability to focus our attention on those background decisions, to bring them to the foreground, and to see previously unperceived possibilities for change. Free action transforms prereflective choices, but never entirely transcends them.

The sedimentation of meaning also lends unity to the various decisions an individual makes without supposing a deliberate intention on his or her part to express the same theme in all conduct. Even though Sartre admits the existence of some such pre-reflective choices he misses the explanatory potential of the body-subject because he believes that "the true choice" is only in a "purifying reflection that assumes [the primary one]."[38] The priority of interpretive freedom rules out the possibility that any "factual state whatever it may be (the political or economic structure of society, the psychological 'state,' etc.) is capable by itself of motivating any act whatsoever."[39] The efficacy of a motive must derive from an individual's perpetually renewed decision concerning its value.

For Merleau-Ponty "the true choice is that of our entire character and of our manner of being in the world" (PP 501, tr. 438). This choice is most genuine in the sense that it is a better indicator of our values than are our verbal claims and in the sense that it is more efficacious. Deliberative choices often yield to the weight of an established way of life. Our prereflective choices give a spontaneous meaning to our perceptions and through that meaning motivate our actions. "Motive" signifies the "situation" in its most immediate, brute, or obvious sense, prior to its being touched by operations of reason. It is "the situation as fact" (PP 299, tr. 259). The situation as given to bodily or habitual ways of knowing is the meaningful ground upon which intelligence constructs the figures of its higher-order significations. There can be no question of a situation causing any type of action because the subject must first be aware of it for it to have any effect on him. Like a cause, "the motive is an antecedent," but unlike a cause, it "acts only through its significance" (PP 299, tr. 259).

A church steeple seen in the midst of an open landscape, for example, will appear smaller and more distant than the same steeple seen through a reduction screen that blocks out the surroundings. The meaning of the steeple changes as it is seen with or without its contextual field. Blocking out the hills, valleys, and rooftops that separate us from the church removes a set of potential "lived"

---

[38] Jeanson, *Le problème morale et la pensée de Sartre*, p. 305. See Sartre, *L'être et le néant*, p. 201.

[39] Sartre, *L'être et le néant*, pp. 510–513.

projects—crossing fields, climbing hills—through which we understand our relation to the steeple. The size of the retinal image remains constant in the two cases, so the change in perception cannot be explained in terms of causes; moreover, the change is spontaneous and so not the product of reflective reason. Rather the different meanings of the steeple motivate the change in its apparent size. Our ability to act on, to reach, or to explore the object is a part of what the object means to us.[40] A situation similarly motivates an action insofar as it offers certain meanings that I validate by my decision to take them up (PP 299, tr. 259).

The durability of perceptual forms and their partial efficacy in motivating behavior mean that action can be described in terms of "probabilities" (PP 505, tr. 442). This term should not be allowed to call to mind highly intellectualized operations and statistical procedures far removed from originary perception. Merleau-Ponty's example is revealing in this regard. A long-standing inferiority complex translates, he says, a sedimentation of attitudes towards one's milieu—attitudes beyond the reach of simple volitional reversal and, hence, ones that will "probably" persist (PP 504, tr. 442). Habits, trends, persistent personality traits, and preferred modes of behavior are the basis of a phenomenological concept of probability. Sartre's radical liberty presupposes at every moment an unvarying ability to tear through the fabric of meaning one has woven into one's life. But if one's choice of friends, living situation, employment, preferences, and goals all interrelate in an *être au monde* (being-in-the-world), then certain types of decisions will be more probable than others in a way that Sartre cannot acknowledge (PP 505, tr. 442). Probable behavior and understanding are characteristic of a being that cannot continually create meanings in disregard of established ones.

Two aspects of this theory of freedom then account for the resistant quality of the background on which it appears. First, the fact that the body spontaneously presents us with a world ordered to support our practice removes our background decisions from easy conscious control. Since every free act requires some background, there will always be meanings inaccessible to change even at the moment we initiate a particular change. Background meanings are experienced passively and, unbeknownst to consciousness, motivate perception and behavior. Second, any one of the orientations of the corps propre is integrated with innumerable

---

[40] Shapiro, "Perception and Dialectic," pp. 255–256; cf. pp. 59–61, tr. 48–50.

others in my being-in-the-world. This makes it difficult to change a given element of my behavior, as the established themes of my life will tend to make the change conform to the sens of my previous behavior. The phenomenon is similar to one familiar in visual perception. When we encounter a strong pattern in our visual field, we tend to overlook imperfections in it unless we expend unusual effort in examining it. Our initial perception of the pattern sets up an expectation that the pattern is continuous, and this expectation suppresses perception of the flaw. Likewise the general structures of my habitual way of being-in-the-world tend to assert themselves against radical changes in my attitudes. General structures resist change by integrating particular elements into established patterns.

Ultimately the reason that Sartre falls short of an adequate theory of passivity is that he attempts to found existential understanding on Cartesian categories. Being-in-itself updates Descartes' conception of a dense material world that is absolutely other to the consciousness. Being-for-itself revives Descartes' pure thinking substance that freely surveys the world. Sartre deliberately sets himself the task of standing between a deterministic positivism and an unconstrained idealism. But he is unable to define that position theoretically because the Cartesian spirit virtually possesses his philosophy. Descartes' spectral cogito makes Sartre unleash a subject with absolute freedom, and Descartes' voice echoes through a political discourse that cannot discriminate between free and unfree situations. It is as if Cartesian categories contained a logic of their own that led their users into self-contradiction: empiricists presuppose absolute subjects, idealists presuppose absolute objects, and existentialists presuppose them both.

It is to exorcize the Cartesian spirit that Merleau-Ponty insists existentialism must find a "third term *between* the for-itself and the in-itself" (PP 142, tr. 122). He shifts the emphasis in existential thought from the free subject to the structure of relationships tying together the perceiver and the perceived. He seeks to begin theory anew at the level at which sens is founded, a level where subject and object have not yet become differentiated. Autochthonous sens cannot diminish human freedom or preempt all areas of human action in freedom's favor because it is prior to freedom. It "forms the ground of all decisional *Sinngebung*" (PP 503, tr. 441).

Merleau-Ponty's treatment of Sartrean freedom is a perfect model of the sort of critique he practices throughout his political theory of the 1940s. He takes up an important concept and argues that only existentialism, not idealism or empiricism, can give an adequate account of it. Moreover, he shows that his revised existentialism, particularly with its notion of the body-subject, is a better foundation for the concept than what alternative existentialisms provide. Finally, he demonstrates that his philosophy offers not only a better metaphysics, but also a firmer grasp of a political phenomenon like repression.

Merleau-Ponty's analysis of freedom thus foreshadows his general argument that a properly founded existentialism supplies the conceptual tools needed to think politically. The very enterprise of describing the constraints that so much political action strives to abolish demands a particular understanding of human consciousness. One must be able to conceive intentionality and passivity together. Empiricists cannot (consistently) speak of the slave's freedom because they view him as an object whose behavior is entirely determined by antecedent circumstances. Idealists cannot (consistently) conceive passivity. Their slave destroys his shackles by suspending the judgments that give the iron its solidity. Sartre's slave either reinterprets his irons as bracelets and slips out along with the idealist or contents himself with rattling the gates of his cell as he proclaims himself a free man. Merleau-Ponty's slave, on the other hand, has a body that feels the cutting edge of the irons and a mind that can be dulled by years of subservient behavior.

Yet Merleau-Ponty's theory of freedom may appear to have its own political weaknesses. Most would assert that the primary political question raised by the existence of slavery is not how to describe it but how to end it, and Merleau-Ponty has only made the latter question more difficult. If the slave's very consciousness is altered by his servitude, how can he ever become free? Does it really matter to anyone who wants to liberate the oppressed to learn that freedom has its foundation in the individual's being-in-the-world? While my discussion so far gives some idea of the transcendental approach that Merleau-Ponty will apply to any subject matter, it has not been explained why there is politics or why freedom is ever endangered. To understand these topics requires analyzing the foundation of meaningful relations, not only between subject and world, but between subject and subject.

THREE

COLLECTIVE MEANING: POLITICS AND VIOLENCE

When Sartre first applied his existential ontology to political questions, the Marxist theorist Henri Lefebvre chided him for posing "the human problem" as "an individual question, abstract and theoretical." This was in sorry contrast to Marxism, which sees man's social condition as "a problem of action founded on objective knowledge."[1] Merleau-Ponty, coming to Sartre's defense, was suspicious of this Marxism that refused to "tarry over the task of describing being and of founding the existence of other people" (SNS 134, tr. 77). His use of "founding" suggests that political theory starts not by assuming that man's nature is social, but by explaining at a perceptual level how a social nature is possible. The theoretical shortcomings are not so much Marx's, he notes, as those of his erstwhile followers. Their conception of "objective knowledge" leads them to "treat consciousness as part of the world, a reflection of the object." Where Lefebvre complained that Sartre's descriptions are too fundamental to be relevant to a radical theory, Merleau-Ponty insisted that any theory purporting to explain social phenomena hovers without support until its transcendental underpinnings are secured.

But he also concluded in this same article with another suggestion for the sequel to Sartre's ontology. "One must analyze engagement, the moment when the subjective and objective conditions of history tie into one another, the mode of existence of a class before the awakening of consciousness, in short, the status of the social and the phenomenon of coexistence. *Being and Nothingness* does not yet give us this theory of the social" (SNS 140, tr. 81). Again Merleau-Ponty will argue that idealism, empiricism, and Sartrean existentialism cannot elucidate a crucial aspect of human consciousness. This time they fail to understand not freedom, but intersubjectivity. Founding an existential politics requires re-

---

[1] Lefebvre, "Existentialisme et Marxisme: réponse à une mise au point," p. 8.

vising existentialism so it can adopt modes of thought that make phenomena like interpersonal solidarity and group behavior intelligible. Building on his conception of the corps propre, Merleau-Ponty shows how the cultural development of meaning answers to this requirement. At the same time this theory explains why violence between differently formed classes is the central problem of collective life.

The Possibility of Community

In *The Structure of Behavior* Merleau-Ponty shows that all animals participate in articulating an environment that is meaningful to their behavior. What differentiates man from other animals is his ability to manipulate his surroundings symbolically, to transform things in light of an idea, even to imagine things present that are not before him. Using a branch as a "club" and as "something to reach with" and as a "cane" involves exercising a peculiar ability to alter the immediate sens of an object such as a tree limb; these usages would be impossible if the only significations we knew were those established in our bodily relation to the environment. Where animal intentionality involves the constitution of a fixed setting, we "humanize" nature by acting on it. We settle new and plural meanings into matter. Following Hegel, Merleau-Ponty gives the name "work" to all activities by which we transform physical and biological nature.[2]

The significance of work goes far beyond its utility. Work creates "a cultural world that constitutes a second level above perceptual experience."[3] We develop new structures that spontaneously orient us in practical activity. Just as the corps propre installs us in a world of natural objects whose wholeness is so familiar that the synthesis of perspectives goes unnoticed, so it takes up human creations and sediments their meanings in the perceptual apparatus so that it takes no intellectual effort to recognize a pile of stones as a "wall," to hear a succession of sounds as "music," to recognize a gesture of the hand as an attempt at communication. Man virtually "secretes culture," creating a non-natural world that is nonetheless *"natural for man"* (SNS 208–209, tr. 118).

This lends a unique dynamism to human existence for "cultural objects . . . cause new cycles of behavior to emerge" (SC 175, tr.

---

[2] SNS 189, tr. 107; SC 176, tr. 162; cf. Hegel, *The Phenomenology of Mind*, pp. 423–430; and Kojève, *Introduction*, p. 140.

[3] Merleau-Ponty, "Le primat de la perception," p. 142.

162). Even if, like other animals, we have a distinctive "a priori of the species" that orients us toward the natural world, it is not this, but the a prioris of our culture that most directly influence our perception. Human life takes place, for the most part, in a world of human construction. Each change in this humanized environment motivates new projects and beliefs. "A milieu of tools, instruments, and institutions . . . fashion[s] how the individual thinks" (BP 160). Cultural objects are therefore much more than the furnishings of the community. By shaping the thought of those who use them, they motivate a way of life common to a particular group of people. What *constitutes* a community is the meaning-saturated milieu that it creates for itself and that it transmits to its members.

This conception of community, however, raises a new question: how it is possible for one person to understand the meanings incorporated in an object that is the work product of another? Merleau-Ponty admits that "properly human acts—speech, work, the act of clothing oneself—do not have their own signification" (SC 176, tr. 163). So how can he assume that others grasp conventional meanings as their maker intended them? To get at this question, he makes an important observation: "The first cultural object . . . is the body of the other [known] as a bearer of behavior" (PP 401, tr. 348). In other words our ability to discover the uses of cultural objects is a secondary instance of our ability to understand the behavior of other persons. Both cognitive operations require that a perceiving consciousness determine the intentions in something of which it is not the source. If he can found the possibility of one person's grasping the meanings of another's gestures, then he can also explain how communities form through the accumulation of meaning. Neither empiricism nor idealism, however, has a conception of consciousness that sheds light on this problem. Sartre's existentialism comes closer, but is in the end too pessimistic to explain successful communication.

The empiricist's assumption that external forces determine perceptual experience sets up a block to understanding how things come to be commonly understood. What makes me believe, for example, that the contorted, reddened face before me is "angry"? By method the empiricist is obliged to interpret my perception as the effect of a series of causal relations. He makes my body and the other's into objects in a world of objects. The face is broken down into sense data that stimulate photosensitive receptors in my eyes. But where is "anger" in this concatenation of sensory impressions? There is no such thing in an objective world because anger is a *meaning*. The phenomenon of one person understanding another's meaning has entirely disappeared. The empiricist cannot, however, simply shrug off that objection by saying that the truths of science often contradict common sense. There is a contradiction in his method: he uses his intuitive, nonreductive understanding of emotion to guide his choice of phenomena to study (PP 68, tr. 55). Merleau-Ponty surprises a conscious subject moving furtively in a world supposedly cluttered only with objects. Theory needs to construct a new passage connecting science and the "cultural world" of commonly understood meanings that the empiricist uses but cannot explain (PP 31, tr. 23).

Idealism in one sense makes the perception of common meanings impossible and in another presupposes that all genuine meanings are common. To understand the first problem one need only return to the Cartesian inspiration of Brunschvicgean idealism. Descartes' cogito is free and self-determining, certain of its own existence because of the impossibility of denying the fact that it thinks. But what of bodies to which it has access only through its senses? The purely observational perspective that the cogito imposes cannot consistently conceive the existence of other egos. When the cogito posits meanings, it does so as a universal, rational mind. The existence of other cogitos then becomes incomprehensible since that would mean to a mind that considers itself the *absolute* source of meaning that there are other, meaning-producing egos. Insofar as things are external to the cogito, the assumption is that they are objects that receive meaning from it; insofar as they are, by definition, cogitos, they are independent sources of meaning (HT 102, tr. 78). The Cartesian conception of consciousness excludes any consistent way of talking about entities that are both "other" and "people." Merleau-Ponty sums up the Cartesian paradox in a pithy formula: "If [the other] is alter, he is not ego; if he is ego, he is not alter" (IN 162). The very manner of reasoning of a rationalistic philosophy breaks down as soon as it tries to conceive collective existence.[4]

Yet, in another sense, idealism makes community seem real before the conditions for it even exist. "Between Kantian consciousnesses agreement is always taken for granted" (SNS 57, tr. 32). Brunschvicg's "reason" is by definition uniform and universal; for

---

[4] For the existentialists' dissatisfaction with Husserl's answer to this dilemma, see Schmidt, *Maurice Merleau-Ponty*, pp. 65–70.

him every mind, insofar as it is truly rational, draws from a common fund of apodictic truths. Where there are failures of communication, they are attributed to poor judgment or unnecessarily ambiguous expression. From the idealist point of view differences between subjects can always be resolved by putting them on different planes: truth and error, right and wrong, developed and primitive, superior and inferior. But this rigid segregation envisions a world in which truth and error never meet. In a profound sense the idealist believes that no conflict is real. Every conflict has its solution predecided, if only we think hard enough about it. This sort of thinking presupposes subjects without countries, histories, or interests—in other words, without points of view. Reflexive analysis "ignores the problem of the other" because it believes that consciousness has "the power, in principle, to go to a universal truth" (PP vi, tr. xii). In effect, it collapses the diversity of humankind into one all-embracing mind. By interpreting mind as an abstract capacity to synthesize experience, idealism underestimates the individuality and contingency of reason. It walls itself off from any profound understanding of intellectual discord and social conflict.

Sartre's ruminations on "the existence of the other" represent the primary alternative to theories that misconceive intersubjectivity. Sartre's reasoning is existential because it portrays what empiricists and idealists do not—intersubjective relations that take place through meaning (not causation) and yet do not end in harmony. At its center is one of the most famous episodes in *Being and Nothingness*, the analysis of "the gaze" (*le regard*).

Beneath the gaze of others, Sartre argues, the for-itself is dispossessed of its liberty and reduced from the richness of its mental life to what it is as mere external appearance. Consider the significance of the gaze for a man who spies on his lover through a keyhole. As long as the man is alone, unobserved, he is but the innocent spectator of a scene. He controls not only what he does, but the meaning that his action has for him. Only the introduction of another's eye—another person's, God's, a superego's—makes him feel shame.[5] Under the gaze of another the external reality of his act becomes that of a jealous or indiscreet lover.

This analysis has a dual significance. First of all, Sartre uses it to explain the emergence of an objectivity that the for-itself does not control. Certain affective and nonetheless indubitable experiences

---

[5] Sartre, *L'être et le néant*, pp. 347–355.

such as shame, fear, and pride cannot be conceived in the solitude of the Cartesian consciousness. A being that could determine the meaning of its world by will would never have these emotions. It could always redefine criticism to render it impotent, and the admiration that it legislated would be worthless. Now, because I am absolutely certain of the reality of these experiences for my own account and because these experiences only arise when I am seen by others, the view that others have of me must be part of my reality.[6] I am forced to recognize that part of what I *am* is what I am for others.

Second, the episode of the gaze speaks to the quality of interpersonal relations. For Sartre the fact that we are seen lays a curse of conflict upon human relationships, as each consciousness tries to reaffirm the exclusive validity of its subjective views against all others. His play, *Huis clos (No Exit)*, most graphically conveys the problem. Three strangers share a locked, windowless room. If one of them talks, another retorts with taunting sarcasm; if one keeps silent, another reproaches him for inflicting the spectacle of his fear upon her; if two of them try to amuse themselves in an amorous relation, the third looks on with irony until self-consciousness tears the lovers apart. Finally, there is a climactic insight on the nature of the situation: "Hell is other people!"[7] Or, in the more philosophical language of *Being and Nothingness*, "the essence of relations between consciousnesses is not *Mitsein*, but conflict."[8]

Dialogue: Thinking Conflict and Communication

The theory of the gaze is existential, but not in an entirely satisfactory way. Merleau-Ponty traces Sartre's errors once again to faulty foundations. He objects that what makes Sartre's antitheses of intersubjective relations seem insurmountable is the same Cartesian misconception of consciousness that weakened his notion of freedom (PP 401–402, tr. 349). If the standard of all certainty is uncovered in the Cartesian inner dialogue that strips existing things to their essence, then it follows logically that nothing else can possibly exist with the same degree of truth as my own ego. With nothing else do I have such intimate contact. Because the analysis starts from the cogito, because thought is made the measure of truth,

[6] Ibid., p. 317.
[7] Sartre, *Huis clos*, p. 75.
[8] Sartre, *L'être et le néant*, p. 502.

everything external to the ego, including other persons, is first as-similated to the status of an object.

Merleau-Ponty exposes the untenability of Sartre's position by suggesting that the terms of its analysis already presuppose a more robust intersubjectivity. From the start, even before the introduction of the look of the other, *Being and Nothingness* uses social categories. The general terms through which the Sartrean consciousness understands itself—as a "man," for example—require that the meaning-giving consciousness be able to see itself as a specific case of a larger social group (PP 512, tr. 449). Figure implies background: an analysis that tries to generate all the structures of consciousness from the cogito cannot avoid reference to a social dimension of life. Similarly, Sartre's notion of the objectifying gaze of others smuggles intersubjectivity into the cogito. If I feel "dispossessed" of my freedom by the gaze of another, it cannot be the case, Merleau-Ponty replies (without naming his colleague), that the other is viewed as an object; I must already recognize the other as one capable of bestowing esteem and value (PP 414, tr. 361). But when defending Sartre (by name) from his critics, he puts the best face on existential relations: " 'Hell is other people' . . . [means that] if others are the instrument of our torture, it is because they are first of all indispensable to our salvation" (SNS 74, tr. 41). There is a more fundamental orientation toward others than the one that Sartre's interpretation of the for-itself explicitly allows. Put philosophically, Merleau-Ponty's corrective lesson is that consciousness must contain within itself the structures of intersubjectivity.

An alternative existentialism views people not as objects external to a constituting consciousness, but as *phenomena*—"structures of behavior" that are spontaneously comprehensible in perceptual life. Because existence always denotes a subject's rapport with its world, the consciousness' openness to others is not particularly mysterious. Merleau-Ponty puts the point rhetorically: "If . . . the perceiving subject . . . draws along with it that bodily thing without which there would be no other things for it, why should the other bodies that I perceive not be inhabited by consciousnesses?" (PP 403, tr. 351). The corps propre is already a mixed existence, a dialectical unity of subject and object. Able to touch itself and to feel itself being touched, as when one hand clasps the other, the body-subject lives outwardly at the same time that it perceives inwardly. At the most basic level it is prepared to encounter others. The child's ability to learn a language (SC 185, tr. 166), sexual inclinations (PP 185, tr. 158), the understanding of facial expression (PP 404, tr. 352) all testify to an a priori human orientation toward the other not as an object, but as a center of meaningful behavior (SC 239, tr. 222; PP 405, tr. 352).

Now, if I am open to meanings in the gestures of others, I can also make out the sens that, by means of gestures, they build into objects. For example, I follow the ways that they manipulate an object as a "tool" and so learn to use the instrument (SC 184, tr. 165). This learning process is what makes an intersubjective world familiar to me. "When cultural objects that fall beneath my glance suddenly adjust themselves to my power, awaken my intentions, and make themselves 'understood by me'—I am then carried into a *coexistence* of which I am not the sole constituent, a coexistence that founds the phenomenon of social nature" (SC 239, tr. 222). A theory of mind that comprehends the exchange of meaning can be foundational with respect to the entire social world because it accounts for the ways that conventional meaning accumulates in the individual consciousness. Whether others show me tools, make signs to me, or address me in speech, they "take hold of my thoughts" in a process that prolongs an established cultural dialogue.

Having grounded the possibility of successful communication, Merleau-Ponty may seem to verge on the idealist's error of prefiguring social harmony in his concept of mind. Seeing how he attempts to avoid that error is vital to understanding one of the more puzzling features of his remarks on Sartre. It is strange to find that, after criticizing Sartre's analysis of the gaze, Merleau-Ponty goes on to incorporate it in his work. He argues that the very sort of generic thought that discovered the other in the subject's reflections and hence made intersubjectivity comprehensible itself requires a certain measure of "objectification" (SNS 237, tr. 134). "The metaphysical structure of the body" dictates that there shall be two fundamentally incompatible perspectives on human action. The body is simultaneously "an object for the other and a subject for myself" (PP 195, tr. 167). He seems to be saying that one cannot deny the legitimacy of the spectator's view. Even to admit that one is a "human being" is to take leave of the intimate flow of perception in order to rise up to an external and comparative perspective on one's estate. This inevitable degree of objectification keeps open an epistemological gap between how one knows oneself (through reflection) and how one knows others (through observation of appearances).

Thus one must emphasize that the uptake of intentions can fail; we never follow the feelings of another perfectly. "Agreement with myself and with others . . . remains difficult to obtain" because our thoughts, our perspectives, and our appearances do not completely converge (SNS 166, tr. 95; cf. SC 239, tr. 222; PP 409, tr. 356). But rather than make disagreement grounds for scepticism, Merleau-Ponty finds that it underscores the urgency of dialogue. We must "work endlessly to reduce our differences, to explain our words that have been misunderstood, to make evident what is hidden from us, to perceive the other" (IN 223). For Merleau-Ponty meaning is always a process of exploration and progressive clarification. No more in the perception of other people than in the perception of a cube is understanding "given" or complete.[9] The challenge of understanding is always that of making our partial perspectives come together to "announce" a whole. If we must discard both the rationalistic model of apodictic truths and the scientific model of purely objective knowledge, then, Merleau-Ponty insists, dialogue is itself the origin of whatever universality we can experience. "Truth [is] not the basis of the agreement between others and myself, [nor] simply the consequence of that agreement; but [it is] agreement through a dialogue with the maximum of clarity where something appears other than a simple common prejudice" (IN 17). All we can do is *search* for truth in the give-and-take of a discussion where various perspectives are explored and differences resolved. Where dialogue constitutes rationality, neither conflict nor successful communication is guaranteed.

Dialogue, therefore, not the gaze, is the category that existentialism needs to describe intersubjective relations. Like the gaze and unlike the empiricist's "causes," dialogue denotes a relationship of meaning. Like the gaze and unlike the idealist's "reason," dialogue presupposes that communicating subjects are not pure intellects. But there are three reasons for existential theory to accept dialogue instead of the gaze as the appropriate concept for the description of collective meaning. First, it grounds a more general theory than does the gaze. Whereas the gaze clearly applies only to human relationships, dialogue is continuous with the concept of "existence" that includes relationships of perceiver and perceived in all species. Merleau-Ponty's theory of the corps

---

[9] Métraux, "Über Leiblichkeit und Geschichtlichkeit als Konstituentien der Sozialphilosophie Merleau-Pontys," in *Maurice Merleau-Ponty und das Problem der Struktur in den Sozialwissenschaften*, eds. Grathoff and Sprondel, p. 145.

propre holds that "all of nature is . . . our interlocutor in a sort of dialogue" and that communication with other people begins when the intentions incorporated in one's gestures and speech are taken up by another in the phenomenon Husserl called "coupling" (PP 370, tr. 320). From nature to culture, dialogue describes the interaction between man and world. Second, dialogue explains how collective existence is possible. That is, since social life depends not only on the individual's ability to give new meaning to matter, but on the ability of others to read these meanings accurately, a theory of dialogue is a theory about the preconditions of the cultural world. Third, while it grounds the possibility of discord, it does not distort the reality of communication. Even if Sartre's for-itself finds the other as an unavoidable fact in its world, the demands of Cartesian clarity make him conceive the other as an unassimilable alien. Only a non-Cartesian starting point does justice to both the understanding and the antagonism found in coexistence.

Gazes and Structures: Contradictions in a Corrective Dialogue

Why then does Merleau-Ponty use Sartre's description of the gaze at all? It seems he believed that he could integrate Sartre's theory into his own even as he corrected it, thus adding a level of dialectical complexity to his account of communication. In his lectures, after setting out Sartre's theory of the other and concluding that competition and conflict afflict man's social existence, he asks whether these Sartrean conclusions should have the last word: "This is psychologically true. But is it a binding metaphysical constraint? Is it partial or total?" (IN 37). Should the problem be only partial, then after an account of conflict there is room in existential theory for an account of mutual understanding. In Hegelian language, Merleau-Ponty turns Sartre's theory of conflict into a "moment" in his argument, an unstable truth that moves toward resolution at a higher stage of understanding.

An exchange between Merleau-Ponty and Emmanuel Mounier gets at the heart of this strategy. Mounier's lecture on "Existentialism and Personalism" criticizes Sartre for thinking of personal relations within a paradigm of possessiveness.[10] Sartre, says

---

[10] Mounier gave the lecture at the Club Maintenant on June 17, 1946. There exist two press accounts of the lecture and the debate that followed. See Regnier, "Ex-

Mounier, views the presence of the other as a violation of the self because he thinks of the self as property. When I am exclusively preoccupied with myself, then the very existence of other free beings carries the threat that my "wealth," the richness of my personal world, will be taken away. If, on the other hand, I start from Gabriel Marcel's concept of "availability" [*disponibilité*], then "I 'am open' to the world and other people, I 'lend myself' to their influence, without systematic calculation or distrust."[11]

In a perfect illustration of the way Merleau-Ponty acted as the public defender of a politicized existentialism, he was present to make the following rebuttal: "Existentialism does not describe man's ideal condition, it analyses his concrete condition, the difficulties he encounters—the ones about which M. Mounier is silent. It is in fact through the body that we communicate, not by pure mind. We are at the start opposing objects and appetites for one another."[12] Merleau-Ponty is saying that the concept of availability, like the idealist's rationality, explains the possibility of communication only by giving up any plausible account of conflict. He knows that existentializing Catholics like Marcel and Mounier are right to insist, pace Sartre, that true communication does occur. Existential theory must grasp the attributes of human perception that make common experience and its transmission possible. Still, the partiality of our situation condemns us to partial understanding, and partiality is the door through which violence enters. Merleau-Ponty hastens to reemphasize the moment of objectification "at the start" of interpersonal relations because conflict is an obtrusively evident element of collective life. A philosophy of difficult communication, as Jean Wahl once labelled Merleau-Ponty's phenomenology, is one that realizes that it must account for the mix of conflict and dialogue that characterizes human existence.[13]

It must be objected, however, that Merleau-Ponty's strategy of transforming Sartrean existentialism without overtly contradicting it confounds his own theory. The problem is that there is a basic incompatibility between his phenomenology of perception and

---

istentialisme et personnalisme," p. 134; and Marc Soriano, "L'existentialisme est-il l'enfant naturel du personnalisme?" *Carrefour*, June 20 1946, p. 6. Mounier's lecture was probably the basis for his *Introduction aux existentialismes*.

[11] Mounier, *Introduction*, pp. 123–124.

[12] Regnier, "Existentialisme et personnalisme," p. 134.

[13] Wahl, "À propos d'une conférence de Maurice Merleau-Ponty sur les aspects politiques et sociaux de l'existentialisme," p. 679.

Sartre's notion of the gaze.[14] Phenomenology achieves under-standing, it will be recalled, by locating particular phenomena in structures that give them meaning. My actions fit into a unifying style that defines what they are objectively. Now there is no obvious place in a structural account of objectivity for the "objectifying" gaze of another. How can another's gaze possibly modify the complex meanings I have woven into my life? What I *am* is a sedimentation of natural and conventional meanings. In *The Structure of Behavior* Merleau-Ponty writes: "[A person's mental] structure is visible from the outside and for the spectator at the same time as from the inside and for the actor. . . . But . . . I can be wrong about the other and know only the envelope of his behavior. I communicate with him by the signification of his conduct, but *it is a matter of getting at its structure*, that is, of *reaching beyond his words or even his actions* to a region where they are prepared" (SC 239, tr. 222, emphasis added). Here it is evident that the other's gaze does not necessarily penetrate to the core of my being. Merleau-Ponty's descriptions of Gestalt experiments and originary perception give no reason to think that my perceiving the other's perceiving me changes the structure of my behavior. To be consistent with his theory of behavior, he should attribute failures of mutual understanding to misinterpretation, not objectification. The gaze fits poorly in a theory of perceptual structures.

That Merleau-Ponty appropriated it nonetheless points, I suspect, to a significant deficiency in his phenomenology—the virtual absence of an account of emotional life. One wonders why two body-subjects conflict. Plato discusses the competitive ethos of those overendowed with spirit; Hobbes points to insatiable appetites and boundless vanity inherent in the human organism; Freud dwells on a death instinct. But references to the passions are rare in Merleau-Ponty's phenomenology. As his comments on dialogue make clear, his primary explanation for conflict is that differences in interpretation result from differences in points of view, from incompleteness in one's view of the object, from a failure to perceive the larger structure that gives an object its distinctive meaning. Misunderstanding comes from disparate perceptions. While this explains disagreement, however, it falls short of accounting for actual conflict. Why are we not, after all, creatures

---

[14] For somewhat different accounts of the contradiction, see Barral, *Merleau-Ponty: The Role of the Body-Subject in Interpersonal Relations*, p. 225; Kruks, *The Political Philosophy of Merleau-Ponty*, p. 78; and Heidsieck, *L'ontologie de Merleau-Ponty*, p. 29.

who quietly accept others' views of the world, without competing with or trying to destroy them? What moves us to try to suppress the perspectives of others?

Sartre's existentialism goes much further than Merleau-Ponty's in developing a phenomenology of the emotions and in using that phenomenology to explain conflict. In his *Esquisse d'une théorie des émotions (The Emotions: Outline of a Theory)*, Sartre contends that feelings like anger, fear, and shame are among the irreducible phenomena of a consciousness that aims at things. Corresponding to various emotional states are worlds with particular "magical" structures, and existential phenomenology describes their peculiar logic.[15] The dynamics of interpersonal relations under the influence of the gaze are an instance of this approach. Self-recognition, mediated by another's judgment, is the existential structure of shame. The subsequent dialectics in which the for-itself tries to suppress the other and regain its possession of the world flow from this analysis of the significance of being seen by another.

What is missing in Merleau-Ponty's theory is even the outline of such a systematic phenomenology of affective life. In this being that correlates to the world, where are shame, pride, anger, joy, courage, indignation, hate, love, or a *Wille zur Macht*? Although he occasionally mentions the passions, he never defines, catalogues, explains, or interrelates them. Merleau-Ponty is so coolly preoccupied with the corporeal conditions of cognition that affectivity goes relatively unexplored. He appropriates parts of Sartre's theory—and, as we shall see, Hegel's also—as surrogates for the theory of the dynamics of emotional relations that his own work neglects.

From Conflict to Violence: Master and Slave

But even Sartre's theory of the gaze, grounded as it is in Cartesian reasoning, is strangely abstract. Two for-itselfs collide not because they differ over particular beliefs that they have acquired as concrete individuals, but because it is logically impossible to conceive of two sovereign sources of meaning. In Hegel's *Phenomenology of Mind* a confrontation is recounted that has greater historical specificity and, because of its dialectical development, greater political import. Hegel's dialectic of master and slave is at the center of Merleau-Ponty's political theory, giving him the clues he needs to

---

[15] Sartre, *The Emotions: Outline of a Theory*, p. 93.

decode the text of intersubjective life.[16] It is useful therefore to sketch out this encounter in preparation for exploring how Merleau-Ponty unpacks its political significance.

In Hegel's story of the odyssey of Geist the episode of the master and slave represents the moment of passage from sensual consciousness to self-consciousness.[17] Hegel teaches that we are at least potentially "für sich," consciousnesses capable of reflection. Alone, however, man is like the animal so attached to the world that he cannot wonder at his own existence. He considers his beliefs and sensations unchallengeable. He is "self-certainty." This certainty is thrown into crisis only by the view of another person, when each consciousness feels its certainty reduced to pure subjectivity. Abstracting from tales of the Greek heros, Hegel describes a battle to the death where two competitors try to reestablish their certainties by risking their biological existence. There is movement toward self-consciousness if one contender is finally gripped by anguish at the prospect of his own extermination and decides to save his life by submitting his existence to the arbitrary will of the other. The victor becomes the master, the vanquished the slave.

This resolution contributes to self-consciousness only indirectly. Although the master gains recognition of his position and certainties, he does so only by reducing another person to subhuman status. How can the master's worth be confirmed by a being without worth? True esteem must come from an equal, not an object. It is the slave who offers a more progressive resolution. In the duel he desired continued life instead of the possibility of heroic death. He chose to live in the world, where now he must restrain his desire in order to produce objects that are not for immediate consumption. From work he learns about a power distinct from the master's arbitrary rule. He learns self-discipline. He experiences the resistance of matter to his will and develops techniques that will liberate mankind from the imperious demands of nature.

Thus the slave represents a step in the direction of humanity's future. The flaw in the master's omnipotence and the power concealed in the slave's labor portend a reversal of roles: "The truth of the autonomous consciousness is the servile consciousness."[18] The real meaning of the slave's life comes not from his immediate

---

[16] See Schmidt's penetrating article, "Lordship and Bondage in Merleau-Ponty and Sartre," pp. 201–227.
[17] Hegel, *Phenomenology*, pp. 217–240.
[18] Ibid., p. 237.

existence as a laborer for the master, but from his role as instigator of an historical movement that creates a world stabilized in culture and institutions. The change in meaning of the slave's existence from servility to civilization comes about through the dialectical development of the structure of his situation.

For Merleau-Ponty's purposes Hegel provides a theoretically more powerful description of conflict than does Sartre. In fact, the dialectic of master and slave serves Merleau-Ponty as the paradigmatic case of violence itself, for Hegel lays bare the structure of objectification common to all forms of violence. Violence always consists in a retreat to a partial perspective, to a subjectivity that knows how to treat everything external to it only as an object. There is violence in perception, Merleau-Ponty says, because the perceiver's assertions about an object always exceed what he really sees; he does violence to the object in its full definition (PP 415, 438, tr. 361, 382).[19] In the struggle for recognition the master's imposition of meaning entails violence against the slave insofar as the latter is prevented from expressing his own meanings and values. In a world where meaning is plural, the temptation always exists to reestablish univocal meaning through domination. To treat others as objects is to gain unquestioned security in one's world view.

One misses one of the most important lessons of Hegel's dialectic, however, if one fails to see that master and slave are not just individuals, but symbols of groups bearing antagonistic values. As Kojève taught, relations between Romans and barbarians or between the nobility and the Third Estate under the ancien régime followed the course of the master-slave conflict.[20] Merleau-Ponty takes this lesson to heart in "The War Has Taken Place." "If we had watched more closely," he writes, "we would have already found masters and slaves in peacetime society, and we could have learned how each consciousness . . . becomes frozen and generalized under a stranger's gaze, how it becomes 'a proletarian' or 'a Frenchman' " (SNS 251, tr. 142). Groups—French and German, worker and bourgeois, imperialist and native—carry opposing ways of life that periodically erupt in violent conflict. War, class struggle, and colonialism are not just disputes over material interests. When victorious Germans demand that the French institute

---

[19] See Geraets, "Le retour à l'expérience perceptive et le sens du *Primat de la perception*," pp. 601–602.

[20] *Introduction*, p. 53.

anti-Semitic laws, when dominant classes propagate economic theories justifying their financial success, when imperialists insist on their "civilizing mission," they do more than extract wealth and power from their victims; they try to make their victims acknowledge the superiority or rightness of their way of life. Human violence takes place through conflicts of meaning and recognition. Only if we understand such connections between violence and *sens* do we see why Merleau-Ponty refers to violence in the most general terms as "the human problem" (HT 158, tr. 147). The goal of a humanistic politics is to eliminate or at least mitigate violence.

It is only possible to think about eliminating violence, however, if violence is not mankind's ontological destiny. In this respect too Merleau-Ponty finds Hegel's analysis more persuasive than Sartre's. Hegel makes it explicit that conflict is only a moment in human relations. The impasse represented by the master's success is that in a struggle where each seeks recognition as an autonomous being, the dialectical process "leaves facing one another a master who continues to live in sensual consciousness and a slave-thing"; there is, at best, "unilateral recognition" (IN 75). The true goal of the dialectic must be "mutual recognition." Merleau-Ponty highlights the potential for mutuality implicit even in violence when he observes that "I do not reduce [another] to a slave unless, in the very moment when I look at him as an object, he remains present to me as a consciousness and as a free being" (SNS 118, tr. 68). Struggle takes place only on a "common ground" where each already recognizes the other as *that sort of being* which can challenge it. To pass from the political predicament of people treating each other as objects to the solution of "mutual recognition" is to approach the ultimate goal of Merleau-Ponty's existential politics.

What is mutual recognition? Unfortunately, he never defines this extraordinarily vague ideal. Some of its meaning, however, can be inferred from the dialectic of master and slave. The concept of recognition stems, first, from Hegel's dialectic of desire. In the first moment of the dialectic, man desires that others desire him: "since he desires a desire, he wants to be recognized" (IN 74). One ego wishes to have its view of the world and its needs acknowledged by another. To treat others as objects means to consider them purely as a function of one's desires, as determined beings unworthy or incapable of making a meaningful contribution to the world except under the direction of another's will. "Recognition," in contrast, is the affirmation of one ego's autonomy and value by another.

Second, mutual recognition stands for the discursive processes through which communities arrive at generally accepted meanings. We are truth-seeking beings. We "need to have our opinions recognized by [the other] and to justify our choices before him" (HT 193, tr. 188). This means that seeking truth is never simply an individual enterprise. Without the recognition of others, the universal claims of our inner certainties lack the stamp of truth. Claims to truth and value, for all their imperfection and contingency, are inherently *public* claims. A public discourse is founded in affirmations that command general recognition because they have been examined, revised, and sustained in discussion.

Third, the essentially discursive nature of truth has egalitarian implications. The master's impasse in Hegel's dialectic shows that genuine recognition is grounded in an equality of status. Recognition extorted from another or given by an inferior is of no value to the autonomous consciousness. Mutuality demands the erasure of social lines that rationalize arbitrary evaluations of individual worth and it forbids counting views obtained under coercive conditions. This lesson must be applied to all discussions of truth and value. Dallmayr, explaining Karl-Otto Apel's writings on communicative interaction, illuminates the connection between equality and dialogue perfectly. "The scrutiny and validation of statements in . . . a[n investigative] community cannot proceed without the 'reciprocal recognition of all participants as equal partners in the discussion,' that is, "without their recognition as moral agents equally committed to the search for truth and both able to justify their arguments and entitled to receive justifications in return."[21] Similarly the most profound insight that Merleau-Ponty gained from Hegel's dialectic of master and slave was that even relations of unremitting hostility and uncompromising domination prefigure the possibility of a truth-seeking dialogue between equals.[22]

In sum, Hegel's dialectic of master and slave neatly fulfills a dual function in Merleau-Ponty's political theory. It identifies the ideal

[21] *Beyond Dogma and Despair*, p. 288. Dallmayr goes on to link Apel's reasoning to Merleau-Ponty. See pp. 292–293.

[22] Jürgen Habermas makes similar but more detailed arguments to show that the very practice of speech implies an orientation toward truth and anticipates, in T. A. McCarthy's words, "a form of life in which autonomy and responsibility are possible." Quoted in Bernstein, *The Restructuring of Social and Political Theory*, p. 213. See pp. 199–200 and 210 of the same work for more on this issue.

of communication implicit in all human relations—thereby setting the goal of a humanistic politics. And it explains why human beings tend toward violence. Emotions like pride and anguish and a fundamental desire for the universalization of our values spawn conflict.

But Merleau-Ponty pays a price for incorporating the master and slave episode into his theory, just as he does for appropriating Sartre's notion of the gaze. Hegel deflects Merleau-Ponty from undertaking an original phenomenology of violence. When he writes that "violence is the common starting point of all regimes" (HT 127, tr. 109), presumably we should call to mind the destruction of human life and possessions in the clash of armies, the guillotine, the pain and despair of refugees. But he also speaks of imperialism and unemployment as forms of violence (HT 122, tr. 103), even though these may not involve direct destruction of persons and property. We have seen that he even mentions a violence of perception. So just what is violence? The dialectic of master and slave suggests that violence has to do with the imposition of meaning. I suffer violence when I am forced to accept a way of life that I do not choose. Yet the future slave chose to fight, so did he not choose to accept the outcome? If the fact that he chose under a mortal threat means that he did not *really* choose, what are the conditions of a real choice? Are we free of violence only when we decide subject to no constraints? Is that even imaginable? We rarely get all that we want, but surely that does not mean we always suffer violence. Behind Merleau-Ponty's concept of violence is an unelaborated theory of consent.

The distinctions that might help to fill in such a theory have been explored in a recent phenomenologically inspired study by Sergio Cotta. He argues that "violent phenomena" are ones that deny "the dialogical nature of existence, and so constitute the . . . radical breakdown of communication."[23] Violence becomes all pervasive when it becomes associated with a "dizziness of subjectivity, that refuses every objective rule."[24] For Cotta, insofar as some non-consensual forms of social control are necessary, there is a favorable alternative to violence. That alternative is force. Force, unlike violence, is measured, proportionate, controlled and is properly a subcomponent of law. Law, he believes, can be grounded in "the

[23] *Why Violence? A Philosophical Interpretation*, p. 66.
[24] Ibid., p. 111.

objectivity of human structure," "the ontological primary fact of life," which is "the relationship of 'I-with-the-Other.' "[25]

Cotta's analysis has obvious affinities with Merleau-Ponty's discussion of coexistence and communication. But it does not appear that Merleau-Ponty could easily adopt Cotta's distinction between force and violence. For Merleau-Ponty law itself, even when it is restrained, is a primary form of violence. At least in capitalist societies, law maintains social structures that perpetuate inequality (HT 9, tr. xiii).[26] From the variety of his examples, it appears that he regards violence as a virtual logical primitive of political commentary. Yet violence cannot be so objective in a phenomenology of perception. Even a concept like violence is value-dependent. While Merleau-Ponty regards unemployment as violence, there are theories of capitalism according to which persons denied jobs suffer no positive harm because their failure to strike a contract makes them no worse off than they were before.[27] The point is not that all concepts of harm are equally plausible; it is that they are theory-laden. Once that is acknowledged, a phenomenology of violence faces two alternatives. One is to conceive violence itself as a concept whose meaning is enmeshed in a web of social practices. Phenomenology would then trace out the emergence of forms of "violence" in the dialectical interchange between the use of force and the imposition of meanings. I will suggest at the end of my study that a phenomenology pursued in this direction would approach Foucault's archeology. The other alternative would be to follow Cotta's lead. He defines violence relative to *right* order. Similarly, Merleau-Ponty could expand on his ideal of mutual recognition, spelling out the conditions under which intersubjectivity is best realized. This, we shall see, is the route he takes in his interpretation of Marxism.

Structure and Class Consciousness

Merleau-Ponty's presentation of Hegel as an existentialist—he wrote an entire essay on "Hegel's Existentialism"—seems to contradict the very reasons for which existentialism arose in the nine-

[25] Ibid., p. 132.

[26] See Hamrick, "Interests, Justice, and Respect for Law in Merleau-Ponty's Phenomenology," in *Phenomenology in a Pluralist Context*, eds. McBride and Schrag, pp. 42–43.

[27] Milton Friedman, *Capitalism and Freedom* (Chicago: University of Chicago Press, 1962), p. 112.

teenth century. Modern existentialism was born in Kierkegaard's revolt against Hegel's massive philosophical system.[28] "There can be no system of existence," Kierkegaard declared. Hegel's system was the antithesis of existentialism because it was a philosophy of totalization. Hegelian history would always absorb individual experience, suffering, and belief into the broader perspective of the development of Geist. Hegel treats the slave's fear of death, for example, only as a moment in historical construction of self-consciousness and freedom. Kierkegaard objects: the slave has lived, suffered, and "existed" in a way that cannot be assimilated in any higher truth. The individual's subjective, passionate experience has a validity in itself that is not reducible to its contribution to world history, and no future accomplishments of mankind can compensate the suffering endured by the individual in the present. For Kierkegaard it is the individual who perceives, who feels anguish, who decides to engage in action, who is free.

This commitment to individualism, however, poses particular problems for a political existentialism. When all choices are reduced to individual decisions, how can one explain the spontaneous cohesion of social groups like classes or nations? Given the existentialist emphasis on the interpretive freedom of the individual consciousness, a satisfactory theory of solidarity will be extremely difficult to conceive. This is evident in Sartre's theory. Sartre denies that human behavior can be founded in any set of social determinations or motives because consciousness can always transcend its immediate surroundings as it gives definition to its project. Furthermore, he rejects the possibility of any "we-subject," a collective source of meaning, since it is always the case that "subjectivities remain . . . radically separate."[29] And yet no theory that is to illuminate politics can deny that social categories have a real existence. Phenomena of the recent war, like anti-Semitism or the differential acceptance of the Vichy regime among the bourgeoisie and the working class, become incomprehensible if seen as the coincidental outcome of millions of separate, personal "projects." A failure to account satisfactorily for group behavior could cripple a political thinker's ability to estimate realistically the prospects of a mass movement. The recently politicized Sartre knows this. To account for the solidity and permanence of group

---

[28] Mounier, *Introduction*, pp. 17–19.
[29] Sartre, *L'être et le néant*, p. 498.

relations, he recurs to the usual source of "objectivity" in his theory—the gaze of the other.

In *Being and Nothingness* Sartre adduces the ontological existence of a "we-object," defined by the appearance of a group in the eyes of another. "The 'master,' the 'feudal lord,' the 'bourgeois,' the 'capitalist' all appear . . . above all," Sartre suggests, "as *Thirds*, that is, as those . . . *for whom* this community exists." Thus "the oppressed class finds its class unity in the knowledge that the oppressing class has of it."[30] Workers form a class less because of their common condition as exploited laborers than because their work is carried out under the supervision of a bourgeois employer. The bourgeoisie, too, even if it seems objectively united through a certain community of interests, is constituted as a class only when it is confronted by the demands of the oppressed class. Workers *look* at the bourgeois and make him into an object with all other members of his social group.

The most directly political passages of *The Phenomenology of Perception* propose an alternative theory of solidarity—one that can better account for the role of classes in social change. Underlining the moment of the "awakening of consciousness" (*prise de conscience*), Merleau-Ponty explains that class formation is a "cultural phenomenon" mediated by meanings sedimented in a way of life (PP 199, tr. 170). His structural concept of class is indispensable to an existential politics because it permits the theorist to conceive the rigidity of social systems at the same time that it suggests the conditions for radical alterations in the quality of political life.

The fundamental problem with Sartre's theory, Merleau-Ponty points out, is that the category of the "we-object" confines the individual in no binding structures at all. "Undoubtedly I . . . am [handsome, Jewish] for others, but I remain free to posit the other as a consciousness whose views touch me in my very being, or on the contrary, as an object. . . . I am still the one who makes Being for myself" (PP 497, tr. 435). If freedom is absolute, it must include the ability to reject or renounce one's social appearance. That others treat me as a "Jew" cannot in any sense compel me to affirm my solidarity with other Jews; the inner cohesion of the social group called "Jews" remains to be explained. Sartre underestimates the depth of the individual's commitment to his or her social class. If he were right, "one could reasonably expect a despot to become a convert to anarchism" (PP 512, tr. 449).

[30] Ibid., pp. 492–493.

With the word "reasonably" Merleau-Ponty brings out the tremendous political liability that such thinking imposes on existentialism: Sartrean freedom deprives political theorists and political actors alike of any way of taking their bearings in the social world. Nothing is firm, everything may change at any moment. All strategies seem equally rational in a world where nothing is fixed. Such a perspective describes poorly historical phenomena like the *persistence* of the British empire or the *repeated* instances in which individuals sought to establish a military dictatorship in France at the end of the eighteenth century (PP 512, tr. 449) The case of Napoléon Bonaparte, in fact, is especially instructive. His accession to power depended on his understanding an "average and statistical signification" in the desires of a people tired of revolutionary government, yet still detesting the ancien régime (PP 513, tr. 449). He managed to take power because he comprehended this aggregated meaning. So a more politicized existentialism, one that is interested in questions of power, must ground group behavior in a different sort of perceptual objectivity than that generated by the gaze of the other. It makes the phenomenon of a "we-subject" central to its theory of intersubjective relations.

Merleau-Ponty's analysis of cultural perception has already laid the groundwork for explaining the development of common structures of perception in groups of individuals. We are creatures who objectify our intentions; we make sens exist in language, in cultural objects, in institutions. When these creations take their place in the world, they become "anonymous." Separated from their creator's will, as when an author's text assumes meanings other than those he intended, they become part of an immense repository of meaning that defines a culture. That such anonymous meanings accumulate in the "objective spirit" of a civilization means that individuals pick up motivations of which they are unaware. They often follow out the norms of their culture as if submitting to the force of an impersonal "one."[31] Class is the primary example of the way "consciousness can *live* in existing things . . . , can have its liberty imprisoned by the inertia" of a structure of memories and attitudes toward objects (SC 239, tr. 222). Reflecting on the growth of revolutionary sentiments in the working class, Merleau-Ponty shows how the phenomenon of perceptual structures makes social class comprehensible.

---

[31] Capalbo, "L'historicité chez Merleau-Ponty," p. 525. See PP 446–447, tr. 390 and SNS 189, tr. 107.

To be a worker is first of all to have a style of life where one lacks control over the basic conditions of personal existence—over the duration of employment, over how frequently one is paid, over the products of one's work (PP 506–507, tr. 444). For each individual the accomplishment of a task is largely habitual, barely noticed: "Facing typical situations, he makes typical decisions" (PP 103, tr. 87). Particular factors in the worker's situation, such as the nature of his job, typical contacts with others, and place in hierarchies, interact with the nature of his subjective choices and judgments (e.g., that his condition is "right," "inevitable," or "barely tolerable") to form an overall structure, a cultural être au monde.

At first the worker does not challenge this condition because it seems inevitable. The sens of his situation is a *fatum*. But the commonality of this situation creates the conditions for shared understanding among all who experience it. "An implicit or existential project" gives "spontaneous meaning" to the action of the numerous members of a social group (PP 511, tr. 511). Their project is only implicit because one worker understands his relation to other workers more through their common tasks and gestures than through intellectual choice. " 'I exist as worker' or 'I exist as bourgeois' in the first place, and it is this mode of communication with the world and society that motivates both my revolutionary or conservative projects and my explicit judgments" (PP 506, tr. 443). A common style of life forms through the cultural uptake of experience.

Yet if the workers interpret their way of life fatalistically, how can there be change? Clearly no objective conditions can determine a revolution because those conditions must be interpreted by a structuring consciousness. Nor is there any question of revolutionary voluntarism because the revolutionary mentality must be built upon the primordial meanings that structure the individual's situation before he has any reflective cognizance of them. Nor, as we have seen, does Sartre's notion of the Third succeed in explaining class consciousness. An existentialism that focuses on the *structures* of consciousness and world offers the following alternative explanation of the awakening of class consciousness:

> The worker learns that other workers in a different trade have received higher wages after a strike, and he notes that subsequently wages are raised in his own factory. The fatum with which he was at grips takes on a clearer form. The day laborer, who does not often see workers and who is not like

them and has little love for them, sees the price of manufactured goods rise . . . and sees that he can no longer earn a
livelihood. . . . If class consciousness is born, . . . it is because
he has seen concretely how his life and the worker's life are
synchronized; he sees how they share a common lot. . . . The
social space begins to become polarized, and a region of the
exploited appears. . . . Class becomes real and we say that a
situation is revolutionary when the connection that exists objectively among the parts of the proletariat . . . is finally lived
in perception as a common obstacle to the existence of them
all. (PP 508, tr. 444)

Why do lived meanings not remain preconscious? What vantage
point permits a worker to see the structure of which he is part?
The answer lies in the figure-background relation. "For knowledge
to progress . . ., what was background must become figure. We
must stop seeing as a fatum that which is a result of our own activity" (BP 113). What happens in the awakening of class consciousness is that changes in the social situation (higher wages for
some after a strike) make the everyday condition of the worker
appear against a new background. Ordinarily workers are a group
for whom everyday life takes place against the background of
threats of unemployment, disrespect, and poverty. But when they
observe concessions made to other workers, this "easing of living
conditions makes a new structure of social space possible" (PP
509, tr. 446). What formerly enveloped the perception of the
worker comes to the foreground: the "fatum . . . takes on a clearer
form," and henceforth he "situates himself in relation to the possibility of a revolution" (PP 509, tr. 446). By focusing on the background meanings of stunted human potentialities rather than on
the foreground meanings of a "natural" lot in life, the worker re-
structures his field of social perception. The situation "motivates"
this new project. Social conditions fall into a configuration that
suggests alternative meanings to the actor (PP 201, 511, tr. 172,
448). The poverty and uncertainties of life that had been imputed
to individual shortcomings or to "nature" are now seen as part of
a system in which the power and wealth of some are obtained at
the expense of the sweat and poverty of others. "Exploitation"
and "revolt" insert themselves as possible ways of understanding
daily existence.

In this analysis the characteristics of "structures" laid out in
Merleau-Ponty's phenomenology transfer directly to the realm of

political theory. Just as an animal's superficially different modes of behavior exhibit an a priori common orientation toward problems in its environment, so human consciousness can carry an "historical a priori"—a class structure—that underlies and gives thematic unity to the individual's choices (PP 104, tr. 88). These class sympathies are *functional* to the maintenance of a particular equilibrium. As long as the worker accepts his condition as part of the nature of things, the prevailing distribution of power in the social system will remain. Prereflective choices interlock into a set of relationships that feed into a structure of power. To transcend preconscious meanings, the agent must gain access to the larger structural meanings of his or her action. In Hegelian terms change occurs when the sens in itself of a situation becomes for itself for the agent. The act of becoming aware of one's situation is possible only because the situation exists as a potential meaning, as a structure, prior to one's awareness. Instabilities in the old structure of existence redirect behavior to establish a new equilibrium. If the workers successfully press for changes in the social order, they illustrate perfectly Merleau-Ponty's argument that freedom comes not from the "nihilation" of existing structures, but rather from using established meanings as a fulcrum in the process of shifting to new collective meanings.

Considered as a response to Kierkegaard's objections to Hegel, this account of the awakening of class consciousness means that it is possible to describe something like a collective subject without ever losing sight of how essential the choices of unique individuals are in constituting this subject. There is no determinism in this political movement. Thousands of workers may, like the day laborer, interpret events in ways that undermine class solidarity. At best individuated, everyday concerns—here a worker laid off, a union winning a raise elsewhere, nearby a strike brutally suppressed—begin to connect up from person to person, giving momentum to a common understanding of political conditions. Where the individual is the locus of perception, there can be no hypostatized process of change.[32]

Were a Kierkegaardian existentialist to complain nonetheless that this theory still submerges a unique individual in a social category, Merleau-Ponty would have a powerful response. An existentialism that cannot even allow that there is a dialectical exchange between an embodied consciousness and a social milieu is

[32] Miller, *History and Human Existence*, p. 227.

itself a form of abstract thought. The Kierkegaardian is right to worry about philosophies that can see individuals only as expendable components of society or history. But that worry does not warrant moving to the opposite extreme of denying a social point of view for the social has value too. Without it the individual is cut off from the background of cultural meanings that alone furnish the material of a truly human existence. Once one understands that even the most heroic or creative personality draws upon meanings common to a particular society, then the important question remaining for an existential theory is how to do justice to *both* components of the dialectic. If Merleau-Ponty's description of class consciousness seems to compromise unduly the uniqueness of the individual personality, it is only because it is being judged relative to a conception of the subject that unrealistically abstracts consciousness from culture.

The Tasks of a Foundational Political Theory

The theory of the awakening of class consciousness is a critical theory in the sense meant by the Frankfurt School. The workers' altered understandings do not represent just a change in their views; they represent enlightenment—movement toward a more *rational* set of beliefs.[33] All of Merleau-Ponty's existential theory is predicated on a "reason more comprehensive than understanding." He shows that what we accept as reasonable in our personal lives and in our politics is a cultural product, the result of innumerable concrete experiences and accidents that, from today's point of view, may appear unreasonable. If today we believe it reasonable, for instance, that workers attain more than a marginal economic existence or if we find racism detestable, it is because people struggled, through strikes and protest and violence, to vindicate those claims. That is to imply that concrete events, not just abstract reasoning and controlled experimentation, are responsible for constituting what is rational. Neither the empiricist's experimental methods nor the idealist's logic can monopolize reason.

Rationality is not, for all that, *simply* a conventionalized mode of understanding—and here we return to Merleau-Ponty's difference with Rorty. Merleau-Ponty's critique of reason is, as Gary Madison has observed, a *rational* critique. "[It] has for its goal not the denial of reason, but rather an enlargement of it; its goal is to enlarge our

[33] Geuss, *The Idea of a Critical Theory*, p. 29.

idea of what makes a discourse or a belief a rational discourse or belief. . . . Any discourse is rational if it enables men to better understand one another and to better coexist."[34] Something genuinely rational takes form through human beings' never-ending attempts to interact successfully with each other. Genuine improvements in our ability to deal practically with our environment and sympathetically with others are made available to the human community through dialogue. Reason is the outcome, not the presupposition, of the discursive processes that are binding together ever larger segments of mankind.

A foundational philosophy that accepts this idea of reason places special demands on political theory. In effect theorists must be able to undertake three different tasks without self-contradiction. They must be able to describe meanings in the social world, to understand their foundations, and to anticipate their evolution.

A phenomenology of politics begins in a description of the contemporary world as its inhabitants experience it. Empiricists and idealists try to ignore lived experience but succeed only in impoverishing their theories or in making them inconsistent. Theory has no substitute for the originary meanings that pervade a people's way of life. Particular understandings of who belongs and who does not, of what constitutes a good and of how it can be acquired, of what can be changed and what cannot—these are irreducible starting points for a theory that does not stand above existence, but is within it. Phenomenological description differs from direct experience, however, in one crucial respect: phenomenology searches out common themes in the various areas of a culture. A political theorist, for instance, will be attentive to the way religious and economic practices form a whole with a group's political activity (SNS 157, tr. 90). Successful descriptions of this sort give theory an "objective" grounding for its interpretations of political phenomena. Theorists are then able to talk about truly public things, not just their own idiosyncratic opinions.

The descriptive demands of existential theory mean in addition that it must come to terms with a world marked by injustice, violence, social stratification, and war. Certainly Merleau-Ponty does not contend that these aspects of experience are immutable or desirable, but he rejects theories of consciousness that implicitly minimize their seriousness or intractability. He requires a notion of

---

[34] Madison, *The Phenomenology of Merleau-Ponty*, p. 296.

political action that, like Hegel's story of the master and slave, describes the prevalence of violence in human relations.

Theory also stretches backward to describe how human consciousness makes political order possible. If phenomenology is to avoid the pitfalls of subjectivistic and objectivistic theories, it must account for the constitution of the social sphere by grounding it in the individual consciousness (the locale of perception) without making the phenomenon of interpersonal solidarity incomprehensible. At the same time, to be able to understand how violence can be the enduringly vexing problem of human existence that it is, consciousness cannot be optimistically conceived with a penchant for harmonious accord. The notions of the corps propre and of its dialogue with others meet these requirements. Merleau-Ponty's interpretation of the growth of a revolutionary movement illustrates the specifically political significance of his theory of consciousness.

Finally, informed by its foundational analysis of human existence, theory stretches forward to anticipate changes in the political order. When theory describes the themes in a group's existence, it also detects probable adjustments in a cultural structure. It looks at the sens of events, not just their instantaneous position. The theorist looks for signs of change in the "average and statistical" meanings of a group's morale. Political transformations pass through the aggregated power of groups, and theory must allow that these groups are brought together less by rational calculations of interest than by common situations and cultural formation.

What existentialism stands to gain in political acuity by accepting Merleau-Ponty's phenomenology of collective meaning is revealingly summarized in a final exchange with Sartre in the *Phenomenology*. Still in his chapter on "Freedom," Merleau-Ponty takes up the assertion common to *Being and Nothingness* and *The Flies* that even in situations of dire constraint, such as the resister under torture, man remains free in a meaningful sense. "No matter what resistance the victim has offered," Sartre once insisted, "he would have been able despite all to wait ten minutes, one minute, one second longer."[35] This was precisely the sort of claim that most irritated the existentialists' political detractors. They found little advantage in a view that, by affirming liberty in all situations, evaded the question of what social conditions actually favor choices leading to political change.

[35] *L'être et le néant*, p. 474; cf. 607.

Merleau-Ponty joins the argument with the following observation: "A man is tortured to make him speak. If he refuses . . . it is not by a solitary decision. . . . He felt himself still to be with his friends, still engaged in a common struggle" (PP 517, tr. 453–454). His reply to Sartre is meant to establish only one thing. It is not enough to say that man is a being who can freely resist an unjust situation; a political existentialism must discover within the prisoner's experience the foundational properties of human consciousness that make it possible for men to coalesce in communities. It is through common action, as exemplified by a revolutionary movement, that men manage to change their condition. Groups alone stand a chance of establishing freer human relationships by transforming the social structures that reinforce violence. When he invokes affective ties between the prisoner and his comrades outside, Merleau-Ponty points to the bonds that create and sustain political *power*.

To say that power can transform social structures is already to point beyond immediately present structures of experience to a temporal dimension of meaning. This dimension has yet to be included in the groundwork of an existential politics. History is the medium that preserves culture and prepares the advent of change. Situating political action in relation to the projects germinating in collective existence and accounting for the intelligibility of the succession of events are the tasks of a philosophy of history that, Merleau-Ponty will contend, is also the proper form of an existential political ethics.

F O U R

VALUES IN AN EXISTENTIAL
PHILOSOPHY OF HISTORY

"We have learned history and we claim that we must not forget it" (SNS 265, tr. 150). This is the most profound lesson that war taught French philosophy. Its violence exposed the hidden dependency of every way of life—economic, religious, artistic, philosophical—on a political sphere whose practices and disorders accumulate meaning almost imperceptibly over generations. If violence is not to rule public life, each domain must become aware of this dependency and alter itself to accommodate "history." Even philosophers must learn to *think* differently—to become sensitive to the historicity of ideas, to foresee impending changes in political forms, to take account of developments in class relations. A philosophy that so understood history would put itself in a position to make politics thinkable.

Yet a radical historical scepticism that was de rigueur in existential thought in the 1930s denies the very possibility of this new sort of philosophy. Merleau-Ponty must demonstrate that the interpretation of man as a corps propre can serve as the ground of a philosophy of history in a way that other existential formulations cannot. He proposes that seeing history in terms of social gestalten that shape the activities and beliefs of individuals is the basis for a rapprochement between philosophical and political thought. History thus conceived also has ethical significance because it inclines individuals to pursue values shared with others of their class.

Why Merleau-Ponty approaches values in this way does not become apparent, however, until one examines the alternative he seeks to displace—an ethics of fixed rules and pure intentions that he calls "Kantian politics" or sometimes "liberalism."[1] One must

---

[1] He speaks indifferently of "Kantian politics" (SNS 180, 298, tr. 103, 168; IN 2, 21, 26); "liberalism" (HT 18, 29, tr. xxiv, xxxvii; "Indochine S.O.S.," p. 1040); "Cartesian politics" (IN 2; SNS 257, tr. 145); "moralism" (IN 21, 26; SNS 272, tr. 154; "Indochine S.O.S.," p. 1040); and "rationalism" (PP 69, tr. 56; HT 103, tr. 79).

agree with Kruks that his description of this politics matches rather poorly the writings of any major liberal theorist.[2] But the frequency with which he applies these epithets to thinkers of every political stripe suggests that his critique is aimed less at a specific body of writings than at a way of thinking that tempts all who confront the perplexities of action in the public sphere. It is a way of thinking that substitutes the comforting certitudes of firm moral precepts for the troubling ambiguities of concrete political judgments.[3] Merleau-Ponty criticizes the Kantian perspective for being unaware of what phenomenology has learned about human intentionality and for being at odds with the character of political action.

Kantian Politics

In a highly condensed passage in his lecture notes Merleau-Ponty summarizes his understanding of "Kantian ethics and politics": "Agreement of consciousnesses, a completely internal morality (do what you must, come what may) because there is a conviction that the course of events does not make this impossible; the universality of morality, the immutability of the moral act; cf. the political problem: truth and agreement of men through reason, . . . the state consists of the minimum number of safeguards necessary to make this rational life possible" (IN 58). The attributes of a Kantian moral perspective are a strictly principled evaluation of decisions; a disregard for the calculation of consequences; a belief that certain precepts apply without exception in political affairs; a conviction that what one person takes as rational is valid for all. It is appropriate to associate these attributes with the name of Kant because his ethical writings best exemplify their theoretical underpinnings.

Kant invokes freedom as the transcendental principle of morality. Human freedom is the unquestionable premise that makes moral judgment possible; only the assumption that man is a being not subject to natural determinations can make moral responsibility meaningful. For a free being a formal test can serve to distin-

---

[2] Kruks, *The Political Philosophy of Merleau-Ponty*, pp. 67–68 and 73–74.

[3] His criticism reaches the most notable philosophy professors of the 1920s— Brunschvicg, Alain, Bréhier; literati like Gide, Viollis, Aragon, Breton, Bernanos (SNS 272, tr. 154); liberals who attack Communist policies (HT 9, 18, tr. xiii, xxiv); and Marxists like Léon Blum and the exiled Trotsky (SNS 280, tr. 158; HT 102, tr. 78).

guish truly moral ends from those that are merely useful or desirable. By asking if our proposed courses of action conform to the categorical imperative, we can see if they unconditionally respect all others as ends in themselves and if they are capable of universal application.[4] What makes an action right, Kant maintains, is not the goodness of its consequences, but its origin in a good will. Good intentions make action conform to the categorical imperative, universalizing the scope of its potential application to all rational beings.

Merleau-Ponty analyzes the Kantian prescription for moral action by asking in essence: what must man, the world, and political action be like such that it makes sense to adopt this theory of value? What is the fit between *Wert* and *Weltanschauung*? It is a question not just of what Kant says, but of the presuppositions necessary to make possible a moral perspective of the Kantian sort.

Merleau-Ponty speculates on a variety of such presuppositions. A Kantian worldview might assume, for example, that "no liberty can encroach on another and that human coexistence as autonomous subjects is assured" (SNS 180, tr. 103). For if all freedoms and all truths were not possible at the same time, how could Kant exalt them without exception? The metaphysical assumption seems to be that there is only one type of freedom, the freedom of judgment—a freedom, so to speak, that takes up no public space (SNS 257, tr. 145). Each can retain his or her judgment in spite of others or even in spite of hostile political conditions. All liberties seem compatible because liberty itself is interpreted in a way that makes minimal claims upon the political order. To sustain his idea that intentions and not results account for the moral worth of an action, Kant may suppose that we live in a "world well-made," where good intentions suffice to produce good results, where abstention from violence is sufficient to eliminate it (HT 116, tr. 97). Or perhaps because the Kantian moral agent is a "pure self-consciousness," he can afford to ignore consequences (IN 4). That is, since reason is in essence the same for every individual, every individual confronted with a given moral choice will intend the same maxim. Thus my rational self-judgment is the same as others' judgment of my action, and my moral worth is secure whatever the consequences of my actions. There is an "agreement of consciousnesses."

[4] Kant, *Foundations of the Metaphysics of Morals*, p. 39.

But if the realities of creating and maintaining the conditions for a common life seriously contradict these assumptions, it becomes urgent to conceive political ethics in different ways. Merleau-Ponty's critique is therefore inseparable from a particular conception of the nature of politics, which in turn derives from the theory of collective meaning reviewed earlier.

First, because of the situated nature of human intentions, mutual understanding is imperfect. In a phenomenology of perception there is no such thing as a universal, rational mind. Intentions are not the activity of a self-lucid consciousness but are instead part of a dialectical conversation with the natural and cultural world. Persons in different situations will therefore have divergent ideas about the development and functions of the community. Their disagreements reflect the particularity of their principles. To act is to posit values drawn from my own situation, interests, and perspectives; to assert those values morally is to apply them to other persons; and if those persons object to my values, my action on them is immoral.[5] Such immorality is an essential part of every known politics: "Political problems come from the fact that we are all subjects and yet look upon other people and treat them as objects" (HT 122, tr. 102). What moralism lacks is the lesson of Hegel's dialectic of master and slave: human relations are based "at the start" not on Kantian mutual respect, but on a struggle for recognition of personal meanings and values (SNS 57, tr. 32).

If struggle and contradiction are inseparable from political action, there can be no question of setting up an ideal of unconditional respect of the individual as the rule of political relations. That is why one who assumes the perspective of the individual consciousness and equates morality with such respect will find politics "unthinkable." Politics seems to demand a "statistical treatment of men" that "treat[s] these singular beings . . . as if they were a collection of substitutable objects" (SNS 256, cf. 81; tr. 145, 45). Giving priority to the consciousness, however, means that it is absurd to add one individual to another. It makes no sense to speak of a collective good because even after the "addition" of individuals, each remains as separate and as complete as before. Plans that require some men to make sacrifices for others are indefensible, since they make the untenable assumption that *my* sacrifices are somehow compensated by *others'* benefits. Such a mode of evaluation risks paralyzing political thinking at the mo-

---

[5] Merleau-Ponty, "Le primat de la perception," p. 134.

ment of crisis: "Kantianism [is] a morality that does not tell us what we must do, right up to the point where there is no choice but between two types of violence, [and then] it rejects them both" (IN 171). Even in more ordinary circumstances, no community allows its members perfect liberty to pursue their personal projects; all communities hem in these unique beings with "general regulations" created to deal with average and predictable problems. So political action, which uses trade-offs and "statistical treatments of man" in order to make collective existence livable, seems unalterably foreign to the Kantian perspective. Politics is a realm where hard choices must be made, involving degrees of respect and degrees of violence. Philosophy must therefore adjust itself to make possible the sort of thinking that politics requires.

Moreover, any ethical measure of political action must envisage its consequences. "One must succeed in politics—not that success suffices to legitimate a humane politics, but because a politics of humane intentions that produces the opposite results is responsible for them. Thus there is, by definition, a certain realism in politics. Not only good will, but efficacy is necessary" (IN 172). A moralism that looks at collective life only from the point of view of the conscience is fundamentally unpolitical; it automatically makes "relieving one's conscience" a higher priority than reaching the ends that make social existence livable (IN 4). Pacificism is the classic example. In Merleau-Ponty's view, it weakened democratic Europe before the Nazi onslaught. The prevention of war would have demanded, paradoxically, the readiness to use warlike means to counter Fascist belligerence (IN 21). It is a condition of political action itself that one set aside questions of moral perfection in order to accomplish something. Since "humane intentions do not save [us from] an inhumane reality" (IN 149), Merleau-Ponty teaches that interpersonal relations create a context in which results can never be ignored.

Kantians might respond that moral intentions actually do promote good political consequences. In general, the argument might go, we are better protected from tragic miscalculations and data manipulated to serve special interests when political actors adhere to firm precepts than when they attempt to weigh consequences on a case-by-case basis. In Merleau-Ponty's view such a defense of moralism still has to answer to the phenomenological analysis of social structures. Moralism blissfully ignores the "malefice of collective life" (S 258, tr. 204; HT 30, tr. xxxviii) that distorts, warps, even reverses the goals set by the moralistic consciousness. The background of cultural meanings that Kantians presuppose while formulating their express intentions create a functional whole with institutional practices that accomplish the very opposite of the morally desired results. At the level of intentions, for example, liberalism signifies respect for liberty and equality, legality, diversity and harmony in society. But these concepts have a different meaning assigned by the social structure of which they are part. "Liberal ideas form a system with the violence [of exploitation in the colonies and the repression of strikes at home]" (HT 9, tr. xiii). Merleau-Ponty is saying something different than that liberal polities, out of dishonesty or lapse of vigilance, temporarily fall short of the goals set forth in their rhetoric and constitutions. Liberal democracies are engaged in a *system* of relations where standards are routinely subverted in practice. However laudable liberal values may be in theory, they are defeated in practice because they are caught up in a structure that continually requires violent intervention to maintain its equilibrium. The function of liberal values is to legitimate the violence that the system perpetuates. The *structural meaning* of political discourse in the Kantian mode consists in its vindication of a system of violence rather than in the purity of its intentions. From a political point of view what counts is not isolated ethical precepts, but a *system* of values.

The third aspect of the political world that is at variance with Kantian moralism is its seeming superficiality. "It is . . . a fundamental condition of politics," Merleau-Ponty believes, "to unfold in the realm of appearance" (S 273–274, tr. 216). Politics does not take place on a chessboard with pieces that have predefined capabilities and rules that have a clear meaning. The assent of others is the basis of power, and this assent is based on the significance that ordinary citizens attribute to action. The intentions of political actors alone therefore never suffice to determine the significance of what they do. "Acts of power intervene in a certain state of opinion that alters their meaning" (S 274, tr. 217). To a political thinker, the reactions that a group has to its leaders' actions are not simply troublesome complications added on to a project; they are *part of* its reality. Those who suffer or benefit from policies inevitably help set their meaning. "Moralism within one group . . . may be oppressive for other groups outside. For example, England and its Constitution or its socialism implies the exploitation of imperialist politics abroad (the Middle East). Conduct that is honorable 'for itself' may be odious 'for others'. We must not look only from our point of view, but assume how our conduct looks for others" (IN 172). So even if there were a set of universal moral values, the fact that we must judge behavior according to how it appears reintroduces moral division. A "well-intentioned" policy like the "civilizing" mission of British imperialism becomes violent oppression for those who bear the consequences of casting off familiar and preferred ways of life. Where others' beliefs are radically different from one's own—a condition that becomes increasingly likely to obtain as one's action affects large numbers of people—appearance "overturns the precepts of private life" (S 274, tr. 217).

For two hundred years critiques of Kant's ethics have been a mainstay of political discourse. Hegel argued that Kant's abstract moral perfectionism was at the root of the Reign of Terror in the French Revolution; Marx treated Kant's emphasis on "good will" as the ideological correlate of the impotence of the German bourgeoisie; Sidgwick complained that Kant's categorical imperative amounted to affirming the moral rightness of whatever maxims an individual sincerely wills to be universalized. Merleau-Ponty makes two new contributions to this critical tradition. First, he argues that those who seek to define an ahistorical, deontological ethics of political life are involved in a sort of practical contradiction. They expect their rules to guide them in politics, while what politics involves—action on others who do not fully share our values, responses to violence, the channeling of popular movements—is at odds with all the premises of those rules. Like naïve visitors who are ignored or cause offense because they use unfamiliar customs in a strange and hostile territory, moralists find their precepts rendered inoperative or even turned into instruments of domination when they enter the political realm. Second, Merleau-Ponty's consequentialism will be of a new sort. Unlike utilitarianism, it will not simply assume that there are objective costs and benefits out there for the political thinker to weigh. Phenomenology demands a consequentialism of *meanings*. It looks to the probable outcome of movements in people's "preconscious" understandings of their situation. It pays attention to the processes through which groups define values for themselves. Merleau-Ponty's "statistical treatment of man" will then seek to assess the size of rival groups and their relative potential to abolish avoidable violence.

On the other hand, in spite of these contributions there are some areas where the existentialist's argument is not yet as clear as it needs to be to challenge liberalism convincingly. For in striking contrast to his reliance on empirical studies of animal behavior to establish his original arguments for a structural approach to understanding, Merleau-Ponty's political views rest on rather meager evidence. The problem is not just that his "data" on colonialism, war, and economic hardship are relatively sparse; it is that he fails even to consider what sort of evidence it would take to establish that violence is structurally *essential* to liberal politics. Defenders of liberalism will point to improvements in the workers' standard of living and to decolonization to show that liberal polities, without ceasing to be liberal polities, can discard the forms of violence that most trouble Merleau-Ponty.

I want to suggest that his weakness here is linked to his vacillation between the structural interpretation of objectivity and Sartre's theory of the gaze. The argument that imperialist politics is "odious" in the view of the colonized borrows Sartre's insight that the gaze of others contributes to the meaning of the for-itself's world. I have already noted that Merleau-Ponty never explains how the gaze can alter perceptual structures. But, in addition, Sartre's theory carries the danger of minimizing the evidentiary demands of a structural phenomenology of politics. For the system *to be* odious it apparently suffices that certain people *regard* it as odious. At least Merleau-Ponty has nothing more to say about how the number of people who judge the system, or their social positions, or their power affect an assessment of the system's meaning.

A structural phenomenology should set forth a more complex, more empirical, and in some ways, more troubling account of those feelings. Feelings of odiousness are originary perceptions; structures of the social field motivate them, just as stagnant economic conditions can motivate proletarian fatalism. Those feelings, however, may not be the "truth" of the victim's position. If imperialism were creating social conditions that would eventually improve the lot of the inhabitants (as Marx once argued of British rule in India), then attempts to preserve traditional ways of life would actually be retrogressive.[6] This is troubling to the extent that it suggests that political actors should tolerate what even Marx called the "devastating effects" of imperialism as a precondition of social development. At any rate, to decide whether imperialism was on balance progressive or regressive would require a detailed

---

[6] "On Imperialism in India," in *The Marx-Engels Reader*, ed. Tucker, esp. pp. 663–664.

empirical study that the Sartrean sense of objectivity does not promote.

Time and Values:
The Problem of an Existential Ethics

If Kantianism is to be rejected, what will an existential ethics look like? What way of life will it favor? What specific choices will it countenance and proscribe? Existentialists like Sartre and Beauvoir purport to offer a radical new ethics. In fact, however, their commitment to the concept of "transcendence" makes answers to the above questions extremely problematic. Transcendence signifies a tendency to surpass anything fixed, a proclivity constantly to create anew. Thus Beauvoir argues that every goal that man sets himself is only a point of departure toward new ends. These ends cannot be given, for the very hallmark of liberty is the ability to throw oneself forward "without calculation" and to define for oneself the measures of one's own action.[7] Sartre's ontological framework, too, makes it inconceivable that a being that is truly free could be bound by any values other than those holding for-itself. A value is no more than a sort of "lack" in human existence. As man strives for "the fullness of being," he seeks a complementary reality to fill up his nothingness.[8]

Where does a "nothingness" search for the reality of its values? Certainly not in facts, since being in-itself can never determine any lived experience. The attempt to ground one's choices in some determinate condition is the very definition of "bad faith." Since "my freedom is the sole foundation of values" and "absolutely nothing justifies me in adopting this or that value," values have no public existence and ultimately no justification.[9] Consequently, Sartre's theory denies any basis whatsoever for distinguishing among values, as long as they are chosen consciously and "authentically." What puzzled the existentialists' readers was how they could possibly offer for *public* approval the strong moral judgments condemning Fascism and collaboration that abounded in their writings. Transcendence seems to preclude any particular prescriptions about what an individual ought to do.

Sartre's first attempt to answer this problem was thoroughly unsatisfactory (as he himself acknowledged later) and surprisingly

[7] Beauvoir, *Pyrrhus et Cinéas*, p. 107.
[8] Sartre, *L'être et le néant*, p. 139.
[9] Ibid., p. 76.

Kantian in tone.[10] True, he criticizes the Königsberg moralist. The account of the "gaze" compels the conclusion that any involvement with other people, even acting on their behalf or for their benefit, is an imposition on their freedom. It is ontologically impossible to meet Kant's imperative to treat no one as a means only.[11] Yet when Sartre comes to moral theory proper, the Kantian air of his prescription is unmistakable. "The man who commits himself," he writes, "realizes that he is . . . a legislator choosing for all humanity."[12] What is this but Kant's idea that moral reasoning pictures the "rational being" as "legislative in the realm of ends" refitted in existential garb?[13] Even Beauvoir admits that an existential ethics strives, in true Kantian fashion, to "treat each man as an end."[14]

Why is an existentialist a Kantian *malgré lui*? Sartre and Beauvoir's uncompromising insistence on personal freedom leaves them with few options. Kant denied the possibility of an ethics grounded in a fixed human nature, insisting that a conception of law alone allowed man the exercise of his freedom while providing a structure for his choices.[15] The temptation of a formalist ethics is that it seems to reconcile the quest for determinate moral choices with absolute human freedom. In this sense it responds exactly to the priorities of existential theory. But even if this manages to give some content to moral choices (which is dubious), the danger is that the existentialists may slip into a Kantian politics of intentions, emphasizing the universalizability of actions rather than their consequences and volatile meanings. Sartre and Beauvoir's postwar attraction to political engagement does not displace an earlier philosophical commitment to modes of reasoning that rank creativity over continuity, coherency of reasoning over efficacy of choice.

Yet Sartre himself supplies the means for identifying the deeper source of failure of an existential ethics and for overcoming it. Underlying the notion of transcendence is a theory of the temporal structure of consciousness. Temporal experience, Sartre says, is

[10] On Sartre's attempts to construct an ethical system, see Archard, *Marxism and Existentialism*, p. 40.

[11] Sartre, *L'existentialisme est un humanisme*, p. 43.

[12] Ibid., p. 28.

[13] Kant, *Foundations of the Metaphysics of Morals*, p. 52.

[14] Beauvoir, *Pour une morale de l'ambiguïté*, p. 188.

[15] Schrader, "The Philosophy of Existence," in *The Philosophy of Kant and Our Modern World*, ed. Hendel, p. 40.

only possible if there is a nonbeing in the midst of being. The for-itself does not have time imposed on it; time is the infrastructure of consciousness.[16] The real status of a value is its presence to the consciousness as something that does not yet exist and that the consciousness will make "to be" through its action. Only a being that can reach for "nonbeing" can have a future and, consequently, have values.[17]

Contrary in some ways to their stated intentions, however, Sartre and Beauvoir radically devalue one dimension of time—the past. Beauvoir claims that an existentialist ethics refuses all justifications drawn from a civilization, an epoch, or a culture.[18] Sartre explains the ontological reason for this. All that "has been" falls into the domain of a "quasi in-itself" that must be "nihilated" by action.[19] "In the world" the past is unable to touch the for-itself.[20] The past cannot affect a person's decisions unless it is carried along by a present intention. There is no point in searching for values sedimented in personal expression or in a cultural milieu. In fact, Sartre maintains that the ontological status of the past is *exactly opposite* that of a value.[21] One's past is gratuitous, whereas one pursues a value with reasons; the past has the density of fact, a value the insubstantiality of something yet-to-be-realized. Sartre's ontology deprives an existential ethics of all recourse to a people's already valued way of life, while offering no source of values more determinate than the individual's volition. Before it can come to grips with values, existentialism needs an account of temporality that does more justice to the historical dimension of existence.

Merleau-Ponty contends that "we must understand time as subject and subject as time" (PP 483, tr. 422). Superficially Sartrean, this formulation is actually intended to preserve Sartre's insights about temporality while not allowing the dichotomy of the in-itself and the for-itself to undermine them. Merleau-Ponty adduces the corps propre as that sort of thinking substance that adheres to a milieu and is open to meanings bequeathed in a culture. The body-subject constitutes time, in the sense that what we designate by

[16] Sartre, *L'être et le néant*, pp. 72 and 180.

[17] Ibid., p. 171.

[18] Beauvoir, *Pour une morale de l'ambiguïté*, p. 199.

[19] Lauth, "Versuche einer existentialistischen Wertlehre in der französischen Philosophie der Gegenwart," p. 246.

[20] Sartre, *L'être et le néant*, p. 193.

[21] Ibid., p. 164.

our reference to "time" *is* the structure of our subjectivity—its ability to aim at and explore the world, to acquire stable meanings, and to become aware of itself reflexively by separating itself from its present to thrust forward into the future.[22] Time has the character of a synthesis wherein the subject lends attention to and seeks out the continuity of a spectacle. The "historicity" of the consciousness is the way perceptual knowledge accumulates through a process of unfolding and exploring perspectives (PP 276, tr. 239). The geometrical definition of a cube implies no time, but the experience of *seeing* a cube can only occur as the succession of perspectives. That succession is not "in time;" it *is* time. A worker who lives according to received attitudes is time, but so is his assertion of freedom in the moment of revolution.

The past is therefore something other than matter for a radical "nihilation." The past remains present in the form of a "sedimentation" of experience.[23] This is true, however, not only of individuals, but also, as the account of collective meaning intimated, of groups like the workers who share an economic situation. Subjects in similar circumstances acquire similar habits and attitudes. Just as an individual's behavior has a structure, so groups take on a general attitude or style. The situation thus represents a finite range of meanings that motivate classes of individuals to make certain sorts of behavior persist—or change. As the example of class consciousness showed, the spontaneous organization of prereflective meanings can also motivate the alteration of social forms. The structure of social relations creates pressures and instabilities that break down one set of social arrangements and prefigure the form that will take its place. The record of a group's behavior over time will show a sens. What gives history meaning and direction "is the concrete project of a future working itself out in social existence" (PP 513, tr. 449). History *is* the evolution of social forms within a gestalt, the transmission and restructuring of fields of collective perception.

The realization that history has sens opens up important opportunities for the understanding of social phenomena. Sens is the condition of a phenomenon's intelligibility. A history with "at least fragmentary meaning" (PP 512, tr. 448) is a history that can be read. A correct description of historical trends grasps the inner norm that binds together various manifestations of social meaning;

---

[22] Sallis, "Time, Subjectivity, and *The Phenomenology of Perception*," pp. 351–357.
[23] Centineo, *Una fenomenologia della storia*, p. 101.

if the dynamic that governs social organization is understood, it should be possible to commence a provisional, historical "reading" of a society's "logic." Modes of intersubjectivity like class are what found the possibility of a philosophy of history. Classes are the collective subjects for whom time exists; they are the human substance that retains meanings and at the same time inclines individual actions toward future outcomes.

The Philosophy of History
as a Theory of Political Reason

A corrected existentialism, which sees the past always "present" in the form of primal structures acquired in a social setting, cannot agree with Sartre in saying that settled decisions are the antithesis of values. Rather, the habitual choices of members of a class represent favored interpretations that sustain the goals of the individual and the needs of the social group. That is why Merleau-Ponty calls a class a "value-fact" (SNS 140, tr. 80). Just as animals have "objective values" that are perceivable in their behavioral tendencies to constitute around themselves environments favorable to their vital processes, so human classes have values that are readable in their efforts to constitute a social setting that reduces widely felt stresses and that conjoins a variety of goods into characteristic patterns of procuration and prohibition. "Values," Merleau-Ponty argues, "are nothing but another way of designating the relations between men such as they are established according to the mode of their work, their loves, their hopes, in a word, in their coexistence" (SNS 268, tr. 152). He locates questions of value in the context of a social-temporal process that synthesizes a past where projects germinate, a present where their meaning is elaborated, and a future where they reach fruition. A philosophy of history contributes to an existential political ethics by giving it a theory of value. Through the concept of class, Merleau-Ponty suggests, existentialism can bridge the gap between the "is" and the "ought."[24]

There is a serious problem, however, in his theory of value at this point. While his phenomenology allows him to describe values, it still does not *justify* adherence to any particular set of values. If class relations are facts and if these facts *exhaust* the mean-

---

[24] For a careful analysis of how Merleau-Ponty's phenomenological ethics depends on avoiding the positivists' fact-value dichotomy, see Spurling, *Phenomenology and the Social World*, pp. 111–119.

ing of value, he should only make note of them, like the animal psychologist who notes the "objective values" of the species he observes. Because factual values do not speak to the observer's sensibilities, they give him no *reasons* to adopt any particular mode of action. Correspondingly, if Merleau-Ponty foresees that an observer can be moved, say, to criticize class relations, he implies that there exist ethical standards against which facts—even other value-facts—may be judged. Merleau-Ponty's indignation about the condition of the working class springs from values that are *his* in a way that the value-facts of an aristocratic class or of the Trobrianders are not. He is caught in the ambiguity he left surrounding the objectivity of meaning. Value-facts are structures of behavior perceived by the external spectator; his humanistic values are aspects of originary meaning. Just as a subject within a structure immediately perceives changes in sens, so Merleau-Ponty immediately grasps the importance of his own values. Still unaccounted for, however, is the sense in which his values are applicable to persons who do not initially acknowledge them.

He formulates his position better when he says, "it is not a question of renouncing our [humanistic] values of 1939, but of accomplishing them" (SNS 268, tr. 152). Here he does not simply conflate facts and values. Rather, he starts from values that his compatriots acknowledge have moral force and demands that they be made more effective in the life of the community. He censures employers who reduce wages to maintain profits, colonialists who deny indigenous populations equal participation in political decisions, the general who "saves" France by capitulating to German demands. These are instances of powerful classes treating others as objects in order to secure partial interests. The sort of theory that Merleau-Ponty accepts is one that abjures the flights of abstraction inherent in attempts to define a transtemporal ethics, instead adhering closely to a developing community's own conception of the good. The philosopher helps the community systematize its conceptions; he objects to practices that unnecessarily perpetuate violence; he selects which of a community's values stand the best chance of being translated into social relationships. But the phenomenologist does not set himself above the historical conditions of his own existence to become the final arbiter of every ethical conflict.

Merleau-Ponty's important essay of 1949, "A Note on Machiavelli," speaks precisely to the issue of how a philosophy of history informs a new political ethics. On the one hand, Machiavelli's realism earns the highest marks as a theory that takes account of the difficulties of political relations in a world afflicted with violence and mutual incomprehension. Machiavelli counsels the prince to use violence because violence is inevitable, but his advice will push the prince to achieve a sort of collectively moral result in the process. Cesare Borgia was, he observes, more humane in his extermination of factionalistic groups "than the people of Florence who, to avoid appearing cruel, let Pistoia be destroyed."[25] Machiavelli's demonstration that political action can give order to human affairs exemplifies a "statistical treatment of man" that an existential politics can endorse.

But Machiavelli was unable to prescribe a way to systematize and give force to such isolated decisions. Merleau-Ponty points to Machiavelli's erratic shifts of political allegiance between the Medici family and Florentine republicans as evidence that his theory lacked a ground in ongoing trends and social forces. Although the Florentine had no illusions about moralistic politics and although he had nationalistic values that he wished to further, he still needed a guideline to give him an alternative to random schemings (S 280, tr. 221). A philosophy of history furnishes this guideline. It leads to the center of Merleau-Ponty's political theory because it is a way of "thinking politics," of conjoining rationality, action, and value in a single framework.

More specifically, it puts any statement of political values under a triple mandate. First, it proscribes personal choices whose underlying values are patently incompatible with the structural values of a system. Merleau-Ponty takes up the cautionary example of Thierry Maulnier's political evolution. Maulnier had been a prominent figure on the right wing of the "nonconformist" intellectual movement in the 1930s.[26] Convinced of France's decadence and of the need for a total spiritual revolution, he turned to the Fascist amalgam of nationalism and socialism (but not racism) for inspiration. The war prompted Maulnier to reject Fascism and take a closer look at Marx in a work titled *Violence et conscience (Violence and Consciousness)*. Discussing the book at length, Merleau-Ponty welcomes the conversion, but objects that Maulnier had *never* been justified in viewing Fascism as a socially progressive force because, "from the very start, by stepping back from the proletarian prob-

---

[25] Machiavelli, *The Prince*, chap. 17, quoted in S 273, tr. 216.

[26] J.-L. Loubet del Bayle, "L'esprit des années trente," *Politique* 33–36 (1966), p. 201.

lem, Fascism chose the 'solutions' of war and conquest" (SNS 177, tr. 101). Maulnier's criticisms of Fascist social policy were naïve and in vain. A more adequate philosophy of history would have required him to study the integral ties between Fascist expansion and its antiproletarian domestic politics. The false compound of nationalism and socialism would then have been discovered.

Second, a philosophy of history should force political actors to examine the larger social meanings of their actions. Merleau-Ponty explains, for example, that nationalism sometimes reinforces the bourgeois political order and sometimes—as in the France of the 1940s—is the vehicle of a proletarian politics. "It is history that transforms national feeling into revolutionary will"—and it is a philosophy of history that will attune action to these changes (SNS 246, tr. 140). It alerts political actors to the structural sens of their initiatives and to their appearance in the eyes of others.

Third and most important, a philosophy of history highlights the true "vectors" that are converging toward social transformation. It is the task of the political actor to "construct an image of the future that is justified only by probabilities"(HT 90, tr. 64). A politics that follows and pushes in the sens of history stands a better chance of success than one that guides policy by moral dictates or one that merely manipulates events opportunistically. In particular, one makes good Machiavelli's defects by attending to the state of class relations in one's society. "It is important not only to know *what principles* to choose, but also who, what forces, what men will apply them" (S 278, tr. 220). Missing from Machiavelli's theory was any means of identifying those who would have the "historic mission to bear [values] in the historic struggle," a group that could "raise *virtue* above opportunism" (S 281, tr. 222).

What theory needs, then, is to align itself with a group whose situation and behavior portend an ethical advance for mankind. A realism that works through a class movement will bypass the insurmountable difficulties of keeping track of all historical trends favorable to its values, for a class is a spontaneous summation of historical experience. And since a class is oriented toward certain goals, it can represent a guideline for a theory that grounds political decisions in probable outcomes. Attending to the state of class relations in a society also resolves the problem of efficacy without giving in to voluntarism. The problem of a discrepancy between principles and their successful translation into social relations does not arise because, if we are talking of the true, lived values of the class, the principles are *already* embodied in its common attitudes and situation. A philosophy of history is a systematic statement in which the thinker identifies key problems and unstable cultural meanings that favor a particular direction of change in society.

The Challenge of Historical Scepticism

Formidable epistemological difficulties beset this entire conception of political thinking. Existential philosophers, notably Sartre and Raymond Aron, have advanced devastating critiques of historical reason. Aron's *Introduction à la philosophie de l'histoire (Introduction to the Philosophy of History)* in particular stresses the inherent subjectivity and historicity of any interpretation of the past.[27] If correct, his analysis would make Merleau-Ponty's theory of value founder under a barrage of sceptical objections. But Merleau-Ponty was acutely aware that Aron had reset the terms for any modern approach to the question of meaning in history. He therefore had to respond to Aron's epistemological challenge not only in order to fortify his philosophical ground, but also to hold at bay a powerful conservative critique of his political theory. As elsewhere when criticizing existentialist thinkers, Merleau-Ponty deals with Aron covertly, but structures his comments to respond to specific elements of the targeted work.[28] Understanding his critique therefore presupposes some familiarity with Aron's arguments.

The *Introduction to the Philosophy of History* explores one major question: can historical knowledge ever claim a degree of "objectivity" comparable to that attained in the natural sciences? Maintaining that there are two essential modes of historical thought, Aron investigates the prospects for historical objectivity offered by the methods of Verstehen and causal analysis. He completes the essentially tripartite structure of his work with some reflections on the existential situation of the historian. In each mode of thought Aron seeks to expose the moments when the historian's subjectivity obtrudes upon a supposedly factual order.

Some of the reasons for believing our knowledge of the past to be always unfinished and subjective are common to all types of historical research. History, first, does not consist of a finite num-

---

[27] Aron noted that his *Introduction* asked existential questions much like Sartre's. Aron, *The Committed Observer*, pp. 48–49. Sartre's historical scepticism appears in *La nausée*, p. 26, and in *L'être et le néant*, p. 582.

[28] Only once do Merleau-Ponty's published works of the 1940s explicitly refer to Aron's *Introduction*. See *L'esprit européen* (1946), p. 253. As the following discussion should make clear, however, the unpublished manuscripts cite Aron often.

ber of neatly arranged facts only awaiting some historian's syn-
optic vision to be made comprehensible. The historian must select
what facts to study—"great men" or socioeconomic data, decisive
battles or influential ideas. Moreover, the historian shapes the conclusions he will reach by his choice of aggregative concepts.[29] Second, the ever-growing interval between a given past and the present constantly changes the observer's perspective on even
"established" facts. For example, while a historian writing in 1925
might see the Weimar Republic as part of a process of the gradual
democratization of German politics, after Hitler's accession to
power he would understand that it was merely an intermediate
phase between two empires.[30] Thus only a Hegel who believed he
stood at the end of history or watched it from an extrahistorical
viewpoint could possibly lay claim to historical truth.[31] For want of
such a position historians must make interpretive choices that cannot be justified absolutely. Not even the application of a more
highly developed methodology will settle these interpretive ambiguities; it will only add new ones.

Advocates of "historical understanding" insist that the intelligibility of historical phenomena depends on seeing them not as the
products of causal regularities, but as the embodiment of human
intentions and purposes.[32] Yet no matter how necessary "understanding" is in historical research, continues Aron, it cannot issue
in universally compelling knowledge. This must be so, since "one
lives one's own experiences whereas one knows those of other
people *objectified*."[33] The recovery of others' meanings is an inherently uncertain affair because it must be based on supposed similarities between one's own intentions and those of others. Since
meaning originates in minds that are always somewhat opaque to
us, the behavior of others can always be explained by a variety of
plausible interpretive hypotheses.

For all his emphasis on the methods of Verstehen, however,
Aron is not hostile to the methods of a more positivistic social science. He simply wants to establish that even rigorous empirical
methods fail to achieve the sort of objectivity expected in the natural sciences. While statistical regularities observed among historical phenomena may suggest causal relationships, these never

[29] Aron, *Introduction à la philosophie de l'histoire*, pp. 163, 167.
[30] Ibid., p. 165.
[31] Ibid., p. 123.
[32] Ibid., p. 90.
[33] Ibid., pp. 81, 86.

have the certainty of physical laws. Aron demonstrates that the data used in such statistical regressions must be grouped in general categories that depend on the will of the researcher and that they can always be inserted in a variety of developmental series.[34]

Aron directs these conclusions especially against a vulgar Marxism and a Hegelianism that purport to show that, "in the final analysis" there is an underlying unity tying the diversity of social forms into a complex, evolving whole. Such philosophical claims, Aron argues, are but vestigial theology. There is no "in the final analysis" in historical understanding.[35] The inevitable intrusion of contingent facts, the multiplicity of possible interpretative schemas, the "dialectical" interpenetration of all social domains frustrate any attempt to discover a total order in history. The historian's task is really only a "mise en perspective" (putting into perspective).[36] Of these perspectives there is an irreducible multiplicity; there is no way of integrating them into a single, valid perspective.

If the phenomena of history offer only an inchoate plurality of interpretive possibilities and if this plurality must be reduced in order to produce an intelligible narrative, on what basis does the historian choose? The historian's perspective-setting, Aron concludes, is the result of a dialectic between an individual's vision and his historical-cultural context. One pole of that dialectic is an essentially personal philosophy. Since historiographical choices lack any final justification in an "objective" order, a philosophy is required to organize the historian's selection of facts, concepts, and modes of analysis into a coherent framework. Ultimately this philosophy translates not only epistemological choices, but also moral and political ones. The historian "seeks out his own ancestors," in one of Aron's striking phrases.[37] By narrating the past in terms that reflect his own moral priorities, the historian in effect makes it sound as if the past anticipates the wisdom of his own point of view.

Approaching the dialectic from the other pole, the historian's choices are not purely personal; they are impelled by the social context in which the historian functions.[38] A focus on "great men" or a "universal class," on positive science or humanistic interpre-

---

[34] Ibid., pp. 221, 223.
[35] Ibid., p. 309.
[36] Ibid., p. 164.
[37] Ibid., pp. 40, 176
[38] Ibid., p. 416.

tation stems from a particular intellectual and cultural milieu. But whether historiographical choices are grounded in personality or culture, the implications for the possibility of objective history are the same. It is because the historian is in history and not above it that there can be no question of a definitive understanding of the course of events.[39]

Aron intended his *Introduction to the Philosophy of History* to go beyond an abstract consideration of the epistemological problems of the historian's craft to serve as an introduction to political thought.[40] Thus the overwhelmingly negative, critical quality of this work is somewhat misleading. Aron was sounding some positive themes that he wanted his contemporaries to hear. First, his proofs of the inherent partiality of historical perspectives establish that any politics presupposing a uniquely valid or totalistic understanding of history is misguided. Uncertainty about ultimate truths makes Aron opt for a politics that respects "particularity," diversity, and an endless renewal of values.[41] Both his epistemology and his politics end in pluralism. Second, Aron criticizes Kantian moralism.[42] Political action requires more than ethical motivation; it demands attention to the limited opportunities available in any given situation and to the probable results of an act.

The problem is, Aron's critical analyses may have undermined the epistemological foundations of even this cautious politics. For a troubling ambiguity clouds his entire work: it is never clear how Aron could defend *any* sort of historical knowledge. He denies that he is a sceptic. He admits, for example, that there are "partial historical laws" and "partial necessities"; there are "permanent conditions of collective life" and genuine probabilistic relationships between events.[43] But the same acid used to dissolve the massive systems of Hegel and Marx must as certainly eat away Aron's fragile assertions. Thus although one of the most important lessons that Aron intended to convey was that political choices are always constrained by the "historical situation" and the "individual's past," no concrete description of those conditions could survive the perspectivist's scrutiny. For example, did Russia's involvement in World War I, its industrial underdevelopment, and

---

[39] Aron later admitted that his early work overstated his critique of objectivity. Aron, *Politics and History*, trans. and ed. Conant, p. xxii.

[40] Interview with Raymond Aron, June 19, 1981.

[41] Aron, *Introduction à la philosophie de l'histoire*, pp. 400, 431.

[42] Ibid., p. 418.

[43] Ibid., pp. 300, 344, 317.

its lack of experience with parliamentary institutions limit Lenin's choices in 1917? But should the historian focus on Lenin or perhaps on local party agitators? What is "underdevelopment"? What was the meaning of "parliament" to Russians—and to which ones? Following Aron's analysis each of these questions must admit of a plurality of responses. Perspectivism endangers his own positive conclusions, even his opposition to Kantianism.

Merleau-Ponty has evident sympathies for Aron's existential approach to history. Their conclusions are similar in their emphasis on the historicity of human existence, the objectification of intentions, and the rejection of deontological ethics. What Merleau-Ponty cannot accept is Aron's account of the irreducible plurality of historical meanings. The gist of his critique is contained in the following elliptical passage from Merleau-Ponty's personal lecture notes for a presentation entitled "The Individual and History." Calling Aron's approach the "Negation of a . . . sens of history," Merleau-Ponty argues that

> Even in this way one is creating an historical tableau (as a mosaic of individual decisions, great men and leaders, accidents, ruses, policelike conception). One therefore puts things into perspective . . . : this view of history translates an a priori of the philosopher . . . How can one act and judge according to this view of history? . . . according to objective factors (geography, economy, elites . . . chosen tacitly and themselves understood as if without subjective impact, as if at rest, for fear that they might have a meaning). . . . Whence a politics that is entirely objective, conservative. At bottom one avoids the problem of the subject-history relation. One gave the subject a power that is total and nothing. . . . Aron goes from history in the future to history in the past. Example: the Russian Revolution of 1917 seen according to Aron's method (several interpretations, accidental encounter of peasants and workers, weak Kerensky, few members of the bourgeoisie) and seen according to Trotsky (all of that is linked to the status of Russia as a semicolonized country). Trotsky: where revolution is concerned, the greatest objectivity is often the subjectivity of he who lived it. (IN 5–6)[44]

[44] Merleau-Ponty probably delivered this lecture on "L'individu et l'histoire" in February 1946 in Brussels. I reproduce the unedited, French version of this same passage in my "Perspectivism and Historical Objectivity," p. 138.

To follow Merleau-Ponty's reasoning in these elliptical notes it is necessary to juxtapose his words with passages in his other works. An argument against perceptual scepticism in *The Phenomenology of Perception* is especially important in understanding his critique of Aron's perspectivism.

Perceptions, Perspectives, and Truth

For the sceptic, Merleau-Ponty observes, the experience of different perceptions of the same thing destroys any rigorous distinction between truth and falsity. Suppose, for example, that I see along the path ahead what appears to be a rock. Closer inspection reveals that the "rock" was nothing but a spot of bright light in an otherwise shaded area. Through the opening of fallible experience, reasons the sceptic, doubt must come to infect all knowledge. Distinguishing between illusory and veridical experience would require comparing sense data with some other, incontestably true evidence. Yet we have nothing but our fallible perceptions to guide us. Thus there is no way of reducing a multiplicity of perceptual experiences to a single true one.

That, for Merleau-Ponty, is a fundamental misunderstanding of the nature of perception and, ultimately, of truth itself. What occurs in my dis-illusionment is that I move from an "epistemologically unfavorable position," in Samuel Mallin's words, to one where my perceptual apparatus has a better hold on the object.[45] At a distance, the light is in a field where the components lack clear articulation and where my senses cannot fully explore the phenomenon. My body then overspecifies the meaning of the bright spot in accordance with the structure of the total situation (e.g., the rockiness of the terrain in general). Up close, in my proximal field, the initial impression is rectified by another perception—not an experience metaphysically different from the one that motivated the illusion, but one whose meanings gain specificity because my body is finally in a position to articulate them through its maximal perceptual capacities (PP 347, tr. 301). The sceptic is right that, in the example above, all that happens is that one perception (that of a patch of light) succeeds another (that of a rock). But I do not conclude that my senses are incapable of distinguishing truth from illusion or that I can only choose indifferently between the two perceptions. I feel that the first was confused, the

---

[45] *Merleau-Ponty's Philosophy*, p. 210.

second certain and stable. The second perception constitutes a genuine *improvement* of my perceptual grasp of the phenomenon. The movement from illusion to veridical perception is experienced as a *process of correction*. (PP 343, tr. 296).

The "internal contradiction" of the sceptical position is that while questioning the certainty of all knowledge, it makes tacit reference to "an absolute knowledge and being in relation to which our factual evidence is considered inadequate" (PP 455, tr. 397). The sceptic assumes that for a perception to be true, it must be absolutely invariant. Therefore, if a phenomenon undergoes any alteration, its claim to truth must be surrendered. In effect, the sceptic is an unconfessed objectivist. He measures knowledge against a standard of absolute objectivity never encountered in human perception. And by using this standard instead of regarding knowledge as a process of correction of structural understandings, he can only affirm the equal partiality of all perspectives. To the sceptic who demands a supraperceptual concept of truth, the phenomenologist points out that our concept of truth must come from distinctions *within* our perceptual experience. Fallibility and perspectivism do not undermine all claims to knowledge as long as they involve us in an ongoing task of approximation and adjustment of perception toward more adequate knowledge. Merleau-Ponty's phenomenology, we have seen, requires not that "objectivity" be abandoned, but that it be rectified to express the structural nature of perception.

From this vantage point the same internal contradiction that discredits scepticism is seen to run through historical perspectivism. "[There is] a dialectic of subjectivity and objectivity. Aron requires absolute, nonphenomenal objectivity and concludes with subjectivity" (IN 104). The most basic fallacy of Aron's argument is to measure the historian's interpretive choices against a perfect, unchanging understanding of events. In comparison to that "nonphenomenal objectivity," the actual practice of historians appears only as a process of putting events into perspective. Merleau-Ponty implies that if the historical enterprise were considered within the limits of real human understanding, then it would make sense to pursue a sort of historical truth. How would "phenomenal objectivity" in history differ from a mise en perspective?

It would entail, first, a sympathetic exploration of the lived experience of people in the society one was studying. Merleau-Ponty cites Lucien Febvre's famous study, *Le problème de l'incroyance au XVIe siècle (The Problem of Unbelief in the Sixteenth Century)*, as an example. Febvre, always deploring anachronism in the study of *mentalités*, draws freely upon anthropology, archeology, and sociology to challenge and refine his understanding of an unfamiliar past. Merleau-Ponty seconds this approach, noting that "true objectivity" requires "reconstituting the atmosphere of an epoch as it lived by its contemporaries" (SNS 160, tr. 91). Because cultural perception is an a priori human capacity, no conventional meaning is inherently beyond the historian's grasp. As opposed to Aron's contention that the "objectification" of the other entailed by the observing position denies to the historian the real ability to understand the intention of historical actors, Merleau-Ponty maintains that the ability to tie into intentions permits genuine communication with the past. Aron's analysis of the limits of Verstehen repeats the sceptical error by requiring of the historian a perfect knowledge of the inner states of other people. In Merleau-Ponty's view such knowledge is inaccessible even to oneself. Phenomenologically much more plausible is a view of historical knowledge regarding it as corrigible and somewhat ambiguous. In this way the historian integrates subjectivity into the object of his study "without imposing on it our values" (SNS 161, tr. 92).

In addition, the historian interrelates the realms of experience he charts. He attempts to understand societies and events in terms of structures. Merleau-Ponty believes that a society's ideologies, politics, religions, and economics all express "the same structure of being," they all converge in a "unique core of existential signification that becomes more explicit in each perspective" (PP xiv, tr. xix). Not simply a mise en perspective or an arbitrary description grounded in idiosyncratic values, the historian's understanding follows the "immanent logic of experience" (SNS 113, tr. 65; cf. PP xiii, tr. xviii). As presumptuous as this mandate may sound today, it is important to realize that Merleau-Ponty does not mean it to sound a call for a history necessarily as comprehensive as Hegel's or Marx's. Again, Febvre's work exemplifies what Merleau-Ponty expects of social analysis. *Le problème de l'incroyance* discloses a unique structure of social behavior in sixteenth-century France. Whether it is a question of philosophy or everyday work, of science or eating habits, the themes of religious belief inform every aspect of sixteenth-century life, fashioning the expectations and actions of every individual. Febvre makes manifest numerous mutually confirming perspectives on cultural life. This is the sort of perspectivism Merleau-Ponty endorses.

This analysis explains Merleau-Ponty's reference to Trotsky in his lecture. A perspectivist analysis of the revolution of 1917 would have to admit a number of possible interpretations. Aron might emphasize alternatively or concurrently the Communists' clever strategy of alliance between workers and peasants, the personal weakness of Kerensky, or the underdevelopment of the Russian bourgeoisie.[46] Which interpretation the historian chose would depend on methodological predispositions and political values he brought to the analysis. According to Aron's metatheory of historical practice, however, isolating any single factor as dominant or reducing the variety of contributing factors to a common denominator would violate the postulate that historical understanding can do no better than offer perspectives on the past. Trotsky's structural view of the events, on the other hand, understood these perspectives as parts of a single syndrome (PP 508, tr. 444; SNS 160, tr. 91). The convergence of the radical demands of the peasantry and the working class occurred, for example, not by chance, but because neither the peasants' nor the workers' demands could be met by the limited reforms instituted by the Kerensky government. The weakness of the bourgeoisie explains the timidity of the reforms themselves.

This explanation would exemplify phenomenal objectivity in the following sense: it would combine the two epistemic vantage points revealed in the study of perceptual gestalten. In effect, the historian would occupy an epistemic vantage point analogous to the psychologist who observes a gestalt experiment. Just as the psychologist learns how particular structures of the visual field motivate a subject's perceptions, so the historian finds social structures that favor decisions by historical actors. "Truth" is found not in a direct, causal link of a subject to an invariant object, but in an observed gestalt relationship that holds constantly between the two of them. Trotsky was in the epistemic situation of the subject who understands the lived, ordinary sens of a phenomenon because it is optimally within his grasp. Trotsky was right to think his understanding more "objective" than other historians' not just because he was there, but because as a participant in the revolution, he had grasped the problems of the Czarist Empire and of the first attempts at parliamentary democracy. On the basis of this understanding he had helped channel social forces and grievances in the direction of radical change (SNS 160, tr. 91). The very success of the Bolshevik Revolution, which few would have ac-

---

[46] Aron, *Introduction à la philosophie de l'histoire*, p. 222.

counted probable before it occurred, tends to confirm for Merleau-Ponty the "objectivity" of Trotsky's understanding.

Reflexivity and Political Conservatism

Phenomenal objectivity, however, puts an additional charge on the historian. Aron claimed that since the historian's personal values color his choices, objective history is impossible. Merleau-Ponty moves to derelativize historical judgment with the remark that Aron is right to say that "we choose our own ancestors," but "it is also true that this choice is motivated by our past" (IN 104). A motive represents a meaning favored by a certain structural configuration, as when the illusion of a rock at a distance is favored by a spot of light in a certain landscape. To understand the motivational structure underlying this illusion is to take a step toward dispelling it or, at least, toward limiting its power to mislead. An illusion understood is one to which expectations can be adjusted. Thus, if our past motivates our "choice of ancestors," then awareness of that motivational structure will help check the incursion of overly subjective historical judgments.[47] Knowing the motive of a perspective, one initiates the process of correction that leads to veridical perception.

Aron's theory lacks just such a moment of corrective reflexivity. Merleau-Ponty therefore joins to his philosophical critique an examination of Aron's practice. To the theorist who argues that true meaning in history presupposes a viewpoint beyond history, it is perfectly appropriate to ask: where do you stand when you make your perspectivistic assertions? How can Aron's metatheory of historical understanding find a place in a perspectivistic philosophy? "One cannot do without a philosophy of history," and so Aron must have one. In fact, he may have two: one associated with his theoretical writings, the other with his work as a political journalist.

The first is represented by a perspectivism that sees only "a mosaic of individual decisions." So long as Aron insists that history is *only* a mise en perspective, his position is indistinguishable from one that sees every sort of understanding and cause as of potentially equal explanatory power. That *is* a philosophy of history. It is a way of saying that historical change must be approached

---

[47] Merleau-Ponty sometimes interrupts his own reflections and questions himself on his position as an intellectual in order to liberate his views from the confines of a distorting situation. See HT 114–115, tr. 95; PP 510, tr. 447.

piecemeal, without an overarching theory of change. Perhaps that is the best way of approaching history. But if so, it presupposes a philosophical justification that Aron's *Introduction* never presents. And he will have great trouble doing so in any other work, for if he can undermine the truth claim of every historical assertion, he must himself be beyond history—that is, in exactly the position his entire theory proves unreachable.

More informative about Aron's methodological and ethical commitments are the choices he makes in his concretely political essays. There, Merleau-Ponty finds, Aron stresses objective social determinants in a fairly conventional sense.

> The sceptic suddenly abandons his methodological scruples when it comes down to practical conclusions. To guide action it is necessary to consider certain facts as dominant and others as secondary. . . . A sceptical politics encloses a philosophy of history ashamed of its own name. For example, it will calculate the future of France as a function of the English Empire, or of the USA, or of the USSR defined once and for all by geographical conditions, natural resources, and unchangeable psychological traits. (SNS 297, tr. 168)

The dialectic of subjectivism folds back in upon its own antithesis, objectivism. The "sceptical politics" to which Merleau-Ponty tacitly refers is found in a 1946 study of France's postwar problems—by Raymond Aron.[48] Accepting the necessity of social elites, analyzing the immense demographic and economic constraints on postwar reconstruction, Aron argues against a revolutionary politics in France. The factors to which he attributes social efficacy are however "chosen tacitly and understood as if they had no subjective impact, as if they were at rest, for fear that they might have a meaning" (IN 5). In practice Aron leaves behind the lessons of the Verstehen school, failing to question, for example, how the concept of "elites" that he uses is constituted in a particular historical context and embodies certain values. The "fear of meaning" has a double significance. First, if Aron pursued his reasoning about the influence of elites or the economy on social evolution, he might have to invent a schedule of priorities in social explanation that specified the most powerful factors in historical change—and this would contradict his view that history is a mere mise en perspec-

---

[48] *L'âge des empires ou l'avenir de la France* (Paris: Éditions Défense de la France, 1946).

tive. Second, he would have to think dialectically, taking account of how such factors can be efficacious only as meanings recognized by political actors. "He does not see, in sum, true subjectivity, which is never without motives, or true objectivity, which is never without evaluation, or the junction of the two in praxis" (IN 104).

For want of this extension of his own thought, Aron veers toward conservatism. He defends a strong executive on the Gaullist model, he establishes the maintenance of the empire as the "primary task" of French foreign policy. Merleau-Ponty views such political stands, not as an accident of personal preferences, but as the existential consequence of Aron's philosophy.[49] "Historical scepticism is always conservative, even though strictly speaking it can exclude nothing from its predictions. . . . Under the pretext of objectivity it freezes the future, it withdraws change and human will from history" (SNS 298, tr. 168). Based on a "realistic" sociological assessment of his country's political options, Aron's L'âge des empires (The Age of Empires) specifically excludes a socialist future for France.[50] His tacit objectivism denies the real condition for social transformation—the subject's consciousness that the current political and economic order is not a fatum, but the product of human will, cooperation, and consent.

This critique goes a considerable distance toward redeeming Merleau-Ponty's hope of developing a philosophy of history that can serve as a new theory of political reason. His notion of phenomenal objectivity means that existentialism need accept neither Sartre's frenetic quest for values, nor Aron's studied conservatism. Notwithstanding Aron's empirical bent, his theory is like Sartre's in making the object evaporate. But an existentialism without a notion of objectivity—a notion of a world not freely constituted by the individual—cannot be truly political. It cannot make political claims of the following sort. (1) *These values are essential to our community.* Certainly an existentialist could espouse certain values and even force them on others. These values would remain nonetheless private and idiosyncratic. Because every person's morality is on a par with every other person's, whenever such a theorist says, "It is wrong that . . . ," he means so only for himself. There is

---

[49] Undoubtedly, this judgment also reflects an assessment of Aron's political career, his change from being an activist in the French Socialist party before the war, to working in the office of his Gaullist friend André Malraux during the latter's brief term as Minister of Information in 1946.

[50] L'âge des empires, p. 216.

nothing in a subjectivistic existentialism that necessarily ties into the traditions and hopes of those with whom one shares a way of life. (2) *These values have been violated.* The infractions that one observes to have taken place become a matter of endless interpretation. All interpretations end up being equivalent because there is no rational way to choose between them. A philosophy asserting that there is always an irreducible plurality of perspectives deprives us of the incentive to reconcile our views as much as possible. (3) *This political situation is likely or unlikely to change.* A theory that stresses the role of will in social relations underestimates both the rigidity and the pliability of social structures. Although Sartre is more guilty of this problem than Aron, even the latter's emphasis on the historian's subjectivity calls into question what he says about "objective mind." (4) *We must plan our actions in relation to their probable efficacy in a given situation.* An existentialism that cannot take seriously the power of social trends must give up on tactical thought. Tactics requires projecting ongoing events and adapting one's activities to them. A sense of probabilities is the basis of the political leader's ability to foresee the local configuration of events for the immediate future. But an existentialism that denies that events even have "an average and statistical situation" could not distinguish "an adventurer from a statesman" (PP 513, tr. 450). It would confuse all who seek a radical change, but who do not want to be misled by utopian dreams. For all these reasons Merleau-Ponty's transformative criticism seeks to make existentialism accept a theory of phenomenally objective historical structures. This will give existentialism a *publicly* defensible account of events and values, thereby allowing it to venture into the realm of politics and yet not compromise its insights about man's interpretive freedom.

It is only fair to acknowledge, however, that Aron raises questions that Merleau-Ponty never adequately addresses. A study of the "limits of historical objectivity" is particularly useful in challenging him to make his concept of structure more precise.

Merleau-Ponty's contention is that the meaning of phenomena is objective relative to the structure of which they are a part. The biologist who knows the structure of behavior of a species can correctly interpret a particular animal's gesticulation as, say, a sign of irritation or a mating signal. The historian who knows the structure of a culture can accurately decipher particular forms of social behavior according to their social meaning. Understanding the structural context of action makes meaning determinate, "objective." Aron suggests, however, that historical phenomena have no "objective" boundaries.[51] If, on the one hand, it is essential that historians comprehend the "objective mind" of a time and place in order to grasp the meaning of a community's acts, artifacts, and institutions, it is true, on the other, that the "time" and "place" of the "community" are without fixed limits.

Merleau-Ponty's unwillingness to face up to this difficulty is evident in his critique of "liberalism." Clearly one assumption of his argument is that he can specify what a liberal polity *is*, for only then can he determine whether violence is really essential to its equilibrium. Yet he never explicitly attempts to explain how the observer delimits such a phenomenon. Is a polity liberal because its constitution guarantees its citizens certain civil liberties? Does liberalism require a free enterprise economy, and at what point does government intervention in the economy become illiberal? Are colonial ventures really necessary for the survival of the liberal polity? The assertion that historical objectivity is possible does not answer such specific questions. Merleau-Ponty has an unfortunate tendency simply to stake out the position of an external spectator who claims to view an entire social system in equilibrium and who then makes generalizations about that system.

This tendency is traceable to his failure to consider how much more complex is the task of observing social phenomena than that of observing animal behavior under the controlled conditions of gestalt experiments. When describing structures of animal behavior, the scientist knows the identity of the existent. This greatly simplifies the problems of forming explanatory hypotheses. If a chimpanzee learns to manipulate tools in more sophisticated ways than Köhler's original experiments indicated were possible, the scientist would not be tempted to say, "this is no longer a chimpanzee," largely because the animal is physically present before him. He would recast his original view of the structures of chimpanzee behavior. But a "liberal polity" stands before no one, and so the question of what it *is* is logically prior to the question of what explains its behavior.

Moreover, while the political concerns that lead Merleau-Ponty to seek an alternative to rationalistic moralism are quite persuasive, one can only be apprehensive about the prospects for developing a philosophy of history that can respond simultaneously to all the demands that he has placed on political thinking. We are

[51] Aron, *Introduction à la philosophie de l'histoire*, p. 94.

approaching here, I think, the greatest flaw in Merleau-Ponty's plans for a new mode of political thinking. It is reasonable to argue that political actors must become aware of a variety of factors connected with "history"—the consequences and structural context of their actions, the appearance of their policies in the eyes of a community with a certain culture, the probable evolution of class relations. A strong case can also be made, as I will discuss later in confronting Merleau-Ponty and Michael Walzer, that the ethics of political action should not stray far from a community's own conception of the good. But having urged these views, Merleau-Ponty does not then undertake, or even encourage, the multitude of empirical and ethical investigations that political thinking seems to require. He does not examine the lived values of classes other than the proletariat. He reprimands Maulnier for imputing to Fascism an unlikely direction of development, but his reproach has the benefit of hindsight.[52] He gives few clues about where to turn to gather dependable information on systems in which one is currently involved. Merleau-Ponty does not pursue questions about the specific meanings that his community gives to values like freedom and equality. Instead he immediately reaches out for a guideline, a *single* thread that will lead him through even the darkest passageways of political life. The problem is that the guideline may simply be a way of dispensing with the difficulties of actually doing the studies and hard thinking that an existential politics makes necessary.

The seriousness of this problem becomes most evident when he argues that Marx combines a theory of historical gestalten with an account of universal values, offering up the proletariat as the indispensable guideline of a humanistic politics. While Marxism supplies the substantive content of an existential politics, Merleau-Ponty also uses it, I will contend, to evade some of its most difficult problems.

[52] Eslin,"Critique de l'humanisme vertueux," p. 12.

F I V E

MARXISM:
THE RADICAL HYPOTHESIS

In his critique of Kantian-liberal politics Merleau-Ponty contends that there is a chronic divergence between the universal values that liberals preach and the self-interested values incarnated in the bourgeois way of life. Yet the precedence of lived values over verbal ones need not destroy all hopes for a more humanistic society. It is conceivable that a different class might exist whose incarnated values are not inherently self-serving. A class might exist that in its very existence stands a chance at actualizing the as yet only ideal claims of the liberal tradition. The symmetrical solution to the problem of a class that systematically subverts its ideals would be to ground political action in a class that systematically sustains them. That is the essence of a startling hypothesis that Merleau-Ponty builds into his postwar writings. Its author is Karl Marx. "Marx thought he had found the solution to the human problem in the proletarian inasmuch as he is detached from his natural surroundings, deprived of his private life, and insofar as there is truly a fate common to him and all other proletarians. The logic of the situation would lead him to join others in a common struggle against economic destiny . . . and to realize with them a *common liberty*" (HT 158, tr. 147). Political reason fulfills its dual vocation of recognizing the necessity of success in collective action and of creating a truly public morality by organizing its theory of intersubjective relations around Marx's notion of a universal class.

Marx stands at the intersection of the two lines of Merleau-Ponty's research. The one, dominated by epistemological concerns, concludes that a new theory of the relation of subject and object is required to found human existence. The other strand, dominated by ethical concerns, connects man's creation of meaning and the problem of social conflict. In Marx, Merleau-Ponty finds a metaphysics consistent with his phenomenology and an ethics responsive to the existential analysis of violence. His objectives are, as

133

always, foundational. He exposes the phenomenological substructure of Marxism in order to support his contention that it is a conceivably valid philosophy of history. His endorsement of Marxism as a radical hypothesis extrapolates his conclusions about the phenomenal objectivity of history to the maximal value still compatible with existential theory.

Whether this rapprochement of Marxism and existentialism is successful has long been the key interpretive controversy surrounding Merleau-Ponty's political writings of the 1940s.[1] My argument that he was founding an existential politics to some extent decenters that question, for it suggests that his interest in Marx is secondary to a larger problematic. Marx elaborates the lessons of thinking politically, but only because he first passes the tests of phenomenological understanding. Merleau-Ponty never relinquishes the priority he gives to phenomenology and so virtually puts Marx on historical probation, waiting to see if events bear out the revolutionary's audacity.

Marx as "Realizer" of Hegel

Merleau-Ponty's analysis of collective meaning concludes that the body's perceptual relation to the world and to others implies a constant tension between communication and violence. Groups refuse to acknowledge the validity of the values and aspirations of other groups. One violates others by unilaterally imposing meanings—a morality, a government, a type of work—on them. Because man is a creature who actualizes his ideas in the form of a way of life and because he seeks public recognition of his always partial values, there is an undercurrent of violence that erodes all attempts to constitute community on the ground of universal ideals. It was Hegel who, for Merleau-Ponty, first explained the conditions under which mankind might escape this problematic. He-

---

[1] For criticisms of his attempt to connect phenomenology and Marxism, see Lefort, *Sur une colonne absente*, p. 97; Miller, "Merleau-Ponty's Marxism: Between Phenomenology and the Hegelian Absolute," pp. 109–111; Viano, "Esistenzialismo ed umanesimo in Maurice Merleau-Ponty," p. 58; Edie, rev. of *Humanism and Terror*, trans. O'Neill, p. 318; Rabil, *Merleau-Ponty*, p. 101; and Pax, "Merleau-Ponty and the Truth of History," pp. 276–277. Others, however, treat his Marxism and his phenomenology as basically compatible. See Waelhens, *Une philosophie de l'ambiguïté*, pp. 350–365; Bien, "Man and the Economic in Merleau-Ponty's Interpretation of Historical Materialism," pp. 121–127; Brockelman, "Sibling Rivalry: The Early Marx and Some Existentialists," pp. 250–262; Poster, *Existential Marxism*, pp. 144–153.

gel begins to redefine the notion of an ethical life in a way that treads a narrow path between the empty abstraction of Kantian moralism and the equally empty scheming of the Machiavellian prince.

Violence must find its remedy in a logic of historical development rather than in an ethic of self-imposed laws, argues Hegel, because the latter is the unwitting accomplice of social destruction. In *The Phenomenology of Mind* he traces the Reign of Terror of the French Revolution to the abstract concept of morality that was put into practice by Robespierre and given purest expression by Kant.[2] The terror begins when the isolated, particular consciousness (Robespierre) mistakes its own certainty for a sign that its moral concepts are universal. It seeks to realize absolute freedom through political action. "Universal freedom becomes a fever of destruction," warns Hegel; "the sole act of absolute freedom is death."[3] Because it disregards the limits upon freedom implicit in a given stage of cultural development, the abstract consciousness is forced to unleash a reign of terror to make the world conform to its moral fantasies.

Hegel's alternative mode of ethics depends on drawing norms from the deeply rooted practices of a culture. He admires the ancient city-state because there the state did not impose its will upon citizens, but rather preserved laws and customs that expressed the collective consciousness of the whole city.[4] The individual practiced an ethical ideal immediately, with no need for "self-legislation" and no anxiety as to the content of his moral choices. But before culture can offer a truly universal ethics—one not only for the privileged few, but for all mankind—history itself must surmount its contradictions in "a long process of maturation" (SNS 119, tr. 69). The slave's progress from the natural desire to preserve his own life to his ability to dominate matter freely through work symbolizes this process. The slave is Hegel's first example of how an individual can be the unconscious agent of mankind's universal destiny. He is the "hero," "the individual of universal history" who, acting from personal motives and passions, has an implicit understanding of the needs of his time. His maturation anticipates the action of the greatest figures of world history. A Caesar who ruthlessly extends the Roman Empire or a Napoleon

---

[2] Hegel, *Phenomenology*, pp. 599–610.
[3] Ibid., p. 605.
[4] Shklar, *Freedom and Independence*, p. 74.

who imposes the achievements of the French Revolution on all of Europe does history's bidding by instinctively directing action toward goals adumbrated in the conflicts rending society. "They accomplish and conquer for others what will appear later as the . . . very sens of history" (SNS 324, tr. 183). Hegel's heroic individual is the person in whom lived convictions and a propensity for action combine to forge new ethical structures for mankind. The liberation of humanity from the burden of violence, partial knowledge, and divided moralities takes place through a dialectical progress of historical stages that extends and integrates the totality of human experience.

Merleau-Ponty's admiration for Hegel's ethical insights collides once more with the established existential sensibility. Sartre charges that Hegel was guilty of "ontological optimism," of describing the relations of other consciousnesses "from the point of view of the absolute."[5] Hegel writes as if he were not himself a consciousness afflicted with the partialities he ascribes to others. His history of ethical development supposes that he is not subject to the existential conditions of knowledge. Merleau-Ponty's often repeated distinction between the early Hegel of the *Phenomenology* and the late Hegel of *The Philosophy of Right* and the *Logic* is his tactical response to Sartre's complaint. For Merleau-Ponty the early Hegel simply described the succession of cultural forms according to their "inner logic" (SNS 112, tr. 65). Only the late Hegel was the spokesman of an idealism that claimed to know the identity of Reason in history (HT 192, tr. 186). The young philosopher of Jena foresaw only the possibility of human reconciliation (SNS 112, tr. 64); the honored professor of Berlin announced the arrival of a final synthesis of all human potentialities in a hierarchical society whose "universal" element was an impartial bureaucracy that mediated the conflicts of civil society (SNS 112, 141, tr. 64, 81; HT 161, tr. 150).

As usual, this modulation of existential views has a political point. Merleau-Ponty's distinctions make available to existentialism a "much more Marxist" interpretation of the *Phenomenology* (SNS 141, tr. 81). Hegelian Reason, he argues, is not something that reveals itself to the philosopher; it is the contingent sens that emerges spontaneously from the multiple, problem-solving activities of individuals and collectivities. But what of the chapter on absolute knowledge that culminates *The Phenomenology of Mind*?

---

[5] *L'être et le néant*, p. 299.

Jean Hyppolite, like Sartre, contends that Hegel's claim to "absolute knowledge . . . that transcends the diverse visions of the world" marks a departure from existential thought.[6] The "more Marxist" Hegel begins to show his face in Merleau-Ponty's reply to Hyppolite's lecture. Merleau-Ponty suggests that absolute knowledge "is perhaps a way of life" (SNS 112, tr. 64). Hegel refers not to the *personal*, all-encompassing wisdom of the sage, but to a *universal social condition* of comprehensive equality and freedom. A condition of freedom does not presuppose an "ontological optimism" that contradicts the existential truths of individual experience. One could say either that Hegel formulated a philosophy of historical development that set the terms for Marx's historical materialism (SNS 141, tr. 81) or that Marx "realized" the potential of the early Hegel (HT 171, tr. 162; cf. SNS 226, tr. 128). For Merleau-Ponty, their common project is clearest in *The German Ideology*, where Marx "reworks the Hegel of 1807" (IN 98).[7]

According to Marx, the division of labor in every society generates social classes with different stakes in the dominant mode of production in their epoch. An exploited, "rising" class eventually throws itself into pitched battles with an exploiting, "declining" class that built its power on an increasingly exhausted mode of production. What is important for Merleau-Ponty in this historical epic is that it depicts how humanity moves toward "universality" through the agency of a class that consummates the logic and resolves the contradictions of the problematic of violence (HT 130–137, tr. 112–118). Marx argues that the historical process has reached a decisive juncture because capitalism has finally spread the forces of modernization and its concomitant alienation and exploitation around the globe. Suffering "not a particular wrong but wrong in general," the proletariat becomes the agent of "the total redemption of humanity."[8] Workers in every country have been thrust into a negative "universality" of dependence, exploitation, and misery that prefigures a positive "universality"—universal

---

[6] Hyppolite, *Figures de la pensée philosophique*, vol. 1, p. 93.

[7] When Merleau-Ponty wrote, Marx's early works had only recently appeared in French. Molitor's translation of *The Critique of Hegel's Philosophy of Right* was published in 1935, followed by *The Paris Manuscripts of 1844* and *The German Ideology* in 1937. Merleau-Ponty's unpublished papers contain a set of detailed notes on the important Introduction to the *Oeuvres complètes de Karl Marx* by Landshut and Mayer that Althusser blames for popularizing a humanistic interpretation of Marx in nonparty intellectual milieus in the 1940s and 1950s. See *Pour Marx*, p. 48.

[8] Marx, "Contribution to the Critique of Hegel's Philosophy of Right," in *The Marx-Engels Reader*, p. 64.

distribution of needed goods, nonalienated labor, worldwide economic cooperation—that will release the individual's full creative abilities. By abolishing private property relations in an international revolutionary movement, the proletariat will abolish the source from which all class relations spring and, hence, class struggle itself. Marx makes the daring claim that the processes of human history are creating a particular class that, by simply living out the tendencies already expressed in its modes of work, belief, and social interaction, will attack directly the root of objectified human relations. Like the Hegelian hero, Marx's proletariat changes the world in ways that expand the area of human freedom.

Foundations of the Metaphysics of Marxism, I: Ethical Theory

Marx presents the paradox of a theorist who derided moralism as mystification and yet who championed the cause of freedom with moral fervor.[9] Merleau-Ponty believes the paradox can be resolved with the following interpretation. "The key idea of Marxism is not the sacrifice of values to facts . . . but the substitution of an effective morality for the verbal one that precedes the revolution; it is to make a society where morality is truly moral . . . by realizing it in effective human relationships" (SNS 287, tr. 162). When Merleau-Ponty maintains that "the revolution directs a violence that bourgeois society tolerates in unemployment and war"(HT 126, tr. 107), he alludes to the possibility of changing the sens of violence, of giving it a different future. Marx's theory shows how this can be done. His philosophy of history is not just a tale of fugitive achievements and inevitable reversals. It is, by virtue of the specific schema of development that it foresees, an ethical theory. The proletariat *incarnates* the Kantian imperative of making behavior conform to universal standards, without relying on individuals' conscious efforts to conform their wills to moral precepts.

The title of the book in which Merleau-Ponty develops this claim, *Humanism and Terror*, effectively summarizes his position.[10]

[9] Lukes documents the paradox in detail in *Marxism and Morality*, pp. 5–12.

[10] Merleau-Ponty apparently contemplated titling his work *Humanism and Violence*. In the unpublished notes, a one-page sketch of ideas for the work is labelled "Passage de l'humanisme à la violence" (IN 16). Also, a literary review announced the forthcoming work as *Violence et humanisme*. See Aimé Patri, "Bibliographie," *Paru 37* (December 1947), p. 51. The shift of terms is significant: "terror" alludes all the more clearly to Hegel's analysis of the French Revolution.

"Humanism" signifies that there are no sources of value and no resolutions to human disputes beyond those that man himself fashions. Marxism is a humanism insofar as it assumes that man creates in his conduct and in his culture whatever absolutes govern his existence (HT 53, tr. 17; cf. SNS 230, tr. 130). Marx also sees that the achievement of humanistic political forms is dialectically related to terror. Marxism—"the only humanism that dares to develop its consequences" (HT 166, tr. 156)—accepts some violence as the premise of any higher ethical theory. Most crucial to his argument is the phenomenological observation that violence can have a sens (HT 116, tr. 97). The history of violence reveals not a movement of pure irrationality, but a scheme of rational evolution. Through conflict mankind gradually puts the natural and political-economic barriers to freedom under the control of reason.

This process depends on the action of the proletariat, a class that is a "value-fact" like no other. Whereas the commitment of the bourgeoisie to existing property relations leads it to combat economic reforms that would equalize political power and extend freedom, the life situation of the proletariat inclines it to dismantle the structures of domination. The proletariat is a "power polarized toward certain values by the very logic of its situation" (HT 142, tr. 127). It makes values real by creating the political-economic infrastructures that motivate nonviolent relations among persons. Mankind achieves morality mediately by means of an evolving cultural formation that is "the concrete bearer of values" (HT 140, tr. 125).

The moral achievement of the Marxian revolution should be "the recognition of man by man" in a new humanistic society (HT 129, 165, 191, tr. 111, 155, 186). By adopting Marx Merleau-Ponty gives his vague concept of "mutual recognition" a little more content. "Mutual recognition" represents an ideal of unimpeded communication (HT 193, tr. 188; SNS 118, tr. 68), where "communication" stands not just for free expression, but for an intellectual and material commerce with all other persons, unrestrained by barriers of class, nation, and ideology. The major instances of violence that Marx identifies—degrading work conditions, war, unemployment, poverty, as well as various forms of political repression—can be interpreted as failures of communication insofar as each involves the use (or acquiescence in the use) of some people as unthinking objects rather than as creators or perceivers of meaning. Merleau-Ponty accepts Marx's contention that socializing the means of production will allow individuals to recognize as their own the material products of civilization. It will create an equalitarian society and reorganize work so that the full diversity of individual talents might flourish. Each person, not just the few, will have the means to make a contribution to the dialogical enterprise of the creation of culture and each will recognize in the work of others a source of enriching self-realization.

But "self-realization" sounds suspiciously unexistential. Self-realization seems to presuppose a human *essence* that is at present unrealized, but can be made to flourish under different circumstances. Merleau-Ponty tries to minimize such essentialist notions. He does so by arguing that class conflict ultimately moves toward a reduction in the alternatives in mankind's historical development to two: either we will establish a society that finally eliminates violence or we will forever tolerate systems that perpetuate it (HT 41, tr. 1). This is an exclusive disjunction. There is, on the one hand, a political-economic order that fosters domestic repression and international aggression. On the other, there already exist patterns of social interaction that are reorganizing human collective life into political forms where the treatment of individuals as autonomous subjects will be the norm.

If the conceivable lines of historical development really are as limited as Merleau-Ponty believes, then it makes sense to ignore most questions about whether morality must be grounded in a particular conception of human nature. What form of social organization benefits an autonomous being? What goods will be produced in the postrevolutionary society and how will they be distributed? What character traits will be fostered in socialist citizens? For the present, when the choice is simply between violence and nonviolence, such questions seem irrelevant. One historical alternative is so clearly morally superior to the other that it must attract our support, regardless of the answers to these questions. For the future, these questions seem presumptuous. According to Marx man has no essence, he has a history. The values of socialist societies will have to result from the imagination and work of future generations.

Thus Merleau-Ponty's ethics is both substantive and existential. Its touchstone is not formalistic "authenticity," but substantive nonviolence. Nonetheless, his ethics remains existential inasmuch as it leaves the task of defining most values to the men and women of future societies. In conception, Merleau-Ponty's argument exemplifies what Mihailo Marković calls an "objective" judgment in political theory.[11] The argument depends not on the avoidance of *any* conception of a human good, but rather on raising value judgments to critical consciousness (as in the critique of Kantian moralism); on reducing them to a necessary minimum (as in the historical disjunction between violence and nonviolence); and on ensuring that its values are of a universal character rather than the expression of vested interests (as in the idea that the proletariat will end violence for mankind as a whole).

But even if the morality of ends is settled, do there not remain vexing questions regarding the morality of means? Do we not still have to anguish over whether it is permissible to precipitate revolution by terrorist means, or to participate in parliamentary government, or to provoke a general strike even when its success seems unlikely? Merleau-Ponty denies that there are moral dilemmas even at this level because questions about means and ends rest upon an unacceptable dualism that phenomenology excludes at the start.

Already in *The Structure of Behavior* he refutes those behavioral theorists who maintain that various animals all seek common "ends" (survival, reproduction, nourishment) and that the diversity of their behavior merely reflects different "means" of attaining those ends (SC 188, tr. 169). He objects that this analysis presumes an abstract concept of what the organism pursues, missing the specific ways in which the organism orients itself toward its goals. The problems that an animal attempts to solve (its ends) can only be known in relation to its unique aptitudes and manners of relating to its surroundings (its means). Marxism sustains the objection. It denounces moralists for deciding, independently of context and likely consequences, what action is right or wrong. Moralists are like empiricists who try to describe behavior without reference to how the surroundings exist for the subject. But in a Marxist revolution, a theoretical outlook itself drawn from historical developments guides the workers. Marxism therefore does not presuppose the dualism of means and ends. Instead it defines the revolution "as the simple extrapolation of a certain practice already at work in history" (HT 141, tr. 126). The Marxist, like the gestalt theorist, grasps the ways that certain settings call forth certain actions. Merleau-Ponty agrees with Trotsky that according to Marx,

[11] "Marxism as Political Philosophy," in *Political Theory and Political Education*, ed. Richter, p. 98.

"the end flows naturally from the historical movement."[12] Properly understood, therefore, Marxism forbids utopian uprisings, terrorist tactics,[13] and Machiavellian maneuvers. It does so not because they are morally wrong, but because they construct schemas of action independently of historical context. So neither the decision to support the revolution nor the choice of tactics involves the individual in Kantian moral deliberation.

This ethical understanding of Marxism is what Merleau-Ponty proposes as the regulative ideal of an existential politics.[14] His existential politics will not be an abstract moralism, but will instead inquire into the overall sens of the violence it encounters. It will seek to place its values in the world by aligning itself with the class that promises to bring them into being. An existential political theory asks how particular events affect the likelihood that a class endowed with lived, humanistic values will "extrapolate" them into political affairs.

Foundations of the Metaphysics
of Marxism, II: Gestalttheorie

How is a theory of this scope possible? Why does it happen that history assumes an ethically relevant sens? What is the nature of the connection of events such that history can be grasped by reason? To answer these questions one must investigate the metaphysics of Marxism as communists and existentialists saw them in the 1940s.

By the early twentieth century Marx's philosophy of history had been widely interpreted as a theory of economic determinism. The story of how Marx's theory of dialectical social practice was transformed to accord with a crudely positivistic view of science is too familiar to bear detailed repetition here.[15] That transformation, partly encouraged by Marx but set more definitively by Engels,

---

[12] Trotsky, Their Morals and Ours, p. 35.

[13] "Terror" differs from "terrorism." André Breton's announcement, in the Second Manifesto of Surrealism, that the true surrealist act would be to shoot at random in a crowded street moved Merleau-Ponty to wonder if there were not a real incompatibility between surrealism and Marxism. Marxism, he said, demands "a minimum of realism," that is, a theory of the discipline of violence toward certain ends. "Le surréalisme." Emission: Tribune de Paris. Débat avec Merleau-Ponty, N. Arnaud, M. P. Fouchet, G. Henein, etc., Radiodiffusion-Télévision Française (RTF), July 21 and 29, 1947. Cf. HT 111, tr. 91.

[14] Invitto, Merleau-Ponty politico, p. 48.

[15] See Miller, History and Human Existence, pp. 103–124, for a recent account.

Lenin, and finally Stalin, ends in a deterministic metaphysics that pictures economic relations as the motor of the historical process. The individual's relation to the means of production, in this view, is the *causative* factor behind social movements, systems of ideas, and political choices. Ideas are merely "reflections" of an underlying material process. Knowledge of this process is possible because the Marxist adopts the objective perspective of the natural scientist: he observes how certain circumstances, defined independently of the subject's awareness of them, rigorously determine the subject's behavior. The scientific Marxist forms hypotheses to explain political events, collects data on the objects of his study, and seeks to verify his findings.[16]

The French Communist party (PCF) became particularly notorious for its unquestioning adherence to the orthodoxy of "diamat."[17] It was from this supposedly scientific perspective that party theorists like Henri Lefebvre and Roger Garaudy, as well as the Trotskyist Pierre Naville, challenged the growing popularity of existentialism in postwar France.[18] Sartre, although sympathetic to proletarian politics, could accept no philosophical position that negated his theory of the free consciousness. In essays on "Materialism and Revolution" in mid-1946, he attempted a definitive response to Marxist critics of his existentialism.[19] Claiming that his dispute was with "neo-Marxist Stalinism," he nonetheless implicated Marx (and even more, Engels) in what he regarded as a crude and outmoded philosophical materialism.[20]

The doctrine of dialectical materialism, Sartre charges, is philosophically incoherent because matter is by definition undialectical. Bits of matter "only have relations of contiguity and simultaneity."[21] Each element in a reaction is considered as if it contributed independently to the final result and it retains its identity after the reaction is complete. True dialectics sees action as a reciprocal process in which each element can be defined only as part of a totality. Sartre's trump, of course, is the Cartesian argument that no reductionist materialism can be foundational because con-

---

[16] Naville, *Les conditions de la liberté*, esp. pp. 86–95, 165–168.

[17] Lichtheim, *Marxism in Modern France*, pp. 151–162.

[18] Poster, *Existential Marxism*, pp. 109–134.

[19] J.-P. Sartre, "Matérialisme et révolution," *Les Temps Modernes* 9 (1946), pp. 1537–1563, and 10 (1946), pp. 1–32. I quote from the reprinted essays in *Situations III*.

[20] *Situations III*, pp. 165 and 147–151.

[21] Ibid., p. 146.

sciousness has the ability to understand and change material relations. At best, he suggests, materialism is a pragmatic myth that has been useful to the revolution by levelling class distinctions (for it means that all men alike are subject to the same social determinations). Today however it needs to be replaced by a new philosophy, one that unites action, thought, reality, and truth—to wit, Sartrean existentialism. Existentialism accepts the historicity of values, it depicts the human predicament as man's being "thrown there" to create his own destiny, it pits the free consciousness against obstacles that it must surmount. Sartre boldly proffers his existentialism as the revolutionary's *substitute for* a philosophically obsolete materialism.

What Sartre overlooks, however, is that "dialectical materialism," in spite of its defects, manages to convey something of what makes Marxism so compelling as social theory. Marx claimed to have discovered the *arché* of historical transformation. Marx offers not only principles of action, but an extended historical analysis that explains why a particular form of revolutionary action is called for by the historical juncture. What makes Sartre's self-proclaimed radicalism so unsatisfactory is its complete inability to posit an alternative first principle that might reveal hidden patterns in social processes.

Worse than this theoretical impotency, from the point of view of some Marxists, is the potential for Sartrean existentialism to rationalize tolerance for ideological defenses of a class-ridden society. Existentialism seems unable to make an analytical distinction between the material conditions of existence and the false ideas that emanate from the economic "base." Henri Lefebvre states the point succinctly."[Existentialism] may very well keep certain spare parts taken from Marxism, but not what is most essential—the method of objective knowledge that allows [the Marxist] to avoid being the dupe of others and to unmask what men are beneath what they say."[22] The very concept of ideology is predicated upon the ability to distinguish between systematically distorted modes of communication, ones that conceal particular class interests behind a "mask" of ostensibly general and impartial formulae, and an objective analysis of the mechanisms of historical movement. Phenomenology's descriptive program, which denies the distinction between appearance and reality, is destined to confuse political ideas and the "real" political world. Lefebvre charges that, by

[22] "Existentialisme et Marxisme," p. 8.

method, existentialism has to accept conservative religious beliefs and economic doctrines as "phenomena" invested with meanings that cannot be reduced to their objective, class content.

In an article appearing at exactly the same time as Sartre's "Materialism and Revolution" (but in a Trotskyist journal), Merleau-Ponty proposes a very different stance toward Marx.[23] Sartre would have the existential account of a consciousness throwing itself forward in the creation of values *supersede* Marxist historical materialism. Merleau-Ponty would *recover* the original Marx in order to discover an authentically existential description of revolutionary man. He regrounds Marxism by cutting it off from the language of nineteenth-century materialism and by explaining its coherence with twentieth-century phenomenology. Merleau-Ponty's most original contribution to the interpretation of Marx is his argument that historical materialism is metaphysics of meaning rather than of matter.

He begins his article with remarks sympathetic to Sartre's critique of the PCF's positivistic Marx. But then, with a discreet footnote to Sartre's essays, he shifts the perspective back to a phenomenological rehabilitation of "materialism." "It has sometimes rightly been asked how materialism could be dialectical. . . . The fact is that in Marxism matter (like consciousness, moreover) is never considered apart; it is inserted in the system of human coexistence, it founds there a common situation of contemporaneous and successive individuals. It ensures the generality of their projects and makes possible . . . a sens of history" (SNS 228–229, tr. 129). The *1844 Manuscripts* reveals that what contemporary Communist doctrine calls "dialectical matter" was originally for Marx a way of talking about how "nature" is humanized by a praxis linking consciousness and substance. It is in effect the "cultural world" whose outlines Merleau-Ponty drew in his earliest phenomenological investigations. Marx and modern phenomenology agree that objects are not simply sense impressions, but are matter impregnated with human signification. Labor is the physical expression of intentions that form matter, and these "incarnated" intentions are the vehicle of cultural continuity.

The importance of this concept of matter is that a dialectic inheres in its very existence. Sartre is right that the "matter" of positivistic theory does not contain an inner principle of contradiction

---

[23] "Marxisme et philosophie" appeared originally in *Revue Internationale* 1:6 (June–July 1946), pp. 518–526.

and synthesis. But cultural objects do. "The spirit of a society is realized, transmitted, and perceived by the cultural objects it gives itself. . . . They suggest to man a way of being and thinking. It is thus understandable . . . that the 'fetishism of commodities' induces an entire mode of 'objective' thought that is peculiar to bourgeois civilization" (SNS 232, tr. 131). Because matter is integrated into networks of human values and needs, it can prompt the formation of attitudes that, in turn, lead to the creation of new objects and new values. Marx's philosophy of history, Merleau-Ponty suggests, develops from an understanding of the conditioning effects of cultural objects.

The Primacy of the Economic

Marx's thesis, one might object, is much more powerful than that. It does not hold that just any cultural objects instigate social development. Historical materialism identifies an economic factor, the nature of a society's productive relations, as the primary one in historical change. So the plausibility of a phenomenological interpretation of Marx depends on its ability to translate the language of economic determinism into its own concepts of meaning and structure.

Merleau-Ponty maintains that the corps propre furnishes a model of how this can be done. "Economic life," he contends, "is the historic bearer of mental structures, just as our body maintains the fundamental traits of our conduct over and above the variations in our state of mind" (SNS 190, tr. 108; cf. PP 201, tr. 172). This parallel stresses a type of relationship. The body is not simply a medium for higher, more reflective forms of behavior; the meanings established in its preconscious intercourse with the world are the background for all higher-level ideation. Similarly, economic life may be the founding phenomenon in the actions of collective subjects, that is, classes (SNS 233, tr. 131). Economically motivated attitudes are the background of all other social attitudes. They are the most deeply rooted, least conscious, and most stable aspects of a cultural structure. Merleau-Ponty, like Sartre, knows that "external" conditions, including economic life, act on the consciousness only through their meaning. Yet meanings associated with modes of work and ownership can become "sedimented" in the consciousness, where they operate as inertial factors in social organization (SNS 189, tr. 108).

Thus, Marx's emphasis on the economic need not be interpreted on the positivist model of causation. Instead, it signifies a theoretical assessment that, among available points of interpretive access in social explanation, economic conditions are more likely to sketch out accurately the course of events over some extended segment of history (SNS 191, tr. 109). So even if in phenomenological description no factor can be isolated from any other because each bears some thematic relation to all others, still the economic text may be more "readable" and more dependable than any other in the total "text" of social life.[24] Economic relations motivate patterns of social choice in a manner allowing probable estimations of the outcome of class conflict.

The corollary to the argument that economic life is the primary sector motivating historical change is that idea systems are secondary sectors. Ideologies are to be criticized not as superstructures emanating from an economic base, but as meanings that give only weak interpretive holds on the direction of transformation of cultural meanings. Drawing on the lessons of Gestalttheorie, Merleau-Ponty develops a nonreductionist interpretation of ideology. In a gestalt experiment in which a subject's perception of an "illusion" is observed, the scientist comes to understand how the structure of the perceptual situation motivated the illusion. Yet the scientist's understanding does not change the experimental subject's perception. The illusion itself is irreducible, a "fact" that can now be explained but not discarded. It reveals a truth about human perceptual faculties.

Ideologies are similar to illusions. They are partial systems of meaning whose full social significance becomes apparent only when one specifies their function in a political structure. Merleau-Ponty cites some of Marx's earliest comments on the religious question as the model of this sort of analysis. Marx knew that, strictly speaking, religion is not "true"; the assertions it makes about the afterlife or about the sources of human misery do not conform to our best knowledge of those subjects. Nonetheless, he recognized religion as "the realization in fantasy of the human essence." It is the *real* expression of human conflict and aspirations, and as such, it contains an element of truth. Marx does not ignore religion. He wants instead to "replace this fantasm of communi-

---

[24] Caillois, "De la perception à l'histoire: La philosophie de Maurice Merleau-Ponty," p. 79. In spite of Althusser's hostility to phenomenology, his own theory of structural causation, according to which the economic "instance" is dominant and yet interactive with political and ideological instances, is very similar to Merleau-Ponty's. Compare *Pour Marx*, p. 111.

cation by an effective communication in this world" (SNS 226, tr. 127). The social theorist's objective is not to suppress "fantasms," but to supply an interpretive context that reveals their partiality and hidden functions. In this spirit Merleau-Ponty reminds those who would censor books according to standards of ideological purity that: "Marx said that the curve of ideologies is much more complicated than that of social and political life. In the novel there are not some errors and some truths, but lives for which errors are on the path of truth."[25] "Ideologies" are a link in a process of correction, that is, in a process of the discovery of the larger schema that fixes their meaning. In a phenomenology inspired by Gestalttheorie, an ideal of the critical interpretation of social phenomena supplants the metaphor of "unmasking."

In fact, the reasoning Merleau-Ponty develops in his analysis of Gestalttheorie guides his entire interpretation of Marx's philosophy of history. Marx puts violence and freedom in the same relationship to classes as illusion and veridical perception to the individual subject. Illusion occurs when what I perceive is out of my optimal perceptual field—the object is too distant, in too little light, at an unfamiliar angle. Illusion exposes me to error in my practical choices. Veridical perception explores the phenomenon, destructures the perceptual field that motivates the illusion, and reintegrates the field in a way that gives me an effective grasp on the world. It allows me to solve problems that the illusion did not. Fox example, I go around this dark spot in my path because I see it is a hole, not a discoloration in the ground.

In *The German Ideology* especially, Marx understands the assimilation of historical experience by classes in the same way. Through modes of work and organization classes develop means to liberate man from cycles of economic crisis, natural disasters, and even the humanly created scourge of violence. But the extension of human liberty is a gradual and lurching process. Class structures become frozen; they cease to restructure cultural acquisitions in ways that increase human power and freedom. Classes whose livelihood depends on a more primitive mode of production then act like illusions in the historical process. They impede the ability of larger and more innovative groups to respond to problems posed by technological, organizational, and political developments. Class struggle represents the perceptual movement toward the historical object. Blocked potentialities inherent in one social form are liber-

[25] "Une enquête d'*action*: "Faut-il brûler Kafka?," p. 14.

ated by a political restructuring that, for a time, facilitates man's practical activities in the world.[26] This movement has a generally progressive direction because of what Merleau-Ponty (following Trotsky) calls a process of "historical selection" (BP 259). Like Darwinian natural selection, in which the struggle for existence among animal species favors species with the best characteristics for survival, so historical selection "eliminates in the long run [social forms] that create diversions in relation to the permanent exigencies of man" (HT 164, tr. 154) and develops those that respond best to human needs. The sens of history evolves from the contact between, on the one hand, human suffering and ingenuity and, on the other, ossified cultural forms.

In the climactic passage of his interpretation of Marx in *Humanism and Terror*, Merleau-Ponty explains the precise "fit" of Marxism to Gestalttheorie (HT 144, tr. 130). A gestalt is a system of mutually determining elements, and "in a Marxist politics, history is a system." Gestalttheorie understands a subject's behavior by seeing it as oriented toward solving certain practical problems in its vital environment. Marx's logic of history is based, at the most fundamental level, on the notion that there are "effective problems" that account for the arrangement of economic, political, and ideological structures (SNS 185, tr. 105). We grasp human history as the story of different organizational and technological attempts to overcome the obstacles to man's self-mastery. Thus "to be a Marxist is to think that economic and cultural or human questions are a single question and that the proletariat is the solution to this problem." The "solution" in a gestalt relation is an adjustment and redistribution of factors to recreate a stable whole: "history is a gestalt . . . , a total process in movement toward a state of equilibrium, which . . . is indicated in present crises as the resolution of these crises." Human needs and aspirations, operating collectively and culturally, may have arranged themselves into an unstable configuration whose resolution would be a social form that will end the problematic of violence.

This analysis has the same implications for the intelligibility of history that the phenomenon of the gestalt has for understanding perceptual structures. Merleau-Ponty speaks of Marx's work as a "perception of history" (HT 117, tr. 98) to stress the cognitive relationship that Marx was able to establish with his subject matter, a relationship that is only possible because the problem-solution

---

[26] Langan, *Merleau-Ponty's Critique*, pp. 103, 106.

dialectic gives history a discernible structure. This dialectic creates in history the two vantage points from which structural meanings can be understood.

The account of the awakening of proletarian consciousness means that the workers are in the primary epistemic situation, that of the subject situated wholly within the structural meanings of history. The proletarian experiences the shift of meanings as the social "background" changes. The Marxist theorist, on the other hand, wants to occupy the secondary epistemic position of the observer who grasps the signifying processes generative of class meanings. If he observes the relationship between historical conditions and proletarian conduct, the disorder of history takes on understandable contours of meaning. The conjunction of these two perceptual situations allows Merleau-Ponty to claim that "a revolution, if it is really in the sens of history, can be thought at the same time as lived" (PP 416, tr. 365). What the proletariat lives, the Marxist theorist thinks, conceptualizes, extends.

The political importance of Merleau-Ponty's refutation of Aron's historical scepticism is now clear: no such claim as Marx's that history has a single, intelligible structure is possible if every reading of the past is an arbitrary mise en perspective. Interpreted as a theory of historical gestalten, however, Marx's philosophy of history is an epistemologically defensible extension of the notion of phenomenal objectivity. "The plurality of perspectives is not an argument against Marxism. . . . Marxism consists precisely in saying that each phenomenon is inseparable in the plurality of perspectives—including economic. . . . He contends that they are all convergent and agree in their existential bearing" (IN 103; cf. SNS 197, tr. 112). Marx's argument is that diverse phenomena like the expansion of markets, technological developments, philosophical and religious movements, and class divisions are all converging toward communism. By using the proletariat as a guideline, Merleau-Ponty redirects the existential project of discovering the sens of human relations to seek the cognitive link between local and universal history.

Merleau-Ponty's Doubt: Transforming Transcendentalism

Raymond Aron was, not surprisingly, the first to criticize the Marxian extension of an existential philosophy of history. He accused Merleau-Ponty of "always confus[ing] two ideas: the idea that history has a meaning, and the idea that the meaning the Marxist assigns to it is the only valid, rationally admissible one."[27] The passage in which Merleau-Ponty is alleged to have slipped from phenomenological interrogation to political dogmatism occurs toward the end of *Humanism and Terror*. "Looked at closely, Marxism is not just another hypothesis, replaceable tomorrow by another. It is the simple statement of the conditions without which there will be neither humanity in the sense of a reciprocal relation between men nor rationality in history. In this sense it is not a philosophy of history, it is the philosophy of history, and to reject it is to give up on Reason in history" (HT 163, tr. 153). How can any assertion that history has a single meaning fit into an existential framework that stresses ambiguity and situated knowledge?

In order to understand Merleau-Ponty's hopes for an existential political theory—and to criticize them fairly—it is vital to grasp the significance of the formulation "the conditions without which" that introduces the possibility of "Reason in history." This wording (and even more clearly, another assertion that "the solution to the proletarian problem is *that without which* there will be no solution to the human problem" [IN 42, emphasis added]), invokes what he had elsewhere used as a catch phrase for Kant's transcendental method, "le ce sans quoi" (PP 501, 506, tr. 439, 442). His formulation hints that the proletariat is the last heir of Kantian transcendental argument, an heir whose inheritance has been rebuilt by its intermediate legatees to stand as an empirical possibility. To understand how a transcendental category can be empirical is to grasp the philosophical explanation of Merleau-Ponty's doubt-ridden commitment to Marxism.

The burden of Kant's epistemological argument is that knowledge is the product not of immediate sensual access to nature, but of a process by which mind gives form to experience. Sense experience is grasped universally in terms of time, space, and causality because reason has applied to it a priori categories of the understanding. The categories are "that without which" there can be no

---

[27] *Marxism and the Existentialists*, p. 36. This remark is from a lecture originally given at the Collège Philosophique in 1947. Merleau-Ponty was present at the lecture and even responded with a defense of *Being and Nothingness*. Charles Delasnerie, "Des actuelles tentatives de synthèse entre l'existentialisme et le Marxisme," *Revue Internationale* 13 (February 1947), pp. 184–185. Sartre notes, however, that Merleau-Ponty—in another example of his publicly argued, transformative interpretation of existentialism—freely used his own political ideas to clarify Sartre's. See "Merleau-Ponty [1]," p. 148.

rational grasp of sense experience; they are its "condition of possibility." In ethics Kant applies the same transcendental form of reasoning. Man must order his conduct according to precepts given to him by reason alone. Heteronomous behavior—acting out of desire or for the sake of any empirical goal—is devoid of moral content because it is not determined by a universal law that reason legislates for itself. Kant does not argue that the ground of empirical experience and the ground of moral reasoning are the same. Indeed he believes that the laws of causality absolutely determine the empirical order and that the ethical order absolutely requires the premise that man makes his decisions freely. An ethical "ought" cannot apply to an empirical "is"; the two orders require different presuppositions. But in both cases Kant maintains that reason acts upon material given in particular form to the senses (disparate impressions, egoistic desires) to make it uniform and universal.

Hegel collapses those epistemological and ethical inquiries into a single problematic. He agrees with Kant that mind shapes the materials of experience but finds Kant's answers lacking in two respects. In the first place, Kant had made the categories the property of a changeless, universal reason, whereas in fact they are cultural and historical acquisitions. Second, rationality is the product not of a purifying reflection, but of a mind realizing its ideas in the world and reapprehending them, always in an enriched and more complex form. Categories are still transcendental, for within a culture and period, they are the a priori organizing assumptions of its cognitive and ethical life. But Hegel refuses to separate the "is" from the "ought": moral as much as epistemic categories develop historically. History (that which "is") actualizes by its dialectical advance the ethical requirements of human life (that which "ought" to be)–freedom.

Marx agrees with Hegel in collapsing the is/ought dichotomy and in regarding rationality as the product of human historical activity, but argues that Hegel ends by overemphasizing the role of mind. Not spiritual activity but modes of production are the primary factors in shaping categories of knowledge and morality. Processes of economic activity produce a logic of historical existence that will eventually impel the workers to reorganize economic and cultural life on a rational basis. Man in history gradually constructs the material and cultural basis for freedom.

Merleau-Ponty's hypothetical Marxism continues this tradition of receiving and transforming transcendental analysis. Throughout his phenomenological research, he argues that there are "conditions of reality" that make experience comprehensible and conduct moral. These conditions relate not to the timeless structure of the human mind, but to the fact of having a body and of living in a particular culture. The theory of the proletariat closes out this series of transcendental perspectives by posing, in effect, the "conditions of reality" of historical rationality. Like a Kantian category, the proletariat is the "filter" through which the chaotic and strife-torn materials of history pass in order to receive rational form. This "filter" could be said to serve the double function of a category of the understanding and of a categorical imperative. The proletariat, with its privileged epistemic position within the gestalt, is the only class to perceive correctly the structure of the historical process. In addition, it gives human collective life the moral structure of freedom in institutions and cultural practice. The transcendental subject survives, since Marx, in empirical form.[28]

Merleau-Ponty's argument is that an historical configuration has made the proletariat the equilibrating agent in a process that will strike down the barriers to the fullest means of human expression. The proletariat is the *condition* of this process in the sense that the moral outcome is *inconceivable* without it carrying out its role in the gestalt. No other class or group can replace the proletariat in this function. When Merleau-Ponty dismisses princes, scientists, intellectuals, bureaucrats, and saints as other candidates for this "historic mission," he is doing more than rejecting specific proposals (e.g., those of Hegel or Saint-Simon), more than rejecting the sceptical contention that any number of groups might have been chosen with equal plausibility. He is saying that each of the other candidates would in fact end up dominating all other groups. Each presupposes a continuing division of humanity between rulers and ruled, masters and slaves. Each would leave civilization in a state of "struggle [and] violence, not reciprocity" (HT 164, tr. 155). Other groups might act in the name of the "common good." Yet acting in another's stead is still a violation of freedom, for existential freedom is *self*-determination. Proletarian universality is unique because it portends the abolition of class division itself.

Portents, however, are not prophecies. The proletariat's promise is lodged in reality, and reality is always contingent. Merleau-Ponty balances the audacity of the Marxian hypothesis with an awareness that the proletariat's mission is vulnerable to diversion.

---

[28] Piccone, "Phenomenological Marxism," p. 26.

Even class values can miscarry. With the example of Germany fresh in mind, Merleau-Ponty realizes that nationalist ideology can grip the working class, stifling its internationalist impulse and impressing its power in the service of war.[29] We shall see in a later chapter that he fears even Communist parties can lead the proletariat in ways that exacerbate violence. He can imagine that "for centuries" history might stumble through a series of diversions (SNS 213, tr. 121). He believes that Marx's schema has some possibility of being fulfilled. He even thinks it must be fulfilled if ever there is to be true freedom. But "that does not mean that it will come to pass; one can only say that if it is not realized there will be no humanity" (IN 9).

So Merleau-Ponty ends even his most confident meditation on Marxism in the subjunctive mood, asking whether "humanity" can be conceived as a "problem." He questions not only whether Marx's vision will come to pass, but also whether history is even structured as Marx believed. *Humanism and Terror* only sets forth "the *question* of our times" (HT 191, tr. 186, emphasis added).[30] "The proletarian problem" is to know whether the proletariat will in fact carry out its role as the universal class in this scheme of historical sens. The important point for an assessment of his Marxism is that Merleau-Ponty never claimed that it offered more than a hypothesis, a statement of the "conditions without which" the end to the problematic of violence is inconceivable. He admits from the start that structures of particular cultures and limited historical epochs may be the most comprehensive gestalten formed by human relations and that history as a whole may be only a meaningless succession of such forms.

Merleau-Ponty's philosophy of history involves, in effect, two related assertions with different degrees of plausibility. Marxism is what I will call the maximal interpretation of historical meaning; the philosophy implied by Merleau-Ponty's refutation of Aron's scepticism is the minimal interpretation. Minimally, historical sens is "fragmentary" (PP 512, tr. 449). Particular cultures or periods are understandable as gestalten. For Marx, in contrast, human his-

---

[29] "Le Manifeste Communiste a cent ans," p. 2.

[30] In what was probably his concluding lecture on the philosophy of history at Lyon, Merleau-Ponty clearly exposes the hypothetical character of his interpretation of Marxism: "Our times are philosophical because they put philosophies of history in question: are they or are they not capable of informing the world? . . . Is this crisis or is it chaos?" (IN 170). For similar claims, see SNS 141, 213, 268, tr. 81, 121, 152; "Réponse à C.L.R. James," p. 2294.

tory itself is an all-embracing structure in which every event, every class, every technology plays a role in the advancement of human freedom. Minimally, history is "rational" in the sense that it is intelligible. It can be penetrated by human reason in a way that exceeds simply putting facts into perspective. But when Merleau-Ponty says that history has "an effective logic that courts contingency . . . and individual freedom and turns them into reason" (HT 143, tr. 129), "reason" implies not just intelligibility, but effectiveness in responding to fundamental human needs. At a minimum, there can be some "objective knowledge" about history, but any particular view may have to be modified by new information. The maximal philosophy of history abides no alternatives; history is either rational or it is "chaos" (SNS 209, 218, 288, 299, tr. 119, 124, 163, 169). If man fails to consummate the tendency toward mutual recognition implicit in the historical gestalt, the result will be "non-sense"—"the power of some, the resignation of others" (HT 165, tr. 155), an infinite repetition of age-old structures of domination. Minimally, Merleau-Ponty asserts that any political program includes an estimate of the most powerful factors shaping social development. Maximally, he speculates that the "objective" meaning of history and the most *valued* form of human relations might be, in the final analysis, the same thing.

Merleau-Ponty's approach to Marxism in the 1940s could be paraphrased as follows. "Marxism rightly understood is only an application and extension of truths that phenomenology has already established. Marx meets the standards of existential philosophy when 'history' is understood as a structure of intersignifying, lived meanings, not as the concatenation of economic impulses; when sens assumes the material form of praxis and is not supplanted by 'causes'; when nature is dialectical because it is humanized, not because matter contains the synthesizing power of intellect; when classes are constituted not as reflections of economic processes, but as nondeliberative ways of life motivated by economic conditions; when the theorist claims not to have absolute knowledge, but only to occupy an epistemic vantage point that favors understanding historical structures. But did Marx occupy such a vantage point? Does history really have an all-embracing structure because of economic meanings? Can one class become universal? No one can be sure. Still, nothing existential phenomenology says can exclude affirmative answers to these questions. There is, moreover, empirical evidence that Marx might be right. The Bolshevik Revolution has survived almost thirty years; the resilience and power of the USSR was crucial in defeating Hitler; in many European countries Communist parties have more working-class support than ever before. So we should take the chance and use the theory as the guideline of an existential politics. We reserve, however, the right to criticize the hypothesis and to determine if necessary the point at which historical evidence speaks overwhelmingly against it."

Critical Observations

In evaluating Merleau-Ponty's Marxism, I want to comment first on its ethical aspects and second on its explanatory ones.

Merleau-Ponty usually reduces the ethical content of Marxism to an assertion that communism will create a completely nonviolent society. Although this keeps Marx within the existential ambit, it barely scratches the surface of Marx's moral sensibility. Marx's argument that the misery of early capital accumulation is compensated by the happiness it creates later, notes Alan Gilbert, verges on a utilitarian notion of justice.[31] Michael Green thinks that Marx is getting at a conception of justice in which "each must earn his way by putting forth according to his abilities the type of effort appropriate to the object he wishes to appropriate."[32] Stephen Lukes believes that when Marx speaks of the autonomy of socialist man, of an enriched individuality with a variety of talents, he presupposes something like Aristotelian perfectionism.[33] In fact, Merleau-Ponty himself occasionally uses phrases like "the permanent exigencies of man" (HT 164, tr. 154) and "the most purely human of men" (HT 14, tr. xix) that seemingly allude to some deeper features of the human character that must be fulfilled in a morally acceptable society. Whether Marx's ethical views were internally consistent is a question I cannot resolve here. But it is clear that Merleau-Ponty was unwilling to probe Marx on this issue, probably because he suspected he might find a concept of human self-realization that does not accord easily with the existential notion of man as an entirely self-determining being.

Merleau-Ponty's failure to elaborate on the telos of historical development, the society of "mutual recognition," cuts his ethical theory short in additional and distressing ways. Drawing on Hegel and Marx, I have tried to fill in some of the features of this telos—

[31] "Historical Theory and the Structure of Moral Argument in Marx," p. 175.
[32] "Marx, Utility, and Right," p. 444.
[33] *Marxism and Morality*, p. 87.

nonviolence, socioeconomic equality, unimpeded communication. It must be admitted, however, that even these specifications hardly tell us what mutual recognition entails. Will the new society permit any distinctions of rank or income? Is it consistent with free communication if every person does not have at every moment equal access to the media? Does one do violence to another by failing to give him all the assistance in one's power, even if that assistance could only come at the expense of more modest benefits for others? There is a tradition among Marxist theorists not to spell out answers to such questions. Like Marx, many are averse to "prescribing recipes to the cookshops of the future."[34] They plead that concrete answers will be found only in the praxis of the future society, as people invent solutions in the context of historical circumstances that we cannot yet imagine. Merleau-Ponty's Marxism accepts that tradition in its most problematic form: "How did Marx know," he asks,"that the free development of each individual is compatible with the free development of all? It would be as audacious to say the contrary. We do not know if human liberty can be accomplished . . . , [but] it is necessary to try to create equality."[35] In other words, because we cannot absolutely exclude Marx's hypothesis that all liberties are compatible, it is reasonable to act as if they are and to do all we can to make them so. On the grounds of one sweeping hypothesis, Merleau-Ponty defers any further thinking about how to accommodate conflicts of values and interests.

This deferral presents a variety of dangers. One is that in a social world beset by innumerable conflicts, revolutionaries who lack any clear idea of their goal will be unable to judge whether a particular trend is progressive or not. They may fail to support a second- or third-best emancipatory force, even though that is all that is genuinely available in their situation. One of the great tragedies of radical politics in the 1930s came from the indecisiveness of Communist parties faced with the rise of Nazism. Should a working-class party ally with bourgeois parties to combat Fascism? Or should workers steadfastly oppose bourgeois parties as the primary obstacle to the realization of Marx's vision? When the German Communist party helped immobilize the Reichstag rather than joining the Social Democrats in making the government work, it contributed directly to its own eventual annihilation by

[34] Marx, quoted in Lukes, *Marx and Morality*, p. 36.
[35] "Le Manifest Communiste a cent ans," p. 2.

Hitler. A different course of action on the part of the Communists would have required, among other things, a greater sensitivity to the fact that, even if the Socialists were "bourgeois reformers," common action with them might be the only way to defeat a growing force whose values were absolutely at odds with communism. To be a political realist is to understand the necessity of working with trends that exist—no matter how imperfectly they embody one's ultimate vision of a just society. Although Merleau-Ponty is undoubtedly a proponent of such realism, his nebulous descriptions of Marxist goals would hardly help a political thinker distinguish in the next crisis the options that come closest to advancing the cause of "mutual recognition."

Another danger is that if the revolution does succeed and if genuine incompatibilities of liberties arise nonetheless, the revolutionary tradition will lack the philosophical resources necessary to think through these problems. How will a genuine communist society treat a call for independent trade unions? What would be done in case a group wished to continue religious practices that placed duties to their god above duties to their society? Can a society of mutual recognition allow citizens to criticize its institutions? To assume that no such conflicts will arise once private property is abolished is to succumb to utopianism in the worst sense. In fact, Merleau-Ponty once seemed to concede that some such questions were valid. "Even if there is an alienation of the for-itself that no revolution will end . . . , this is not a reason to turn [the individual] away from the revolutionary act . . . that . . . has the chance to reduce the constraints of existence to an inevitable minimum" (SNS 10, tr. 5). Here he claims only that the realization of Marx's vision would constitute such a radical improvement over the present order of violence that even if certain forms of conflict survive, there is still more than enough reason to endorse the proletarian cause. He gives no hints, however, about how postrevolutionary theory might treat residual alienation.

The greatest danger, however, is not that theory will have nothing to say in the face of social conflicts, but that it will use the only tool it has left itself—the bloody logic of historical development—to correct its deficiencies. In the most disturbingly unqualified passage of *Humanism and Terror* Merleau-Ponty states: "Among men considered as bearers of situations that together make up a single *common situation* . . . , it is permissible to sacrifice those who, according to the logic of their situation, are a menace and to promote those who offer a promise of humanity" (HT 128, tr. 110). Perhaps this passage bears an acceptable interpretation. There are situations where some people pose such an extreme danger to freedom (the Nazi regime's attempt to conquer Europe is the most obvious example) that the only moral course is to "sacrifice" them. Even so, one would want to add numerous caveats concerning the conduct of the war, the extremity of the situation, the availability of alternatives, the responsibility and numbers of those to be "sacrificed," the possible corrupting effects of the "sacrifice" on the "promise of humanity" itself, and so forth. But Merleau-Ponty here adds no such qualifications. So suspicious is he of the abstraction of Kantian politics and so credulous is he with respect to his idea of a self-equilibrating historical structure that he will not deign to formulate *reasons* for his positions. Yet reasons are precisely what he needs to confront the moral dilemmas that will arise in postrevolutionary society. He needs to make connections between the community's broader purposes and its specific actions so as to be able to correct imperfect policies or to rally citizens to important causes. With reasons, moreover, he would bring his own views into that "process of correction" that is essential to his phenomenological conception of objectivity. Were he to try to debate what "mutual recognition" is, for example, he might be obliged to think seriously about problems a socialist revolution is unlikely to solve. He might then revise his ideas to take account of objections, rather than evade them with references to a vague "promise of humanity."

One might think that Merleau-Ponty's Marxism is even less satisfactory at an explanatory level than at an ethical level. In comparison with many technical works in Marxist philosophy and economics, Merleau-Ponty's writings seem to be filled with paltry generalizations. To cite only one example, one might contrast his historical materialism with G. A. Cohen's much lauded study, *Karl Marx's Theory of History: A Defence*. It is in Cohen's work, not Merleau-Ponty's, that one finds a distinction between class position and culture that is "required to protect the substantive character of the Marxian thesis that class position strongly conditions consciousness, culture, and politics."[36] Merleau-Ponty's political essays borrow gestaltist conceptions of the relation of function and form (e.g., he argues that Kantian moralism is functional to the maintenance of capitalist structures), but it is for Cohen to sort out the logical characteristics of such explanation. Cohen is a more re-

[36] *Karl Marx's Theory of History*, p. 73.

liable guide to Marxist notions like "productive forces," "means of production," and "production relations" than Merleau-Ponty, who refers more generally to "economic life" and "modes of production."[37]

And yet it would be rash to reject Merleau-Ponty's Marxism on account of its imprecision. For he never claims to refine the technical concepts of Marx's theory. His contribution is to establish that the *foundation* of Marxism is—and must be—a phenomenological conception of consciousness. Only phenomenology has a concept of human existence that embraces simultaneously freedom and conditioning, conflict and consensus, meaning and function, individual and class. A work like Cohen's presupposes such theoretical flexibility, but does not explain how it is possible. To define a productive force Cohen refers to "someone's purpose" to use a facility to contribute to production. He therefore implies a concept of intentionality.[38] His "development thesis" ("the productive forces tend to develop throughout history") posits a rational structure for history as a whole.[39] But the nature of the connection between the notion that we are "rational beings who know how to satisfy compelling wants" and the rational structure of history is not entirely clear.[40] Merleau-Ponty's ideas on intentionality, sedimentation, and historical gestalten are meant to supply the theoretical ground for precisely the sorts of technical arguments Cohen makes.

Still, one crucial aspect of the Marxian hypothesis is at best confusingly defended in Merleau-Ponty's phenomenology: it is the notion that economic relations are the founding ones in the historical process. We must ask why the destiny of beings whose behavior is above all symbolic (as Merleau-Ponty says in *The Structure of Behavior*) should be so decisively governed by their efforts to satisfy their material needs. It is symbolic capacities, after all, that give us the ability to act independently of our immediate environment and even of immediate bodily sensations like pain or hunger. We are beings who not only pursue life, but who create art, worship divinities, seek honor. Is there any reason to expect economic matters (even leaving aside the question of what is and is not "economic") to be more important in shaping collective life than aesthetic, religious, or political ones?

[37] Compare SNS 189, 231, tr. 107, 130 with Cohen, *Karl Marx's Theory*, pp. 31–34.
[38] Cohen, *Karl Marx's Theory*, p. 32.
[39] Ibid., p. 134.
[40] Ibid., p. 152.

It is tempting to respond by recalling that Merleau-Ponty always maintained that people are working beings who create their own milieu (SC 175, tr. 162; SNS 189, tr. 107). He thus agrees with Marx in *The German Ideology* that "the social structure and the State are continually evolving out of the life-process of definite individuals . . . as they work under definite material limits."[41] But that would be to equivocate on the meaning of "work." Work in Merleau-Ponty's sense has no necessary connection with the satisfaction of material needs. Its essence is to alter something in light of an idea, to attribute a new meaning to what is present. Writing poetry is just as surely work as pouring steel at a foundry—regardless of whether either activity is a means of subsistence. This concept of work elects no particular domain of human life as one likely to be "founding." Perhaps "economic life" really does represent "the inertia of human life" more often than other areas of existence (SNS 189, tr. 107). But if so, that fact seems to point to some particular structure of human being that a philosophy of self-transcending, symbolic behavior has yet to explain.

Alternatively, Merleau-Ponty might say that there is nothing *necessary* about the importance of economic relations; they just *happen* to be particularly powerful in our era. That seems to be his leaning in the *Phenomenology*. "In the sphere of coexistence, one period of history can be seen as especially cultural or primarily political or economic. To know if our time has its main sens in the economy . . . is a question that belongs no longer to philosophy but to politics" (PP 202, tr. 173). But that is an extraordinarily weak interpretation of historical materialism. It leaves mysterious why history *as a whole*—which is what the Marxian hypothesis is about—should have a particular structure.

This is not the last criticism to be made of Merleau-Ponty's Marxism. Indeed, later chapters will show him in the 1950s launching compelling arguments against his own former views. Yet there is an important sense in which none of these criticisms get at the essentials of his political project. In 1960, long after he has abandoned the Marxian hypothesis, he will say that Marxism "is an immense field of sedimented history and thought where one goes to practice and to learn how to think" (S 18, tr. 12). There is the essential function of his Marxism—"to learn how to think" or, better, to learn how to think *politically*. It is because he dared to join Marxism and existentialism that he had something more to

---

[41] *The Marx-Engels Reader*, p. 156.

say about political affairs than that man is a free being or that man universalizes whatever values he chooses. There is, in effect, a dialectic between his Marxism and his existentialism that enriches them both. His existentialist predispositions elicit an interpretation of Marx in which the themes are freedom, individuality, culture, and sens. His respect for Marx makes him look into the conditions under which violence might be ended; it makes him think about consequences and conceive society in not entirely individualistic terms.

Finally, if his political essays are not detached and meticulous like scholarly monographs, it is because they are in some measure political *acts*. This aspect is important for understanding both their content and their style. Merleau-Ponty's failure to fill in all of the steps between his phenomenology and his Marxism does not lead him into a political dead end, at least not in the 1940s, because questions surrounding Marxism—the growing power of the Communist party, relations with the Soviet Union—were at the top of the political agenda in the postwar years in France. In a sense, to be political was to take a stand on Marx and vice versa. Marxism is the vehicle that brings Merleau-Ponty into contact with the most powerful political forces of his day and that challenges him actually to *practice* political thinking. It gives him a credible evaluative standpoint, one that is missing in Sartre's and Beauvoir's writings of those years. A political existentialism will now regard the concrete events of its epoch in light of their prospects for the realization of Marx's vision. The first "incarnation" of that vision in the USSR is then the natural focus of Merleau-Ponty's existential politics.

S I X

PRINCIPLES AND PREJUDICE
IN LIBERALISM

In September 1944 Sartre and Merleau-Ponty brought together the editorial committee for a new journal.[1] Its title, *Les Temps Modernes* (*Modern Times*), was a sign that its journalism would be enmeshed in current affairs.[2] Merleau-Ponty stressed that a review "plays its role . . . by favoring a political awakening of consciousness."[3]

Because of cold war tensions, this awakening required vigilance on two fronts.

> *Les Temps Modernes* . . . battle[s] against the pathetic and pro- phetic spirit, every day more widespread, which requires blind choices and tortured commitments from our contempo- raries. It is not true that the world is divided into two empires, one good and one evil. . . . It is not true that good intentions justify everything, nor that we have the right to do the oppo- site of what we want. The comedy of history, the switching of roles, the frivolity of the actors does not prevent us from dis- cerning a sufficiently clear path.[4]

Indirectly "two empires" is a metaphor for a simplistic moral dual- ism and directly it is a reference to worsening relations between Communists and the Western liberal democracies. Merleau-Ponty implied that cold war judgments are not merely reflections of the interests of rival powers; they partake of a philosophical problem. Political dualism has the same logical structure as the subject-ob- ject dualism that phenomenology criticizes, and it has the same effects: it blinds observers of social phenomena to the lived mean- ings at the foundation of judgments and it inclines interpreters of

---

[1] For an account of the journal's origins, see Burnier, *Choice of Action*, pp. 29–37.
[2] Beauvoir, *La force des choses*, I, p. 28.
[3] "Indochine S.O.S.," p. 1052.
[4] This statement, written by Merleau-Ponty, was reprinted on the back cover of numerous issues of the journal starting in May 1950.

political affairs to overemphasize either the subject's freedom or the object's deterministic power.

The distorting simplifications of cold war Manicheism are especially troubling once existentialism accepts the Marxian hypothesis. Pressures to "choose the god of the East or the god of the West" make men "ready for propaganda and war" rather than for discussion and sober assessment (HT 33, tr. xiii). Only if the existentialists' contemporaries can be made to question habits of thought that prejudge communism is there any hope of impartially assessing the Soviet claim to embody the proletariat's "mission." Here the position of a journal is crucial.

The political essays that Merleau-Ponty writes for *Les Temps Modernes* show him trying to dismantle cold war dualism by engaging in corrective dialogues with representatives of the primary political formations of the day. Not only do phenomenological lessons inform the content of these dialogues; they dictate their strategies, or what I have called the politics of Merleau-Ponty's theory. He uses his grasp of others' values to expose hidden assumptions and to reveal unsuspected relationships between beliefs and interests. He presses his interlocutors to restructure their values in order to accommodate new meanings. In a style poised between the philosophical and the polemical, he seeks to bring interlocutors of varying political persuasions to conceive political problems in the way laid out by his theory. As a journalist, the philosopher *participates* in constituting a nondualistic interpretive framework for contemporary politics. This chapter focuses on Merleau-Ponty's dialogues with liberals.

The Existential Imperative: Engagement in Modern Times

The lifting of Vichy censorship in 1944 saw the flowering of dozens of monthly reviews of varying political colors. Among them was an *Esprit* more left leaning than before the war, the Trotskyist *Revue Internationale*, the Catholic *La Vie Intellectuelle*, the communist *La Pensée*, and the *Revue de Paris*, which sought a generally lenient policy toward Vichy collaborators.[5] Writers in these journals often addressed to each other "intellectual polemics [that] had the inti-

---

[5] For a detailed analysis of the place of *Les Temps Modernes* among postwar journals, see Boschetti, *Sartre et "Les Temps Modernes": Une entreprise intellectuelle*, pp. 185–205.

macy, urgency, and heat of family quarrels."[6] When substantive editorial debate is a living institution, the format of a monthly review perfectly accommodates political argument. Journal articles are shorter than books and more rapidly composed, and yet can still be written with time for reflection and attention to detail. A journal, although less frequently published than a newspaper, nevertheless appears often enough to allow commentary on pressing issues and responses to criticism. As de facto political editor of *Les Temps Modernes*, Merleau-Ponty was in a position to profit from this argumentative mobility to construct a quintessentially dialogical form of writing.[7]

Emmanuel Mounier astutely remarked that *Les Temps Modernes* was the first postwar journal to give coherent representation to the new generation whose unity derived less from a single political program than from a common political consciousness born of war and defeat.[8] Sartre explained the politics of its staff. He and Simone de Beauvoir were its centrists, Raymond Aron was on the right, and Merleau-Ponty on the left.[9] Its unifying theme was not an ideology, but an idea traceable to Mounier himself—the idea of engagement, a commitment to change the status quo while retaining critical judgment.[10] The existentialists, however, add several nuances to what might otherwise have been only an exhortation to political activism.

They connect engagement, first, to a theory of how man constructs around himself a value-laden world. Sartre has nothing but contempt for the doctrine that art is justified for its own sake. He points out that this idea found its logical extension in the excuses offered by the collaborationist writers of the Vichy regime. Accused of abetting political repression and racial destruction, they reacted with surprise and dismay. In perfect bad faith, they said that their writings were of no political consequence. They claimed that literature belongs to the domain of expression, not action.[11] But if writing does have social consequences (as the hate cam-

---

[6] Beauvoir, *La force des choses*, I, p. 73.

[7] For all practical purposes Merleau-Ponty, not Sartre, managed the journal from 1945 to 1950. Sartre, "Correspondance," *Les Temps Modernes* 194 (July 1962), p. 183.

[8] "Le message des 'Temps Modernes' et le néo-stoicisme," p. 957.

[9] Leenhardt, *Les yeux ouverts*, p. 147.

[10] Schalk, *The Spectrum of Political Engagement*, p. 25. For Mounier's role in developing this idea, see Merleau-Ponty, "Mort d'Emmanuel Mounier," p. 1906; La revue: *Les Temps Modernes*, Merleau-Ponty interviewed by Georges Charbonnier, RTF, 1959.

[11] Sartre, "Présentation," p. 3.

paigns of some Vichy journalists had tragically proven), then concludes Sartre, a theory recognizing "the identity of word and action" is needed. Words do not simply reflect reality; they mold the way we view the world by suggesting the possibility or impossibilty of change, by infusing action with value judgments. *Les Temps Modernes* takes responsibility for the power of the word.

Engagement has, in addition, a deeper ontological meaning. Sartre does not want to say that had the collaborationist writers abstained from explicit political commentary they could have been innocently disengaged. No, "the writer is 'in the fray,' *whatever* he does, marked, compromised."[12] All writing is *engagé*, all writing has social meaning and political consequences.[13] Even bourgeois writers attest to their participation in a particular social order by their choice of audience, their perspectives, their style of life. But while their choices are unavowed, the truly "committed writer" acts in full cognizance of the social significance of his values.

Finally, engagement implies a methodology for the understanding of personal and social phenomena. Existential analysis explains how author and oeuvre form a thematic whole. Every engagement, whether deliberate or unconscious, expresses a person's fundamental attitude toward the world. For example, in an essay on the personality of the collaborator, Sartre shows how Drieu la Rochelle (the extreme right-wing author who directed Gallimard's leading journal, *La Nouvelle Revue Française*, during the Occupation) practiced a rejection of law, a hatred of man, and an idolization of iron rule in his life as much as in his literature.[14] Drieu represents "the collaborator," a social type, and his attitudes stand for those of a social stratum. To understand the logic of social themes expressed in his conduct is to understand a collaborationist milieu.

Les Temps Modernes takes advantage of the Hegelian insight that "in human coexistence, ethics, doctrines, thought and customs, laws, works, and words express one another" (SNS 269, tr. 153). Sartre announces in the first issue that the review will try to grasp synthetically the meaningful relations between all sectors of contemporary life, from fashions and criminal trials to political facts

---

[12] Ibid.

[13] See Merleau-Ponty's ironic comments on a journal that prided itself for being *dégagé*, while publishing "des apolitiques" like Malraux, Camus, Giono. "Les cahiers de la Pléiade, avril 1947," pp. 1151–1152.

[14] Sartre, "Qu'est-ce qu'un collaborateur?" in *Situations III*, pp. 43–61.

and works of the mind.[15] Since phenomenology places partial truths in a meaning-giving context instead of seeing them merely as secondary effects of social relations, a philosophical investigation of all of the facts serves the existentialists' political causes. It is set to detect in the facts of every domain of life the chances for radical change.

Merleau-Ponty announces the journal's credo in a slightly different formulation: "if all truths are told, none will have to be hidden" (SNS 268, tr. 152). He adds the second phrase because engagement could easily be mistaken for a call to put journalism at the service of a political party, accepting the lies and half-truths that such subordination might entail. In a lecture on "The Signification of French Existentialism," he explicitly denies that engagement as practiced by *Les Temps Modernes* fosters such partisanship. On the contrary, it "forbids no subject" of investigation; it "does not at all oblige that one take a given position"; and it "neither sacrifices literature nor transforms it into propaganda" (IN 44). The last stipulation applies only obliquely to Merleau-Ponty since he wrote no novels or plays. But, an admirer of Malraux and Saint-Exupéry, he was as sensitive to the political power of literature as any of the other existentialists. In fact, his major political work of the 1940s, *Humanism and Terror*, originally appeared as a commentary on a novel, Arthur Koestler's *Darkness at Noon*. It was a work that fascinated Merleau-Ponty because, through its depiction of the mind of a revolutionary, it went to the heart of the question of evaluating the progress of the world's only socialist state toward a humanist political order.

Reading Darkness at Noon

For seven years, from 1931 to 1938, Koestler had been a member of the German Communist party. As a correspondent he had witnessed firsthand the process of collectivization and industrialization in the USSR. It was in Spain in 1938, where he was fighting for the Republicans in the civil war, that he quit the party, discouraged by the news from Moscow of the trials of the few remaining leaders of 1917, disillusioned by Communist exploitation of events in Spain.[16] He took asylum in France and set about writing the novel that was to become his masterpiece.

---

[15] Sartre, "Présentation," p. 20.
[16] "Arthur Koestler s'explique: Interview avec J. Duché," p. 2.

Darkness at Noon opens with the arrest of Rubashov, an old Bolshevik leader whose character is styled after Nicholai Bukharin. In prison Rubashov ruminates upon incidents in his political life, upon his willingness to sacrifice individuals who had devoted themselves to the revolution. He comes to realize that he had ignored the irreducible worth of the individual for the sake of the revolution. But a harsh, manipulative interrogator finally overcomes Rubashov's new-found moral sentiments. He appeals to the old Bolshevik's deep devotion to a cause that is mankind's only chance to end exploitation. In a public trial Rubashov confesses not only to acts of political opposition in which he engaged, but also to crimes he never committed. He does so in order to make opposition seem despicable. The ultimate reason for his confession is "to do a last service for the Party."[17] Koestler's work is a provocative example of engaged literature. Fictional in presentation, *Darkness at Noon* is an emotionally powerful and deeply political work about contemporary events; the story of a personal experience, it aims to illuminate the culture of an entire society.

When Koestler's novel appeared in France in February 1946, translated under the title *Le zéro et l'infini*, it quickly became the literary event of the year and the center of political debate. Only a few months later, Koestler followed up his success by publishing a collection of essays under the title *Le yogi et le commissaire* (*The Yogi and the Commissar*). While every newspaper and journal wrote about Koestler's works, it was *Les Temps Modernes* that gave them the most extensive review in the French press. Merleau-Ponty's articles on "The Yogi and the Proletarian"—articles that now make up the bulk of *Humanism and Terror*—inquire into the significance of Koestler's works for an era when the promises of communism are, according to some, finally being redeemed and, according to others, revealing their fundamental falseness.

That Merleau-Ponty's review of *Darkness at Noon* is critical there is no doubt. But it is important to the interpretation of his criticism to know at what points and to what extent he disagrees with Koestler. Much recent interpretation assumes that *Humanism and Terror* represents Merleau-Ponty's purely negative response to a work that crystallized anticommunist feelings in France.[18] Two facts argue against seeing his primary motivation in those terms. First, he

---

[17] *Darkness at Noon*, p. 205.
[18] See, for example: Cooper, *Merleau-Ponty and Marxism*, pp. 56–59; Poster, *Existential Marxism*, p. 154; Hughes, *The Obstructed Path*, p. 200; Rabil, *Merleau-Ponty*, pp. 92–93.

annotated *Darkness at Noon* in the English edition in 1945, before the translated version even appeared in France and, hence, before it became a public issue.[19] Second, Koestler's views and Merleau-Ponty's are similar on an astonishing number of issues.[20] I want to suggest that Merleau-Ponty's interest in this novel was from the start not polemical, but genuinely philosophical. He was taken with Koestler's reasoning for and against Communist practice in the Bolshevik experience.

Koestler wrestles with what he takes to be the central enigma of the Moscow trials. Some confessions, he is sure, were extracted by threats and torture. "[Yet] there still remained a hard core of men like Bukharin . . . whose total and gleeful self-abasement [at their trials] remained inexplicable. It was this 'hard core' that Rubashov was meant to represent."[21] Koestler asks what could have moved men of unimpeachable revolutionary credentials to confess to treasonous actions that they obviously never committed. In answering that question, he does far more than fictionalize a mass of historical details. He explains the moral logic of the communist mentality and pits that logic against what he sees as its sole ethical alternative.

Ivanov, Rubashov's first interrogator, lays out the rival viewpoints. "There are only two conceptions of human ethics, and they are at opposite poles. One . . . declares the individual to be sacrosanct and asserts that the rules of arithmetic are not to be applied to human units [who, in our equation, represent either zero or infinite]. The other starts from the basic principle that a collective aim justifies all means and . . . demands that the individual should in every way be subordinated and sacrificed to the

[19] Lefort, "Introduction" to *Humanisme et terreur* (1980), p. 20.

[20] Compare *Darkness at Noon* and *Humanism and Terror* on the following topics: motives in a revolutionary trial (DN 18; HT 65, tr. 33); the objective meaning of political action (DN 79; HT 62, tr. 29); the notion of revolutionary honor (DN 144; HT 86, tr. 58); the idea that war may justify suppression of political opposition (DN 193; HT 74, tr. 44); the different tasks owed to those who fought in the revolution and to those who are responsible for building the economic base of society (DN 150–151; HT 75, tr. 45); the concept of a philosophy of history that progresses toward the reconciliation of mankind and the recognition that the course of history would likely contain detours where sacrifices seem out of all proportion to the social good obtained (DN 79; HT 144, tr. 130); the question of whether our epoch of executions and deportations and war represents history's ultimate deviation (DN 46; HT 158, tr. 147) and whether today's traitors will be rehabilitated tomorrow as heroes (DN 10; HT 94, tr. 69).

[21] *The Invisible Writing*, p. 395.

community."[22] As the novel unfolds, Rubashov repeatedly slips into the more individualistic ethics. While working for the creation of a new humanity, he had never before allowed himself to look at his actions through the eyes of those whom he sacrificed.[23] His experiences in prison, while facing the reality of death, tempt him to reject the logic of means and ends and to adopt the perspective of those individuals who would never enjoy the fruits of the revolution because they were crushed in its path.[24] What finally defeats this temptation and makes him confess to crimes he never committed is yet another set of powerful arguments from social utility: the USSR represents the sole hope for socialism in the world; it is surrounded and threatened by capitalist states; in the situation of imminent war all opposition must be stamped out. This ethical debate gives Koestler's work an explicitly philosophical dimension.

It also gives the novel a curious ambiguity. Witness its reception by the French in early 1946. Doubtless numerous critics saw in the novel a trenchant indictment of communist practice. But there were many others who believed the work had been cast in the communist mold. Claude Mauriac, for example, refused to be "converted" by Rubashov's sacrifice, and it was widely admitted that *Le zéro et l'infini* had won a fair number of readers *over to* communism.[25] Koestler knew this and in 1946 even boasted of it as proof of his success in presenting convincingly both sides of the issue.[26] Depending on which morality its readers found most persuasive, the morality of individual worth or the morality of social utility, *Darkness at Noon* could be understood as an apology for the revolution or a blistering indictment of it. I will call this possibility of alternative readings "the dual interpretation."

It is in the context of this divided reception of Koestler's novel that we must read the very opening lines of the first essay of *Humanism and Terror*. " 'There is what they want to set up in France,'

---

[22] Koestler, *Darkness at Noon*, p. 128. The phrase in brackets, from which the title of the French translation is drawn, is omitted in the English version.

[23] Ibid., p. 18.

[24] Ibid., p. 106.

[25] Claude Mauriac, rev. of *Le zéro et l'infini, La Nef* (April 1946), pp. 156–159; "André Breton parle," *Le Littéraire*, October 12, 1946, pp. 1, 3; E. Borne, "Koestler: Signe de contradiction," *L'Aube*, February 9–10, 1947, p. 1; Louis Beirnaert, "Mais où sont les révolutionnaires?" *Études* (September 1946), p. 284; André Boy, rev. of *Le zéro et l'infini, Gazette des Lettres*, March 2, 1946, p. 11.

[26] "Arthur Koestler s'explique: Interview avec J. Duché," p. 1. In 1963 he denied this assertion. Compare "Darkness at Noon Again: An Interview," pp. 173–174.

said an anticommunist after reading *Darkness at Noon*. 'How excit-
ing it must be to live under that regime,' said, on the other hand,
a Communist sympathizer of Russian origin. . . . The first forgot
that all regimes are criminal . . . the second forgot that violence
. . . is not attractive" (HT 41, tr. 1). From the start, Merleau-Ponty
alerts his reader to the dual interpretation of Koestler's novel and
gives notice that his essays are going to be an intervention in a
public debate. They will concern the nature of communist action
and an evaluation of the Soviet regime. The conversation reported
by Merleau-Ponty conveys, however, yet another impression—
that the writer's audience consists of two very partial communities
whose standards of evaluation are self-comfirming. Each side "forgets" part of the truth about violence.

Les Temps Modernes and the Divided Audience

In the preface to *Humanism and Terror* Merleau-Ponty alludes to
one of Sartre's articles that examines the theoretical issues surrounding the relationship between an author and his audience
(HT 37, tr. xlvi). In "For Whom Does One Write?" Sartre tries to
demonstrate that since a contemporary audience only understands
literature that speaks to its mores, ways of reasoning, and experiences, the writer's style is of necessity somewhat constrained. The
writer is forced to accept certain limits on the choice of genre,
theme, and morals.[27] One of Sartre's examples is highly suggestive
with respect to the dual interpretation of *Darkness at Noon*. The
eighteenth-century Encyclopedists, Sartre argues, had to develop
an ideology relevant to two publics, the nobility who paid them
and the bourgeoisie whose values they favored. They devised the
idea of "universal" or "natural man" then to free them from the
particular prejudices of the two classes that divided their loyalty.
To the bourgeoisie, the doctrine of universal man sounds as an
invitation to revolt; to the nobility, it is a call for the abandonment
of privilege.[28] Because their commitments were divided between
two classes, the Encyclopedists could not simply adopt the literary
genres of a single class. They developed a discourse that, while
serving their purposes, spoke to two audiences.

The writer's audience in postwar France was no less divided
than that of the Encyclopedist. There was, however, a significant

[27] *Qu'est-ce que la littérature?* pp. 88–89, 91, 99.
[28] Ibid., pp. 132–136.

difference: both groups, the liberals and the communists, *rejected* the efforts of writers who were not decisively of their own camp. Sartre put the dilemma for *Les Temps Modernes* in the following way.

> Insofar as the Communist party canalizes . . . the aspirations of any oppressed class, . . . we are with the party against the bourgeoisie; . . . insofar as certain bourgeois milieus of good will recognize that intellectual production must be simultaneously free negativity and free construction, we are with the bourgeoisie against the Communist party; insofar as a decrepit, opportunist, conservative, determinist ideology is in contradiction with the very essence of literature, we are against both the Communist party and the bourgeoisie.[29]

The task of *Les Temps Modernes*, as Sartre saw it, was to compose an audience from among those who did not fit into the primary social formations: bourgeois of good will, intellectuals, teachers, noncommunist workers.[30] It would do this even at the risk of "speaking in the desert."

That programmatic conclusion is unacceptable in light of Merleau-Ponty's political realism. A conviction that one must *always* reason from the forces present in the historical structure means that one *must* talk to the two dominant political formations. Merleau-Ponty's problem is rather like the Encyclopedist's. He must conceive a discourse that is understandable and illuminating to two rival groups and yet distinctly favorable to only one of them. Somehow, he must "recall to the democracies their fundamental hypocrisy" (HT 186, tr. 179). He must appeal to lived experience in a way that changes liberal *perceptions* of the relationship between revolutionary violence and human freedom.

The success of *Darkness at Noon* suggests an alternative to Sartre's aspiration to assemble intellectuals at the margin of French politics. The moral ambivalence in the plot of Koestler's novel had already allowed it to speak to the two primary political formations in France. Unfortunately, the public's spontaneous dual interpretation merely indicated the partiality of each group's reading. *Darkness at Noon* did not so much call into question as mirror whatever political views the reader brought to it. But that was a problem of interpretation that Merleau-Ponty could try to remedy.

[29] Ibid., pp. 318–319.
[30] Ibid., p. 325.

Through *Les Temps Modernes* he had immediate access to the journalistic circles in which interpretive biases were being formed and
to audiences which turned these biases into political behavior.
With his review of *Darkness at Noon* he tries to manage the interpretation of Koestler's novel in order to change liberal habits of
thought about political action and violence.

Given this project, it is a logical first step to devote a half dozen
pages to recapitulating the plot of a familiar work. Merleau-Ponty
proposes his own interpretation of *Darkness at Noon* because the
partiality of opinion in the divided French republic had denied the
novel a fair reading (HT 42, tr. 2). His commentary then proceeds
to do nothing so much as foster the dual interpretation. He
stresses the vacillation between moral viewpoints that keeps the
novel from ever arriving at a final judgment on Communist politics. Rubashov's career shows a man who, in the service of the
revolution, forgets his own subjectivity. Arrested, he discovers the
value of the individual. Interrogated, he admits that the individual
must be sacrificed to secure an egalitarian society. Condemned, he
cannot decide whether the revolution has left mankind a mon-
strous abortion or the material base of a new, moral society. Merleau-Ponty insists that "the greatness of Koestler's book is precisely that it makes us see that Rubashov does not know how to
evaluate his own conduct" (HT 29, tr. xxxvii). Note: great because
ambiguous. To those who would search Koestler for a confirmation of their political sentiments, Merleau-Ponty suggests that the
novel always returns to the forgotten complement of their moral
position. The anticommunist who condemns political violence
should find a justification for violence on the pages of the very
novel he admires.

Why then does Merleau-Ponty go on to criticize Koestler? An
earlier essay on the metaphysical novel clarifies his strategy. "The
function of the novelist is not to state ideas thematically, it is to
make them exist in front of us like things. . . . When writers do
take a deliberate interest in philosophy, they recognize . . . poorly
their own affinities" (SNS 45–46, tr. 26). When Merleau-Ponty
turns from praising the greatness of Koestler's novel to regretting
the mediocrity of his Marxism, what he criticizes most are the
quasi-philosophical interruptions in the literary art which are scattered throughout *Darkness at Noon*. Dilemmas of ends and means,
utilitarian logic, and a mechanical philosophy of history—the ideas
of Koestler's Communist characters—are foreign to Marx's dialectics
(HT 50–57, tr. 14–23).

Such criticism and interpretation might have been sufficient to salvage the novel's existential lessons had Koestler not published *The Yogi and the Commissar* later in 1946. Essays like "The End of an Illusion" and "Soviet Myth and Reality" dispel any questions about his political commitments. In the title essay Koestler charges that Marxism cannot account for a necessary mystical element in human relationships.[31] In other essays he catalogues the horrors of the Soviet regime: inequalities, prison camps, poverty, deportations. By the time Merleau-Ponty's first essay appeared, the French recognized Koestler, who was now living the life of a celebrity in Paris, as the spokesman of an implacable anticommunism.[32]

That is why Merleau-Ponty was at pains to recuperate the unresolved ethical dilemmas of Rubashov's conduct.[33] *Darkness at Noon* was useful inasmuch as the plot captured the drama of subjective and objective moral reasoning in the revolutionary situation. It was useful, furthermore, insofar as it had stirred a genuine public debate. But Koestler's "mediocre Marxism" and his penchant for moralism meant that *Darkness at Noon* could always invite a misrepresentation of the issues involved in assessing the role of violence in politics. Neither the sanctity of the individual nor calculations of ends and means illuminate the character of action at the moment when a regime is born. The interpretation of *Darkness at Noon*, no matter how sympathetic, could be only a first move in a plan to reorient the liberal view of revolutionary violence.

The Enigma of Historical Responsibility

Merleau-Ponty proposes a competing interpretive standpoint from which to address the problems of revolutionary action. "True liberty," he says, "takes others as they are, tries to understand those doctrines that are its negation, and never allows itself to judge before understanding" (HT 19, tr. xxiv–xxv). Phenomenological un-

---

[31] *The Yogi and the Commissar*, p. 19.

[32] In fact, Merleau-Ponty knew Koestler, and they debated each other privately in the cafés of St. Germain des Prés. Interview with S. Merleau-Ponty, June 8, 1981.

[33] It is even probable that Merleau-Ponty changed his own mind about the message of *Darkness at Noon* between 1945 and 1946. In lectures in February and March 1946, Merleau-Ponty rehearses the plot of the novel without the slightest word of criticism (IN 7–9, 24–25). His first critical remarks on Koestler appear in a short sketch for *Humanism and Terror* (IN 10–15) written later in 1946, after he had read *The Yogi and the Commissar*. The very positive assessment of its plot in *Humanism and Terror* (HT 42–50, tr. 2–12) probably rests upon an earlier conviction that the novel never compromised its ambiguous message.

derstanding, it should be recalled, implies that the knower examines lived experience before intellectual conceptions, heeds not only intentions but also the appearance "for others" of action, and takes account of the structural significance of behavior. When Merleau-Ponty sets out to "understand Bukharin as Koestler sought to understand Rubashov" (HT 11, tr. xv), his goal is to make liberals face up to the potential rationality of a doctrine that is the "negation" of liberalism.

For Koestler, the enigma of the Moscow trial of 1938 is that Bukharin confessed to being a traitor to the cause he had served all his life. What makes sense of the confession in *Darkness at Noon* and, more broadly, characterizes the emergent values of Soviet society is an unmeasured, strictly disciplined commitment to collective ends—ends against which personal interests carry no weight. For Merleau-Ponty, in contrast, the enigma consists in the *pattern* of acceptance and rejection of charges in Bukharin's plea. "Bukharin admits personal responsibility for all the acts of the 'block of Rightists and Trotskyists.' He considers himself already condemned to death. And yet he refuses to regard himself as a spy, saboteur, and terrorist. . . . How can he at once declare himself responsible for acts of treason and yet reject the name of traitor?" (HT 75, tr. 45) What gives internal coherence to this strange pattern, Merleau-Ponty decides, is the assumption that Bukharin took "historical responsibility" for his political actions. He was willing to be held accountable not only for what he *intended* to do, but also for what he found he *had done* in light of subsequent events (HT 73, tr. 43). Bukharin did not fall victim to blind discipline. He vigorously denied accusations of criminal acts that he never undertook or supported. Yet even if he had committed no crimes by normal juridical standards, he was no simple innocent either. As a political actor he counted upon social forces whose opposition to Stalin was quite explicit. Without ever intending to undermine the revolution, Bukharin had mobilized political forces in favor of a comparatively liberal economic policy (the NEP) while Stalin launched his policy of rapid collectivization. He relied on counterrevolutionary social groups (the kulaks) and effectively weakened the country in the face of the Fascist threat (HT 80–81, tr. 52). Thus, he admitted that he was a traitor "in the historical context." He patterned his responses at the trial to acknowledge his accountability for the historical role he had played in "the logic of the struggle."

To a certain extent Merleau-Ponty is a critic of the Moscow trials.

He condemns the regime's attempt to disguise a political act as a juridical one; he uses the trials to expose a disfigurement of the communism of 1917.[34] Still, his account of Bukharin's confession is problematic in the extreme.[35] To appreciate the difficulties Merleau-Ponty creates for himself, let me separate three different functions of his argument.

He interprets Bukharin's confession first to improve the explanation of an historical event. Koestler's idea that a perversion of utilitarian reasoning motivates the confession fails to explain why Bukharin disputes the prosecutor's accusations at all. If the defendant believed only in social utility, he would have confessed to any crime that would blacken the idea of political opposition. Instead, Merleau-Ponty contends, the trial transcript shows a man who knew he acted in good faith for the revolution, but who judged his acts by their historical consequences. With war close at hand, he realized that he had to admit that the facts spoke against the policies he had once favored.[36]

It is important to understand Bukharin's confession correctly since, as Merleau-Ponty and Koestler agree, it casts considerable light on the character of Soviet society. Koestler believes that revolutionary culture in the Soviet Union has deteriorated. Rubashov's confession indicates that the humanistic inspiration of the Old Bolsheviks has given way to an exclusive concern with questions of technique and efficiency. Merleau-Ponty's notion of historical responsibility gives evidence of a different cultural theme. The prosecutor *and* Bukharin expect leaders to take responsibility for the historical consequences of their actions. In spite of its grave procedural faults, the trial evinces a *moral* dimension in the communist's concern for his objective role (HT 57, tr. 23). Communists do not hide behind good intentions to excuse their political failures.

This first level of interpretation is empirical and therefore subject to revision in light of new evidence. One area in which recent research questions Merleau-Ponty's interpretation concerns Bukharin's motivations. Merleau-Ponty's detailed discussion of the

[34] His criticisms of the trial are forceful enough to give some support to claims that his intent was entirely censorious. See Goyard-Fabre, "Merleau-Ponty et la politique," pp. 250–251. But for reasons that become evident below, I cannot concur with this view.

[35] For powerful critiques of it, see Kolakowski, "Obsolete Therefore Instructive:" Review of *Humanism and Terror*, trans. John O'Neill, pp. 15–16; and Shklar, *Legalism*, p. 202.

[36] Brena, *Alla ricerca del Marxismo: Maurice Merleau-Ponty*, p. 91.

Moscow trials makes sense only on the assumption that Bukharin confessed of his own free will, that he intentionally set up the pattern of his responses as a reflection of certain values. That premise is in error. It is now quite certain that the confessions were extracted by force—if not by torture in Bukharin's case, then by threats against his family.[37] When Merleau-Ponty wrote, some such evidence was available but it was far from universally accepted.[38] Still, he would have been truer to his methodological principles had he inquired more systematically into the function of political trials throughout the USSR in the 1930s rather than tried to infer a cultural theme from a single example that even he knew was potentially highly flawed.

At a second level, Merleau-Ponty sets forth historical responsibility as a genuine ethical doctrine. It surpasses the liberal emphasis on motives and intentions, so that it can take account of both the subjectivity and the phenomenal objectivity of political action.[39] Thus he emphasizes that, unlike Koestler's Rubashov, Bukharin did not lay out the course of events as if history were an ineluctable force; he *interpreted* history in terms of class struggle and set about "synchroniz[ing] existing forces" (HT 85, tr. 58). Only the prospect of war changed the sens of the NEP. It went from being a valid political compromise to a policy that could impede necessary industrialization (HT 87, tr. 60). Bukharin then transcended the tension between the meaning for itself and in itself of his actions (between intentions and consequences) by *consenting* to view them simultaneously from the two perspectives (HT 89, tr. 62). Before the revolution has laid all the economic foundations that will mitigate social conflict, the ethic of socialist man converges with that of Hegel's tragic hero, whose "self-reliant solidity . . . does not wish to share the guilt and knows nothing of the opposition of subjective intentions and objective deeds."[40] Tragedy comes from the confrontation of two legitimate and yet

---

[37] Cohen, *Bukharin and the Boleshevik Revolution*, pp. 372–375. A few commentators still find an explanation based on historical responsibility to be credible. See Pavel Kovaly, "Merleau-Ponty and the Problem of Self-Accusations," pp. 225–241, and Somerville, "Violence, Politics, and Morality," pp. 241–249. Neither really disputes the sort of evidence adduced by Cohen to prove that Bukharin's confession was forced.

[38] As one critic remarked, he could have consulted Victor Serge's *Seize fusillés* or the *Mémoires* of General Krivitzky. Patri, rev. of *Humanisme et terreur*, p. 146.

[39] Wiggins, "Political Responsibility in Merleau-Ponty's *Humanism and Terror*," pp. 276–278.

[40] Hegel, quoted in Walter Kaufman, *Tragedy and Philosophy* (New York: Doubleday, 1968), p. 245.

mutually exclusive ethical perspectives. Bukharin was like the ancient hero, with a crucial difference: he confesses not out of "self-reliant solidity," but because he understands the conditions for creating universal values according to Marx's philosophy of history. For Merleau-Ponty, the pathos and the greatness of Bukharin's confession was that he accepted this violence, even as it was exercised on him, because it reaffirmed his solidarity with an historical community whose emergent values he endorsed. The Bukharin of *Humanism and Terror* symbolizes the ideal political actor—one who grounds his politics in calculations derived from an ethically regulative philosophy of history and who takes full responsibility for the ramifications of his acts.

There is a partial truth in this ethical stance. We do want politicians to take risks and even to act, as Machiavelli said, "against humanity" if such action is essential to secure things of the greatest importance to the community. Scruples do not suffice where a community's survival and well-being are at stake. One might even take this further by imagining a society that made politicians legally responsible for the consequences of their decisions in order to discourage foolish risks and "moral" inaction. But because the effects of action are endless, it would make no sense for this community to hold people responsible for *every* consequence connected in any way to their decisions. The acceptability of a theory of historical responsibility depends on how it delimits accountability and how it specifies procedures for its determination.

Merleau-Ponty fails this test of acceptability with the equivocal assertion that "political acts must be judged not only according to the meaning that the moral agent gives them, but also according to the meaning they take on in the historical context" (HT 65, tr. 33). The "historical context" signifies at times the real consequences of an act, its concrete impact upon others, its success or failure in achieving its goals. Merleau-Ponty contends that responsibility and guilt vary as a function of historical outcomes. At some points Bukharin seems responsible for *actually* weakening Soviet defense efforts. He counted upon peasant revolts (HT 81, tr. 52); perhaps he relied upon defeatist generals as part of his plan to remove Stalin (HT 84–85, tr. 57). On this interpretation, determinations of responsibility call for a careful examination of what did happen and of what the political actor could reasonably be supposed to have known might happen.

At other times the "historical context" denotes some sort of interpretative assessment of consequences. "Our historical responsibility . . . [is] but our responsibility in the eyes of others," explains Merleau-Ponty. Plausibly this might be interpreted to mean that consequences are never objective in a positivist sense; they depend on the understanding and values of a certain population. Being a "traitor," for instance, is not simply a matter of committing some abstractly definable act like turning over secret weapons plans to an enemy power. Whether the plans were rightly "secret," whether the foreign power was truly an "enemy," and so forth are complex questions of meaning bound up with a society's concepts of rightful holding and office and its interpretations of the quality of its relations with the foreign power. Such reasoning would support Merleau-Ponty's contention that neither individual intention nor objective fact can determine the extent of responsibility.

But he does not pursue his argument in this way. Rather, he gives the notion of historical responsibility a peculiarly Sartrean twist. Instead of accepting the individual's intentions, Merleau-Ponty continues, historical responsibility "substitutes . . . a role or a phantom in which he does not recognize himself—but in which he should since this is what he was for his victims and today his victims are right" (HT 73, tr. 45; cf. SNS 254, tr. 144). Like Sartre's jealous lover caught peering through a keyhole, Merleau-Ponty's political actor understands the meaning of his deeds only when they are objectified by others. Yet the Sartrean notion of objectivity has the bizarre effect of reducing evidentiary demands to a minimum. Here it convicts Bukharin simply because others *believed* he stood in the way of a certain political program. Merleau-Ponty fails to ask for independent evidence showing that their beliefs were *right*. It would have been a far different trial had Bukharin been allowed to introduce evidence to refute charges of conspiracy, of treasonous agreements with Nazi Germany, of intentions to provoke peasant resistance to collectivization.[41] Nothing in Merleau-Ponty's phenomenological Marxism requires him to mitigate the moral unacceptability of the legal circumstances of Bukharin's defense. A phenomenologist who decried moralism for failing to investigate the chasm between verbal and actual behavior ought to have been far more sensitive to the suppression of evidence at the Moscow trials. At any rate, his argument leaves even politicians who *want* to assume historical responsibilities unsure of whether

[41] For a factual assessment of the charges, see Tucker and Cohen, eds., *The Great Purge Trial*, pp. xxi–xxiv.

to look to factual consequences or simply to defer to another's judgment.[42] The ambiguity of Merleau-Ponty's notion of objectivity ends up depleting "historical responsibility" of its prescriptive force.

It also harbors an extremely dangerous tendency that is exposed when we ask: who are the "others" who determine what "really" happened? Merleau-Ponty asserts that "the trials only acquire a definitively criminal character when they are viewed from the perspective on the future held by the men in power" (HT 61, tr. 28). More bluntly, "they posit as absolutely valid the Stalinist perspective on Soviet development" (HT 62, tr. 28). It is true that in these statements Merleau-Ponty is only setting out an interpretive supposition designed to make sense of the trials. But even suppositions should conform to their author's sense of appropriate evidence. A phenomenology of perception that stresses the inevitable partiality of viewpoints ought to have ruled out the idea of any "absolutely valid . . . perspective." Indeed, there is a strong case for supposing that those in power are *especially likely* to have distorted perspectives. Their reliance on bureaucracies to distill information and on advisers to interpret it all too often insulates them from disturbing realities.

Finally, Merleau-Ponty's willingness to consider relying on Stalin's point of view reveals the ultimate price of his indifference toward a phenomenology of the emotions. Typically emphasizing cognition rather than affect in perception, he seems at times blind to the personal motives and psychological traits that distort political leaders' beliefs. When he praises Trotsky's "historical objectivity," he does not even mention that Trotsky's desire for world revolution might have been at the root of his erroneous estimates of the chances of a successful revolution in Germany. As the next chapter will show, Merleau-Ponty asks no questions about authoritarian traits in Lenin's character. When he comes to Stalin, he fails even to ask what role ambition, spite, or paranoia might have played in the "perspective" of one who named himself the "man of steel." Whatever their ultimate explanation for the purges, few authors writing since Khrushchev's speech to the Twentieth Party Congress have entirely omitted mention of Stalin's pathological suspicion of potential rivals.[43] Of course Merleau-Ponty lacked

---

[42] Stojanovic, "An Ideology of 'Objective Meaning' and 'Objective Responsibility,' " in *From Contract to Community*, ed. Dallmayr, pp. 114–115.

[43] See Tucker and Cohen, eds., *The Great Purge Trial*, p. xxxviii.

such information. But a well-elaborated theory of the relationship of affect and perception might at least have made him more sceptical with regard to the truth claims of revolutionary leaders. The key lesson is that a notion of political perception without such a theory is singularly ill equipped to anticipate the irrationalities that individual leaders can introduce into political life.

While historical responsibility fails as historical explanation and as the postulate of a new political ethics, it plays an important role in Merleau-Ponty's politics of theory. When he emphasizes that responsibility in the Moscow trials must be understood according to political, as opposed to legal or moral categories, it is his conception of the political even more than of responsibility that is striking (HT 29, 61, 63, tr. xxxvii, 28, 30). As part of his communicative project of insinuating a new understanding of politics into liberal discourse, Merleau-Ponty develops a parallel between Bukharin's fate and an episode in the lived experience of his French audience. The choice between collaboration and resistance during World War II illustrates the nature of decision making during the most intensely political moments in a regime's existence—the moments when its institutions are founded or when they are in mortal danger. An adroit interpretation of this episode should make liberals perceive political action in other than strictly moral terms.

Political Lessons of the Extreme Situation

The purge trials of French collaborators, which had begun in October 1944, kept the public eye on the agonizing choices all had faced during the war. Prosecuting the high officials of the Vichy government was, from a legal point of view, no easy matter. The transition from the prewar government of Paul Reynaud to the wartime regime of Marshal Pétain took place through prescribed constitutional procedures. There was an obvious argument that the collaborationist regime acted within the limits set by the formal criteria of a legal order. Collaboration, some claimed, was not a crime, but rather a difficult and unpleasant political choice, one realistic way of facing up to France's defeat. Reference to incriminating motives was equally shaky as a prosecutorial strategy, for the defendants could plead that their motives were analogous to those of the Resistance. The collaborators sought to preserve French independence and to regenerate national self-esteem. For many the purge trials did not radiate legal virtues. They reeked of vengeance.

181

Les Temps Modernes took great interest in the purge trials. Simone de Beauvoir sat in on the trial of one of the most notorious anti-Semitic journalists of the Vichy period, Robert Brasillach. In "An Eye for an Eye" she reflects on the rationality of punishment. The goal of punishment, she argues, is to make the malefactor understand the nature of his action as he would have if he had been the victim.[44] Her view is implicitly Kantian: the criminal's moral judgment was defective since he did not ask if he could endorse his conduct if it were universalized. Punishment brings to his attention what he ignored.

The existential point of view, however, reveals a troubling paradox: the fact of human freedom makes punishment seem futile. Physical suffering, Beauvoir admits, cannot force a free consciousness to see its action in a new way. No penal system can determine how a person interprets his sentence—with resignation, remorse, or irony.[45] In addition, after the fact and in changed circumstances, judgment seems superfluous. One sees not vile traitors but weak old men.[46] Still, Beauvoir concludes, punishment is necessary. It is a matter of affirming the freedom of the individual. Freedom implies that we can push away the most urgent temptations; punishment insures that if we do not resist evil, we are at least held responsible for our action.[47] To fail to punish is to denigrate freedom itself.

Merleau-Ponty comments upon this article in a lecture on "The Social and Political Aspects of Existentialism." With characteristic tact he brings out Beauvoir's ideas affirmatively, only to draw them toward his own vision of an existential politics. Punishment, he agrees, strives to reestablish reciprocity between the victim and the accused, but its significance is more collective than individual. Punishment "affirms a single history, our truth with others and with the criminal" (IN 30). The criminal engaged himself—and more seriously, others—in the task of making a "single history." *Humanism and Terror* incorporates this perspective. "When the collaborator of 1940 made up his mind according to what he believed to be the inevitable future," Merleau-Ponty writes, "he committed those who did not believe in that future or who wanted none of it; thereafter, between them and himself, it was a matter of force"

---

[44] Beauvoir, "Oeil pour oeil," in *L'existentialisme et la sagesse des nations*, p. 135; originally published in *Les Temps Modernes* 1:5 (February 1946), pp. 813–830.

[45] Ibid., p. 138.

[46] Ibid., pp. 146–151

[47] Ibid., p. 160.

(HT 12, tr. xvii). The purge trials represent less the confirmation of individual freedom than the community's affirmation of its ethical identity. Even if the trials do not affect the free individual, they establish that "rapport between individuals in which unreason becomes reason" (IN 24). A community constitutes an identity radically distinct from its predecessor's by *imputing* liability to key individuals who acted against its values.

Merleau-Ponty's argument concerns not everyday politics, but action during an "epoch, one of those moments when the traditional ground of a society collapses and man . . . must reconstruct human relations" (HT 12, tr. xvii). Normally there is at least some minimal consensus about the sorts of action that are permissible in a community and about the procedures for resolving conflicts. But in the absence of this fundamental consensus, politics reverts to a naked confrontation of groups fighting for mutually exclusive visions of an ethical order. Choices are then absolute and mortally serious. "To be a collaborator was not to take one of two possible positions on French national interest, it was to affirm that there was only one, and it was to take responsibility for the *milice* and the execution of resisters" (HT 72, tr. 42). For the values that constitute a regime to be taken seriously, those who made the radical choice against them must continue to be subject to violence even after the time of decision has passed. It is not for political man to commit the lives and welfare of others to certain goals, to fail, to disavow his actions, and to begin anew with impunity. The purge trials secure a single history by ensuring that radical choices stay radical.

There is a strange tension in Merleau-Ponty's argument at this point. On the one hand, he makes it appear that history has a knowable, moral structure *even in advance* of the action that accomplishes its ends. Thus he calls the resisters heroes because "they carried out . . . what history was waiting for and what was to appear afterwards as the truth of the time" (HT 71, tr. 40). Implied is a structural argument that the Allied victory stood closer to the point of historical equilibrium for the values of freedom than did Pétain's France. On the other hand, he is equally emphatic that during the war all bets were off concerning the future. The resisters are to be admired, he says, for making a decision in defiance of the *probable* outcome of events (HT 71, tr. 40). They could succeed only because "at certain moments . . . nothing is absolutely fixed by the facts, and it is precisely our withdrawal or intervention that history awaits in order to take form" (HT 91, tr. 65).

In Merleau-Ponty's eyes, however, this is no contradiction. It is a way of depicting a tension that characterizes *all* political decision making. Action that is truly political derives from the conjunction of choice and calculation that the resistance experience exemplified. Common to his interpretations of Koestler, the Occupation, and Bukharin's confession is the lesson that political action operates at the ambiguous frontier between freedom and facticity, intention and structural appearance. To accept the meaningfulness and ambiguity of politics is also to acknowledge its violence. Choices are divergent and calculations only probable. At certain times of extreme conflict opponents can only stake their futures on different predictions, on different groups, and on different values. What is victory for one is violent defeat for the other.

At an explicit, thematic level Merleau-Ponty's discussion of the purge trials and Bukharin's confession emphasizes the moment when a regime is founded in order to *make manifest* the connection between violence and cultural values (HT 65, tr. 33). He does this because the liberals' moralism prevents them from taking this connection seriously. "We do not criticize liberalism for being a form of violence," he explains, "but for not noticing it" (HT 67, tr. 35). He reminds moralists who automatically condemn violence that violence is pervasive and can be progressive. Their own approbation of the Resistance proves this. Liberals should not therefore condemn revolutionary violence before inquiring carefully into its *sens*.

But, it may be objected, it is one thing to tell liberals that they see violence prejudicially, quite another to make them change their views. Misguided values are not superficial matters of rhetoric or misinformation. Phenomenology teaches that values are a part of our perceptual relationship to the world. They support and are supported by a complex ensemble of preconscious decisions concerning our work, family, laws, and religion. It is "natural" to take one's personal situation, with its level of comfort, security, and power, for granted while evaluating other situations. Were Merleau-Ponty to believe he could change his contemporaries' political views merely by asserting a connection between violence and established culture, he could rightly be accused of ignoring in his method of argument one of the most important lessons of his phenomenology.

If he can defeat this accusation, it is because he implements a particular politics of theory designed to make liberals *perceive* the connection that he asserts to exist. His argument invokes the perceptual logic of the "limit situation." Karl Jaspers introduced the concept of the *Grenzsituation* in the second volume of *Philosophie*, (*Philosophy*), published in 1932. The meaning of a "limit situation" stands in contrast to the existential interpretation of a "situation" in general. The "situation" refers to the theater of action and knowledge. It is the set of factors—for instance, location, lighting, emotions, class values—that condition perception. We live in an environment of inexhaustible meaning because we are enveloped in unique and constantly changing situations. Usually this situationality escapes notice because it is the background on which the figures of conscious perception stand out. The limit situation, however, *reveals* the intrinsic, inescapable situationality of the human condition. It momentarily tears one free of the familiar meanings that make up one's spontaneous interpretation of the world. The experience of another's death, of guilt, of conflict, says Jaspers, finally makes one *aware* of the *limits* of one's personal existence. This awareness invites the subject to push at those limits and give new significance to a situation hitherto taken for granted.[48]

Merleau-Ponty politicizes the concept and ties it back to his own theory of existence.[49] For liberals natural rights, regular elections, and legal procedures are the background of violence. Violence *appears* by virtue of its contrast with such rules. In that perceptual structure all violence, even violence designed to institute a more just political order, is darkened. In this sense, "liberalism excludes the revolutionary hypothesis" (HT 12, tr. xvii). It confirms the legitimacy of its own institutions insofar as they regulate conflict without violence, and it automatically condemns the presence of violence in moments of historical change. But the war precipitated a new awareness of "the dogmatic ground [fond] of liberalism" (HT 67, tr. 35). France's defeat meant that suddenly each citizen was thrust into a situation where he had to "argue within himself over the social pact and reconstitute a state by his choice" (HT 68, tr. 36). Where before there had been habitual allegiance, now there was necessarily a deliberate decision for or against the Vichy re-

---

[48] Dufrenne and Ricoeur, *Karl Jaspers et la philosophie de l'existence*, pp. 173–194. For a discussion of the relation between Jasper's concept and its use in French existential milieus, see Wilkinson, *The Intellectual Resistance in Europe*, pp. 14–15.

[49] Merleau-Ponty joins the name of Jaspers to "situation-limite" in a lecture on "La tradition française de l'existentialisme" ("The French Tradition of Existentialism") (IN 17).

gime. The Occupation brought to the foreground a truth usually ignored: the state rests upon nothing other than the collective effect of choices made by individuals. To live through the limit situation of war was to witness "the contingent bases [*fondements*] of legality" (HT 68, tr. 36). At a regime's origin not law, not morality, but violence decides the character of political existence. Merleau-Ponty reverses the relation of figure and background that rules liberal perception. Violence does not appear on a background of political-moral order. Order appears on a background of violence.

What makes this argument particularly appropriate to an existential politics is that it does not operate wholly at the level of intellectual conviction. Merleau-Ponty starts with what his compatriots know and have seen—their own lived experience from the past war. Next, he makes them see that chaotic, conflictual situation as the background of their political views. A new understanding of the unity of the object emerges. A gestalt switch opens liberals to a truth that moralism obscures: since *every* regime emerges from a violent ground, the presence of violence at the origin of a regime cannot count decisively against it. Merleau-Ponty's interpretations of Bukharin's confession and of responsibility during war are designed to respond to the practical problems of communicating with liberals and of *actually changing* how they perceive political situations.

First Dialogues concerning Humanism and Terror

Not everyone ventured to participate in Merleau-Ponty's political gestalt experiment. His articles on "The Yogi and the Proletarian" drew a spate of extremely negative critical reviews.[50] Many

[50] It is an index of his success in gathering attention for his existential politics that he attracted more commentaries than he could answer. Immediately published critiques, in addition to those mentioned below, were Gaetan Picon, "La politique et la morale," *La Gazette des Lettres* 3:38 (June 14, 1947), pp. 8–9; J-D. Martinet, "Les intellectuelles et le goût du pouvoir," *La Révolution Prolétarienne* 303 (May 1947), pp. 43–45; Louis Pauwels, "Du scandale existentialiste au scandale surréaliste," *Une Semaine dans le Monde*, May 24, 1947, p. 12; Aimé Patri, "Philosophie de la police politique: À propos de Arthur Koestler et M. Merleau-Ponty," *Masses: Socialisme et Liberté* 7–8 (February 1947), pp. 28–30; E. Liénert, "Koestler et l'intelligentsia de gauche," *La République Moderne* 27–28 (May 15–June 1, 1947), pp. 13–15; Georges Braud, "La nouvelle justice," *Écrits de Paris* (October 1947), pp. 47–52; Emmanuel Mounier, "Y a-t-il une justice politique?" *Esprit* 8 (August 1947), esp. pp. 234–236; Robert Campbell, "M. Merleau-Ponty et ses lecteurs," *Paru* (December 1947), pp. 49–51.

showed more outrage than comprehension. But the polemical traditions operative in the journalistic milieu in which Merleau-Ponty
wrote gave him one additional chance to shift his opponents'
viewpoint. In an essay that is now the preface to *Humanism and
Terror*, he pursues the pedagogy of violence in a virtual dialogue
with his critics. Never identifying his interlocutors (they are
named for the first time in the discussion below), he characterizes
his inquiry as "sociological" (HT 34, tr. xlii). Just as Sartre sees
social themes running through all the behavior of collaborators
and anti-Semites, so Merleau-Ponty picks out a coherent set of
personal "engagements" in the opinions and lives of his critics.
Since they do not appreciate the reversibility of figure and background in his interpretations of Bukharin and the resistance, he
carries the argument to a more personal level. He shows them that
there is violence not only in war and revolution, but also in *their*
manner of existence.

Emmanuel Berl, first in "The Innocent and the Phantom" and
then in *On Innocence*, was Merleau-Ponty's most eloquent critic.
Berl was a personality of some notoriety. In the late 1920s he had
written books on the death of bourgeois thought and morality and
entered into journalistic collaboration with Drieu la Rochelle. During the 1930s he edited the radical newspaper *Marianne*. In the first
months following the armistice of 1940 he helped write Pétain's
speeches. Being Jewish and anti-German, however, he soon abandoned the Vichy regime to take refuge in the south of France for
the duration of the war.[51]

Berl brings an outraged sense of justice, polemical style, and
considerable historical learning to his comments on *Humanism and
Terror*. On Berl's reading, Merleau-Ponty defends a viciously rela-
tivistic notion of justice according to which " 'to be right' means
'to be in power,' 'to side with the strongest.' "[52] To Merleau-Ponty's argument that an individual could be accountable for his
"phantom" Berl opposes a moralistic conception of justice. Morality implies "a sentence . . . equitable to an eternal consciousness,"
whereas Merleau-Ponty's appeal to history asks the accused to
surrender to his accuser. For Berl the standpoint of the "eternal
consciousness" is occupied, in practice, by established laws and
procedures. Like morality, fixed rules fairly applied discover an
"innocence" that no historical context can alter.

[51] Berl, *La fin de la IIIe République*, pp. 12–14.
[52] *De l'innocence*, p. 20.

A second source of criticism was the liberal Dominican journal, *La Vie Intellectuelle*, in which Merleau-Ponty had published his very first articles in the mid-1930s. The editor of the journal, "Christianus," discloses a dark irony in the fate of humanism: just when the Church has finally adopted liberal humanist principles and disavowed the Inquisition, atheistic humanists have turned to designing justifications for a new one. Merleau-Ponty's ultimate lesson is that "history will eventually absolve those who have helped the Communist party make history."[53] Merleau-Ponty makes history the judge of right and wrong, implying that in revolution "any citizen who is arrested is a traitor." By denying any transcendent source of value, Merleau-Ponty makes fallible and interested man the sole arbiter of good and evil.

In 1946, the sociologist Jules Monnerot was only beginning to set forth the analyses of Marx, communism, and French intellectuals that were to provide the cornerstone, in such later works as *The Sociology of Communism* and *The Sociology of Revolution*, of a career of academic anticommunism. He prefigures many of the themes of his career in his response to Merleau-Ponty, "Liquidation and Justification."[54] Of the three liberal critics, Monnerot manages the closest reading of *Humanism and Terror*. He nods in the direction of Merleau-Ponty's insistence on the abolition of violence. He recognizes that Merleau-Ponty uses a philosophy of history to ground his discussion of the trials—but criticizes him for confusing two notions of history. "History, according to Merleau-Ponty, is sometimes what has happened and is happening, sometimes the idea that our author has of what should happen but which may never come to pass."[55] The latter conception Merleau-Ponty entrusts to a group of "the elect" who, having privileged access to the secret of history, can justify tyrannical practices.

The dominant theme of Merleau-Ponty's response is that liberals tend to overlook the complicity of their principles with the violence of political life.[56] Liberalism is an ideology in the phenome-

[53] "Sainte-Antigone," p. 4. "Christianus" was probably either Étienne Borne, one of Merleau-Ponty's classmates from the École Normale and a frequent contributor to this journal under this pen name, or R. P. Maydieu, who solicited Merleau-Ponty's articles for this same journal in the 1930s. See Rémond, *Les catholiques dans la France des années trente*, pp. 261 and 264.

[54] Monnerot later responded again to Merleau-Ponty in "Réponse aux *Temps Modernes*," *La Nef* 4:37 (1947), pp. 32–43.

[55] "Liquidation et justification," p. 18.

[56] This is also the implicit charge in Merleau-Ponty's only recorded exchange with Albert Camus. "Le destin de l'individu dans le monde actuel," p. 31. It may seem

nological sense—not a "mask" for practice, but the existential accompaniment of concrete political decisions. Thus Berl's "ostentatious cult of values, of moral purity is secretly akin to violence, hate, and fanaticism" (HT 175, tr. 165). The secret kinship, as we have seen, is that liberal principles form a functional whole with institutional practices that perpetuate domination and destruction. Deftly alluding to Berl's political activities from before and during the war, Merleau-Ponty tries to make his critic confront at a personal level the import of this critique of liberalism. Berl's plea, sometimes on behalf of law, sometimes on behalf of eternal justice, in fact serves as a defense of "the irresponsibility of political man" (HT 34, tr. xliii). Berl forgets his connections with Drieu and Vichy because he had done nothing illegal and nothing to trouble his conscience. Yet this journalist's moralism postulates "a shallow world in which nothing would be irreparable" (HT 35, tr. xliii). The moralist can only afford to ignore the historical consequences of his action because he assumes there are no decisive junctures in history when personal choice makes the difference between the development of humane institutions and the furtherance of violence. If there are circumstances when the damage of bad choices cannot be undone, the criteria of legality and conscience are inadequate to judge the extent of political responsibility. Political actors have an obvious interest in avoiding such responsibility, and their principles can help them do so. Berl's moralism and his political biography are complementary. The one excuses the consequences and the mistakes of the other.

One could avoid Berl's vacillation between politics and morality by turning decisively from man-made law to a fully transcendent ethics. That was Christianus's approach. For Merleau-Ponty, Christianus demonstrated only that religion too had yet to learn the lessons of historical responsibility.

There are Christian critics who now blithely dissociate themselves from the Inquisition because they are threatened by a Communist inquisition—overlooking the fact that Christianity has not condemned the principle of the Inquisition and was

odd that Merleau-Ponty did not elsewhere pursue his corrective dialogue with Camus, whose moralizing essays were often seen as existential. But their differences were apparently too deep and personal to support an edifying exchange. The two writers once even came to blows in an argument over *Humanism and Terror*. For tacit criticisms of Merleau-Ponty in Camus' writings, however, see Weyembergh, "Merleau-Ponty et Camus: *Humanisme et terreur* et 'Ni victimes, ni bourreaux,' " pp. 53–99.

even able, during the war, to profit here and there from the secular arm. How can they ignore that the Inquisition is focused on the suffering of an innocent man, that the tormentor "knows not what he is doing," . . . and that the conflict is thus placed solemnly in the heart of human history? (HT 31, tr. xxxix–xl)

This dense passage contains three essential ideas. First, irrespective of the Church's claim to embody a transcendent mission, it associates itself with agents of power who shape mundane existence. Parts of the hierarchy cooperated with the Vichy authorities; now the Church fears communism and so cooperates with the liberal-democratic regime. There is a reminder here that the Church does not avoid the politics of the earthly city and therefore cannot avoid the responsibility that goes along with it.

The allusion to the Inquisition contains the second essential idea of his response: the suffering of the innocent Christ was the condition of mankind's redemption from sin. Merleau-Ponty's analysis of the Moscow trial was meant to suggest that the prosecution of the "innocent" Bukharin had a role to play in the redemption of humanity from exploitation. The Church should know that the suffering of some innocents is to be understood in a larger context than that of the immediate justice of the charges against them. Finally, Merleau-Ponty paraphrases Christ's words on the cross to stress that the agent's intentions are not decisive even to the Christian's evaluation of the moral character of action. Even if Christ's tormentors "know not what they do," they are not innocent in the eyes of the Church.

Merleau-Ponty apparently knew of no compromising institutional connections in Monnerot's past. Deprived of the "sociological" strategy of argument, he turns to arguments with a distinctly academic air. He insists that his phenomenological interpretation of Marx denies the Grand Inquisitor "the only justification he can tolerate—namely a science of the future" (HT 28, tr. xxxvi). Yet the cogency of Monnerot's critique forces him to try to attenuate the radicalism of his argument. "Pascal said bitterly three centuries ago: it becomes honorable to kill a man if he lives on the other side of the river, and concluded: things are so. . . . We shall not go so far. We say: one could take this road if it were in order to create a society without violence" (HT 29, tr. xxxvii). He seems to be saying that he has less tolerance for violence than one of France's most esteemed philosophers—surely an argument only professors could appreciate. But Pascal's pessimism does not extricate Merleau-Ponty from the difficulties in his arguments. He admits in this passage that his defense of violence holds on one condition only: it must contribute to the creation of a society without violence. And since he believes only Marx has ever sketched out such a possibility, he means that only imputations of historical responsibility premised upon Marx's theory can be legitimate. Monnerot had already objected, however, that the admission that Marx's schema "may never come to pass" vitiates Merleau-Ponty's entire argument. If a society without violence should never come to pass, Merleau-Ponty would be deprived of any ethical standard for ascribing "historical responsibility." His argument would reduce to Pascal's and the liberal's horror at Bukharin's execution would be justified.

The problem with Merleau-Ponty's account of historical responsibility is the same that detracts from his Marxist ethics: it is long on ambiguity and short on reasons. Frederick Olafson made this case convincingly thirty years ago. Merleau-Ponty wants to say that there was something morally wrong with collaboration *and* that the Resistants' victory was a necessary condition for validating this moral judgment. Olafson points out, however, that if the collaborationists' defeat was morally objectionable, we would want them to admit that they had done wrong and that they should have done otherwise. But Merleau-Ponty offers no reasons why they should decide against the rightness of their actions.[57] His doctrine of historical responsibility will only lead them to conclude that they should have fought harder or changed their strategy so that they could have won. As I will argue at greater length in my conclusion, Merleau-Ponty does not realize that giving moral reasons for actions is a necessary form of existential political engagement.

What remains valuable in his analysis of liberal judgment, however, is its warning that apparently neutral evaluative standards can translate a programmatic hostility to revolutionary regimes and incline politics toward war. Judging communism by the criteria of abstract liberty amounts to "a symbolic destruction of the USSR" (HT 18–19, xxiv). For liberals the existence of violence in nonliberal countries suffices to condemn them. For Merleau-Ponty such condemnation, grounded in an unreflective moralism, leads to the premature abandonment of regimes that might eventually

---

[57] Olafson, "Existentialism, Marxism, and Historical Justification," pp. 126–134.

advance the freedom of their peoples. If liberals can be made to understand that primordial violence is the background condition of political order, their entire framework of political assumptions and reasoning will shift. Injecting the "revolutionary hypothesis" into their reasoning would perhaps alter their stance toward revolutions.

Koestler's essays in *The Yogi and the Commissar* reveal the dismal alternative. To protect Western democracies against possible Communist aggression, Koestler advocates a firm military posture toward the USSR. What he does not want to acknowledge is that "however peaceful [the West's] ends, the adversary is unaware of them; he sees only tanks, artillery, a naval fleet, and draws the consequences of that situation" (HT 180, tr. 173). "For others" preparation for war announces war, not peace. And when the Communists undertake military counterpreparations, the liberal will only see confirmation of his fears of the Communists' aggressive intentions. It is such refusals to *understand* the Soviet experience that set in motion a mechanism of politically simplistic choices, a spiral of misunderstandings that could plunge the world into war.

None of this is to say that the USSR *is* the fulfillment of proletarian humanism. Even once one understands the problem of originary violence, "it remains to be seen whether communist violence is, as Marx thought, progressive" (HT 181, tr. 175). An *empirical* transcendental must be evaluated empirically. The social structure actually engendered by the revolution must be measured against the Communist claim to advance human freedom. To this end Merleau-Ponty tries to draw Communists, even more than liberals, into a conversation on the relationship between humanism and terror.

THE COMMUNIST PROBLEM

Marxism is not only a philosophy *of* history; it is a philosophy *in* history. Marx's assertion of the unity of theory and praxis means that theoretical knowledge and practical change are inseparable. Understanding the workings of reality initiates a process that alters it, as when the proletariat's "awakening of consciousness" changes it into a force for its own emancipation.[1]

Theory inserts itself into this process of historical change through a pedagogical function: it brings its interpretation of reality to the working classes to catalyze those changes in outlook that will set in motion a revolutionary transformation of social structures. In Marx's celebrated phrase, "theory itself becomes a material force when it has seized the masses."[2] This is not a matter of words acting as might inflammatory propaganda that incites a mob to riot. The practical bent of Marxist theory presupposes a Hegelian epistemology in which mind and reality are in reciprocal relation. Theory can become practical because it ties into a latent consciousness already active in existing social relations.

The Marxian hypothesis necessarily directs most of Merleau-Ponty's attention to the local representative and current pedagogue of revolutionary practice—the French Communist party. He once revealed his strategy with respect to that group. "We had to work . . . with the Communists against a Nazi victory. This we did while keeping our freedom with regard to them, while initiating a discussion that we could pursue after the war—a discussion that could favor the tendencies of 'western Communism' inside the PCF."[3] "Western communism" denotes the ideology of those who preserve some critical distance from the USSR, who speak of dialectics and subjectivity rather than positive science, who balance discipline with discussion. With a select group of Communist in-

[1] Aviniri, *The Social and Political Thought of Karl Marx*, pp. 131–144.

[2] Marx, "Contribution to the Critique of Hegel's *Philosophy of Right*: Introduction," in *The Marx-Engels Reader*, p. 60.

[3] "L'adversaire est complice," p. 7.

terlocutors Merleau-Ponty pursues a conversation whose political function is to develop whatever is left of truth in the Marxian hypothesis. What necessitates dialogue in this case is not the moralist's suppression of violence, but the revolutionist's excessive recourse to it. To those who *already* recognize the inevitability of conflict, Merleau-Ponty teaches that Marxism-Leninism is a theory that, by its very logic, also implies limits to violence.

Difficult Relations:
Existentialists and Communists

The Liberation of France seemed to hail a new political era. Collaborationist activities discredited large segments of the elite of the Third Republic, while the leading role of Communists in the Resistance won the party greater prestige than ever before. In membership the PCF was, briefly, the largest party in France; for the first time it held ministries in the government. A coalition of Communists, Socialists, and Catholic Democrats was to oversee the design and implementation of a new constitution. In the cultural sphere the party was in a relatively tolerant phase. While defending the family and the nation, it showed some willingness to listen to philosophies other than dialectical materialism.[4] It was with a not unfounded hope, therefore, that *Les Temps Modernes* directed its voice with insistence to the second half of its divided audience. The party seemed to be willing to keep up its end of a conversation on diverse political values.

Coincident with the new openness of the PCF, however, Sartre began to win substantial popularity. The Communists, fearing that the bohemian attractiveness of existentialism would divert potential members from the party, unleashed a series of newspaper articles and pamphlets attacking Sartre's philosophy in 1946 and 1947.[5] Curiously, the existentialists were able to keep up friendly private relations with the Communists even as they were attacked in the party's publications, and Merleau-Ponty, benefiting from his Communist connections and Marxist inclinations, was largely spared the bombast.[6] But an ominous duplicity had begun. The

[4] Caute, *Communism and the French Intellectuals*, pp. 163–164.

[5] Poster, *Existential Marxism*, pp. 110–113.

[6] Sartre, "Merleau-Ponty vivant," pp. 311 and 314. Sartre forgets only Merleau-Ponty's exchange with Pierre Hervé, discussed below. René Scherer responded to Merleau-Ponty's "La querelle de l'existentialisme" in "Ou bien, ou bien" ("Either/

growth of cold war tensions, moreover, quickly withdrew this un-even margin of amicability.

Nineteen forty-six and 1947 were years of escalating crisis. They heard Churchill's call for increased military preparedness in his "iron curtain" speech. The French bombed Haiphong; the Greek monarchist regime was foundering in a civil war; and Truman sent a flotilla into the eastern Mediterranean to convince Stalin that the U.S. would not tolerate Soviet control of the Dardanelles. The Tru-man Doctrine offered U.S. aid to countries needing to resist "at-tempted subjugation by armed minorities or by outside pres-sures." When the U.S. extended the Marshall Plan to support the reconstruction of Europe along lines conforming to the Western model of free institutions, the USSR denounced it as an imperialist ploy. In September 1947 the Kominform was created.

With events attesting to the proximity of war, *Les Temps Mo-dernes's* allies on the Right and Left assumed more partisan stands. Sensing that in case of war Merleau-Ponty and Sartre would sup-port the Eastern bloc, Raymond Aron and Albert Ollivier quit the editorial committee of the journal around June 1946.[7] Both were soon working in support of General de Gaulle's political party, the Rassemblement du Peuple Français (RPF). In a series of six radio broadcasts in the fall of 1947, various collaborators of *Les Temps Modernes* harshly denounced Gaullist politics. Characteristically, however, Merleau-Ponty also added marked criticism of the USSR, and Sartre berated the Communists' "worst case politics." Too controversial for the tense political atmosphere of the time, the Schumann government silenced these public announcements of a politics "between the [Great Power] blocs" in late November 1947.[8]

Les Temps Modernes's relations on the Left deteriorated just as rapidly. When Henri Lefebvre and Louis Aragon accused Paul Ni-zan of being a police spy and a traitor (Nizan had quit the party after the Nazi-Soviet pact was signed and died a soldier for France at the Battle of the Marne), Sartre spearheaded a defense of his friend. He left the Communists with resentment, but no convinc-

---

Or"), *action*, December 21, 1945, p. 12. But his complaints were directed at Sartre, not Merleau-Ponty.

[7] Aron remembers first perceiving the distance between him and *Les Temps Mo-dernes* when he read Merleau-Ponty's claim that the existentialists' quarrels with the PCF were merely "family disputes." *Mémoires*, p. 312. See also Burnier, *Choice of Action*, p. 30; Beauvoir, *La force des choses*, I, p. 135.

[8] *Le Monde*, December 3, 1947, p. 3; Cohen-Solal, *Sartre*, pp. 386–390.

ing reply.[9] The real watershed in relations between existentialists and Communists came with a speech by Soviet Politburo member Andrei Zhdanov in September 1947. In an inaugural address for the Kominform Zhdanov declared that the world was divided into two camps: the imperialists, who were bent on war and controlled by American monopoly capital, and the socialists, who were peaceful, anti-imperialist, and democratic.[10] Party members were summoned to break off personal relationships with the ideologically impure.[11] After this the Communists no longer exempted Merleau-Ponty from attack. The party founded a new journal, *La Nouvelle Critique*, which was more polemical than the long-established *La Pensée*. In the first issue J.-T. Desanti liberated himself from the shackles of phenomenology and launched a frontal assault on *Humanism and Terror*.[12] Merleau-Ponty's nuanced argument was, he said, but the subterfuge of an intellectual afraid to give unequivocal support to the proletariat.

So although the early postwar liberalization of the party had been grounds for optimism, it never progressed far enough to entice Merleau-Ponty to join.[13] He charged in 1947 that, far from letting intellectuals "tell all the truths," the Communists "prefer those who never write a word of politics or philosophy and let themselves be listed in digests of newspapers" (HT 21, tr. xxvii). A critique of contemporary Communist practice was an unavoidable part of the program of an existential politics. But his rejection of liberal modes of criticism meant that he could not measure Communist practice against the precepts of advanced Western democracy and ignore the foundation of political order in violence. Before *judging* communism, one must attempt to *understand* it as it understands itself, as a theory of revolutionary praxis.

The Failure of Proletarian Spontaneity

In postwar France the "communist problem" had a very conventional meaning. Conservatives pointed to the danger of over

[9] Contat and Rybalka, *Les écrits de Sartre*, p. 164. Merleau-Ponty wrote the introductory note to Sartre's protest and signed it. "Réponse à Olivier Todd," p. 17.

[10] André Fontaine, *History of the Cold War: From the October Revolution to the Korean War, 1917–1950*, trans. D. D. Paige (New York: Vintage Books, 1970), p. 334.

[11] Interview with Dominique and J.-T. Desanti, April 8, 1981.

[12] J.-T. Desanti, "Le philosophe et le prolétaire," pp. 26–36. This article won Desanti praise in the highest circles of the party. See D. Desanti, *Les Staliniens*, p. 363.

[13] *Humanisme et terreur*, Merleau-Ponty interviewed by Georges Charbonnier, RTF, 1959.

one-quarter of the electorate voting for a party committed to the overthrow of the constitution and to the paradox of such a party participating in the government. From the perspective of an existential philosophy of history, so restricted a context is misleading. The "communist problem" is, for Merleau-Ponty, the third movement in a suite of philosophical problems that establish the proper context for understanding revolutionary practice.

The first problem, the "human problem," is that of a consciousness endowed with a body and with a cultural formation attempting to impose its truths on others. It is the problem of violence. Marx states the "proletarian problem." He raises the question of whether the historical conditions for ending violence—a proletarian revolution—will be fulfilled. The "communist problem" concerns the possibility, once history has failed to realize proletarian values spontaneously, of preserving the Marxian vision by using a party apparatus to push the workers toward revolution. The communist problem signals, in Malraux's phrase, that "the age of parties has begun."[14]

It is well known that Marx himself was suspicious of theories of revolution based on the conspiratorial action of a political party. Merleau-Ponty's historical Gestalttheorie implicitly accentuates this suspicion. In his interpretation the Marxian hypothesis is that the arrangement of social power and human interests is such that their present, unstable configuration will tend to readjust itself by a process of "historical selection" into an order supportive of human freedom. He concedes that this belief in a spontaneous process of historical adjustment is a sign of "Marx's optimism" (IN 16, 183). But spontaneity is an essential element of the ethical appeal of Marxism. After becoming aware of its exploited condition, the proletariat must carry out its own emancipation. Any group that pretends to act in its stead prior to its *prise de conscience* has to *force* the workers to adopt new patterns of political conduct against their will. That is the very definition of violence.

The century that had elapsed since the writing of the *Communist Manifesto* had proven Marx's confidence in spontaneous revolution misplaced. The broad lines of change that he had traced out on the map of history had grown faint in the harsh light of twentieth-century events. Where Marx talked of "the" proletariat, historical experience revealed a class fractured by internal divisions. Merleau-Ponty follows Lenin in discussing territorial, religious, and

[14] André Malraux, *L'espoir* (Paris: Gallimard, 1937), p. 493.

197

professional differences within the proletariat (HT 133, tr. 116). So heterogeneous a class could not be expected to revolt at a single moment, with everywhere the same political competence. Furthermore, experience showed that it was possible to divert proletarian values. Fascism, for instance, "politically nullified broad social strata that would been capable of revolutionary action" (SNS 207, tr. 117). Even Lenin's own theory that the political instincts of the working class would take it only so far as a reformist trade unionism underscored the precariousness of the revolutionary movement. Finally, October 1917 demonstrated that a Marxist revolution could take place in a country where "the economic premises of socialism" (especially the development of heavy industry and capitalist methods of economic organization) were not yet in place (HT 95, tr. 70). The success of the Bolsheviks depended on combining the power of the peasantry and the workers.

Had Merleau-Ponty been more sceptically inclined in the immediate postwar years, he might have used these examples to question Marx's theory of class or at least to demand that it be refined. If the proletariat, where it is strong, can be "nullified" by an ideology that is opposed to communism, in what sense is it necessarily a revolutionary class? Merleau-Ponty could have taken Nicos Poulantzas's route—that of specifying lines of cleavage within "the working class" to separate out those elements most likely to support proletarian objectives from those likely to support the bourgeoisie.[15] Or he might have asked in what sense it can still be said that the mode of production is uniquely important in favoring class formation in a world in which ethnic, religious, and national motivations can be as powerful as economic ones.[16] He ought to have wondered about the degree to which the attributes of the working class under developed capitalism really matter, when peasants can make a socialist revolution possible in an economically underdeveloped country. But those are not Merleau-Ponty's questions. He asks only whether, given recent historical experience, it is still conceivable for the proletariat to fulfill its "historic mission" without having to practice violence on a substantial segment of the population.

Merleau-Ponty discovers a theoretical solution to this question

---

[15] With distinctions between productive and unproductive labor and between mental and manual labor, Poulantzas identifies members of the truest working class as those who labor productively and manually. See *Les classes sociales dans le capitalisme aujourd'hui* (Paris: Editions du Seuil, 1974).

[16] Parkin develops this criticism tellingly in *Marxism and Class Theory*, pp. 29–42.

in Lenin's response to the untrustworthy record of historical spontaneity. Lenin proposed to harness the immanent power of the proletariat by putting it under the leadership of a highly centralized party. At the summit a small group of professional revolutionaries would direct the day-to-day activities of the entire group. A revolutionary vanguard would assist the proletariat in strikes, help prevent penetration of workers' organizations by agents of the state, print revolutionary newspapers, and promote all forms of social protest. Even after the seizure of power, the party's emphasis on leadership and discipline would not immediately abate. To control the classes of small proprietors that were integral to the economy and to check the resurgence of petit bourgeois tendencies in the proletariat, the party would have to exercise "the strictest control . . . of the quantity of labor and the quantity of consumption."[17] Although Lenin foresaw the eventual "withering away" of the state, he believed a prolonged period of party dictatorship would be necessary to effect the transition to communism.

Lenin and the Limits of Violence

Are Lenin's ideas really consistent with Marx's theory of historical change? Can a party claim both to follow the movement of history and to shape it? Reconciling Marx's theory of the spontaneous development of the revolution with the necessity of a centralized party are two conditions that, according to Merleau-Ponty, Lenin imposed on the party's leaders. First, the party must "recognize the proletarian spirit as it appears at a given historical moment" (SNS 291, tr. 164). Neither Marxist theory, which reveals only the general direction of history, nor mass sentiments, which too easily stray from the revolutionary path, suffice to guide revolutionary politics when history is riddled with contingent circumstances. A Leninist leader supplements Marxism with a theory of political tactics—"man's responses to the detours of historical logic."[18] A tactical plan does not proceed directly from the certainties of radical theory. It starts by estimating "an ensemble of probabilities" concerning the evolution of historical circumstances (SNS 293, tr. 165). Leaders first discern constellations of factors that affect the probable success of revolutionary action—the weakness of one class, the likelihood of foreign intervention, the degree of worker discon-

[17] V. I. Lenin, *State and Revolution* (New York: International Publishers, 1974), p. 80.
[18] Merleau-Ponty, "Indochine S.O.S.," p. 1049.

tent. They then plan to intervene in this conjuncture to favor the outcomes foreseen in Marx's general reading of history. Leadership presupposes those "statistical treatments of man" that Merleau-Ponty's phenomenology salvages for an existential politics. Leaders relate the Marxian outline of history to particular political conditions.

While "recognizing . . . the historical moment" allows leaders to deviate from Marx's scenario for revolutionary change, it also constrains their tactics. "The contact which was lost between the spontaneous life of the masses and the requirements of proletarian victory as conceived by the leaders must be reestablished at the end of a foreseeable lapse of time. . . . Local history must have a visible relationship with universal history" (HT 134–135, tr. 118–119). Leaving aside the easy conflation of "the masses" and "the proletariat" (more evidence of Merleau-Ponty's unwillingness to enter into the complexities of class theory), the critical point is evident. Marx's concept of a logic of history depends on the idea that those in direct contact with the dominant problems of an era tailor their own, historically appropriate solutions to those problems— and it is the workers, not the party leaders, who maintain such contact. Since only the proletariat's own "awakening of consciousness" makes the logic of history operative, the party can do no more than "clarify the proletariat to itself" (HT 133, tr. 116). It makes workers see more interconnections between political and economic phenomena than they might have unguided. It sets up channels of communication to unify workers geographically. It proposes policies to strengthen the revolution. The party leads, but only by "one step ahead" (HT 106, tr. 84).

It follows that if revolutionary enthusiasm among the masses wanes, the party should make concessions to the popular will. Lenin knew that "the force of tradition among millions of men is the most fearsome force" (HT 125, tr. 106). The Bolsheviks could not oppose pure violence to mass sentiments. In the face of preconscious meanings, strategic compromise and well-timed retreat are as necessary as constraint to achieve revolutionary objectives. Merleau-Ponty's favorite example of this is Lenin's tactical retreat in the face of the economic hardships associated with War Communism (HT 137, tr. 121). Mass insurrections in 1921 signalled that the party had tried to force economic changes too quickly. Rather than pursue what might have seemed the most ideologically correct, "leftist" policy, Lenin decided to relax centralization. In his New Economic Plan he allowed some private enterprise and managed to revive the economy. The lesson is that if the party crafts its policies in response to mass attitudes, it can act successfully without imposing undue violence on an unwilling population.

What allows the leaders to perceive this consciousness are free channels of communication with the people. Candor is the second condition of reconciliation between leadership and proletarian freedom. Merleau-Ponty maintains that "the secret of Leninism was in the communication that it managed to establish between the masses and the leaders, between the proletariat and its 'consciousness.' This presupposes leaders . . . who know how to explain to the masses what is proposed to them, it presupposes a dialogue and exchange among the masses that indicates at every moment the condition of the effective revolution" (SNS 206, tr. 117). So when party slogans fail to be "immediately understood and to find agreement all around," it is not the workers who are at fault (PP 508, tr. 445; cf. SNS 319, tr. 180). The assumption must be that the party has misgauged the revolutionary situation; it is time to improve channels of communication so that it better understands the state of the revolutionary movement. Thus the requirement that the proletarian consciousness be the moral anchor of the revolution limits the allowable tactical moves of the leadership. Consistently deceiving the proletariat about the party's tactics would prejudice the workers' spontaneous interpretations and baffle the historical process.

This is the sense in which Merleau-Ponty asserts that naming violence openly is a necessary condition for eliminating it (HT 66, tr. 34). When Lenin spoke of retreat to the Party Congress, he acknowledged the exact meaning of his policy vis-à-vis the party's immediate goals and the total sens of history. Such candor "transforms compromise into awareness of compromise . . . , it makes detours knowing and saying that these are detours" (HT 136, tr. 120). It protects a Marxist politics from cynicism and opportunism by opening itself to challenge and criticism. Lenin's practice exemplifies the conditions of a revolutionary politics that remains rational, even after all necessary concessions to historical contingency are made.

Why focus on Lenin? The author of *Materialism and Empiriocriticism*, who maintained that all reality is composed only of matter and that the mind merely reflects an objectively existing, exterior reality, seems an unlikely ally of existentialism. Yet from Merleau-Ponty's perspective Lenin has two marks in his favor: the revolution that he led succeeded (and success can never be ignored in a philosophy of praxis), and as the hero of the communist movement, he is an object of valuation common to all party members. This established valuation makes it possible for Merleau-Ponty to use Lenin's revolutionary *practice* to legitimate in Communist eyes a set of criteria for Communist action.

His rhetorical strategy is the mirror image of his handling of liberal views. Liberals are so preoccupied with moral norms that they cannot see the violent background of politics. Calling on their valued memories of the Resistance, he brings violence to their attention. Communists are so preoccupied with revolutionary violence that they often ignore the common ground of dialogue. Calling on their valued memories of Lenin, Merleau-Ponty brings dialogue to their attention. He seeks to shift some aspects of Communist practice by inferring from Lenin's behavior certain norms that the party's current leaders have forgotten. These norms are not the moral "oughts" that Communists ridicule; they are conditions of rationality of their praxis. Merleau-Ponty's Lenin is not a positivist, but rather a perspicacious reader of historical structures, a man who listened to the masses, an artful political tactician who accepted a phenomenological conception of dialogue.

From an existential point of view, Lenin's leadership was legitimate because it can be explained in terms consistent with a phenomenology of perception. In a remark on Lenin's practice-oriented pamphlets, Merleau-Ponty alludes to this possibility. "It would be appropriate to extend the practical conclusions that [Lenin] adopts [in *Left-Wing Communism*] onto the theoretical plane. One could draw a theory of contigency in history from his Marxist 'perception' of situations" (SNS 217, tr. 123). Lenin's manner of communicating with the masses represents an additional answer to the problem of finding an epistemological standpoint from which to perceive the structural meaning of history. Yet another resolution was necessary because the necessity of an *organized* revolution complicates the perceptual issue. The general problem, it will be recalled, is to explain how the subject can be certain of his knowledge when he is part of the very structure he is investigating. The answer in Merleau-Ponty's phenomenology is to move into an epistemologically advantageous position, for instance, a position close enough to an object that one's perceptual faculties can explore it easily. Marx assumed that the logic of history put the proletariat spontaneously into such a position. But Lenin's theory that the workers' spontaneous political demands lead them no further than trade unionism means that the proletariat pulls up short of the point where it can understand its historic mission.

Hence a party is necessary to "clarify the proletariat to itself." "The masses" are like a subject who can perceive an object, but only vaguely. The party is comparable to the active element in the subject's perceptual capacity that directs him to focus in on the object in order to improve his perceptual grasp. The dialectic of leadership and led duplicates in political affairs the concept of existence that Merleau-Ponty used to describe the rapport between organism and environment. The party does not impose action upon the workers; it gauges the possibilities for action from the current state of proletarian consciousness. Proletarian consciousness is not a datum; it can be prodded, enhanced, shaped. Ideally, there is a fit between leadership and masses that makes them but two poles within a single, structural process. In a phrase worthy of Malraux, Merleau-Ponty calls their relationship an "organic unity of will and destiny" (IN 7).

It must still be objected that the strategy of Merleau-Ponty's interpretation of Lenin does not excuse its disturbing partiality. Where is the "sociological" analysis of Lenin's life to parallel what Merleau-Ponty said of his liberal adversaries? Why do we not hear of some of Lenin's more authoritarian inclinations? The Lenin who "communicated" with the masses in 1921 is also the man who dispersed the Constituent Assembly of 1918, who closed down the non-Bolshevik press, who banned intraparty factions at the Tenth Party Congress. No matter how flexible his leadership, this tactician of revolution was still the author of a philosophical work that is rigidly materialist and that subordinated philosophy to *partiinost*. Add what explanations that one may for these aspects of Leninism, the point is that Merleau-Ponty ignores them. And to the extent that he simply omits what might spoil his picture, he exposes his strategy to failure. His Communist interlocutors will probably prefer to gaze at the official portrait, however mythic, because it purports to depict the man's entire life, not just a few carefully selected details. Merleau-Ponty's strangely angled profile of Lenin hardly lends credence to a phenomenology committed to telling "all the truth."

What Merleau-Ponty does recognize even in his partial account of Lenin's practice is that the Bolshevik variation on the Marxian hypothesis carries substantial dangers. To the extent that the party must represent a class consciousness that does not exist in some sectors of the masses, "these sectors could only be said to think by proxy. . . . To act according to another's deepest convictions, such as one has oneself defined them, is quite precisely to do violence to him" (HT 106, tr. 84). Especially where situations impede the awakening of revolutionary consciousness of the masses or where dialogue breaks down and the leaders' perceptiveness falters, the "communist problem" assumes a disturbing form: the revolutionary gestalt decomposes into a dualism of subject and object. The working class remains the objective base of the revolution, its "material force," while the party becomes an arbitrary subject directing the revolution by will. Such an eventuality sunders the relations that shape history into a rational structure.

Significantly, Merleau-Ponty circles back to Hegel's later works to describe this outcome. Should dialogue fail and discipline prevail, communist politics would look like nothing so much as the Hegelian state. It would be directed by "a few bureaucrats of History, who know for everyone and who actualize what the World Spirit desires with the blood of others" (HT 135, cf. 26, tr. 119, xxxiv). The irony of this assertion is that Marx himself had exposed the sham involved in Hegel's portrayal of the Prussian bureaucracy as a "universal class." The bureaucracy portrays itself as working in the interest of the whole society, but in fact treats the state as its private domain, a domain of authority and careerism. It is as if the philosophy at the origin of the Marxian perspective hosted a logic intrinsic to any theory based on a reading of world history—foretelling even the theory's possible deviations. The empirical question that Merleau-Ponty's existential politics is driven to address by its own logic then is this: has the political organization that Lenin bequeathed to the USSR become precisely such a sham universal class?

The Problem of the Ambiguous Form: Trotsky's Fate

Even though reliable information was scarce, evidence on the condition of the USSR painted a grim picture. Merleau-Ponty's criticism of Soviet policy is sweeping (HT 151–153, tr. 139–141). Thirty-five years after the revolution, he finds not a thoroughly egalitarian society, but one stratified along lines of political power and economic position. He mentions that the use of the profit motive in large enterprises has led to large differences in salary between workers and administrators. There are special schools for the sons of bureaucrats. The party itself shows a diminishing rate of participation by workers. Bureaucratic administration of the economy has burgeoned to the point where the "social revenue [of the USSR] remains saddled with a state apparatus more burdensome and more imperious than any other."[19] Most horrific of all is the finding that the Communist regime "permits a system of concentration camps as an essential element," a fact Merleau-Ponty exposes publicly during *Les Temps Modernes*'s second radio broadcast in October 1947.[20]

However, an evaluative course apparently headed for an outright condemnation of the USSR in fact veers away at the last moment. He calls the statistical portrait of the USSR "un montage" (HT 149, tr. 136) to suggest that its truth is partial and perhaps contrived. Reasons both phenomenological and historical preclude at this point an absolute condemnation of the USSR.

Gestalttheorie trains the observer to characterize a structure at *equilibrium*. Judging the state of the revolution in the USSR is then a question of assembling positive and negative perspectives on its development, of taking account of the conditions of the revolution and of the possibility that the negative aspects of the current society are part of a temporal process of adjustment toward an acceptable equilibrium of incarnated values. The suite of problems—human, proletarian, and communist—serves as an evaluative context that suggests possible explanations for Soviet conduct. In accordance with the human problem there is violence in the USSR; yes, but creating a new society demands violence. If resistance rather than mass enthusiasm greets the revolution, one must seek the explanation partly in the fact that the USSR faced the double task of completing the bourgeois revolution by giving the country an infrastructure of heavy industry and at the same time of carrying out the socialist revolution (SNS 215–216, tr. 122). From Lenin's *State and Revolution* Merleau-Ponty learns that sweeping society clean of the traces of bourgeois society is an affair of many years; "no one can set a date [for the beginning of] the highest stage of communism" (IN 184). Moreover, Lenin set precedents for most of Stalin's policies, so it cannot be said that Stalin purely and simply betrayed the revolution. For Stalin's Nazi-Soviet pact, there was Lenin's treaty at Brest-Litovsk; for the social stratification of Stalinist society, there was Lenin's tolerance of monetary incentives during the stage of socialism; for Stalin's purge trials, there were expulsions from the party that Lenin countenanced (IN 185).

[19] Merleau-Ponty, "Le Manifeste Communiste a cent ans," p. 2.
[20] *Communisme et anticommunisme*, interview, October 1947, RTF.

Between Lenin's dialogue and Stalin's protracted terror, Merleau-Ponty finds only a difference of degree (HT 111, 116, tr. 91, 97). His key point is that, in spite of its horrors and hardships, the Russian Revolution succeeded in laying the basis of a socialist society (SNS 285, tr. 161).

But as for the redemption of Marx's pledge of a new humanism, it was too early to tell: "we do not know if a universal socialist production will reach its equilibrium" (SNS 214, tr. 221). The outcome of so many evaluative scruples is a judgment that the USSR is a "mixed reality" (HT 154, tr. 142; cf. SNS 296, tr. 167). It is an ambiguous form that, for the present, eludes accurate perception and unequivocal evaluation.

How can Merleau-Ponty be satisfied with so indecisive a conclusion? In an important sense he is confounded not by a lack of information, but by his own views on violence. He confuses the thesis that violence is inevitable with the conclusion that no useful ethical distinctions can be drawn between types, degrees, and circumstances of violence. The cost of that confusion is now painfully apparent. He is unable to come to any clear (even if provisional) assessment of the Soviet experiment. Surely it makes a difference that Stalin used purge trials systematically to eliminate all opposition, while Lenin rarely used the procedures of expulsion against party members. Surely Merleau-Ponty could distinguish between economic policies that allow some accumulation of private wealth and the deliberate construction of a system of privilege for party members. Surely it makes a moral difference whether violence is deliberate or accidental, wanton or restrained, chosen as a preferred policy or accepted only after other means have been tried. It is not to lapse into a smug liberalism to insist on such distinctions. For political actors these are internal guideposts that preserve their sensitivity to the cruelty of violence, even as they recognize its occasional necessity in the pursuit of morally worthy objectives.[21] From the point of view of a political critic such guideposts demarcate territories that are extremely dangerous to enter. Erasing boundaries rather than enforcing them with circumspection makes the critic unsure of his own whereabouts. Merleau-Ponty's tolerance for conceptual ambiguity repays him with ambiguous commitments.

His undecided critique of the USSR then leaves an existential

---

[21] Walzer defends such a perspective in "Political Action: The Problem of Dirty Hands," in *War and Moral Responsibility*, eds. Cohen et al; esp. pp. 80–82.

politics facing the delicate task of defining a stance toward a form whose violence might or might not be progressive. The stakes are extremely high. A premature judgment that violence in the USSR disproves the Marxian hypothesis would condemn the only potentially humanistic society in existence. Undue delay in that judgment would mean justifying a retrograde terror in the name of a purely nominal humanism. In these respects, the existentialists' position is similar to Leon Trotsky's and they have lessons to learn from this revolutionary who developed serious doubts about the course of the revolution.

Merleau-Ponty's political theory evinces throughout a careful reading of Trotsky's works. The image of history as a process of "natural selection," the argument that means and ends form a homogeneous alloy in revolutionary morality, the defense of terror, the insistence that a participant might have a more objective view of the 1917 revolution than a detached observer: all of these ideas are Trotskyist in origin. Less obviously, Merleau-Ponty's references to the mitigating conditions of Bolshevik violence and to the simultaneous critique and defense of the USSR crosses territory that Trotsky had charted. Most important, however, is Merleau-Ponty's description of the USSR as "an enterprise that is out of order." Like Trotsky's parallel characterization of the USSR as a "degenerated workers' state," this simple phrase implies an entire political stance.[22] What is "degenerated" or "out of order" is something unacceptable in its present form. It needs to be changed and revitalized. It is nonetheless a "workers' state," something closer to Marx's vision than any other state and thus to be defended against imperialist aggression.

No doubt these parallels testify to Merleau-Ponty's considerable admiration for Trotsky as a political thinker.[23] They do not, however, tell the whole story. It is significant that when he published *Humanism and Terror*, he added only one entirely new chapter to the series of articles that had appeared earlier in *Les Temps Modernes*. The new chapter dealt with "Trotsky's Rationalism." "Rationalism"—always a critical term in Merleau-Ponty's philoso-

---

[22] Merleau-Ponty mentions Trotsky's phrase in "L'adversaire est complice," p. 6 and IN 181. Merleau-Ponty's own phrase appears in a rebuke to Lefort for having too strenuously condemned the Soviet Union. "Note de la rédaction à 'Kravchenko et le problème de l'URSS' par Claude Lefort," p. 1516.

[23] Lukacs's charge that Merleau-Ponty is essentially a Trotskyist thus strikes me as more than mere cold war rhetoric. See *Existentialisme ou Marxisme?* pp. 188, 221–228.

phy—refers to a set of reservations about the Russian revolutionary that have to be balanced against the preceding remarks. He sees, in effect, two Trotskys. "They" were men of differing significance for a humanist politics.

The first Trotsky represents communist politics at its most authentic. He was the leader of the Red Army and Lenin's closest political ally. He was a flexible leader, notable especially for his willingness to depart from the most obviously "socialist" policies in order to preserve revolutionary gains. Organizing a centralized and conventionally hierarchical army, he opposed those who argued that the communist fighting corps should be rigorously egalitarian in structure (SNS 291, tr. 164). Suppressing the revolt of the Kronstadt sailors in 1921, he ordered military action against workers who were calling for the decentralization of power. Trotsky's defense of the repression of "counterrevolutionary elements," his advocacy of a controlled press during a period of intense class struggle, and similar positions were a rejection of a politics deduced directly from abstract theory—one written on "Kautsky's work table," in Trotsky's derogatory phrase (HT 110, tr. 90).

To a certain extent, Merleau-Ponty admits, this Trotsky's lucidity persisted even in exile. He inquired into the reasons for his political defeat. As a good Marxist he looked into the historical meaning of Stalinism and described its politics in terms of bureaucracy, regimentation, and political repression. He investigated the historical-social conditions that made a political leader like Stalin possible or even necessary. His answer—Stalin's "Thermidor" is part of the revolutionary cycle. "Thermidor" is the moment when the revolution consolidates itself into institutions, builds material strength, and disciplines society in preparation for the next revolutionary impulse (HT 98–99, tr. 74). It is this perspective that justifies Trotsky's programmatic defense of the USSR. Only because Stalin maintains the *essential* socialist trait of the USSR—the collective appropriation of the means of production—does it make sense for his adversaries to expend the effort to defend the USSR against capitalist aggression (HT 104, tr. 81; S 320, tr. 255).

But there is a second Trotsky, out of power and thus out of contact with the regulative problems of Soviet experience, who repeatedly slips into moralistic "rationalism." This Trotksy formulates a rule for conduct when all else fails: "do what you must, come what may." Beyond a certain point he gives up on seeking creative, tactical responses to historical contingency and hopes no more than to "pass on to our children an unstained flag" (HT 102–

103, tr. 79). Merleau-Ponty rejected such an option with regard to liberalism, and it was no more suitable for revolutionary politics. Trotsky lost sight of the fact that politics is *always* about doing something, *never* simply a matter of relieving one's conscience. Trotsky erred by trying to discover a concrete politics in Marx's philosophy of history. Then, when the broad lines of history temporarily escaped him, nothing remained but to settle into moralism.

That liberalism and communism are massive, historically accredited phenomena worthy of the examination that Merleau-Ponty gave them is presumably clear. But why did he direct so much attention to the relatively impotent Trotskyist movement? It seems there was a danger and a temptation close at hand. Collaborating on *Les Temps Modernes* were Sartre's former student J. Lefebvre-Pontalis and Claude Lefort, Merleau-Ponty's protégé. Both leaned toward Trotskyism, although Lefort alone was actually an activist in the Fourth International.[24] David Rousset, also a Trotskyist, published in *Les Temps Modernes*. The journal's quasi-Marxism, critical position between the power blocs, and direct political affiliations put it on a band that overlapped with Trotskyism on the political spectrum.[25] From the days of resistance in "Socialisme et liberté" to the time of regular collaboration between *Les Temps Modernes* and Trotskyists, the existentialists flirted with the Soviet exile's movement.[26]

Merleau-Ponty's analysis of Trotsky's fate posts a warning to those who would try to trace out a Marxist politics completely independent of the mass organization of the Communist party. Realism calls for the sympathizer to rally to the only existing formation that enjoys mass support and is *engaged* in Marxist politics. Trotskyism, Merleau-Ponty tells his collaborators, verges on abstraction. It reads Marx at the expense of reading contemporary history. It no longer makes contact with the existing structure of power in the world situation.[27]

And yet, Merleau-Ponty's own realization that the Soviet regime

[24] J. Lefebvre-Pontalis, April 29, 1981.

[25] Sartre acknowledges this quite specifically. See "Merleau-Ponty vivant," p. 332.

[26] J.-T. Desanti believes that the Trotskyists in "Socialisme et liberté'" aspired to make Sartre's group their "organe de masse." Interview, April 8, 1981.

[27] See, for example, Merleau-Ponty's disagreement with Lefort over whether a compromise agreement signed by Ho Chi Minh in the Indochina War included too many concessions to French colonial power. "Indochine S.O.S.," p. 1049.

is an "enterprise out of order" counsels distance and criticism. The upshot of his dissatisfaction with Trotskyism is that an existential politics needs a theory with a different sort of practical link to power than that represented by either Trotsky's ambivalent external criticism or by the PCF's direct political organization of the proletariat. Communist popularity vouches for its historical significance, so realism commands that Merleau-Ponty accept the party in some sense as the focal point of an existential politics. For this, he takes advantage of his position as theorist and journalist. His instrument is the word; his preferred medium, *Les Temps Modernes*; and his only concrete contact with Communist politics, the party's intellectuals. As with the other half of his divided audience, an actual dialogue is necessary. But as in that case too, dialogue is not a simple exchange. Contemporary Communism, like liberalism, has an ideological form that excludes existentially validated types of reasoning. To read the dialogue that ensues is to perceive how to use existential political theory to alter the train of Communist thought.

Dealing with Neocommunism

Merleau-Ponty names the general syndrome of contemporary party reasoning "neocommunism" (HT 155, 156, tr. 144, 145; IN 11). Neocommunism is the ideological form complementary to the mixed reality of the USSR. Its hallmarks are a strict subordination of discussion to discipline; the assumption that all spheres of culture are weapons in an ideological battle whose objective is the absolute defense of the USSR (S 328–329, tr. 261); a zigzag policy, sometimes supporting the French government, sometimes precipitating crisis.[28] Instead of frankly admitting its violence, the party conceals it, as when it dismisses Nizan's resignation as the act of a common traitor in the pay of the police (HT 19, tr. xxv). Finally, the neocommunists espouse a strict scientism, "as if [the dialectic] left too large a margin of ambiguity and too broad a field for divergences" (HT 15, tr. xx; cf. SNS 223, tr. 126). Scientism means that for every question there is a single answer. It is the ideology of the revolution in retreat, trying to shore up its position by force of unquestionable discipline. It is the death of political dialogue.

To counter this tendency among Communists, Merleau-Ponty chooses to debate at length not with the party's prewar luminaries

---

[28] "En un combat douteux," pp. 961–964; HT 119, tr. 100.

like Henri Lefebvre or Georges Cogniot, nor with its most rigid new converts like Georges Mounin or Jean Kanapa. Instead, his privileged interlocutor is Pierre Hervé, a man who wanted as much to infiltrate the democratic spirit of the Resistance into the party as to infiltrate the party into other groups.[29] Merleau-Ponty respected Hervé as a thinker[30] and admired him as a man of action. Hervé had been a Communist since age fifteen and during the war had been a leader of the Resistance in southern France. In the postwar period, he was for a while at the very center of a liberalizing movement within the party.[31] Hervé became director of *action*, a weekly paper whose staff was largely Communist, but which showed considerable editorial independence from the party.

In 1946, the party tried to counter the existentialists' popularity by creating an offshoot of *action*. The first issue of *Cahiers d'action* contains several indignant letters to the editor objecting to one of Merleau-Ponty's articles, as well as two articles criticizing Sartre.[32] One article is by Hervé, the other by Georges Mounin. Interestingly, Hervé undertakes to refute Sartre's Husserlian idealism by using as his counterexample not only Marx, but Hegel. Hervé contrasts Husserl's "bracketing" of the world with Hegel's conception of "concrete reality," Husserl's "essences" with Hegel's processes.[33] Hegel and Marx, he says, share a notion of "collective praxis."[34] Differently reasoned was Mounin's critique of existentialism, which repeated the code words of neocommunism: matter, the brain, consciousness reflecting the world.[35]

Merleau-Ponty drives a wedge between the two styles of criticism. Mounin's position amounts to a disregard of "philosophical culture" itself and so gets no more than brief polemical attention. But Hervé he takes seriously. Merleau-Ponty carefully separates misconception from insight and finally complements Hervé's "Hegelo-Marxist," "passably phenomenological" philosophy (SNS

---

[29] Lacouture, *André Malraux: Une vie dans le siècle*, pp. 310–311.

[30] Merleau-Ponty cites Hervé's book, *La libération trahie*, as evidence that an individual can make his integration into the party an engagement combining critical judgment and obedience in good faith (SNS 320–321, tr. 181).

[31] For example, an article he wrote proclaiming that there was "no communist aesthetic" raised eyebrows in the party hierarchy. Desanti, *Les Staliniens*, p. 70.

[32] "Correspondence à propos d'un article de Maurice Merleau-Ponty, 'Le culte du héros,' " *Les Cahiers d'action* 1 (May 1946), pp. 55–61.

[33] Hervé, "Conscience et connaissance," pp. 1–9.

[34] Ibid., pp. 2–3.

[35] Georges Mounin, "Position de l'existentialisme," pp. 36–37.

241, tr. 136). In another article published at about the same time, he explains why tolerance of Hegel is so important. All of the great philosophies of the past century, he claims, from Marx to Nietzsche, from phenomenology to existentialism and psychoanalysis, have Hegel as their source (SNS 109, tr. 63). However, many of these philosophies were anxious to enter the twentieth century unencumbered by their "idealist" paternity. They turned their backs on their origins, settled on different frontiers, and learned to speak new languages, like immigrant children determined to cut their old-world roots.

Yet this heritage means it is possible to avoid incomprehension of the sort represented by Hervé's dismissal of Husserl. Merleau-Ponty suggests that in Hegel "a common language will be found" through which "a decisive confrontation [among contemporary doctrines] can take place" (SNS 110, tr. 63). He encourages Hervé's Hegelianism first because it is the lingua franca that permits the exchange of ideas between existentialists and Communists. More important, one who speaks or even stammers the Hegelian tongue in the party gives voice to a conception of mind that does not exclude dialogue. And dialogue hits the PCF squarely in its scientism.[36]

Merleau-Ponty is most interested in changing the party's stance toward those outside the Politburo who can contribute to the formulation of policy. Here Hervé's attitude toward honesty in politics is the opening for Merleau-Ponty's dialogical strategy. He cites an article in which Hervé responds to detractors who accuse the party of hypocritically invoking the values of democracy in the service of dictatorship (SNS 285, tr. 161). "Does the party engage in double-dealing?," Hervé asks. "No, because the party of freedom is universal and does not hide its goals. More than that, it explains, demonstrates, and shows itself for what it is even through its tactical maneuvers."[37] Hervé claims that the party practices Leninist honesty. Communists are not obliged to pursue a single policy with absolute consistency, but to make their tactics *intelligible*. So far, so good.

Yet neither *action* nor the Communists honored this commitment consistently. Merleau-Ponty selects for criticism an editorial in which *action* approved "without reservations" the outcome of

---

[36] The party soon condemned the Hegel Renaissance. See Jean Kanapa, "Chroniques philosophiques: Les interprètes de Hegel," *La Pensée* 17 (March–April 1948), p. 121.

[37] "Doubles jeux," p. 3.

negotiations between France and the Soviet Union for a mutual assistance treaty.[38] This necessarily endorses the conventional methods of "secret diplomacy," leaving *action* with the role of giving an a posteriori, Marxist gloss to whatever results the negotiations yield (SNS 276, tr. 155). By pushing a patriotic line, the Communists even strengthen the established order without justifying that policy in a revolutionary perspective.

These criticisms elicit a revealing response from Hervé. Without responding to the substance of Merleau-Ponty's complaint, Hervé accuses the philosopher of being a mere "solitary spectator," unconcerned to take an active stand on political issues, unwilling to join a party, unable to see that Communists defend the fatherland because that concept has recently taken on revolutionary signification.[39] What Merleau-Ponty regards as a corruption of Marxist practice is, he says, simply the illusion of an isolated thinker who keeps himself "above the mêlée."

In *Humanism and Terror*, Merleau-Ponty reviews their exchange to show how Hervé's reasoning has taken an undialectical turn. For all the emphasis on political activism, Hervé still neglects to put "the detours and compromises [of Communist politics] back into a general line" (HT 157, tr. 146). By sidestepping the entire issue of making Communist tactics comprehensible to others, Hervé makes further rational discussion impossible. Merleau-Ponty astutely points out that in conversation with the workers themselves, Hervé's evasiveness translates into a manipulative paternalism. "The condition for a valid compromise was, for Lenin, 'to raise . . . the proletariat's general level of consciousness.' For Hervé, it is to 'watch over the permanent interests of the workers.' It can be seen that the criterion has changed. It has moved from the subjective to the objective, . . . that is, toward the consciousness of the leaders" (HT 157, tr. 146). Hervé's reference to "permanent interests" postulates, in contradiction to Marx's theory of the continual evolution of human needs, the existence of certain static requirements of the working class. Hervé asserts, in contradiction to Lenin's theory of communicative leadership, the ability of the party to discern these interests independently of their expression by the workers. His paternalism legitimates the role of leaders who demand the unquestioning obedience of those whose interests they oversee. The Communist who was tolerant of He-

---

[38] Victor Leduc, "Alliance de peuples," *action*, December 15, 1944, p. 1.
[39] Hervé, "Sommes-nous tous des coquins?" p. 3.

gelian dialectics just after the war had now accepted the premises of a scientistic diamat.

Merleau-Ponty concludes that "there is perhaps still a dialectic [that justifies the party's tactics] but it is visible only to the gaze of a God who comprehends universal history" (HT 155, tr. 145). The ironic reference to a comprehending God means that Hervé's new version of party politics presupposes an epistemic position unavailable to any human knower. To be simply a "man situated in his time" (HT 155, tr. 145), as Merleau-Ponty views himself, is to stand in a position more general and representative than that implied by a "solitary spectator." He stands where the limiting conditions of historical knowledge place *all* men. From that vantage point the PCF's politics look more like cynical maneuvering than rationally justified tactics.

So neocommunism follows through on the logic of objectivism. Its manipulative cynicism, like the liberal's moralism, is the consequence of a flawed foundational concept of mind. Where the liberal grounds truth in introspective reason, the Communist adopts the empirical objectivity of positive science as the foundation of knowledge. Those who hold the objective truth on human relations treat others, by method, as objects. To them individuals are like atoms, moving, colliding, subject to attractions and repulsions. But the inconsistency of this perspective discloses its violence: observers who see others as determined objects to be manipulated exempt themselves from their model. Their projects of social engineering proceed from a will not bound by the same laws they see governing the behavior of others. Unchecked by others' opinions, their views stray toward utopias to be imposed by violence on all who disagree with them.

The flaw in Merleau-Ponty's criticism is that his own interpretation of Lenin comes dangerously close to invoking the point of view that his phenomenology declares inaccessible. The problem connects two weaknesses in his philosophy—the residual objectivism in his phenomenology and the vagueness of his concept of dialogue. He believes that he secures the epistemological legitimacy of Lenin's "perceptions" with a theory of historical objectivity that takes account of subjectivity. But the looseness with which Merleau-Ponty speaks of dialogue makes it seem that subjectivity belongs all to the masses and phenomenal objectivity is all Lenin's. Merleau-Ponty gives no evidence that the "dialogue" that produced the NEP was the result of *discussion* within the party or with the people who suffered from War Communism. What he

admired was Lenin's *perceptiveness* with regard to popular senti-
ment and his subsequent openness in confronting the failures of
party policies. At bottom, Merleau-Ponty seems to be building directly on the metaphysical sense of "dialogue" that he employs in
his phenomenology, where dialogue signifies *any* exchange of
meaning between human beings (SC 239, tr. 222; PP 407, tr. 354).
In this sense, if Lenin adjusts his tactics because he is apprehensive about mass opposition, a "dialogue" can be said to have taken
place. But to transfer this general conception of dialogue directly
to politics is to slight any concrete description of the means of in-
stitutionalizing discussion (e.g., political structures that allow information to reach leaders, protections for an independent press)
and of the norms that make institutions of communication work
well (e.g., tolerance for dissent, a certain degree of scepticism
about truth claims). Leninists receive almost a blank check to "constitute" the object of their political action.

If it is objected that this criticism ignores Merleau-Ponty's insistence on the incompletion and ambiguity of every reading of history, one may concede the point—but also remark, with Hervé,
that the philosopher is staying strictly "above the mêlée." One
who simply says that political judgments are difficult or multifac-
eted is not engaging in political judgment. Defending Merleau-
Ponty by reference to ambiguity would reveal him as more interested in characterizing the nature of political perceptions than in
determining conditions for their accuracy. It places him once more
in the position of the Gestalt scientist who studies the process of
perception, but who does not consider his own views as the result
of such a process. At any rate, it does not restrain activists simply
to distract them from their understanding of the political terrain
and to remind them that all perceptions are ambiguous. Unless
one explains better what they have misunderstood, unless one
gives a rationale for norms of dialogue to which they should adhere, they will justifiably respond: we must act, and your uncertainties only delay our action without helping us succeed. It would
have been more engagé for Merleau-Ponty to have related his theory of historical rationality to concrete measures to promote dialogue. Greater democratization of the party apparatus and procedural protections for dissenters go further toward assuring the
sensitivity of leaders to followers than admonitions about ambiguity.

Merleau-Ponty is truer to the deepest inspiration of his philosophy when he criticizes the presuppositions of neocommunism. In

a sense what is at issue between an existential politics and the PCF is the meaning of Marx's dictum, "you cannot transcend philosophy without actualizing it." The PCF interpreted this to mean that the advent of the organized revolutionary class supersedes philosophy as independent criticism. Since philosophy is only a sublimated expression of class interests, the elimination of classes spells the end of philosophy. Prior to that event, any philosophy that claims to support the proletariat while refusing its subordination to proletarian objectives (as set by the party) is hypocritical. Recalling his attitude from his days as a Communist, J.-T. Desanti explains that since the party represents truth in history (it sets in motion those changes that will make social organization respond to man's truest needs and aspirations), the party *itself* stands for philosophy. As a member of this "collective subject," the party philosopher serves his function by obeying; his goal is "not to clarify fully opposing positions, but to keep them away from the masses."[40]

Behind this reasoning lurks an idea that Merleau-Ponty never ceased to contest in his phenomenology—the idea of a final truth. For only if the will of the party is identical with the rational course of history can the subordination of philosophy to leadership be correct. The process theory of truth holds that such identities are never complete. The philosopher contributes to truth by questioning, by engaging in the give-and-take of dialogue, by taking new perspectives. So when Merleau-Ponty paraphrases Marx's formula he introduces a telling nuance: "Philosophy realizes itself by eliminating itself as *separate* philosophy" (SNS 236, tr. 133, emphasis added; cf. PP 520, tr. 456). He once explained this sense of "separate" in an article suggesting that modern metaphysics replaces the distinction between induction and reflection with a continuum of knowledge running from naïve to explicit. The new philosophy is not a "world of separate knowledge" like idealism or science; it seeks to think all phenomena "to the limit" (SNS 171, tr. 97). Merleau-Ponty pursues meaning in novels as much as in philosophy, painting, film, science, and politics. His point is that through phenomenology philosophy becomes worldly and the world becomes philosophical. Marx eliminates philosophy not in the sense of making it disappear, but only in the sense that he joins phenomenology by supporting conditions in which philosophy will no longer constitute a discipline distinct from many others.

[40] J.-T. Desanti, *Le philosophe et les pouvoirs*, pp. 215–218.

So an existential politics is not about to efface itself in obedience to any party. True, as long as the USSR remains an ambiguous form, the Marxian hypothesis commands a position as close to the Communists as philosophical integrity allows. But given the party's emphasis on obedience, an existentialist could only be the party's "external opposition," sympathetic to its goals, critical of its organization and policies.[41] Programmatically an existential politics culminates in "a practical attitude toward Communism of comprehension without adherence and unfettered examination without denigration" (HT 159, tr. 148).

Bloc Thinking

In fact, the existentialists' suspicion of parties was so great that at the first meeting of the editorial board of Les Temps Modernes Sartre asked everyone not to belong to any of them.[42] The existentialists abided by this rule throughout the 1940s, with one minor exception. In 1948, Sartre and Merleau-Ponty joined the Rassemblement Démocratique Revolutionnaire. Formed by men of the non-Communist Left (including Merleau-Ponty's Trotskyist friend, David Rousset), the RDR criticized both Stalinist Communism and capitalist democracy.[43] But the exception was minor because the RDR took pains to stress that it was a "gathering" of members of other parties, not a new party, and Merleau-Ponty held largely aloof from it, quitting the group shortly after its creation. So it is easy to wax ironic about committed philosophers who avoid concrete political commitments.[44] But Merleau-Ponty explains the rationale of their position and the sense in which it remains activistic. "Today's politics is truly the domain of . . . questions posed in such a way that one cannot be part of either of the two forces that are present. We are called to choose between them. Our duty is to do nothing of the sort, to demand clarifications . . . to explain maneuvering, to dissipate myths"(HT 22–23, tr. xxx). The duty of criticism ranks above the desirability of partisanship when the major political formations demand simplistic commitments. Beholden to neither East nor West, the praxis of dissipating myths locates Merleau-Ponty "between the blocs." He inveighs as much against

[41] Beauvoir, La force des choses, I, p. 19.
[42] Merleau-Ponty, La philosophie, émission de André Parinaud, RTF, December 20, 1952.
[43] The best account of the RDR is in Burnier, Choice of Action, pp. 54–64.
[44] Aron, Marxism and the Existentialists, p. 40.

France's colonial policy in Indochina as against the futile manipulation of strikes by the PCF.[45] He warns of the potential for U.S. imperialist penetration into Europe concealed in the Marshall Plan, while pointing out the conditions that could increase the plan's proletarian significance.[46]

Les Temps Modernes shared with other left-leaning reviews such opposition to the Eastern and Western blocs.[47] But only Merleau-Ponty developed the theoretical grounds for distinguishing such a comprehensively critical stance from a typically moralistic way of keeping one's hands clean in a world that demands commitments to some existing structure of political power.

His analysis starts from an observation about structures. He argues that liberalism and neocommunism form a general system of bloc thinking.

> There is an ambiguity in communism that consists in passing off the Russian system as socialist and in confiscating popular movements for its own benefit. But there is a symmetrical and complementary ambiguity of anticommunism: it consists in bringing together into the same camp those who criticize the USSR for good reasons and those who do so for bad ones. To pose the political problem in terms of [a choice] for or against the USSR is to condemn oneself to alliances in confusion. . . . The Enemy Number One ends up being the only one, and one is led by imperceptible degrees to compromise with the others.[48]

Merleau-Ponty's warning is that each bloc, in its eagerness to form massive political fronts, minimizes differences between itself and potential allies. Each side excuses faults, demurely closes its eyes to the nature of the social forces on whom its erstwhile allies depend. The two sides form a single system in the sense that each needs to portray the other as absolute evil to justify its own expansionist moves.

In three editorial dialogues Merleau-Ponty tries to make his con-

[45] Respectively, "Indochine S.O.S." and "En un combat douteux."
[46] "Complicité objective," pp. 1–11.
[47] For instance, Les Temps Modernes and Esprit cooperated in printing appeals for an independent socialist Europe and in protesting the French government's refusal to negotiate with Ho Chi Minh in 1949. Winock, Histoire politique, pp. 272, 323; Boschetti, Sartre et 'Les Temps Modernes', pp. 196–198.
[48] "Preséntation de 'Pages de journal de Victor Serge' " pp. 973–974.

temporaries aware of the distorting pressure that the cold war atmosphere exerts on their thought. The first is with the Catholic novelist and editorialist for *Le Figaro*, François Mauriac. When *Les Temps Modernes* published an anonymous editorial condemning the reassertion of French colonial power in Southeast Asia, Mauriac took up his pen. He begins by defending French rule as the work of a "beneficent civilization, . . . charged with an educative mission with respect to the lesser peoples."[49] But along the way he intimates a deeper concern. He fears that, should France fail its mission, a communist regime will take its place. Merleau-Ponty calls such reasoning "political nominalism": "each chooses his position according to whether it will weaken or strengthen the USSR and does as best he can with his ideas. That is why there are no longer any political problems or true political discussions."[50] Discussion presupposes differentiation—not only the differentiation of minds, but the differentiation of complex phenomena. But when one chooses for or against the USSR, it is not a question of distinguishing progressive from retrograde tendencies in its policies, nor is it a question of focusing on the oppressive practices of a "civilizing" colonialism. Unwilling to examine political phenomena in detail, bloc thinkers erect an impenetrable barrier between themselves and those who challenge their perspectives.

A second effort to expose the corrupted logic of cold war reasoning so outraged André Malraux that he forced Gallimard to expel *Les Temps Modernes* from its office in the publishing house.[51] Merleau-Ponty analyzed the nominalist absurdities in an interview that Malraux had given to the *New York Times*'s C. L. Sulzberger. The revolutionary of *Man's Hope* had evolved since the 1930s into one of the most articulate spokesmen of anticommunism in France. In his interview, however, Malraux claimed he would now be a Trotskyist (rather than the Gaullist that he was) had Trotsky defeated Stalin. Merleau-Ponty objects that such pretentions hardly stand up before the evidence. In the 1930s, when Malraux could have actually contributed to Trotsky's political cause, he effectively supported Stalin. He refused to testify for Trotsky in the

[49] "Le philosophe et l'Indochine," p. 1. Mauriac apparently thought Merleau-Ponty wrote the editorial. It was in fact by Jean Pouillon.

[50] Merleau-Ponty, "Indochine S.O.S.," pp. 1043–1044; cf. SNS 283, tr. 160; "L'adversaire est complice," p. 8.

[51] Lacouture, *André Malraux*, pp. 138, 219–220; Beauvoir, *La force des choses*, I, p. 236.

Dewey investigation, and never publicly denounced the Moscow trials. But Sulzberger outdoes Malraux's nominalist convolutions, reasoning that Malraux's *current* anti-Stalinist/pro-Gaullist stand is, at a deeper level, Stalinist. Sulzberger says that Malraux's opposition to Stalin from within a right-wing party gives the Soviet regime the much needed but specious appearance of being revolutionary (S 314–315, tr. 251).

Far from the ideal of a politics in which things have "one name only," the cold war makes men tread on a slippery terrain where meanings shift with every step. Instead of designating realities, political labels come only to serve them and transform themselves as service requires. The discourse of political nominalism bypasses the moment of reflexivity that stabilizes meanings. It neglects the existential demand that one take on the meaning one's action has in the eyes of others. Political nominalism is but another form of the human problem of the universal imposition of personal meanings.

A third confrontation with bloc thinking, however, was the most significant. While it calls into question the cold warrior's intellectual integrity, it also forces on Merleau-Ponty a reflexive moment he had delayed exercising in his own thinking. In what were to be his last political articles for *Les Temps Modernes*, he begins a process of reassessing the role of violence in Soviet society. David Rousset's exposé of labor camps in the USSR plays a crucial role in bringing about this change of perspective.

By 1949 Rousset had reached the midway point in a postwar evolution that carried him from Trotskyism to Gaullism. It was in part because of his attempt to turn the RDR toward American trade unions that Sartre and Merleau-Ponty ended their affiliation with that group.[52] Their definitive break with Rousset did not come, however, until November 1949, when he published an appeal for an investigation into labor camps in the USSR. *Le Figaro Littéraire* devoted its entire front page to this single item.[53]

It is not because he disputes Rousset's facts that Merleau-Ponty ironically titles his response "The Days of Our Life."[54] (Rousset's

[52] Burnier, *Choice of Action*, p. 63; Beauvoir, *La force des choses*, I, pp. 245–246.

[53] David Rousset, "Au secours des déportés dans les camps soviétiques: Un appel de David Rousset aux anciens déportés des camps nazis," *Le Figaro Littéraire*, November 12, 1949, p. 1ff. I quote from a reprint in *Révolution prolétarienne* 333 (November 1949), pp. 27/347 to 30/350.

[54] The article appears in *Signs* as "The USSR and the Camps." Sartre originally

fictionalized account of the two years he spent in a Nazi concentration camp is titled *The Days of Our Death.*) Irony is a response to bloc thinking. Rousset claims disingenuously not to be charging that Soviet concentration camps do in fact exist. "All" he asks is that a group of former prisoners of Nazi camps be invited by the Soviet government to come to inspect their camps. This investigative committee would inspect only the USSR. Rousset fears diluting its efforts by having it look into allegations of human rights violations around the world.[55]

Rousset isolates the USSR for criticism, Merleau-Ponty charges, in order to ensure the widest support for his attacks. His goal is not to find the truth, but to humiliate one bloc and reinforce the other. He knew that if he had asked for a simultaneous inquiry into Western colonialism or racism, if he had investigated structural forms of violence *in general* rather than in the USSR *in particular*, "his audience would steal away" (S 341, tr. 272). Bloc thinking circumscribes phenomena artificially. It simplifies reality, not because reality is simple, but because it desires to strengthen its political position. Like the neocommunist, the anticommunist bloc thinker subjugates thought to power.

And yet Rousset's articles on Soviet labor camps profoundly upset the program of an existential politics. They move Merleau-Ponty to recant an assessment that had been crucial to the *realism* of the Marxian hypothesis: "Two years ago . . . [I] wrote that Soviet society is ambiguous and that signs of progress and symptoms of regression are found there. . . . If there are ten million in concentration camps . . . , then . . . the entire system changes meaning" (S 333, tr. 265). If the USSR is not an at least potentially socialist polity, then Merleau-Ponty loses what he had accepted as the strongest evidence that history is structured as Marx believed.

What did Rousset say that differed from what the existentialists had known at least since 1946?[56] His article apparently met for the first time a strict evaluative requirement that Merleau-Ponty had always placed on political criticism.[57] An existential politics re-

cosigned the article, but wrote none of it. Sartre, "Merleau-Ponty vivant," pp. 320–332.

[55] Rousset in *Révolution prolétarienne*, pp. 27/347 and 30/350; Rousset, "Le grand retentissement de l'appel de David Rousset," *Le Figaro Littéraire*, November 19, 1949, p. 1.

[56] Koestler discusses the camps in *The Yogi and the Commissar*, p. 265. Merleau-Ponty first mentions them explicitly during a radio broadcast in 1947, cited above.

[57] The dating is somewhat muddled, however, since Merleau-Ponty appears to

quires that a political system be evaluated not according to the amount of violence it perpetrates at a given moment, but by the sens of its violence, by its tendency to perpetuate or abolish itself through time, by its function in a society. Rousset does this. He carefully documents a system of prison camps in the USSR. Using known Soviet law and the testimony of eyewitnesses, he exposes a set of *institutions* for the management of violence in the USSR— special trains to move prisoners, the rule of common-law prisoners over political ones, an administrative Gulag using the camps to finance police activities, camps outfitted for industrial labor and scientific research. Rousset shows that the camps are integral to the "socialist" economy that Merleau-Ponty considered possibly the only positive accomplishment of the revolution to date.

Merleau-Ponty is obliged to reverse many of his findings in *Humanism and Terror*. He agrees that the mitigating circumstances of economic backwardness or the persistence of class resistance cannot account for a system of forced labor. If the Soviets continue to imprison many of their citizens, then the system must engender its own internal opposition. He now states unequivocally that the camps show a system whose meaning has swerved. "There is no socialism when one citizen in twenty is in a camp" (S 332, tr. 264). He goes further. He draws together all the strands of his critique of contemporary Communism. He sees links between work camps and trials where men are forced to repudiate their opinions. He sees the logic of a system that combines harsh inequalities and a "materialism that has always been scarcely dialectical at all" (S 335, tr. 266). From ideology to values, to modes of work, to the exercise of justice, Soviet Communism has given birth to a self-perpetuating *structure* of violence.

Strangely, however, he does not at this point bring himself to reject his notion of Communist *ideals*. Refusing as always any assimilation of Fascism and Communism, he notes that "no Nazi was ever burdened with ideas like the recognition of man by man, internationalism, a classless society. . . . [The Communist] has values *in spite of himself*" (S 337, tr. 268). But this plea was in such strong tension with a philosophy that insisted on judging actions

---

reach the same conclusion in an unsigned editorial in July 1948: "We believe that forced work or work in concentration camps in the USSR . . . has become a permanent element of Soviet production (and correlatively, the police have become a state power) . . . ; consequently, the system has no chance of realizing socialism." "Complicité objective," p. 10.

according to the lived values they embodied, not according to the "nominal" values used to defend them, that it could be no more than a briefly held, transitional opinion in Merleau-Ponty's career. One additional shock was all that was necessary to cut the last ties joining an existential politics to the Soviet Union.

E I G H T

IN SEARCH OF
MERLEAU-PONTY'S
LATE POLITICS

In *The Adventures of the Dialectic*, Merleau-Ponty explains how successive confrontations with the somber realities of the revolutionary experience finally forced him to call into question the guiding assumptions of his politics of the 1940s.

> Could we continue to think, with all necessary reservations concerning the Soviet solutions, that the Marxist dialectic remained valid negatively and that history should be put into perspective, if not according to the proletariat's power, at least according to its lack of it? We do not want to present as a syllogism what became clear to us gradually, in contact with events. But an event was the occasion of an awakening of consciousness and not at all one of those accidents that upsets without enlightening. (AD 337, tr. 230)

The "event" was the outbreak of the Korean War in June 1950, and his enlightenment led to a repudiation of the Marxian perspective. Where before the hypothesis of a revolutionary *sens* of history had informed all of his political thinking, now proof of inexcusable violence and historical disorder set the course of a new politics.

Does the rejection of Marx's philosophy of history compel the theorist to alter his views on the need to avoid moralism, to perceive the violence in the equilibria of political systems, or to join individual action to collective, historically significant movements? Does it compromise the philosopher's tasks of elucidating the foundations of political praxis and of carrying his understanding of social phenomena into a transformative dialogue with others? It is far from obvious that it should. Yet there is a profound sense in which Merleau-Ponty's repudiation of revolutionary politics distances him not only from what was romantic in his Marxism, but also from the most important demands that he put on political

224

thinking. I will contend that from the middle of 1950 until his death in 1961, Merleau-Ponty ceased to work on the foundation of an existential politics in the sense developed in the preceding chapters.

Supporting that conclusion involves two sorts of inquiry. The next chapter asks whether Merleau-Ponty's late political writings are grounded in an alternative theory of meaning and history that conduces to political thinking. But first it is essential to understand the political issues addressed in those late writings and to appreciate the theorist's criticisms of his own assumptions. This chapter examines why the Korean War should move Merleau-Ponty to put Marxism itself into question. There follows a brief chronology of his political activities in the 1950s and then a review of the three key themes of his late politics—a revised conception of the philosopher's engagement, a critique of revolutionary theory, and an endorsement of a new liberalism.

War and Historical Meaning

Merleau-Ponty held the USSR responsible for the Korean War. At the very least, it permitted North Korea to reinforce its own strategic position when it could have intervened to stop the conflict. Sartre recalls Merleau-Ponty's conclusion: "He thought he saw Stalinist doctrine without its mask, and it was Bonapartism."[1] So decisive was this revelation to all of Merleau-Ponty's subsequent political views that Sartre speaks of his friend's "conversion" to a non-Marxist politics.[2]

But why should war be so important to him? Is war not merely another form of the violence that Merleau-Ponty knew afflicted all politics? Could he not reason, like Hegel, that violence between nations (e.g., Rome's imperial conquests) might help universalize man's sense of culture? Such reasoning would make a place for war in the equilibrating processes that advance human freedom. But these questions and Sartre's religious imagery ignore the fact that war had always haunted Merleau-Ponty's theory. War jolted his political consciousness in 1939, and so his existential politics began with the observation that "the war has taken place." He admired the treaty of Brest-Litovsk with which Lenin withdrew Russia from World War I. He charged that only the assumption

---

[1] "Merleau-Ponty vivant," p. 338.
[2] Ibid., p. 347.

that war has already begun made bloc thinking credible.[3] Missed by Sartre and by those who follow his account is what is most important about Merleau-Ponty's choice—not its biographical but its *theoretical* antecedents. Only an examination of the unique place of war in his theory can explain why the Korean conflict is the logical point of closure of an existential politics.

For Merleau-Ponty, war is chaos. It is the polar opposite of historical sens as described by Marx (SNS 218, tr. 124). Several reasons support this judgment. First, in a limit situation like war, historical structures become subject to unpredictable changes of form. According to the Marxian hypothesis historical rationality depends on one condition. It is that the proletariat as a class develop values by tackling the problems of its own situation. Marx believed that one class happens to have been formed whose particular conditions motivate it to discover and to dismantle the principle obstacles to freedom. Its orientation toward progressive change comes only from experiencing its conditions to the full. The workers learn solidarity in the capitalist factory and become radicalized by the exploitative logic of a system that maximizes productivity while minimizing pay. The transition to socialism comes about when this logic finally makes the proletariat the largest class in society while steadily worsening its standard of living. According to this scenario, it is predictable not only that revolution will occur, but that the workers will institute a more just society precisely because they are the first class in history to have the experience, the incentives, and the power to do so.

Modern warfare suspends this historical logic. Now conflicts are decided not by the power of classes, but by the technological sophistication of the combatants. There is thus little assurance that the most humanistically progressive side will win. Likely as not, war issues in political forms hostile to freedom. That is why the threat of "chaos" looms over the proletariat's project. Thus even though World War II ended on terms relatively favorable to the working class, Merleau-Ponty adds that it had the effect of baffling Marx's schema of history to the extent that it "put on the sidelines the most politically mature and class-conscious nations, Italy, Germany, and Russia" (IN 186). Moreover, defense policies skew social priorities in the dominant political systems. If the USA and the USSR are both mixed realities—the one with formal liberties but acting as an accomplice in economic exploitation, the other with a

---

[3] Merleau-Ponty, "L'adversaire est complice," p. 11.

potentially more rational economy but still wearing the stains of a terror exercised against its own people—it is not war that is going to resolve their contradictions.[4] Investments in arms hardly promise an economy of abundance.

Second, since Merleau-Ponty held the USSR responsible for North Korean aggression, the invasion was a coup de grâce for any lingering belief that the USSR might be a nonexpansionist type of state—a premise he had stressed at least since 1947.[5] While one could explain the nonhumanist traits of the USSR by such contingent factors as the country's isolation or lack of industrial development, there were no extenuating circumstances that could explain how an expansionist war might play a role in the development of socialism.[6]

Third, war generates the maximum degree of polarization in political relations. By reducing political choices to two, for or against, war and its propaganda create a gap that communication cannot cross (HT 188, tr. 182). War is the moment when even the dissenters within each camp rally to the official position in order to fend off the greater evil. Nuance and impartial criticism become impotent. That is why "there will be no clarity in history except by peace." That is why the danger of war so preoccupies Merleau-Ponty in his conclusion to *Humanism and Terror*. He underlines the importance of not anticipating war, of not employing habits of thought that are its symbolic equivalent, of opposing any preventive war against the USSR (HT 186–190, tr. 179–184).

It is not implausible then that he would see a renewal of armed conflict between East and West with the utmost concern. On the very eve of the Korean War he wrote:

If a war occurs tomorrow or in two years . . . our effort will make little difference. But if, as is possible, the cold war lasts twenty years . . . , we will have . . . kept and serviced the instruments of a political discussion in a time that knows less and less how to use them because it is haunted by power blocs. . . . Perhaps a day will come when [the generals and

---

[4] I am elaborating on the second factor that Merleau-Ponty cites in his notes as an explanation for an "accentuation of the role of the will" in the USSR since 1917. The entire list reads: "(1) Industrialization, forced collectivization; (2) preparation for war, with correlative measures that lead to a lowering of living standards; (3) introduction of nonsocialist incentives . . . ; (4) suppression of the Komintern and proletarian politics; (5) strengthening of denunciations" (IN 106).

[5] HT 190, tr. 184; SNS 275, tr. 155; "Complicité objective," p. 10.

[6] Interview with Claude Lefort, May 22, 1981.

the ambassadors] alone will be able to speak. In our opinion, that will be a day of misfortune because the victor, whoever he may be, will carry everywhere *his* evil along with *his* good.[7]

The outbreak of war literally made "non-sense" of his existential politics. It forced him to make the judgment on Communist values that he had avoided when learning of the work camps. Finally admitting that the USSR was a state like any other knocked the wind out of the project of steering *Les Temps Modernes* alongside Communist politics, or even of engaging in the subtle praxis of trying to tie Communist thought back to its humanist roots in dialogue. Furthermore, war collapsed the ever-shrinking space that *Les Temps Modernes* had cleared for itself between the blocs. It made a search for disinterested interlocutors on either Right or Left futile. With the outbreak of the Korean War, Sartre reports, Merleau-Ponty decided that their journal would have to impose silence on itself in political affairs. Not dialogue, but naked force was about to settle the differences between the blocs.[8]

Merleau-Ponty's interpretation of the Korean War thus fits into an overall perspective that commanded a change in his political orientation. That is why Sartre's characterization of his change of attitude as a "conversion" is misleading. The theory of war and the commitment to evaluate a system according to the structural character of its violence were among the most deeply entrenched components of Merleau-Ponty's existential politics. His choice in 1950 was consistent with his ideas and his perception of the facts, which is to say that they have as valid a claim to being theoretically motivated as human choices ever do.

Postexistential Politics

After abandoning the Marxian hypothesis, Merleau-Ponty never again took up a revolutionary cause. His belief in the uniqueness of that hypothesis and his political realism spared him some of the more embarrassing turns in radical theory in the coming decades (e.g., with certain members of the Frankfurt school, seeking an alternative universal class in Third World peasants, or in students, or in exploited ethnic minorities). Did he, however, become apolitical or socially conservative toward the end of his life, as a num-

---

[7] "L'adversaire est complice," p. 10.
[8] Sartre, "Merleau-Ponty vivant," p. 338.

ber of interpreters have implied?[9] A brief biographical review of his activities in the last decade of his life sets the context for my argument that while he maintained a political presence in the 1950s, his late writings do not measure up to the *theoretical* tasks that he knew an adequate politics must fulfill.

Merleau-Ponty wrote no more political commentary for *Les Temps Modernes* after July 1951. His last article for the journal, "Indirect Language and the Voices of Silence," published in mid-1952, concerned primarily the history of art and linguistic theory. It was an excerpt from a larger work on the creation of meaning in literary language titled *The Prose of the World*. Claude Lefort believes that this work, which Merleau-Ponty had worked on from 1948 but never finished, is the "index of a new stage" in the philosopher's thought; it contains "the first signs of the 'indirect ontology' " that is the subject of Merleau-Ponty's late philosophy.[10]

It would be wrong to infer, however, that aesthetic preoccupations entirely displaced political ones in Merleau-Ponty's works of this period. *The Prose of the World* contains important reformulations of his ideas on history, dialogue, and the perception of other people—topics that are central to his political theory. In September 1951 in Geneva he devoted the last third of his talk on "Man and Adversity" to a very concrete discussion of the problems of juridical politics, ambiguities in the policies of the great powers, and economic development in the Third World (S 299–303, tr. 236–239). If there is a period of political silence in the last decade of Merleau-Ponty's life, it lasted only for about a year and a half following these publications—and it was far from a time without political controversy for him.

That period saw Merleau-Ponty's departure from *Les Temps Modernes* and Sartre's decision to collaborate closely with the French Communist party. The story of Sartre's "radical conversion" is too well known to bear repetition here.[11] Still a director of a journal that was growing closer to the PCF, Merleau-Ponty silently attended its editorial meetings and accepted tendentious articles on colonialism, Korea, and the United States. Two incidents finally

[9] Sartre's "Merleau-Ponty vivant" is again partly at fault (esp. pp. 359–360). Cf. Kruks, *The Political Philosophy of Merleau-Ponty*, pp. 125–126; Langan, *Merleau-Ponty's Critique of Reason*, p. 94; Tilliette, "Une philosophie sans absolu," p. 226.

[10] Claude Lefort, Editor's Preface to Merleau-Ponty, *The Prose of the World*, trans. O'Neill, pp. xviii, xix; and Madison, *The Phenomenology of Merleau-Ponty*, pp. 89–94.

[11] Sartre, "Merleau-Ponty vivant," pp. 347–349; Burnier, *Choice of Action*, pp. 71–75; Poster, *Existential Marxism*, pp. 164–173.

provoked his departure. The first involved Sartre's treatment of an article by Claude Lefort. The French government's clumsy attempt in May 1952 to control an anti-American demonstration organized by the Communists so enraged Sartre and so hardened his sympathy for the PCF that he was moved to write a series of articles—with Merleau-Ponty's encouragement—on "The Communists and Peace." Sartre's conclusion that peace is the highest goal of the Soviet camp is less startling than his assessment of the situation of the working class in France. He argues that the Communist party is *identical* with the working class because only the well-defined leadership that it provides can unify the workers into a whole and thereby create the politically effective force necessary to overcome exploitation. Lefort, then a regular contributor to *Les Temps Modernes*, was highly critical of this reduction of workers to the passive instruments of a bureaucratized, Stalinist party.[12] When Sartre wrote a bitter rejoinder to Lefort's proposed article, Merleau-Ponty faced the unpleasant task of mediating the dispute and convinced both to remove some of their most violent passages.[13] That "le grand Sartre" would treat the young Lefort so harshly added to Merleau-Ponty's alienation from the journal. The second incident involved Sartre's decision to print Pierre Naville's "États-Unis et contradictions capitalistes" ("The United States and the Contradictions of Capitalism"). Merleau-Ponty agreed to publish the Trotskyist's article, but joined to it an editorial caption mentioning "the contradictions of socialism." Sartre eliminated the caption. Upon receiving the page proofs, probably in April 1953, Merleau-Ponty phoned Sartre to terminate his association with the journal.[14] This move was unlikely to send a man of his stature into the political, philosophical, or journalistic wilderness. But, for purposes of understanding the relationship of his subsequent political reflections to an existential politics, it did have three effects worth noting: it removed him from direct contact with his closest interlocutors; it distanced him in the public eye from the "existential" milieu; and it disaffiliated him from the journal most directly associated with "engagement."

In January 1953 Merleau-Ponty was awarded the most prestigious official distinction a philosopher can earn in France, a chair at the Collège de France. Jules Monnerot, no doubt recalling his

---

[12] Lefort, "Le Marxisme et Sartre," pp. 1541–1570.

[13] Sartre, "Merleau-Ponty vivant," pp. 353–354.

[14] Ibid., p. 355. Naville's article continued in the May issue of *Les Temps Modernes*.

debate with Merleau-Ponty over *Humanism and Terror*, saw this appointment as "un Waterloo universitaire." But those who selected him esteemed him as much for his political sensibility as for his sensitivity to the relationship between science and metaphysics.[15] In his inaugural address to the Collège, "In Praise of Philosophy," Merleau-Ponty went beyond the traditional bows to those who had held this chair before him—Henri Bergson and Louis Lavelle—to use the example of Socrates to discuss the role of the philosopher in the city. Once more he took up Hegel, Marx, Machiavelli, the mainstays of his political meditations. And he pursued his interest in the philosophy of history by suggesting that it be modelled on Saussurean linguistics. Among his first courses at the Collège were ones on a Weberian theory of history, on institutions, and on dialectical philosophy.

Of a less formal character were his contributions to *L'Express*. This popular weekly magazine sought to develop a program for the non-Communist Left and was especially supportive of Pierre Mendès-France's short-lived reformist governments.[16] Through his friend Madelaine Chapsal Merleau-Ponty made known his desire to "speak to a greater number" of people than his chair at the Collège permitted.[17] Frequently in 1954 and 1955, and sporadically until 1959, Merleau-Ponty wrote columns on political topics such as the future of the communist revolution, majority rule, and French colonialism.[18]

He published his last exclusively political work, *The Adventures of the Dialectic*, in 1955. Declaring himself a liberal in the tradition of Max Weber, he blames Marx for the tendency of revolutionary movements to vacillate between subjectivistic and objectivistic understandings of history. Over half of the work is an explicit critique of Sartre's essays on "The Communists and Peace." His polemic stirred critical reactions from some of his most distinguished interlocutors of the past—from Communists like Georges Lukacs, Henri Lefebvre, and J.-T. Desanti,[19] from the Sartrean Simone de Beauvoir,[20] and from liberals like Brice Parain and Raymond

---

[15] Bataillon, "Éloge prononcé devant l'Assemblée des Professeurs du Collège de France, le 25 juin 1961," p. 38.

[16] Rabil, *Merleau-Ponty*, p. 108.

[17] Siritzky and Roth, *Le roman de l'express*, p. 75.

[18] Cooper reviews these columns in *Merleau-Ponty and Marxism*, pp. 143–158.

[19] In Lukacs et al., *Mésaventures de l'antimarxisme*.

[20] "Merleau-Ponty et le pseudo-Sartrisme," in *Privilèges*, pp. 185–250.

Aron.[21] This time, however, Merleau-Ponty did not respond to his critics as he had in *Humanism and Terror*. In fact, he did not respond at all. *The Adventures of the Dialectic* reads less like a call for continuing dialogue than like the closing statement of a man satisfied with his position and uninterested in reopening the debate.[22]

The mid-1950s were years of travel for Merleau-Ponty, and most of these travels had a political point. In Venice in October 1956 he attended a conference of writers, scientists, and philosophers from Eastern and Western Europe. Their purpose was to promote mutual understanding of social and cultural conditions in their countries. Merleau-Ponty contributed extensively to debates on the relation between the truth of ideas and socioeconomic systems. Curiously his most important exchange on this topic was with a man who was normally only a few metro stops away in Paris— Jean-Paul Sartre.[23] In 1955 and 1956 the Alliance Française sent Merleau-Ponty to speak in Africa and in 1957 to Madagascar. In such countries as Tunisia, the Belgian Congo, Rhodesia, and Kenya, he did not hesitate to discomfit his colonial audiences by lecturing them on three sensitive topics: race, the sociology of colonization, and underdevelopment.[24]

In early 1959 Merleau-Ponty began working intensively on *The Visible and the Invisible*. This book, which was unfinished at the time of his death, was intended not merely to make the conclusions of his earlier phenomenology of perception more profound, but to "recommence everything" by exploring the ontological signification of the coupling of body and world while rigorously avoiding all dualistic categories (VI 172, tr. 130). Even the abstractness inherent in an ontology of "brute Being," however, did not divert his attention from political affairs. In a series of twelve interviews with Georges Charbonnier, broadcast on the French national radio network in 1959, Merleau-Ponty promulgated his

[21] Parain, "Querelle de Khâgneux," p. 44; Aron, "The Adventures and Misadventures of Dialectics," in *Marxism and the Existentialists*, pp. 45–80.

[22] Susanne Merleau-Ponty was indignant when the Communists held a conference criticizing *The Adventures of the Dialectic* while her husband was out of the country. When he learned of it, however, he was not at all perturbed. Interview, April 13, 1981.

[23] "Discordia Concors: Rencontre Est-Ouest à Venise," pp. 216–217. See Rabil, *Merleau-Ponty*, pp. 145–147.

[24] *Les voyages du philosophe, II*, Merleau-Ponty interviewed by Georges Charbonnier; cf. S 408–423, tr. 328–340. His lectures drew heavily on Claude Lévi-Strauss's *Race et histoire*.

opinions on changes in the Communist world and on colonialism. He worked in the provisional bureau of revived Mendesist groups and presided over one of their debates about "the relationship between democracy and socialism."[25] In 1959 France was mired in a colonial war against Algerian independence; Merleau-Ponty and Sartre agreed in their opposition to the war.[26] Disgusted by the Socialist Prime Minister Guy Mollet's Algerian policy, Merleau-Ponty returned his red ribbon of the Légion d'honneur.[27] Sartre, now far to his left, lent his support to the "manifesto of the 121," which declared the right of French conscripts to refuse to fight in the Algerian war.[28] Sartre's colleagues Jean Pouillon and J. Lefebvre-Pontalis tried unsuccessfully to persuade Merleau-Ponty to support the manifesto. Ever the realist, he feared that it would have too little popular appeal since it exposed any signatory to the threat of prosecution.[29] He then helped draw up a more moderate manifesto underlining the moral seriousness of the choices that the government was imposing on the young and calling for a negotiated peace.[30] By promoting this manifesto—his last political act—Merleau-Ponty enabled thousands of teachers who would not have signed the "manifesto of the 121" to make known their opposition to France's Algerian policy.[31] He asked for and got Raymond Aron's signature.[32]

Late 1960 saw the publication of his last book, *Signs*, which gathered together many of his political essays from the 1950s. It also contained a significant new preface, in which he deepened his critique of communist politics and gave a few hints about the relation between his recent ontological speculations and politics. The last of his writings that he saw published was a defense of this preface against Olivier Todd's charge that his personal reminiscences about Paul Nizan contributed to an apolitical reading of the works of the young revolutionary.[33] Merleau-Ponty's reply exposes the bad faith of Todd's assumptions, his "communist attitude without

---

[25] "L'avenir du socialisme" (debate directed by Maurice Merleau-Ponty), pp. 27–42.

[26] Sartre, "Merleau-Ponty vivant," p. 371; S 338, 341, tr. 252.

[27] Audry, "La vie d'un philosophe," p. 35.

[28] Burnier, *Choice of Action*, p. 125; Beauvoir, *La Force des Choses, II*, p. 312.

[29] Interview with Jean Pouillon, July 20, 1979.

[30] "Maurice Merleau-Ponty est mort," *Le Monde*, May 6, 1961, p. 1.

[31] Suffert, "Chronique: Maurice Merleau-Ponty," p. 82.

[32] Aron, *Mémoires*, p. 391.

[33] Todd, "Nizan et ses croque-morts," pp. 15–16.

communism."[34] In a discussion with Madeleine Chapsal, he returned to his critique of Marx's philosophy of history and called for a "pure politics" based on the spread of information and knowledge.[35] He attended a lecture that Sartre gave on his *Critique of Dialectical Reason* and visited an exhibition of paintings on Hiroshima for which Sartre wrote the accompanying commentary.[36] His last interview insisted on the interdependence of philosophy and politics.[37] His final lecture at the Collège de France—the very day before his death—reviewed how the Marxist notion of praxis becomes a "technique of power" once the revolution has succeeded and asked whether the Soviet Union was not itself about to realize that a socialist society cannot be pure positivity.[38]

In no sense then do we discern the reticence of an apolitical man in Merleau-Ponty's activities and writings in the decade after his disillusionment with communism. He was neither at a loss for political views, nor opposed to political activism, nor as a defender of government intervention in the economy and as an opponent of the Algerian war, inclined to conservatism. We see a man who continued to believe that a philosophy in contact with lived experience has an obligation to take account of the political world. But what *sort* of account of politics is necessary, and what is the relationship of the *philosopher* to political action? Merleau-Ponty's answers to those questions reveal that what he sought in the 1950s was not exactly *dégagement*, but a stronger differentiation of the roles of activists and philosophers.

The Philosopher and the City

As the political editor of a journal whose theme was engagement, Merleau-Ponty believed in the 1940s that writing could contribute to progressive action. He emphatically rejected intellectual life conceived as autonomous reflection. "The intellectual who refuses his [responsibilities] on the pretext that his function is to express everything there is to say is in fact contriving to live a pleasant life

---

[34] "Réponse à Olivier Todd," pp. 17–18. Todd replied in "Réponse à Merleau-Ponty," *France-Observateur*, March 9, 1961, p. 14.

[35] Chapsal, *Les écrivains en personne*, p. 162.

[36] Interview with Jean Pouillon, July 20, 1979, and with Michel Contat, May 20, 1981; Cohen-Solal, *Sartre*, p. 576.

[37] Weber, "Un entretien avec Maurice Merleau-Ponty: La philosophie et la politique sont solidaires" (1960), p. 9.

[38] "Philosophie et non-philosophie depuis Hegel" (II), p. 173.

under the guise of obeying a vocation. His conviction is to be without conviction. . . . But such sincerity is deceitful. . . . From the moment we do something, we turn toward the world, stop self-questioning, and go beyond ourselves in action" (SNS 317, tr. 179). Merleau-Ponty's own action, I have argued, took place in the politics of his theory, in his dialogue with Communist and liberal critics. The rapprochement of phenomenology and Marxism, the encouragement of Hegelianism, the depiction of Lenin as the perceiver of the historical situation—such interpretive moves were designed to correct those tendencies in the Communist party that cut it off from the legitimating conditions of historical rationality and to convince liberals to reexamine the relationship of violence and freedom. He did not equate dialogue with direct political action, but the practical intentions guiding his political commentary nonetheless presupposed that writers and philosophers could aim at political influence without betraying their vocations.

In his inaugural address to the Collège de France Merleau-Ponty begins to differentiate the roles of the philosopher and the politician in ways that contradict this earlier understanding of engagement. The philosopher, he says, pays the closest attention to men of action and passion, but does so precisely because he is not one of them. True politicians live within the dialectic of coexistence. They work with the ruses of power—and use them to hide their actions. The philosopher, on the other hand, is one who bears witness and who explains the dialectic (EP 68, tr. 58–59). The loyalties of even that sly enthusiast of political life, Niccolò Machiavelli, were more intellectual than political. He was anything but Machiavellian, because he exposed the cruel techniques of power for all to see. The philosopher is thus "a stranger in the fraternal mêlée" of politics. He is one who "even if he has not betrayed, gives the impression by his manner of being faithful, that he could betray" (EP 69, tr. 60).

In a most profound discussion of the trial of Socrates, Merleau-Ponty illustrates his view of the tension between the philosophical and the political vocation. Hardly one to pursue power, Socrates is nonetheless decidedly part of the City's public life. He questions its citizens, he obeys its laws. Accused of a crime, he does not flee. He remains to *testify*. Yet in his defense before the City's tribunal, his testimony is also a form of defiance. "He appears before the judges . . . to explain to them what the City is"—because they do not know (EP 46, tr. 38). He lives his relationship to the City at a distance, defending the community that made him what he is, but justifying the City only "for reasons that are his own" (EP 43, tr. 35). This is what the authorities cannot accept. As one who inquires into the reasons for what the City does, the philosopher is not a participant in its politics in the same way as others. If he is to confront the City with its truth, he cannot join its intrigues and speak in the simplifying language of the politician. Socrates anticipates Merleau-Ponty's ideal of "a philosophy that is all the less tied down by political responsibilities to the extent that it has its own, one that is all the freer to enter everywhere to the extent that . . . it does not *play* at passions, at politics, and at life" (S 20, tr. 13).

We have seen that a melding of the obligations of the writer and the political actor is an integral part of a philosophy of praxis. Merleau-Ponty and Sartre agreed that since *vérité* is always *à faire*, no writer can claim simply to reproduce truths that already exist. What was so serious in the actions of resisters and collaborators, Merleau-Ponty contended in *Humanism and Terror*, was that each was fighting, and often writing, for a society that would come into being only by virtue of their efforts. Their "truths" were creative assertions of a community's desires, not representations of an immutable natural order. In a philosophy of engagement words and deeds are similar in ontological status. It follows that if Merleau-Ponty strongly differentiates the philosopher and the politician in the 1950s, his reasoning must be grounded in some deeper distinction that calls into question the premises of engagement. That deeper distinction is between seeing and doing.

"Inasmuch as he sees, [man] . . . is present everywhere without distance, even among those who do, and he obstinately imposes his presence on them even while knowing they do not want it" (AD 260, tr. 177). To see is to be present to objects without being in contact with them. Seeing dominates things. It glides around objects, it knows what they are without feeling their resistance. But when one does something, contact is unavoidable. Reshaping something requires handling it and being sensitive to the particularities of its materials. The sculptor knows that the marble has qualities unimaginable to those who merely gaze at its surface. Likewise, the political actor is one who tries to shape events and behavior, while the writer is one who by vocation analyzes and represents whatever phenomena he sees.

This abstract distinction has a very concrete target—the most famous philosopher of an engaged literature, Jean-Paul Sartre. In *The Adventures of the Dialectic*, Merleau-Ponty sets forth his position on the issues that provoked his departure from *Les Temps Modernes*.[39] His book is not, for all that, another corrective dialogue. With a bluntness and firmness of tone absent from his earlier writings, he explains why Sartrean engagement is not just misformulated (and therefore susceptible of correction), but fundamentally misconceived.

The central fallacy of engagement comes from confusing the writer's seeing with the activist's doing.[40] Just as when we see we forget that we do not perceive absolute objects and mistake our bodily syntheses for what is really there, so the writer who is wholly involved in reporting forgets that he is part of the spectacle. The ease with which vision surveys the world gives rise to a complementary dream of pure action (AD 259, tr. 177). Pure action, like vision, seems to meet no resistance from the world. Its initiator claims to escape the conditions of emotion and appearance. His action, as Sartre said in "What Is Literature?" is an unveiling. As such it accommodates every nuance and reservation. Sartre the journalist *writes* that the Communist party is a force of pure negation and then he thinks he can still judge the party freely. Ultimately, Merleau-Ponty charges, Sartre's idea of direct engagement is based on the same sort of epistemological fallacy that misleads traditional liberals and neocommunists—the myth of the "spectatorial consciousness" (AD 259, tr. 177).

Free judgment lasts only so long as the writer does not try to *do* anything in the party (AD 257, tr. 174). Accordingly, if the Communists sometimes tolerate Sartre, it is because he has temporarily muted his differences with the party and because circumstances have created a situation in which the party finds the writer's contemplative stance useful. Yet such tolerance, far from confirming the wisdom of engagement, only means that doers profit from the illusions of seers. This is not shocking. Merleau-Ponty would even agree that a party is not completely wrong to be impatient with writers for its obligation is "never to lose contact with events." To shore up its popularity it must simplify its views and dissimulate changes of direction. What is disturbing, however, is a party that silences all internal criticism for the sake of truths that may never take shape, precisely because they are never challenged and discussed.

[39] *Les aventures de la dialectique*, Merleau-Ponty interviewed by Georges Charbonnier, RTF, 1959.
[40] Goyard-Fabre, "Merleau-Ponty et la politique," p. 256.

In other words, because action and vision are so different, asserting their equivalence threatens the integrity of both. Bringing the attributes of vision into action turns politics into oppression. It makes politicians inattentive to the capabilities and needs of those who are governed (AD 260, tr. 177). It leads to a politics that tries to mix opposite forms (like democracy and revolution) because, with no understanding born of practice, it does not appreciate their incompatibilities (AD 280, tr. 190). Bringing the attributes of political action into cultural production, on the other hand, restricts the writer's imagination and prevents him from testifying truthfully about what he sees.[41] Thus, Merleau-Ponty concludes, "recognizing literature and politics as distinct activities is perhaps the only way to be as faithful to action as to literature" (AD 294, tr. 201). Not just an editorial quarrel with Sartre, but a revision of his own idea of the relationship of politics and culture was at the root of his departure from *Les Temps Modernes*.

It should be emphasized that while his arguments repudiate Sartrean direct engagement, they still allow for two forms of indirect engagement. One form is personal. Max Weber, for example, favored "the political engagement of professors, provided that it is outside of the classroom, in essays that are offered up for discussion" (AD 43, tr. 26). This engagement is indirect in that it does not let political passions infuse the content of teaching and it does not presuppose the immediate efficacy of ideas. In a sense it is no longer the philosopher or the sociologist who is engaged, but the citizen. That is why Merleau-Ponty immediately follows up his discussion of the philosopher and the politician with the observation that the distinction he is drawing is not between two types of person; it is a distinction "within man himself, the difference between one who understands and one who chooses" (EP 69, tr. 60). He is arguing that, at a given moment, it is possible to be faithfully one or the other, but not both. Merleau-Ponty's numerous political essays of the 1950s presuppose such differentiation. Typical is an article on De Gaulle's accession to power after an uprising of Algerian colonists, in which Merleau-Ponty argues that "our role is to understand what has just ended and what is beginning" (S 422, tr. 340). Understanding proposes no solutions. At most it outlines the conditions for a clarification of French politics. Even this lim-

---

[41] Merleau-Ponty addresses this problem most fully in his encounter with Sartre in 1956. See "Discordia Concors: Rencontres Est-Ouest à Venise," pp. 212–213.

ited engagement, however, is pronounced not ex cathedra, but from the editorial page of *Le Monde*.

There is, nonetheless, an efficacy of the philosopher's understanding—the second form of indirect engagement. "If the philosopher makes known right now something that the great man says as an aside, he saves truth for everyone, even for the man of action" (EP 70, tr. 61). The philosopher's truth is a form of action, but its effect is for the long term.[42] Merleau-Ponty does not cease to see philosophy as praxis, but he denies that its effects are immediate or can be intended. How many individuals have had more influence on Western civilization than Socrates? Yet certainly he would have nullified his importance at the start had he sought to curry favor at his trial by renouncing his religious views or by bringing his weeping children to capture the jury's sympathy. It is precisely the philosopher's distance from the norms of action that permits him to function *effectively* as critic and witness.[43] Fulfilling the philosopher's role, in other words, depends on *not* calculating the consequences of one's statements, on not adjusting ideas to suit the views of others, on not attenuating criticism for "reasons of state."

This conception of the philosophic vocation distinguishes Merleau-Ponty's project of the 1950s from that of the 1940s in an absolutely crucial way. It means that his late work rests on a claim that the integrity of philosophy depends on its *not thinking politically*. It is important not to misunderstand this point. This is not to say that his early political essays are dishonest or manipulative or that his late works disregard the complexities of political affairs. But in the 1940s he wrote in constant awareness that efficacy and appearance were not defects of the political world, but its defining characteristics, and therefore that any statement claiming to truth in that world had to be shaped in light of those characteristics— whence the obliqueness of his dialogues with existentialists, liberals, and Communists. In the 1950s Merleau-Ponty's political truths will be much more straightforward. They take place within the parameters of indirect engagement. As witness, he seeks to understand the complex structures of meaning in the contemporary world. As critic, he seeks to expose above all the reasons for the disastrous "adventures" of revolutionary politics.

[42] Merleau-Ponty in Chapsal, *Les écrivains en personne*, p. 145.
[43] Rabil, *Merleau-Ponty*, p. 149.

The Critique of Marxism and Revolution

In his critical guise Merleau-Ponty brings essentially three charges against Marxism. The first rests upon the concept of "adversity." After arguing that neither American capitalism nor Marxian socialism provide schemata suitable for understanding the problems of Third World economic development, Merleau-Ponty introduces this new concept: "When our initiatives get bogged down in the thick pulp of the body, of language, or of the world . . . , there is no *malin génie* who is opposed to our wishes; there is only a sort of inertia, a passive resistance, a falling away of meaning, an anonymous *adversity*" (S 304, tr. 239).[44] Adversity signifies the dead weight of established practices and meanings; it stands as much for the preconscious sexuality that motivates behavior as for the difficulty of expressing new ideas in a language burdened with literary formulas. In a sense "adversity" is only another name for one of Merleau-Ponty's most familiar themes. Ever since writing *The Phenomenology of Perception*, he had criticized theories that were unable to conceptualize the resistance of social structures, and he had always conceded that such resistance could block necessary political transformations.

But adversity has a newly pessimistic connotation. It expresses a feeling that what human initiative does not control almost inevitably opposes itself to our conscious projects. Marx made a very different assumption. He believed that a single class could be a spontaneous summation of the progressive forces of history and therefore that, even if theory could not chart every turn of the historical process, the revolution stood a good chance of reaching its term. Praxis draws in the lines between points of historical reference that theory locates. Merleau-Ponty's revised concept of social inertia holds that such confidence is unfounded. It implies that no political movement has the momentum to carry it on a straight line between two widely separated points.

In *The Adventures of the Dialectic* he argues that the vagaries and the violence of Marxist politics are due to its confrontation with an anonymous adversity in social relations (AD 142, 213, tr. 95, 145).

---

[44] The term was from *Being and Nothingness*, where Sartre spoke of a "coefficient of adversity." Merleau-Ponty added in an interview: "It seems to me that [Sartre's] idea should be generalized. I have called 'adversity' . . . that which opposes itself in fact to the realization . . . of harmony, of agreement with oneself, with others, but what opposes these things without being an adversary that one can name." "L'homme et l'adversité," RTF, broadcast on September 15, 1951.

The German revolution of 1918 failed; the proletariat never emerged as a global force; the Bolshevik revolution generated a bureaucracy that put an end to revolutionary spontaneity. The problem is that Marx postulated the existence of a force of *pure negation* in history (AD 133, tr. 89). He assumed that the proletariat would suppress itself and, with itself, the entire class-ridden dynamic of history. But the disappointments of the revolutionary experience show that "the proletariat as 'self-suppression' cannot be found; we only find proletarians who think and want this or that, who are exalted or discouraged, who see well or poorly" (AD 133, tr. 89; cf. S 14, tr. 8). What the theorist fails to include in his historical schemata is precisely what drags the proletariat away from its "mission." The workers are part of the positivity of the social order. They partake of its partialities and foibles. Even the bureaucratization of the revolution reflects this truth. At some point revolutionaries must cease their destruction in order to create regular procedures and lasting institutions designed to cope with the exigencies of everyday life.[45] But an institution, because it must accomplish something—keep order, distribute goods—cannot be in a state of perpetual revolt and destruction. This denial of pure negation is the result of adversity: any social group carries within itself and encounters in its experience "positive" inertial forces that prevent it from simply recreating the world.

Marxists themselves are not unaware of the problem of adversity. But their very attempts to express the dead weight of social practices elicits Merleau-Ponty's second criticism: Marxist writings and practice frequently recur to a violent objectivism. Merleau-Ponty finds the best proof of this assertion in the careers of two Marxist theorists whom he greatly admired, Georges Lukacs and Leon Trotsky. Faced with an event such as the failure of the German revolution, Lukacs was forced to admit that his idea of history in *History and Class Consciousness* lacked "the means to express the inertia of infrastructures" (AD 98, tr. 64); it failed to anticipate the resistance the proletariat would meet.[46] After 1923 Lukacs frequently bowed to the pressure of party orthodoxy and spoke of

---

[45] Miller, *History and Human Existence*, pp. 220–221.

[46] For an explanation of possible lines of influence between Lukacs's *History and Class Consciousness* and Merleau-Ponty's Marxism of the 1940s, see Miller, *History and Human Existence*, p. 205; and Schmidt, *Maurice Merleau-Ponty*, pp. 123, 201. Merleau-Ponty may have learned of Lukacs's work first through Raymond Aron's *La sociologie allemande contemporaine* (Paris: Presses Universitaires de France, 1936), pp. 77–78.

consciousness as a "reflection." Trotsky's virtual capitulation to Stalin came from a similar theoretical inadequacy. The primary advocate of regulating revolutionary activism through a dialogical reading of the proletariat's consciousness, Trotsky refused to appeal to the proletariat against Stalin's designs to dominate the party in the mid-1920s. Why such circumspection? Because, Merleau-Ponty contends, he believed in a "scientific socialism" that treats the revolution as immanent in "things." This revolution, whatever its deviations, will necessarily end exploitation as long as the party remains proletarian in composition (AD 125–126, tr. 84).

Merleau-Ponty most clearly departs from his earlier interpretations when he attributes responsibility for the naïve realism of the French Communists, Lukacs, Lenin, and Trotsky to Marx himself. Following the defeat of the revolutions of 1848, Merleau-Ponty now observes, Marx began to speak of "matter," "relations of production," "positive knowledge," and technical action (AD 124–125, tr. 83; cf. EP 61–62, tr. 53). The 1848 revolutions must have failed because the material conditions were not ripe. Marx struggled to account for the "thickness" of social relations by placing them out of easy reach of human will, in "things." That theoretical choice has grave consequences. The counterpart to extreme objectivism is extreme subjectivism: the party claims unique access to the truth, places itself beyond criticism, and treats others as passive objects of political control (AD 99, 101, 140, tr. 65, 67, 94). The myth of pure negation leads the party to assume that it has the right to destroy all opposition. A party that holds the key to truth and to all future happiness will justify any means in pursuit of its ends.[47] The charge is the same as in the 1940s, only now Merleau-Ponty sees objectivism not as an avoidable deviation from Marxism, but as its inherent flaw.

That Sartre, the philosopher par excellence of the free consciousness, falls into the same dilemmas when he declares his solidarity with the Communists is the strongest evidence of the complicity of subjectivism and objectivism in political thinking.[48] In "The

[47] Centineo, *Una fenomenologia della storia*, p. 129; cf. AD 140, 303, tr. 94, 207.

[48] I am deliberately foregoing a detailed exposition of Merleau-Ponty's flawed polemic with Sartre, which has been abundantly reviewed in sources mentioned below. His attempts to relate Sartre's political positions to his ontology are by most accounts strained, and he ignores what is new in Sartre's essays—their historical analyses of class structure and repression of workers in France since 1848 and their theory of class relations under conditions of "massification" (the isolation and dis-

Communists and Peace" Sartre reasons that a proletariat atomized by economic competition and by liberal freedoms cannot on its own find the unity to act as a collective subject. Only the party can bring workers together in a common project that will dismantle the obstructions to man's self-realization. Since the workers' only alternatives are atomization and frustration on the one hand or collective action under the party on the other, it can be said that the party "is an order that makes order reign" and that without the party the proletariat "falls back into dust."[49] Making order reign is a matter of giving orders. The proletariat's role is to follow them.[50]

This reasoning, Merleau-Ponty points out, is perfectly symptomatic of the intellectual condition of contemporary communism. Having faced "adversities" that defeated their revolutionary projects, Marxists adjusted their theory by making historical "forces" seem ever more objective and implacable. This objectivism, however, heightens the subjective role of the party in deciphering historical trends and in commanding the proletariat. In this conjuncture it is understandable that the party welcomes Sartre's conclusions. Sartre's theory misses all the mediations that Merleau-Ponty had emphasized in the 1940s.[51] There is no consistent view of a common meaning germinating within a group that shares a situation; there is no call for dialogue between the party and the proletariat. Indeed, dialogue is devalued in advance, since the workers have no sense of a collective project with which to inform the party. In spite of Sartre's misunderstanding of Marxism, his "ultra-Bolshevism" is not a corruption of contemporary communist thought, but its apotheosis.

---

persion of proletarians brought about by their interchangeability in the workplace). See Sheridan, "On Ontology and Politics: A Polemic," pp. 449–60; Whitford, *Merleau-Ponty's Critique of Sartre's Philosophy*, pp. 41–51; and Dufrenne, *Jalons*, pp. 169–173.

[49] Sartre, *The Communists and Peace*, trans. Fletcher and Berk, pp. 128, 130.

[50] Ibid., p. 128.

[51] To a great extent, Merleau-Ponty's tediously lengthy chapter on "Sartre's Ultra-Bolshevism" merely makes explicit those same criticisms of *Being and Nothingness* that had been implicit in his earlier transformative dialogue with Sartre. He charges that the Sartrean free consciousness arbitrarily imposes meaning on things, it knows no passivity, it reduces relations with others to interplay of competing gazes, it misconceives the nature of social classes, it misses intersubjectivity, it cannot understand history, it makes liberty ubiquitous and therefore politically irrelevant. For the relevant textual comparisons, see Whitford, *Merleau-Ponty's Critique of Sartre's Philosophy*, esp. pp. 41–42, 48, 50, 63, 74, 77, 89, 98.

Moreover, Merleau-Ponty for the first time implicates Sartrean freedom in political evil. In the 1940s he objected that Sartre's conception of freedom was unable to comprehend political phenomena, but defended its value as a first step toward an ethics and a theory of freedom (SNS 81, 126, tr. 45, 73). In *The Adventures of the Dialectic* he contends that Sartre's subjectivism "tends toward violence" (AD 235, tr. 161). A free consciousness is not rooted in the world. It confronts circumstances that bind it and against which it must rebel. "When negativity descends into the world, takes possession of it by force . . . , then all that is opposed to it appears as negation and can be put pell-mell into the same bag" (AD 239, tr. 163). Without a notion of probable success and without an appreciation of the value of others' views, freedom is left to invent a social order according to its own imperatives. The reaction of pure freedom to the world is negation, and negation in human affairs is violence. Sartre's conception of pure action—action unconstrained by dialogue and probabilistic readings of events—is perfectly realized only in suicide or murder (AD 174, tr. 118). Connecting Sartre to the essence of revolutionary politics therefore does more than underline the theoretical infirmities of contemporary communism; it explains the latter's often bloody history and its abiding intolerance of opposition.

The third level of Merleau-Ponty's critique of Marxism concerns its underlying antipathy to independent creation in the realm of culture. He discovers that "*The German Ideology* spoke of destroying philosophy rather than realizing it" (AD 94, tr. 62). In the 1940s Merleau-Ponty interpreted Marx's dictum generously as a call to bring criticism to bear on all domains of culture rather than to isolate it in abstract philosophy. But in 1955 Merleau-Ponty interprets the destruction of philosophy more literally. Marx meant that critical thought would be unnecessary in the pure positivity of a communist society. In light of that interpretation the fate of philosophy in revolutionary movements no longer seems accidental. Early in his career, Lukacs argued that literature could have a certain truth independent of the social conditions under which it was produced (AD 66, tr. 42). Not all consciousness in a presocialist society is false consciousness because writers like Stendhal or Balzac could at least capture the truth of their times in their depiction of social relations. But by the 1940s the party claimed that "no production of a class society can be worth as much as those of Soviet society" (AD 107. tr. 71). At a meeting with Eastern bloc writers in 1956, Merleau-Ponty describes the result of that idea:

"As regards art, painting, culture, philosophy, there are no internal criteria. Thus the discussion of a philosophy or of a work of art can never consist in understanding it first and discussing it from inside; it consists more or less in confronting it with an external discipline."[52] The revolution's penchant for censorship and its intolerance of internal opposition follow from its crude realism and its postulate of pure negativity. How could a theory that interprets thought as a reflection of matter ever value thought as an independent contribution to truth (S 320, tr. 254)? Why would a party that represents the total negation of capitalism ever accept cultural productions sullied by their origins in a class society? This distrust of thought itself is, in Merleau-Ponty's eyes, what blinds the revolution. It means that "there is no revolution that is critical of itself."

Politics after Marx

This critique of Marxism does not necessitate a total rejection of it.[53] "What is obsolete is not the dialectic, but rather the pretension of terminating it in an end of history or in a permanent revolution, in a regime that, because it is contestation itself, no longer needs to be contested from the outside" (AD 301, tr. 206). Merleau-Ponty retains some of Marx's ideas—his thoughts on class, violence, and a generally progressive scheme of historical development. But the rejection of the hypothesis that one class might consummate world history opens the way to what is most laudable in his late politics. It frees up his reasoning to become more convincingly monitory and exploratory.

In a cautionary mood Merleau-Ponty warns that taking one's bearings by the Marxian hypothesis, even staking one's hopes on it as a bold gamble, cuts short political thought. It hides rather than lays bare what binds the revolutionary class to the traditions of everyday life. Detecting "false consciousness" everywhere, it does not take seriously the complexity or the sincerity of others'

---

[52] "Discordia Concors: Rencontre Est-Ouest à Venise," p. 211.

[53] In the *Adventures* Merleau-Ponty often uses the same dialectical language to describe Marxism-Leninism that he had developed in the 1940s. He seems to want to use his previous interpretations to criticize Sartre for misunderstanding Marx and at the same time to say that Marxism rightly interpreted is wrong. This leads to the confusing result that Aron has pointed out, that "Merleau-Ponty writes half of his book as if he were still a Marxist" when he clearly no longer believes in Marx in the way he did ten years earlier. See *Marxism and the Existentialists*, p. 78.

reasons for opposing radical change and thereby betrays a hostility to opposition per se. Sighting revolutionary tendencies in every protest, it reads its own meanings into the intentions of others and thereby deprives itself of a genuine understanding of the complex motives for social order and unrest. Any thought based on the logic of identity—the idea that what was negative or different becomes positive and identical by a dialectical movement of self-transcendence—is a logic of domination.[54] It carries violence within it because it foresees a condition of total actualization in which thought will no longer be differentiated and self-critical. Merleau-Ponty is probably right that even the ferment of a contingent, doubt-ridden belief in a "universal class" yields a brew heady enough to dull the empirical and ethical senses of those who sample it. Political actors must know that they are not en route to the end of history.

There is also in Merleau-Ponty's late works an important warning against using ossified categories of social thinking and conventional ways of delimiting social phenomena. One of the factors that provoked his break with Marxism and traditional liberalism was the inappropriateness of their models of economic development for the Third World. Marxism, he maintains, does not illuminate the problems of modernization for countries without a large proletariat; liberalism does not easily apply to cultures that lack experience with formal liberties.[55] Social theorists are invited to deploy greater creativity in thinking of systems of power as composites of symbols that structure the understanding of particular groups. At the same time this very fragmentation of historical understanding moderates the ambitions of political theory. The number and complexity of historical forms, as well as any person's immersion in only a few of them, limit the possibilities of political knowledge. Every project encounters unanticipated "adversities"; no social science forecasts every form of "inertia." Marx foresaw a society of transparent personal relations because he mistakenly believed his own theory enabled him to penetrate the superficial phenomena of social life and to see the actual mechanisms of historical change. After Marx, Merleau-Ponty reminds us, the invisible is the very condition of visibility. Opaqueness, not transparency, is the lot of social life.

[54] Dufrenne, "Comment voir l'histoire?" p. 50.

[55] S 47, 378–379, 409; 411, tr. 35, 302, 329, 331; "Un entretien avec Maurice Merleau-Ponty," p. 9; *Les Voyages du philosophe, II*, Merleau-Ponty interviewed by Georges Charbonnier, RTF, 1959.

More positively, renouncing the Marxian hypothesis opens Merleau-Ponty to the recognition that there is more to freedom than economic autonomy. In the 1940s he refused to question the possibility that all freedoms are compatible. He assumed the primary forms of oppression to be essentially economic: unemployment, poverty, imperialism. Marx's hypothesis explained how these problems could be resolved simultaneously by bringing economic forces under rational control. No further speculation seemed necessary about other possible impediments to freedom. There was no question of needing to prevent those who controlled the economy from abusing their power. If all liberties were compatible, it was inconceivable that one person's speech could unjustly interfere with another's welfare or that one group's desire to choose its own members could unjustly exclude others from important means of self-actualization. After repudiating the Marxian hypothesis, political thinkers need a more nuanced theory of liberty. They must rethink the relationship between radical change and political criticism. They will have to reconsider the value of institutions that promote popular participation and political accountability. These are the functions of the "new liberalism" that Merleau-Ponty espouses in the 1950s (AD 329, tr. 225).

The New Liberalism

A new liberalism recognizes above all the virtues of parliamentary government and political freedom. "Parliament is the only known institution that guarantees a minimum of opposition and truth" (AD 331, tr. 226). Revolutionary movements suppress opposition and belie their claims to engage in continual self-criticism. Representative institutions, on the other hand, create a forum in which politicians must explain and justify their policies. Politicians then know that opponents will scrutinize their claims and expose their mistakes (S 399, tr. 320). Moreover, under conditions of "political liberty" citizens participate in political debate and share knowledge about the successes and failures of policies (S 332, 270, tr. 265, 213). The apprehension that voters may throw them out of office at the next election restrains parliamentary politicians. And they cannot complain of the voter's stupidity. The voter's choice is right because "each man is infallible" in what concerns his happiness or misfortune. So even if "the majority is not always right . . . in the long run, no one can be right in opposition to it" (S 400–401, tr. 322).

In spite of its rejection of the myths of revolution, the new liberalism has learned important lessons from radical theory. There is no question of "returning to the optimistic and superficial philosophy that reduces the . . . political struggle to exchanges of views on a clearly posed problem" (AD 329–330, tr. 225). A new liberalism is a chastened one. With Max Weber, it appreciates that "all politics is violence" (AD 42, tr. 26). From Marx it has learned that "there is and must be class struggle because and as long as there are classes" (AD 330, tr. 226). And a liberalism that understands class struggle is especially solicitous of the interests of the working class. It defends their right to strike (AD 270, tr. 185); it is critical of capitalist exploitation and economic disorder (AD 332, tr. 227; S 8, tr. 4). In line with the politics of Pierre Mendès-France, Merleau-Ponty favors regulating capitalism through economic incentives rather than through state directives.[56] Committed neither to free enterprise nor to nationalization of the economy, the new liberalism maintains that "what is essential is that the functioning of the political and economic system as a whole serves the public interest."[57]

Pragmatic judgments, not ideological preconceptions, guide a postrevolutionary politics. The premise of revolutionary politics was that all social evils were manifestations of a single problem and were tightly bound together in a single, self-sustaining structure. It was conceivable therefore that a restructuring of the social field could lead to the simultaneous resolution of all problems of inequality, exploitation, and violence. Having denied that possibility, Merleau-Ponty views political action strictly in terms of incremental reforms (S 384, tr. 307). His final statement to Madeleine Chapsal suggests a willingness to look at political problems one at a time: "We will have to consider the problems of modern society—from urbanism (or even traffic), employment, the new farming class, and planning, to the incentives, the movement, the life of the nation."[58] He says that France needs more statisticians, engineers, and economists to regulate capitalism.[59] Not a formula, or a party, or a class, but the creative responses of trained minds will solve the problems of a mass society.

No doubt this account of Merleau-Ponty's liberalism is unsatisfyingly sketchy. The fault, unfortunately, lies with Merleau-Ponty

---

[56] Merleau-Ponty, "Où va l'anticommunisme?" p. 12.
[57] "L'avenir du socialisme" (debate directed by Maurice Merleau-Ponty), p. 31.
[58] Merleau-Ponty in Chapsal, Les écrivains en personne, p. 163.
[59] Ibid., p. 154.

himself. He devotes relatively little attention to the justifications or the conclusions of his later politics. He never manages to face squarely the questions that historically have most troubled liberals. How can a self-interested being be induced to respect the public interest? How can institutions be devised that are neutral as between different visions of a good life? How much equality is compatible with liberty? How can a state that intervenes in the economy be prevented from invading its citizens' property rights? Although "liberty" is obviously essential to liberalism, Merleau-Ponty never explains which "political liberties" he believes are most important or how to resolve conflicts between them. This could be particularly problematic when it comes to defending the freedom of Communists since he argues that the PCF has a right to exist *and to oppose democratic politics*, but not to install itself as a dictatorship of the proletariat (AD 330, tr. 226). What would happen, then, if a revolution seemed imminent? Would the state be obligated unconditionally to protect a Communist's right to free speech? Must it do so when the party organizes a general strike that endangers the regime? On these sorts of questions Merleau-Ponty's belated defense of political liberties is silent.[60]

Nor does he ever clarify what he means by the "democratic regulation of the economy" (S 8, tr. 4). Nationalizing industry, using tax and regulatory policies to influence private enterprises, promoting worker management of firms, and any number of other policies conceivably fall under this rubric. An agnostic with respect to the specific methods of democratic control, Merleau-Ponty advances only a pragmatic criterion for choosing among them: what matters is that a form of property be *"socially* profitable."[61] He seems unaware, however, that there are other values than productivity and fair distribution involved in the ways a society regulates property. Traditionally liberals have regarded the right to make and reinvest profit as an important aspect of personal freedom. Advocates of autogestion often put less emphasis on productivity than on securing the workers' sense of control over vital decisions affecting their daily lives. Perhaps social profitability should rank over these other values. But to be convinced of this we would need to see an argument that explicitly compares the goods of produc-

---

[60] See Hamrick, "Interests, Justice, and Respect for Law," in McBride and Schrag, eds., *Phenomenology in a Pluralist Context*, pp. 43–45.

[61] "Où va l'anticommunisme?" p. 12, n. 2.

tion, distribution, freedom, and participation—an argument that Merleau-Ponty's new liberalism does not provide.

Most disappointing of all, this incrementalist reformism evades the principal charge that Merleau-Ponty levelled against liberalism in the 1940s—that liberalism forms a *system* with violence. This meant, for instance, that changes in the voting system designed to increase the power of ordinary citizens would probably be quickly scuttled and, if they passed, that those with economic power would find new avenues to influence legislators. It meant that industry's need for profit rather than the people's need for protection against foreign aggression was likely to structure the defense policies of capitalist democracies. In the 1940s Merleau-Ponty would use these sorts of examples not only to argue that capitalism is a system polarized to benefit the few, but to show that any politics that ignores the linkages between social problems is doomed to see its initiatives defeated. When he calls for parliamentary government and piecemeal reform, however, he makes no mention of their roles in a structure of violence. Perhaps he came to believe it possible for some institutions to resist being deflected toward violent ends. Perhaps he abandoned entirely the notion of a system of violence in favor of a notion of sporadic, unfocused violence. Perhaps he continued to see liberal democracy as a system of violence, but one whose violence was less severe and therefore more acceptable than that of socialist systems. Not only do we never learn which of these possibilities underlies his liberalism; we are never presented with the evidence or reasoning that would be required to support any of them. Characterizing his "new liberalism" as an "a-communism" (AD 329, tr. 225), he reveals that his views in the 1950s are defined more by what they reject than by their positive aspirations. Neither confident nor vigorous, this is a liberalism *faute de mieux*.

It is not necessarily true, however, that the *foundations* of his liberalism are equally shallow. I have argued that Merleau-Ponty's political work is usually most penetrating when it tries to connect the foundations of meaning to problems of political knowledge and decision. Whatever the doctrinal shortcomings of his liberalism, there still may be great profundity in his exploration of its ground as a mode of thought. This level of his analysis will therefore retain most of our attention.

N I N E

POLITICS AND EXPRESSION

The argument cannot be made that, having become liberal, Merleau-Ponty suddenly forgot what it meant to think politically. In *The Adventures of the Dialectic* he repeats once again the litany of requirements that he places on truly political thought: it begins with a probabilistic reading of events, it needs a philosophy of history, it treats people statistically, it aims at success (AD 239, 9, 226, 251, tr. 163, 3, 154, 172). Chastising Sartre for his notion of "pure action," Merleau-Ponty reminds him that political actors cannot use the fact that history is "overflowing with meaning" to justify an arbitrary perspective favoring just the meanings they prefer. They know that there are more realistic perspectives, ones "that take account of all preceding perspectives (especially those of the actors in the drama) . . . , that try to understand them even if it means putting them in their proper place and establishing a hierarchy among them, and that owe to this contact with the perspectives of others . . . if not a demonstrative value, at least a certain weight of experience" (AD 284, tr. 194). It is a statement that Merleau-Ponty could have written as well in 1944 as in 1954.

Yet by the latter date he has spoken lessons that should be applied to his own thought. He taught that verbal formulas, no matter how lucid, and political positions, no matter how attractive, do not reveal everything important about a political theory. One must also ask whether the categories and logic of a theorist's philosophical presuppositions really support the stances he takes. In the 1940s he charged that empiricists, intellectualists, and existentialists used theories of the relation between consciousness and the world that were in contradiction with what they *did* politically and ultimately led them to take positions at odds with the requirements of a humanistic politics. Ironically, there are grounds for a similar charge against Merleau-Ponty's new liberalism. The conclusion of an analysis of his writings of the 1950s is that the way he revises his philosophy of history after rejecting the Marxian hypothesis ends up hindering political thinking.

Merleau-Ponty might well have reached a more satisfactory synthesis had he lived, like Sartre, another twenty years. He was in the middle of a profound rethinking of his entire philosophy at the time of his death. But his last writings are so incomplete, especially as regards politics, that attempts to infer a politics from them end up saying more about the interpreter than about Merleau-Ponty. Even if he aspired to a new politics, we do not know what it is. Consequently, this chapter addresses his last writings only briefly and focuses instead on the relationship between his liberal reformism, his philosophy, and the problem of thinking politically in works that he wrote between 1951 and 1958.

Language: The Obstacle
to a Cultural Phenomenology

Merleau-Ponty points to the grounding of his reformism in a passage in *The Adventures of the Dialectic*: "If one thinks that the social world is 'obscure and overflowing with meaning'—obscure because it does not indicate its meaning by itself, overflowing with meaning because . . . it indicates several meanings of which none is truer than another . . .—there would be something on which to found a liberal rather than a revolutionary politics" (AD 210, tr. 143). He had always talked of a surfeit of meaning in the perceived world; that was the significance of his perspectivism. What is new in this passage is the idea that these several meanings *do not converge* to establish a truth that is superior to any one of them. His earlier theory of phenomenal objectivity understood truth as a principle of thematic and functional wholeness. The truth of a cube consists not in a view of one of its facets, but in a common style synthesized through a multiplicity of perspectives on it. An assertion that social meanings are irreducibly plural and nonconvergent must signal an important shift in the way he conceives meaning. That shift begins with a change in his preferred model for the concept of structure.

During most of 1940s Merleau-Ponty interprets historical structure in the same terms as biological structure. "History," he asserts, "is comparable to a living being" (HT 110, tr. 89). He elaborates on this conception by saying that "just as in an organism, a given state of the respiratory system demands a particular state of the cardiovascular system . . . if the whole is to function with the greatest efficiency, so also in a Marxist politics, history is a system that goes . . . toward the power of the proletariat" (HT 144, tr.

130). He believes that the proletariat is possibly in the optimal perceptual situation in history, like an observer who sees things at just that distance and in just that lighting that permits him to grapple successfully with problems in his environment. The proletariat's action tears down blockages to freedom and erects a new social order more conducive to human flourishing. Both biological and historical structures translate the idea of a logic within contingent, intentional behavior.

In a course in 1949 Merleau-Ponty suggests that a model of structure drawn from Ferdinand de Saussure's linguistics has those same properties: "Saussure saw [in language] that meshing of chance and order . . . that one could apply to all history . . . : just as the motor of language is the desire to communicate . . . , so what moves all historical development is man's common situation, the desire to coexist and to recognize each other" (BP 259). He goes on to point out affinities between the linguistic model of structure and "the Marxist conception of history." This model recurs in 1953 during his inaugural lecture at the Collège de France. By this time, however, he is prepared to accuse the late Marx of succumbing to scientism (EP 62, tr. 53). His contrasting use of Saussure suggests that the Swiss linguist developed a way of thinking that is less vulnerable to objectivist temptations: "The theory of the sign . . . perhaps implies a theory of historical meaning that goes beyond the alternative of *things and consciousness*. . . . Saussure could well have sketched out a new philosophy of history" (EP 63–64, tr. 54). What Saussure could have done becomes part of Merleau-Ponty's next philosophical project. Assessing the advantages and disadvantages of his turn to a conception of history modelled on linguistics requires some consideration of what attracted him in Saussure and of Saussurean linguistics itself.

In a prospectus of his work written in 1952, Merleau-Ponty acknowledges a significant flaw in his early phenomenology: "The study of perception could only teach us a 'bad ambiguity,' a mixture of finitude and universality. . . . But there is in the phenomenon of *expression*, a 'good ambiguity' . . . , a spontaneity . . . that brings together into a single tissue . . . the past and the present, nature and culture." He mentions two forthcoming works, *The Prose of the World* and the longer study of *The Origin of Truth* for which the former was to be the introduction, in which he will explain how "the characteristic operation of the mind is in the movement by which we take up our bodily existence and use it to *sym-*

bolize."[1] The chapter on "The Body as Expression and Speech" in his *Phenomenology* apparently no longer satisfies him as an account of the transition from the relatively stable originary meanings rooted in the perceiving body to the more diverse meanings found in the realm of culture and history.[2]

The problem in his early phenomenology of speech comes from its attempt to find the ground of expression in the perceptual syntheses of the corps propre. In Stephen Watson's words, "Merleau-Ponty's argument . . . is based upon the necessity of an original 'text' for all signs to refer back to, the necessity of a 'pre-text' which would unconditionally account for all meaning and would be itself unconditioned."[3] The body has primordial capacities to create and communicate meaning. Before language there are sexual gestures, grimaces in anger, the ability to orient oneself in space. The body spontaneously uses itself to develop meaning. Its movements are not just objective displacements of flesh; they are oriented toward goals and therefore can be read as *expressions* of those goals. Speech builds upon this original ability. Speech is therefore "only a particular case" of the body's expressive functioning (PP 221, tr. 190). Merleau-Ponty calls it "a true gesture" in order to emphasize that meaning is not something that thought adds to words (PP 214, tr. 184).[4] Meaning is as inseparable from the symbol as the goal is from the gesture. Like a gesture of a hand directing one's glance toward a distant object, the expressive sign *points at* a fundamental reality.[5] By grounding expression in the gestural relationship between a sign and a pre-text of incarnate meaning, Merleau-Ponty brings speech within his general interpretation of sens as orientation or directedness. He makes language into a secondary function that sublimates the silent meaning of things into expression. Perception alone gives us our primary experience of meaning.[6]

The problem is not that he *reduces* speech to an activity of the

---

[1] "Un inédit de Merleau-Ponty," p. 409, emphases added. For a discussion of these works, see Lefort, Editor's Preface, in *The Prose of the World*, pp. xi–xxi.

[2] "Un inédit de Merleau-Ponty," p. 405.

[3] "Pretexts: Language, Perception, and the Cogito in Merleau-Ponty's Thought," in *Merleau-Ponty: Perception, Structure, Language*, ed. Sallis, p. 149.

[4] Madison, *The Phenomenology of Merleau-Ponty*, p. 49.

[5] Schmidt, *Maurice Merleau-Ponty*, p. 112.

[6] Taminiaux, "Über Erfahrung, Ausdruck, und Struktur: Ihre Entwicklung in der Phänomenologie Merleau-Pontys," in *Maurice Merleau-Ponty und das Problem der Struktur in den Sozialwissenschaften*, eds. Grathoff and Sprondel, p. 96.

body-subject.[7] Already in *The Structure of Behavior* Merleau-Ponty had explained how his phenomenology avoids reductionism by examining hierarchies of meaning. Lower levels of sens (for example, the orientation of a palpitating heart to maintain a vital equilibrium for the organism as a whole) are integrated into higher ones (the heart beats faster in a moment of "rage"). Therefore higher dialectics cannot be reduced to lower ones (anger is not just its physiological manifestations and the quickened heartbeat of an angry person is not "the same" as that of a runner because the functions of the quickening are different in the two cases). Higher dialectics must be understood on their own terms according to their own intrinsic meanings. So Merleau-Ponty realizes that "language transcends itself" (PP 449, tr. 392) and integrates all human activity into a world of verbal expression. He knows that the relatively static and uniform categories of perceptual life are ill suited to describe a domain of perpetual change and creativity.

But the fact is that in the 1940s, when Merleau-Ponty takes up questions of social existence, he most often employs examples derived from perceptual-biological or even physical existence. He speaks, as above, of the cardiovascular system. He mentions the systemic properties of waves and soap bubbles (HT 193, tr. 188) and electrical conductors (HT 144, tr. 130). He compares the habitual actions of political actors to "reflexes" (PP 104, tr. 88; SNS 190, tr. 108) and the intersignification of social phenomena to the unity of "the parts of the body" (PP 202, tr. 173). With the important exception of his notion of dialogue, he had not yet elaborated the categories distinctive to the social sphere that his theory required. At most, his phenomenology demonstrated the impossibility of symbolic meaning in the absence of originary meaning. But as he conceded in 1952, the fact that the body gives us a "primary language" tells us almost nothing about the forms that human life might or should take once the dialectic of language has been initiated.[8] And that is an especially damaging admission with respect to his politics of the 1940s because only the hypothesis that social life was oriented toward one particular equilibrium gave his theory specific ethical content.

A second problem is that, for an avowedly holistic philosophy, a theory of expression that uncovers the roots of meaning in the corps propre is strangely atomistic and individualistic. Its gestural

---

[7] Madison, *The Phenomenology of Merleau-Ponty*, pp. 116–117.
[8] "Un inédit de M. Merleau-Ponty," p. 406.

notion of signification purports to explain how *isolated* signs take on meaning.[9] Viewing speech as a particular modulation of the body implies that, at least at the originary level, individual words, like the pointing gesture, contain their meaning in themselves. One would expect Merleau-Ponty's usual concern for structure to make him more attentive to how some larger context conditions the meaning of verbal elements. An uncharacteristic individualism marks his theory insofar as most of its examples of expression concern individual speakers—the aphasic patient, "a writer," Proust (PP 204, 212, 213, tr. 175, 182, 183).[10] Missing is his usual concern for the effects of culture, history, and class on behavior.

Linguistics and Social Structure

It is likely that Merleau-Ponty began his study of Saussure's *Course on General Linguistics* quite independently of any intention of revising his philosophy of history. Impressed by Sartre's *What is Literature?* he became increasingly interested in questions of expression and language after 1947—the year when Saussure is first mentioned in one of his essays (SNS 173, tr. 87).[11] His course at Lyon on "Language and Communication" in 1947–1948 dealt with Saussure, as did a course titled "Saussure" that he gave at the ENS in 1948–1949.[12] Perhaps not coincidentally, around this same time he became closer to Claude Lévi-Strauss, whose anthropology was starting to show the influence of the linguist Roman Jakobson.[13]

Whatever the source of Merleau-Ponty's interest, the important point is that studying Saussure's linguistics brought him to reject

[9] Schmidt, *Maurice Merleau-Ponty*, p. 131. Cf. PP 206, tr. 177, "The word has a meaning."

[10] I do not wish to exaggerate this point. Merleau-Ponty does allude to the uniqueness of different languages to different cultures (PP 217, 229, 218, tr. 186, 196, 187). But on the whole, Madison's conclusion is fair: "Merleau-Ponty concentrates primarily on speech, as the individual act of expression, rather than on language itself, as the signifying intersubjective system in which speech occurs." *The Phenomenology of Merleau-Ponty*, p. 119.

[11] Merleau-Ponty might have been at least superficially acquainted with Saussure before this. See Watson, "Merleau-Ponty's Involvement with Saussure," in *Continental Philosophy in America*, eds. Silverman et al: pp. 210–213.

[12] Ibid., p. 212.

[13] Clark, *The Foundations of Structuralism*, pp. 60–61; Claude Lévi-Strauss, "De quelques rencontres," in *L'Arc*, no. 46, pp. 80–87. Merleau-Ponty and Lévi-Strauss had first met in 1929 when both were student teachers, along with Simone de Beauvoir, at the Lycée Janson de Sailly. See Beauvoir, *Mémoires d'une jeune fille rangée*, p. 411.

the idea of the meaningfulness of isolated signs and to discover a way of thinking that could unify the speaking subject and the cultural-historical world. He explains the first realization in "Indirect Language and the Voices of Silence": "What we have learned from Saussure is that signs taken singly signify nothing, that each one of them does not so much express a meaning as mark a divergence of meaning between itself and other signs. . . . Language is composed of differences without terms" (S 49, tr. 39). For Saussure the "sign" in its technical definition is "the combination of the concept and the acoustic image." The combined elements are designated, respectively, the "signified" and the "signifier."[14] What was revolutionary in this part of Saussure's theory was his argument that even though all that can be said of signified and signifier in isolation is that they differ and are opposed, "their combination is a positive fact," it brings into being a "system of values."[15] Meaningless components arranged "diacritically" become expressive. As Merleau-Ponty makes Saussure's conception his own (and I ignore numerous idiosyncracies in his reading of Saussure),[16] he steps away from a theory that sees meaning as a polarization toward an end and toward one that sees meaning emerging out of a differentiation of previously meaningless elements.

The "new philosophy of history" that could be drawn from Saussure's theory would come from viewing not just phonemes and concepts, but also social practices and values in terms of diacritical oppositions. "Just as language is a system of signs that have meaning only relatively to one another . . . , so each institution is a symbolic system that the subject incorporates as a style of functioning, as a global configuration." (EP 65, tr. 55–56). The drawback of a phenomenology that tries to build upward from perception to social meaning is that it is unable to get a grip on the complexity of human life once it becomes fully symbolic. In Saussure Merleau-Ponty discovers the potential for unifying perception and expression from the opposite direction—not from perception to symbolization, but from symbolization to perception. Perception would be a "tacit symbolization of life" while a "conscious symbolization" would characterize social life (EP 66, tr. 56). Both are governed by the same logic in which meaning emerges from diacritical opposition (RC 11–12, tr. 3–4). Phenomena like lan-

---

[14] *Cours de linguistique générale*, p. 99.

[15] Ibid., pp. 166–167.

[16] See Lagueux, "Merleau-Ponty et la linguistique de Saussure," pp. 351–364, and Schmidt, *Maurice Merleau-Ponty*, pp. 108–137.

guage, political institutions, kinship relations, and modes of production form a symbolic system in which the types of "logic of conduct" become similar (EP 65–66, tr. 56).

Merleau-Ponty clarifies this new mode of thinking in *The Adventures of the Dialectic*, where Max Weber's *The Protestant Ethic and the Spirit of Capitalism* supplies grist for his interpretive mill. The emergence of capitalism, asserts Weber, presupposes the presence not just of economic factors like the availability of financial resources or free wage earners, but also an ethos that favors rationalization (i.e., the control and careful organization of activities), productivity, accumulation, and reinvestment. He argues that certain theological beliefs of Puritan groups promoted precisely this "spirit." Weber's study shows that no sphere of life, be it economic, religious, political, scientific, or artistic, is autonomous. There are "affinities of choice" through which each sphere penetrates and influences the others. Thus, Merleau-Ponty argues, religious and economic practices are part of a symbolic system in which the meaning "rationalization" arises while "each of these elements gains that historical signification only through its encounter with others" (AD 29, tr. 17). Diverse elements in a way of life enter into a differentiated, diacritical relationship that gives them a particular *sens*. The accumulation of these elements then makes a certain line of development in the system more probable than others. Puritanism did not cause capitalism, but it contributed the logic that tied together people's decisions in various spheres of their life in such a way that capitalistic production was likely to form.

The allusion to a line of development in the preceding discussion should already have suggested that the study of a social system cannot confine itself to the synchronic relations of its symbols, that is, to the relationships among its symbols at a given moment in time. "Since synchrony is only a cross section of diachrony, the [synchronic] system . . . always involves latent or incubating changes" (S 109, tr. 87). Merleau-Ponty's interest in historical change, in the diachronics of symbolic creation, is central to his consideration of Weber. *The Protestant Ethic* not only maps out the rationalist ethos that suffuses the capitalist way of life; it also emphasizes the "advent" of that ethos. The *sens* of capitalism does not precede the accretion of choices expressed in economic or religious practices. Instead, the "affinities of choice" they represent are over time "developed by human intentions" such that they eventually "form a whole" (AD 30, tr. 17; RC 50–51, tr. 33). *Sens* is neither eternal, waiting only to be discovered, nor time-bound, speaking only to its contemporaries. "Advent," a term that Merleau-Ponty borrows from Paul Ricoeur, signifies the process whereby meanings created at a given time virtually demand a succession; their fecundity founds a tradition of thought.[17] Previously discrete elements of social life settle contingently into a configuration from which a new, transhistorically significant meaning arises. Thus to read Weber's account of rationalization is to witness the gradual setting into place of an ensemble of meanings that continue to be effective centuries later—but that equally may disintegrate with the passage of time. History is like "spoken language" (AD 30, tr. 55), writes Merleau-Ponty, modifying his earlier comparisons of it with a "living being."

At first glance this "histoire avènementielle," as James Schmidt has aptly termed it, seems only to change the metaphor for the notion of a logic in contingency that was the mainstay of Merleau-Ponty's philosophy of history in the 1940s. Speakers use language freely, distinctively, contingently. They rearrange the elements of a language so as to make new meanings possible. Language is their means to express their autonomy. And yet all the while speakers draw upon a limited set of phonemes, words, rules of syntax and grammar, and traditions of expression that reflect their membership in a particular cultural community.[18] As Saussure demonstrated, these linguistic resources have a structure of their own. Even as speakers express their individual thoughts and styles, their speech is formed by the general possibilities for symbolization contained in their language. Finally, this general structure itself undergoes intelligible transformations through the advent of new expressions. "The contingent fact . . . becomes a new means of expression that takes its place and has a meaning in the history of that language" (EP 64, tr. 55). So it may seem that Merleau-Ponty has only repeated, not fundamentally altered, his philosophy of sens in history.

Saussurean History

The essentials however have changed. With respect to empirical history, Merleau-Ponty's Saussurean conception sees it as hyper-

---

[17] See Ricoeur, "Objectivity and Subjectivity in History," in *History and Truth*, trans. Kelbley, pp. 33–36. Cf. S 85, tr. 68. Schmidt argues that Merleau-Ponty's use of "advent" stems from a creative misreading of Saussure's distinctions between synchronic and diachronic linguistics. *Maurice Merleau-Ponty*, pp. 134–137.

[18] O'Neill, *Perception, Expression, and History*, p. 58.

contingent, fragmented, and without a founding impulse. With respect to ethics, this new history tolerates as many different values as the world does languages. Consider first its altered empirical vision.

In Merleau-Ponty's works of the 1940s the contingency of history denoted that free choices or unpredictable accidents might intervene in an evolving pattern of meaning in such a way that the pattern was never completed. Still, the pattern could be seen *prospectively* because one could understand the problem that structured its elements. Like a living body striving to maintain a vital equilibrium, mankind in history strives to solve the problems of exploitation and inequality that threaten human existence. In the 1950s the advent of meaning is contingent in a much more radical way. Sens does not preexist the completed pattern; a fortuitous combination of discrete elements generates meaning through interrelations and oppositions of the elements. A problem exists only in relation to the completed pattern and can be detected only *retrospectively*. Not just the completion of the pattern, but the formation of the pattern itself is contingent.

Perhaps an analogy will clarify the difference. The completion of an architect's blueprints for a new building is contingent in the sense that he or she might fail to finish them. Yet, if the blueprints were almost done, a knowledgeable observer might still comprehend the pattern that those designs were fulfilling. One could see the problems the design was trying to solve and fill in the blueprint in a way that could plausibly be said to complete the original architect's plans. Likewise, Merleau-Ponty had argued that Marx saw history's plan: it was moving toward a "society of mutual recognition." Contingencies like nationalist sentiments or war could make history deviate from its course, but that would not compromise the sens Marx discerned. For the 1950s, Merleau-Ponty's idea of the contingent advent of meaning can only be conveyed by analogy with a less predictable form of art. In an article arguing that the painter's use of color follows the same sort of diacritical logic as the writer's use of words, he describes how Matisse developed meaning as he painted: "Matisse . . . looked at the open whole of the work he was beginning and brought his brush toward the line that called for it, so that the painting could finally be what it was in the process of becoming. . . . The chosen line was chosen so as to observe twenty conditions scattered over the painting, conditions that were unformulated and unformulable for anyone but Matisse because they were not defined and imposed except by the intention to execute *this painting that did not yet exist"* (S 58, tr. 45–46). If Matisse alone could formulate the objectives of his painting, it is because he alone controlled the contingent arrangement of the parts that made a particular meaning appear. No other observer has such privileged access to his intentions, and so for all who look on Matisse's meaning can appear only retrospectively, after the work has been completed.

Now, according to Merleau-Ponty's Saussure-inspired philosophy of expression, historical meaning too results from a hypercontingent logic. But with respect to history there is not even this one intending intelligence capable of formulating meaning prospectively. The actions of even the most successful political leader are more analogous to the individual daubs of the painter's brush than to the painter's intending intelligence, for in history domains of culture over which leaders had little control, like religion and literature, contribute to the significance of their actions. Hence Weber finds "rationalization" in law, science, technology, and religion, "but *only after the fact*: each of these elements acquires its historical signification through its encounter with the others" (AD 29, tr. 17, emphasis added). Prospectively, historical *sens* is not only unformulated, but *unformulable*.

On this model, moreover, history is local, fragmented, disconnected. Purging his theory of any remnants of the maximal philosophy of history, Merleau-Ponty now makes historical phenomena seem linked in only limited and temporary ways. There is no single "problem" that orients its movement. "Historical epochs become ordered around an interrogation of human possibility, of which each has its own formula, rather than around an immanent solution of which history would be the advent" (AD 40, tr. 24). Where history is hypercontingent, it harbors no immanent universality. At most, "local histories take form . . . , and begin to regulate themselves, and haltingly link themselves together" (S 47, tr. 35). The advent of capitalism demonstrates what is meant by "local history." Weber notes that many of the elements of capitalism—the impulse to trade and to make loans, the spatial separation of workplaces and residences, the keeping of accounts—have existed in other societies. Nonetheless, capitalism was originally the local economic system of Western Europe. Only there did the idea of the rational, capitalistic organization of free labor develop.[19] The economic history of the West therefore cannot be merged with that of the rest of the world.

[19] Weber, *The Protestant Ethic*, trans. Parsons, p. 22.

In spite of his continued emphasis on economic phenomena, Merleau-Ponty further alters his earlier theory by removing their foundational status. What supported his hypothesis of a unified world history in the 1940s was a notion that had been crucial to his assimilation of Marxism as a mode of political thought—the idea that one sector of human life could serve over time as the founding phenomenon with respect to all other sectors. His very decision to turn to Weber's work indicates a rejection of that idea, for Weber intended his study of the *spirit* of capitalism to challenge the economic reductionism current in most Marxist scholarship.[20] On Weber's model, "the relationship [of motives] is supple and reversible" (AD 31, tr. 18). The Protestant ethic carries along capitalism at certain times, and at others capitalism perpetuates the logic of Protestant behavior. If history is an "exchange of all orders of activity, none of which can receive the dignity of exclusive cause," then historians must avoid preconceptions about the logic of systems they study (RC 44, tr. 28).

In the 1940s Merleau-Ponty's philosophy of history, because it was modelled on the behavior of a "living being," was also a theory of value. He argued that an organism's "structure of behavior" oriented it to take vitally optimal positions in relation to its environment. The equilibrium point of a gestalt makes the components of the organism's behavior into "value-facts." Likewise, he argued, the proletariat may be a "value-fact" in an historical gestalt. Its revolutionary action may finally end violence in social relations. I have shown that Merleau-Ponty could let this hypothesis displace any other ethical speculation only by assuming that the proletariat was in a position to resolve "the human problem" *as a whole*. The proletarian revolution would be a concrete, empirical action that promised universal values. But if history is like "spoken language," the most that can be said to unite mankind's diverse and changing symbolisms is that they are all manifestations of "the permanent exigency of communication" (EP 64, tr. 55). As Merleau-Ponty uses it, this exigency foreshadows no alternative theory of universal values. Just as my use of a language does not imply the existence of a universal language, so my system of values—or anyone else's—does not imply the existence of universal norms. Our urge to communicate exists as much under communism as under capitalism; it is as developed in a so-called primitive society, as Lévi-Strauss might teach, as in an "advanced" one. The

---

[20] Freund, *The Sociology of Max Weber*, trans. Ilford, p. 203.

exigency of communication picks out no political or economic form as preferred. It tolerates instead every form as a mode of expression with its own unique values.

What little Merleau-Ponty says about values in the 1950s echoes Weber. He is now persuaded by Weber's argument for the complementarity of an ethic of responsibility and an ethic of ultimate ends (AD 45, tr. 28). The political actor must attend both to the consequences of action and to moral principles. No ethical formula and no philosophy of history reconciles them. They come together in the personal qualities—the intelligence, the foresight, the moral sensibility—of political leaders. Leaders are those who facilitate the advent of new moral meanings. "To succeed, it is necessary to have that capacity to live history of which Weber speaks, and truth in politics is perhaps only that art of inventing what will appear later as that which was required by the times" (AD 46, tr. 29). But any authentic political action, Merleau-Ponty contends, requires not that I try to redefine myself according to a "premeditated signification," but that I "live naïvely what offers itself" to me (AD 288, tr. 197). If history is like one of Matisse's unfinished paintings, then it is folly for me to hope to complete it as Matisse would have done. My own experiences and style inevitably intervene. I will distort Matisse's intentions and stunt what is original in my own means of expression. It would be better simply to embrace what I am. Because I am necessarily the expression of innumerable historical sedimentations, my style, if explored with originality and courage, has the best chance of making contact with my contemporaries. Politicians, says Merleau-Ponty, like artists, do their most universal work when they "are not too aware that they are founding a human community" (S 78, tr. 62). Both aim, not at a given public, but at one that their works will elicit. There is an advent of political meaning when a leader draws people "toward values in which they will only later recognize their values" (S 92, tr. 74).

The stress on an irreducible multiplicity of values and historical forms, the admiration for Weber, pragmatism—in these respects Merleau-Ponty's late political thought resembles nothing so much as Raymond Aron's philosophy of history of the 1930s.[21] It also suffers the same defects.

[21] This fact was noted in several reviews. See Nadeau, "MM. Aron, Merleau-Ponty, et les intellectuels," p. 903; Beauvoir, "Merleau-Ponty et le pseudo-Sartrisme," in *Privilèges*, pp. 243, 245. Significantly, in 1955 Merleau-Ponty defended Aron's philosophy of history without repeating his earlier criticisms. See "À quoi

New Impediments to Political Thinking

I argued in the preceding chapter that Merleau-Ponty's late political thought advances a number of cautionary themes. These rightly lower the sights of a theorist who too often spoke as if every event in human history was part of a single structure destined to actualize a society of perfect freedom. Nonetheless, from the perspective of his reflections on the problems of political thinking, it is difficult to be encouraged about his later works. In what follows, I contend that Merleau-Ponty's Saussurean conception of history undermines what he believed essential to political knowledge and action and yet does not found a credible alternative way of thinking politically.

Most of the problems in Merleau-Ponty's late political thought stem from his adoption of a philosophy of history implying that meaning can be read only retrospectively. Thinking politically, he always insisted, demands realism and realism demands foresight. Political thinkers gear action onto perceivable trends in history. Every responsible leader must be able to contemplate the retreat of power when failure seems likely and its daring advance when possibilities in the present situation adumbrate the social forms of a desired future.

Particularly vital in such readings of history is a conception of "founding" phenomena. In the 1940s Merleau-Ponty would not follow the neocommunists in reducing all noneconomic motivations to mere epiphenomena. At the same time, his dialogue with Aron taught that political thinkers know that some things count more than others (SNS 297, tr. 168). He argued that economic factors, although not determining, were nonetheless generally the meanings most likely to structure social life in our time. Some such intuitions are essential to political action because action aims at success, and success depends importantly on not squandering energy and resources, on concentrating efforts on people who are likely to respond, on anticipating probable lines of fracture in the social system. It was precisely the function of Merleau-Ponty's philosophy of history to draw up a schedule of motives that would identify those aspects of society most likely to influence the course of events.

But a Saussurean philosophy of history obstructs precisely these judgments. By positing that a contingent association of any social

---

sert l'objectivité?" p. 4. Aron still saw important differences between himself and Merleau-Ponty. See *Marxism and the Existentialists*, pp. 45–80.

phenomena can create meaning, it makes it impossible to regard any particular domain of existence as inherently more likely to influence political affairs than any other. And by asserting that *sens* appears only after the fact, it makes it futile to try to read contemporary events, which are by definition unfinished. It is hard to see how political actors who cannot read historical *sens* could even choose among proposed objectives, since they lack any solid grounds for their judgments about the likely success or failure of their projects. Merleau-Ponty's new philosophy of history promotes not a new caution in political judgment, but a paralyzing bewilderment. It is significant that in his entire discussion of the advent of rationalization, for example, he never suggests that anyone might have grasped this meaning and used it to political advantage. He does well to warn us about a certain one-dimensionality in his political diagnoses of the 1940s. But without an alternative schedule of motives or some ideas about how to construct one *à l'improviste,* his late thought sheds no further light on the nature of the factual assessments that go into political choice.

Lost along with the idea of foundational motives is the thinker's own reflexive analysis. The determination that economic motives are founding does more than tell theorists what social phenomena to scan for historical *sens;* it calls for them to try to understand the conditions of their own thought and, to the extent possible, to correct for their own biases—especially class biases. For intellectuals, who are particularly prone to believing that it is possible to translate ideals directly in practice, this reflexivity is essential to political thinking. Merleau-Ponty's Saussurean history, however, gives no clues about what factors in personal experience are especially likely to distort the thinker's understanding. In fact, he appears simply to cease worrying about such distortions. How strange it is to find this political realist joining Mendès-France, but paying no attention to the weakening social forces—largely the traditional Radicals—that support the Mendesist party.[22]

What is most troubling is that conceiving history on the model of a diachronic linguistics of speech falls into something resembling the dilemmas of subjectivism and objectivism that Merleau-Ponty so long strove to avoid. On the one hand, a theory of hypercontingent advents commits something like the subjectivist error. It does not help us understand how emergent meaning reaches beyond the present to shape alternatives for the future. It

---

[22] Invitto, *Merleau-Ponty politico,* p. 106.

attenuates the apparent resistance of social forms. It suggests that almost any combination of meanings might or might not settle fortuitously into a meaningful structure. How different is this from Sartre's error of making it seem that "a social revolution might be possible at any moment" (PP 512, tr. 449)?

On the other hand, Merleau-Ponty commits something like the objectivist mistake. He uses vague concepts like "adversity" and "inertia" to denote *every* sort of resistance that a project may encounter. Adversity groups together psychological and economic forces, errors in prediction, intractable materials, people's attachment to cherished traditions. It is as if he is hurrying to the conclusion that no amount of knowledge, no methodology, no reading of social trends will ever penetrate the "thickness" of history and allow those who act to get a grip on the direction of political change. He is aware, for example, that Weber worried about the disenchantment and mystification that rationalization spread. But he never hints that Weber's understanding of rationalization might have allowed him to oppose it in any way—as if rationalization were simply an ineluctable force. How different is this from placing the dialectic "in being, beyond debate, and beyond practice" (AD 109, tr. 72)?

If Merleau-Ponty were interested in facilitating political action or even debate, one would expect him to differentiate the forms of "adversity," for surely they are not all equally immovable. Their differences are precisely what will interest one who acts politically. In the 1950s, if he believes that the revolutionary experience has encountered previously unperceived sources of social inertia, he should be able to *specify* them. He might have concluded, like Poulantzas, that traditional Marxist theory insufficiently appreciates the "opacity and resistance" of a state that is not merely the expression of class contradictions.[23] Or he might, like Adorno and Horkheimer, have seen the ways that "the culture industry" throws obstacles in the path of radical social change.[24] Or, in a more liberal vein, he could have reopened the question of whether his phenomenology underestimated the rationality of ordinary citizens, who might resist political initiatives because they have a better understanding of their own needs than any party. The important point is that in the perspective of action, one seeks to per-

---

[23] *Political Power and Social Classes*, p. 131.

[24] "The Culture Industry: Enlightenment as Mass Deception," in *The Dialectic of Enlightenment*, pp. 120–167.

ceive obstacles as precisely as possible in order to devise ways to break or avoid or modify them. Merleau-Ponty's imprecision about the nature of the social "positivity" on which the revolution founders suggests an unwillingness to look at political problems from the point of view of one who, while trying to give new values an institutional form, must work to overcome impediments to action.

The entire problem of the status of values in an existential theory is hardly clarified by Merleau-Ponty's late ruminations. The ethical import of political thinking as he conceived it in the 1940s was the reduction or elimination of violence. Violence—the objectification of others—was *the* political problem (HT 128, tr. 110). He criticized liberalism for perpetuating violence by hiding it in its statements of principle and by profiting from it in its economic life. At the same time, he admired Marxism for admitting the political necessity of violence while placing its use in the context of prospects for creating a nonviolent social system.[25] Although his early thought must be criticized for refusing to evaluate the moral acceptability of different types and degrees of violence, still it has the virtue of keeping in front of political thinkers an ideal of nonviolence. By not implicating every conceivable regime in the principal political evil, it leaves political thinkers with the responsibility of devising ways of countering violence wherever it occurs. Merleau-Ponty himself worked on a theory of the limits of the violence that party leaders might exercise on the workers.

It is to be feared that his post-Marxian work, however, inadvertently diminishes this responsibility. He agrees with Weber that "*all* politics is violence, even democratic politics, in its own way" (AD 42, tr. 26, emphasis added). No doubt he came to believe that parliamentary regimes practice less violence—less censorship, less political imprisonment, and so on—against their citizens than Communist ones. But he continues to avoid any detailed comparison of regimes on this issue. Worse, when he talks of democracy's "own way" of violence, he can be interpreted as suggesting that it is not worth trying to eliminate violence wherever it occurs because some is inherent in the system. By regarding violence as a universal aspect of politics, he diminishes the incentive to push at the social system in order to find the inessential forms of violence it harbors. Moreover, since he no longer supposes any group to prefigure an ethically superior form of social existence, there is no

[25] See Eslin, "Critique de l'humanisme vertueux," p. 11.

obvious reason why leaders must observe a dialogical check on their truthfulness. While his late writings throw out the unconvincing idea of an absolute end to violence, they fail to add to a political thinker's understanding of the limits to its use.

These writings also erode the lessons of his political consequentialism. Merleau-Ponty had emphasized in the 1940s that the responsibilities of political actors must extend to the consequences of their acts because they alter the course of events in a public's name and for its good. If consequences are not to be evaluated according to a crude calculus of ends and means, he argued, they must be read from an interpretation of historical trends that are favoring the establishment of certain values. Merleau-Ponty's later writings do not renounce political consequentialism. But neither do they acknowledge that a Saussurean philosophy of history works against *any* consequentialism in two ways. First, since historical sens appears only after the fact, there can be no question of political leaders sorting among present trends to detect those that will fulfill moral goals in the future. Just how one can act as a consequentialist without being able to foresee the development of events is very unclear.

Second, consequentialism requires political actors to choose their commitments after somehow calculating likely effects of different courses of action. But to say that leaders invent "what will appear later as that which was required by the times" seems dangerously receptive to every sort of political adventurism. It sounds as if Fascists and fundamentalists, liberals and communists alike are invited to see if they can make their preferred meanings prevail. What blocks that conclusion in his earlier work is the contention that the sens of history is prospectively perceivable and morally acceptable. Where moral meanings are purely adventitious, however, there is nothing obvious to save theory from a vicious relativism.

Similar problems bedevil the rest of his late political counsel. To advise us to "live naïvely what offers itself" makes moral sense if one believes, as he did in the 1940s, that lived existence contains in embryo the values of a humanistic politics. But that premise is now gone. Merleau-Ponty's advice seems much less tenable in a world in which people's "naïve" selves are fashioned in the schools of Stalin, Franco, and Hitler. To argue that "what makes a politics important is . . . the human quality that . . . makes the most personal acts [of the leaders] everyone's affair" (AD 46, tr. 28–29) is to establish a moral criterion of leadership, but only if "everyone's affair" does not happen to be barbarism and repression.

I do not mean that Merleau-Ponty actually intends to sanction every form of political life. He probably still believes that existence somehow "naturally" confirms good ways of life and condemns bad ones. He does not discard his old Trotskyist formula according to which history contains a principle of selection that tends to eliminate errors (AD 46, tr. 28; S 92, tr. 74). But that implies that there is an ethical ranking of forms, at least as between those conducive to human development and those that mislead it, and that history has enough positive structure to promote relatively good forms. We then have a right to demand from Merleau-Ponty an account of those values to which he has alluded and an account of how a local, fragmented history can have this global structure.

A final index of the setback of political thinking in Merleau-Ponty's writings of the 1950s concerns not its explicit themes but its rhetorical approach. His rejection of direct engagement entails his foresaking that calculated presentation of his views—partial interpretations, arguments structured by the figure-background relation, dialogical exchanges—that constituted the politics of his theory in the 1940s. For there can be little doubt that his earlier political engagements stood in a certain tension with a commitment to truth telling. When he defended Sartre, he often deliberately gave his friend's philosophy a new accent. In his interpretation of Lenin, he willfully ignored the scientism of *Materialism and Empiriocriticism*. In Merleau-Ponty's unpublished notes are found doubts about bureaucratic tendencies in Leninism that never made their way into his writings of the 1940s.[26] He once as much as admitted the intervention of political motives in the way he stated the conclusions of *Humanism and Terror*.[27] What is at stake in such

---

[26] In personal reading notes on *State and Revolution*, Merleau-Ponty complains that Lenin's theory of the dictatorship of the proletariat "has the disadvantage of not specifying . . . how the workers will control it and consequently leaves the door open to the formation of a bureacracy" (IN 127).

[27] This admission comes in an interview in 1959. "I could show [my conclusion] to you in the book, but I recall quite well that I drew it verbally in a conversation with Sartre. *It is not something I would have said in public at that time*, but I can quite well talk about it now. We were talking about the book, which was finished, and I said to Sartre: 'Well, you know, when all is considered, when one has gone through all these events, the trials, communism, nothing more remains than to be a radical—a radical in the traditional sense in France, that is a member of the Radical party, or something of this sort. I remember that Sartre was very shocked by this conclusion—but it was indeed my conclusion." *Humanisme et terreur*, Merleau-

matters of presentation is not simple deceptiveness, but an attempt to make thought politically effective in a dialogue of a certain structure. In fact, it would be disingenuous for a philosophy in which "vérité" is always "à faire" to exclude political concerns from its own presentation.

There is no such obliqueness in Merleau-Ponty's late writings. They contain blunt critiques of Sartre and Lenin, unvarnished admissions of earlier errors, bald assertions of the virtues of liberalism. If the philosopher's engagement is for the long term, then a much more direct form of truth telling is in order for the present. Concluding his lecture "In Praise of Philosophy," Merleau-Ponty cites with approval a saying by Alain: "[The truth] belongs to a situation and to an instant of time; one must see it, speak it, do it at that moment, neither before nor after" (EP 72, tr. 62). That is exactly the sort of maxim that he had rejected in the 1940s as *unpolitical* because it takes no account of the circumstances in which the truth is spoken, the possible biases of the truth teller, and the appearance of this truth in the eyes of others. Yet if this is the sort of truth at which he aims in essays on the Hungarian revolt, colonialism, and the Algerian uprising, then it is not surprising that they show no subtle interplay between argument, the views of selected interlocutors, and the norms of political action. The structure of these writings, in other words, cannot enlighten us further about the problems of thinking politically since political thought is for those who act, while Merleau-Ponty now joins those who see and understand.

An Invisible Politics?

The Adventures of the Dialectic predates the radical renewal of his thought that he undertook at the end of the 1950s. His unfinished work, *The Visible and the Invisible*, was to begin everything anew in his philosophy. The *Adventures* is not a final statement of his ideas, but a transitional work, one that still uses the language of the 1940s while anticipating his late ontological speculations.[28] It is

---

Ponty interviewed by Georges Charbonnier, RTF, 1959, emphasis added. I am still unable to find this conclusion in the book. Perhaps what Merleau-Ponty meant is that the Radical party, with its support of civil liberties and its "flirtation" with the Communists around 1945, was the party closest to his own programmatic conclusions. See Williams, *Crisis and Compromise*, p. 126.

[28] For development of this argument, see Schmidt, rev. of *The Adventures of the Dialectic*, trans. Bien, pp. 463–478.

conceivable that he would have eventually addressed some of the questions that his political writings of the mid-1950s left unanswered.[29] What evidence is there that he was, or was not, on such a path?

Two related problems in his earlier work prompted the radical rethinking embodied in *The Visible and the Invisible*. He was dissatisfied, first, with a latent dualism in his phenomenology. His concept of a being-in-the-world was meant to convey the indissoluble unity of a being and its world. But his critics made a telling observation: the very definition of the relationship in these terms presupposes a prior dualism of subject and object.[30] By 1959 he apparently agreed. "The problems posed in *The Phenomenology of Perception* are insoluble," Merleau-Ponty writes in a working note, "because I begin there with the consciousness-object distinction" (VI 253, tr. 199). Phenomenology makes objects secondary to reflective apprehension. It successfully counters the empiricist view of mind as a passive register of objective sense data. But it then quickly flees into the subjectivist camp. It regards perception as the outcome of a consciousness' intentional *acts* (VI 297, tr. 243). Unavoidably it ascends to that "high-altitude" perspective that surveys the world rather than participates in it. Merleau-Ponty's last works attempt to explain how both consciousness and objects are secondary to a more fundamental unity.[31]

The second difficulty addressed in his last writings is the ontological status of the world and consciousness. Husserlian phenomenology suspends the ontological question. In order to analyze the structure of appearance, it brackets the question of what makes appearance possible. Yet if consciousness and world are "for" each other, clearly it makes sense to ask what "upholds our life and the life of the world" (S 208, tr. 165)? A philosophical interrogation of Saussurean linguistics leads in a similar direction. Saussure's emphasis on the synchronic structures of language shows that the individual is not the center of the creation of meaning. We think

[29] Asked in 1960 whether he would write any more books on politics, he replied that "political philosophy will come with the rest." Merleau-Ponty in Chapsal, *Les écrivains en personne*, p. 163.

[30] Merleau-Ponty had to defend his phenomenology against this charge even at his dissertation defense. Interview with Jean Pouillon, July 20, 1979. Émile Bréhier also pressed him on this point at a public lecture. See "Le primat de la perception," p. 138.

[31] Taminiaux, "Phenomenology in Merleau-Ponty's Late Work," in *Life-World and Consciousness*, ed. Embree, p. 320.

within a framework of diacritical oppositions that our language makes available to us. But if the individual is not the source of speech, it is not overly enigmatic to ask "what . . . speaks?" (VI 230, tr. 176). There must be in being itself a tendency toward expression. Merleau-Ponty's answer to the ontological question and his alternative to consciousness-object dualism is a philosophy positing that the body and the world are "made of the same stuff" (OE 21, tr. 164).

He calls this primordial unity "flesh" or "brute being." Neither matter nor idea, flesh is what makes consciousness and world present to each other (VI 193, tr. 147). The seeing body and the seen thing are, in Gary Madison's words, "but differentiations of the same fabric, the same primordial Being."[32] Together they form a "chiasm," an intertwining and reversibility in which meaning arises and articulates itself. This articulation, it must be stressed, is still a temporal process, although it has no definable goal. Merleau-Ponty's Being is not static or perfected. Being is a "thrust" (S 21, tr. 14), a perpetual ferment of symbolic expressiveness. In this perspective, consciousness takes place within Being by its self-transcending acts of creation because "Being is that which requires creation of us so that we can experience Being" (VI 251, tr. 197).

What does this talk of flesh and chiasms amount to politically? It is hard to know. Attempts to extract a politics from Merleau-Ponty's last writings have yielded numerous vague and contradictory formulas. An ontology that treats Being as an "intrinsically harmonious unity . . . implies that there can be no fundamental disharmony of human being" and this in turn ends in a rather complacent pluralism says Kruks.[33] Not so, replies Schmidt; there is no reason to assume that Merleau-Ponty's ontology has any such implications for human social arrangements.[34] Langan believes that Merleau-Ponty's last published article, "The Eye and the Mind," contains a "condemnation of activism."[35] And yet, as Howard points out, there is an activism implicit in a concept of history that sees the future as "our present: a task always to be begun anew."[36] Nonetheless, "the practical ethical implication that Merleau-Ponty drew from his later theoretical reflections was that one must learn to moderate one's indignation at suffering or be-

[32] *The Phenomenology of Merleau-Ponty*, p. 172.
[33] *The Political Philosophy of Merleau-Ponty*, p. 121.
[34] "Maurice Merleau-Ponty: Politics, Phenomenology, and Ontology," p. 300.
[35] *Merleau-Ponty's Critique*, p. 116.
[36] *The Marxian Legacy*, p. 217.

holding injustice," concludes Cooper.[37] A theory in which silence is an integral part of expression, argues Dauenhauer, embraces a politics that is "perpetually interrogatory and self-critical."[38] It is a politics of hope.[39] Yet, says Eslin, since history is "capricious, cynical . . . , mendacious," this hope is grounded at best in a sort of Machiavellian virtue that seeks only to "put a little more truth in the relations of the strong and the weak."[40] Wisely, none of these interpreters attempts to apply Merleau-Ponty's late thought to concrete political situations.

If we eschew broad inferences from his ontology and stick close to what he actually says about politics in his last writings, we find that he still has not extricated himself from the theoretical impasse created by the Saussurean philosophy of history. The most important consequence of an ontology of the flesh for a study of Merleau-Ponty's political theory is its emphatic refusal of any mode of thought that aspires to completion or transparency. To say that "I am of it" ("j'en suis") is to claim that the intertwining of my vision with the thing seen makes impossible any experience of the whole of a phenomenon. But it also forbids philosophy simply to merge into the stream of life. This is the sense in which the only direct mention of politics in *The Visible and the Invisible* occurs: "[There is] 'no purely philosophical politics, for example, there is no philosophical rigorism when it is a question of a manifesto. However, philosophy is not immediately nonphilosophy . . . , which would reduce history to the visible, which would deprive it precisely of its depth on the pretext of adhering to it better' " (VI 319–320, tr. 266). Philosophy cannot immediately join praxis, for the attempt to fuse with objects of knowledge is self-defeating. It abolishes the critical distance that allows objects to appear, it brings to an end the creative dialectic that is born of difference.[41] The visible inevitably leaves a fecund invisibility unperceived. Every advent of meaning calls forth new symbolizations that no thought can fully anticipate. "Being, by the very requirement of each of its perspectives . . . [is] a system with several entrances. Therefore it cannot

---

[37] *Merleau-Ponty and Marxism*, p. 176.

[38] "One Central Link between Merleau-Ponty's Philosophy of Language and His Political Thought," pp. 77–79.

[39] Dauenhauer, "Merleau-Ponty's Political Thought: Its Nature and Its Challenge," in *Phenomenology in a Pluralist Context*, eds. McBride and Schrag, p. 23.

[40] "Critique de l'humanisme vertueux," pp. 16–17.

[41] Silverman, "Re-reading Merleau-Ponty," p. 110.

be contemplated from the outside and in a single instant, but must be gone through" (VI 123, tr. 89–90).

Returning to Marx and Hegel in his final set of lectures at the Collège de France, Merleau-Ponty finds that Marx came close to this conception of thought, only to miss it for believing "too soon that he had found the key—the proletarian philosophy of history."[42] Marx's notion of praxis is a philosophy of "carnal man," not a Hegelian philosophy of consciousness.[43] Merleau-Ponty first discussed such a mode of thought in 1958, when he said that "something comes to an end with Hegel" and intimated that, with Marx, Nietzsche, and Kierkegaard, "we enter into an age of nonphilosophy" (RC 141–142, tr. 100). Nonphilosophy borders on pure interrogation, a search for the very possibility of philosophy. Unlike philosophy, where, up until Hegel, the thinker claims to be able to *formulate* a metaphysics (and thus claims to be above the individuating conditions of human knowledge), nonphilosophy focuses on the everyday life from which philosophy is born. Marx regards the revolutionary activities of the proletariat and the logic of the capitalist economy as the experiential form of philosophy. If history is a productive milieu in which nature, the individual, and others are in a perpetual process of redefinition and creation, then the nonphilosophy of praxis converges with the characteristics of Merleau-Ponty's new ontology: "[There is] no cleavage between matter and idea, object and subject, nature and man, in itself and for itself, but a single Being in which negativity works. . . . [History is] the very flesh of man."[44] Where Marx went wrong was in foreseeing an end to negativity, in enclosing it between Nature and self-adequation.[45]

The claims Merleau-Ponty makes in 1961 in favor of Marxian praxis are not substantially different from those he advanced in 1946 (cf. SNS 231, tr. 130), and the complaint that he lodges against Marxian negativity hardly departs from what he said in *The Adventures of the Dialectic*. What is different is that he now believes that the political failures of Marxism stem from not having pursued its insights at the level of being.[46] "Marxism suffers for not having expressly posed itself the [ontological] problem. . . . It re-

---

[42] Merleau-Ponty in Chapsal, *Les écrivains en personne*, p. 156.

[43] Merleau-Ponty, "Philosophie et non-philosophie depuis Hegel," p. 159.

[44] Ibid., p. 168.

[45] Ibid., p. 172.

[46] I cannot agree therefore with Kruks, who charges that Merleau-Ponty depoliticizes Marx by studying him only for what he contributes to the new ontology. *The Political Philosophy of Merleau-Ponty*, pp. 130–131.

lied on the Hegelian categories of the subject and the object, whose relations it limited itself to reversing. That overturned and yet preserved Hegelianism was profoundly obscure. One could show that in that initial obscurity is to be found the origin of *all the surprises* that Marxism held in store for those who were to follow it on the historical terrain."[47] He hints at the "surprises" of Marxism in the preface to *Signs* when he connects "the Marxist ontology" to the "unlimited use of authority" that manifested itself tragically in Budapest in 1956 (S 14, tr. 9). Today, Merleau-Ponty concludes, we should regard Marxism as one of the most powerful advents of meaning. No longer true in an immediate sense, Marx's writings remain "an immense field of sedimented history and thought where one goes to practice and to learn how to think" (S 12, tr. 5).

Fair enough. But what would post-Marxian political thinking look like? What would it examine first and what would it practice? This is where Merleau-Ponty lapses again into unhelpful generalities. The role of philosophy is to "unveil the being that we inhabit," to disclose "fundamental meaning-structures" (S 20, tr. 13). Philosophy is perpetual interrogation. But is *perpetual* interrogation not as contradictory as the "permanent revolution" that he criticized in *The Adventures of the Dialectic*? Was he not right to say in 1946 that "as soon as we do something, we turn toward the world, stop self-questioning, and go beyond ourselves in what we do" (SNS 317, tr. 179)? Just as vision requires a "perceptual faith" (we act as if we are certain of what we see, even though our perspectives are always partial), so there must be an activistic faith that promotes a particular vision of justice even though it may become outmoded. The problem with Merleau-Ponty's late philosophy is not that it directly denies the necessity of such an activistic faith. Rather, the problem is that he develops an all-embracing ontology in which there is no obvious place for specific political demands.[48] The faith may continue, but it has no ends toward which it might aspire even provisionally.

The Fate of a Project

Eight months before his death, Merleau-Ponty reflected back upon the confidence with which he once sought to "penser la politique."

[47] Merleau-Ponty in Chapsal, *Les écrivains en personne*, p. 157, emphasis added.
[48] Cf. Sichère, *Merleau-Ponty*, p. 163.

Everything we believed to be thought through [*pensé*] and thought through well—liberty and authority, the citizen against authority, the citizen's heroism, liberal humanism, formal democracy and the real democracy that suppresses and realizes it, revolutionary heroism and humanism—all of that is in ruin. But we should be careful. What we call disorder and ruin, others who are younger experience as natural and perhaps they will master it with ingenuity precisely because they no longer take their bearings where we took ours. (S 31–32, tr. 22–23)

Optimistically, he believes that the exhausted guides of his generation may finally be dismissed and a path out of the ruins discovered. Yet there is pessimism too, for he implies that it will be a younger generation, not himself, who will break the impasse. His quandary at the end of his life was strangely similar to Sartre's in the 1940s: while he had criticisms and political positions to advance, the philosophical groundwork that he adopted did not help him *think* them.

We do best, I think, not to fabricate a politics from his late works, but rather to see them as a corrective to what was most implausible in his earlier thought and then to acknowledge that, with respect to a new synthesis in political thinking, he made little progress. He began a new era in his politics in 1951 with a critique of Marxism and a "call to invention."[49] Nine years later he was still saying "everything needs to be started over, in politics as in philosophy."[50] That he covered so little distance in the reconstruction of political theory is directly connected, I think, to his having dulled most of the tools for "thinking politics" that he had fashioned in the 1940s. Not only did he reject the notion of an end of history, he adopted a theory making any prospective scrutiny of the course of events seem futile. Not only did he deny that economic motives found the structures of social relations, he refused to look further for any founding phenomena. Not only did he deprive the proletariat of any claim to be the essential value-fact for all humanity, he made all values seem like adventitious aspects of symbol systems whose validity is simply local. What is so dissatisfying in his late political writings is that, while not denying the necessity of political thinking, they conceive meaning and history in such a way that politics seems once again "impensable." Mer-

---

[49] Merleau-Ponty, *La connaissance de l'homme au XXe siècle*, 1951, p. 242.
[50] Merleau-Ponty in Chapsal, *Les écrivains en personne*, p. 163.

leau-Ponty's calls for us to "live naïvely" what presents itself to us or for us to depend on political leaders whose "human quality" animates a party apparatus come uncomfortably close to a conclusion that we do better simply to follow our instincts than to *think through* our political problems.

At best, his ontological reflections are a sort of meta-metatheory of human activity. Unlike a first-order political theory (at least of the Marxist or Leninist sort), they do not conceptualize what is taking place in the social world and coordinate action accordingly. In truth, Merleau-Ponty never wrote much in this vein. But in the 1940s he did make his phenomenology into a genuine metatheory of politics. His existentialism explains how and under what conditions *thinking about* political action is possible. His late ontological writings do not even do that. They tell us only how to *think about thinking about* responding to the problems of collective existence. A philosophy of flesh attempts to account for the possibility of a phenomenology by reference to an elementary unity that makes meaning be. Merleau-Ponty's ontology is thus at two removes from any political argument about "what is to be done." One can charitably interpret a philosophy of "perpetual interrogation" as a call for us to do our own political thinking.[51] That, however, takes us only to the threshold of political theory. We come to a theorist in the first place not to be told how we *must* think about political problems, but to receive some instruction about what political phenomena are important, about what unsuspected relationships may hold between them, about what action is necessary or permissible, about what values are worth pursuing and why. To be told that "the task of the philosopher [is] . . . to elaborate such a concept of being that contradictions—neither accepted nor 'surpassed'—find their place in it" is to encounter a mode of thought does little to help us think politically (RC 128, tr. 90).

The problems of a "politique pensable," however, do not disappear for the theorist's exhaustion or for his having adopted a philosophy that distances itself from political thinking. Had Merleau-Ponty used his critiques of Marxian and Sartrean dualism to develop a more modest theory of historical objectivity, had he worked on a more complex theory of "founding" phenomena (or perhaps on a theory of how to orient political action in the absence of foundations), had he proffered some justification and elucida-

---

[51] That seems to be Dick Howard's approach in *The Marxian Legacy*, p. 213.

tion of the values he endorsed, then he might have strengthened his political thinking rather than undercut it. In the concluding chapter, I want to suggest how his thought might be reinforced in precisely such ways. But the significant fact remains that, whatever his plans for a new political theory, he had not developed it by the time of his death.

For this reason, if one wishes to appreciate the cognitive and ethical problems of thinking politically, it is appropriate to focus on Merleau-Ponty's writings of the 1940s. That is not to say that his views in those works are always right, clear, consistent, or plausible. Manifestly they often are not, and it is important to criticize them. But it is the boldness of their vision—bold, at times, to the point of pressing beyond their own assumptions—that gives them a productive tension missing from his later political commentary. Some would argue that the phenomenological viewpoint is unable to promote particular values.[52] But Merleau-Ponty, aware of the inevitability of values in a political thought, brings values into his analysis through a combination of Marxism and Gestalt-theorie. For the existentialist, historical interpretation is always open to new perspectives, but Merleau-Ponty, aware of the activist's need for a concrete understanding of developing social phenomena, insists on an objectivity grounded in subjectivity. Existentialism usually defends the meaning of the individual's life against any attempt to reduce his existence to its significance for some larger whole. But Merleau-Ponty, aware that any notion of a public good requires individuals to make some unwanted sacrifices, seeks a mode of thought that permits, within limits, a "statistical treatment of man." Finally, believing that any statement, to be true in the public realm, must be consequential, he uses rhetorical strategies in his writings designed to change the perceptions of his interlocutors. But he is also a man of great integrity, who by dint of his own sense of propriety never allows this politics of theory to become mendacious. His later works are arguably more consistent than his earlier ones. He becomes more open to non-Marxist values and less attached to a single reading of history, more emphatic about the unique value of a man like Socrates and less inclined to temper his views to achieve practical effects. But that is also to say that he purchases philosophical consistency at a certain expense in political percipience.

So the defects of his early works are of a piece with their

---

[52] Bernstein, *The Restructuring of Social and Political Theory*, p. 168.

achievements. It is when Merleau-Ponty felt the urgency and inescapability of thinking politically, when he believed that there was something vitally important that could yet be *achieved* in politics, that he elaborated his *political* thought in the most compelling way. This is not particularly surprising. But it does justify returning to the foundation of an existential politics for some concluding remarks about what is most enduring in his political theory.

T E N

CONCLUSION:
THINKING POLITICS IN
CONTEMPORARY THEORY

A convincing case for Merleau-Ponty's importance to contemporary political theory could be made by documenting his direct impact on a variety of influential thinkers. Michel Foucault was his student at the Sorbonne and often used his teacher's phenomenology as a foil in constructing his own archeology of the human sciences.[1] His inspiration is found in the social theories of Claude Lefort and Cornelius Castoriadis.[2] In the United States, a number of those interested in postbehavioral political inquiry gratefully acknowledge debts to Merleau-Ponty.[3] And of course, Sartre's understanding of history and class in the *Critique of Dialectical Reason* owes much to his corrective dialogue with Merleau-Ponty in the 1940s.[4]

But I believe we do more to establish the vitality of a theorist's work by actually confronting his ideas with those of a few currently prominent theorists than by sketching out his influence on many. A discussion of the former sort will help me clarify some of Merleau-Ponty's arguments, pinpoint his principal strengths and weaknesses, and show where his ideas could profitably inform recent theory. Of course, no selection of a small number of theorists for comparison can possibly be immune from the criticism of having omitted an important figure. I would argue, however, that what matters most is simply that those selected be widely respected for having posed significant political questions and that they represent a wide range of theoretical approaches. I conclude

---

[1] Dreyfus and Rabinow, *Michel Foucault*, pp. 33–34.

[2] Howard, *The Marxian Legacy*, pp. 223, 249, 287.

[3] See, for example, Jung, *The Crisis of Political Understanding*, p. xv; Dallmayr, *Beyond Dogma and Despair*, pp. 11–17, 166–168; Warren, *The Emergence of Dialectical Theory*, pp. 102–129, 181.

[4] Sartre, "Merleau-Ponty vivant," p. 322; Hayman, *Sartre*, p. 343.

therefore by assessing Merleau-Ponty's theory in relation to the work of Michael Walzer, John Rawls, and Michel Foucault—three thinkers who, in addition to meeting the criteria just mentioned, elaborate in particularly interesting ways patterns of thinking at issue in an existential politics.

At the end of my study, this conclave of theorists must be kept brief. Difficult interpretive controversies involved in understanding another set of complex works undoubtedly will not get all the attention they deserve. Still I think there is enough truth in my sketches of these theories to indicate accurately what might be the results of an exchange of views between the existentialist and those whose renown has spread since his death. If I am right, even this short meeting will support my belief that today's theorists would do well to keep closer company with Merleau-Ponty.

Particularity and Justice: Michael Walzer

What defines an existential approach to political thinking is implied in Merleau-Ponty's reply to charges that existentialism is an irrationalist philosophy. "Today's philosophers do not renounce rationality," he responds; "they renounce only an impostor of reason that is satisfied to be right for itself and to withdraw itself from the judgment of other people." Existential reason opens itself to the alterity of culturally specific categories and values. It "seeks out agreement . . . , not only in . . . solitary thought, but also in the experience of concrete situations and in dialogue with others" (HT 192, tr. 187). This conception of reason places existential political theory in opposition to a philosophical tradition (or rather, to one interpretation of that tradition) stretching from Plato to Kant. Ever since Plato condemned sophistry, political thinking and philosophy have generally followed separate paths.

If political philosophy signifies an effort to discover the proper purposes and the best form of government, then in comparison political thinking—the reasoning of those who directly seek power, achievement, and influence in and for their community— seems like a bastard form of thought. Where philosophy is noble (it describes perfection), political thinking is base (it can condone scheming, lying, even killing). Philosophy is eternal, political thinking is contingent. The one speaks of natural laws and transcultural categories of regimes, the other deals in passing values and rough estimates of momentary trends. Philosophy claims to be disinterested; it seeks only the general good. Political thinking acknowledges its interest in particular goods for particular people. Philosophers distrust power and so prefer to see it exercised by the virtuous for lofty purposes. Political thinkers pursue power avidly and listen intently to the petty, everyday concerns of all who can help them govern. To use the time-honored distinction, philosophy deals with the essence of politics, political thinking with its existence. That distinction implies a ranking: philosophy judges political thinking, not vice versa.

But what if philosophers who thought they spoke of eternal essences in fact expressed the narrow norms of a particular nation and class? And what if our best evidence and philosophical reflections generalized that lesson, concluding, as in Merleau-Ponty's phenomenology, that essences are constituted out of existence? No longer measured against a standard that is beyond human experience, political thinking would appear no more defective than the perspectivism inherent in vision. Just as the fact that our views are always partial is not evidence that perception gives fundamentally defective knowledge (because no knowledge is conceivable apart from perceptual experience), so the fact that reasoning draws upon contingent social meanings is not evidence of inherently defective thinking (because particularist understandings of social phenomena are the necessary stuff of human reasoning). In this view there is no absolute subordination of political thinking to political philosophy; the one shades into the other. Political thinking supplies the values and categories that philosophers refine, and the philosophers' refined formulations work their way into common discourse, eventually reshaping the choices of those who use them. Reflection on this dialectic of political particularity and philosophical generalization yields an existentialist, as opposed to essentialist, political theory.

At times, it is true, Merleau-Ponty obscured this lesson. In the 1950s he opted for liberalism without exploring its roots in French culture and without clarifying how it should handle direct challenges from value systems like communism. In the 1940s an overly idealist interpretation of Marx sometimes confounded his commitment to political particularity. By arguing that a resolution to all problems of social justice is at least conceivably immanent in the historical process, he escaped a confrontation with the philosophical consequences of ethical pluralism. An existential theory without the Marxian hypothesis would acknowledge that the contingently formed values of different groups of people collide in ways that no cultural evolution is likely to avoid. Nonetheless, to offer any guidance to political thinkers, it would have to justify certain values because of their importance in the ways of life of particular communities. How one might develop such a theory is illustrated in the recent work of Michael Walzer.

In *Spheres of Justice* Walzer denies that there are universal, transcultural, and transhistorical principles of justice. Just distribution, he maintains, depends instead on the meanings that goods acquire in particular cultures at particular times.[5] If we understand the values that people build into their conceptions of goods like needs, office, education, and political power, we will appreciate that, for this community, there are particular just ways of acquiring them. To know whether bread is justly distributed or not, for example, we must find out whether, among these people, it is primarily considered a basic food stuff, a luxury, a religious symbol. A luxury is rightly an object of bargaining on the open market. But where a community recognizes a good as a need, it commits itself to a provision of that good to all its members in proportion to need. Goods, Walzer concludes, belong to different "spheres of justice" that define the specific considerations relevant to their rightful distribution.[6] The task of the theorist is to stand inside a culture, to grasp the meanings it creates, and to evaluate the degree to which that community adheres to the distributive criteria implicit in its own understanding of its social goods.

Numerous theoretical commitments that Walzer shares with Merleau-Ponty make it appropriate to read the former's work as "existential."[7] Both start from a recognition of the historical and cultural specificity of values. Both believe that groups and the meanings they create, not isolated individuals and causes, must be the matter of political reflection. The two thinkers concede that political action sometimes demands violence to achieve the community's good.[8] Both conceive that good in terms of equality. Neither is an epistemological relativist. Walzer, like Merleau-Ponty, thinks it possible to discover the actual themes of a community's way of life. Both have been active journalists who see their pedagogical role as a form of political praxis.

[5] *Spheres of Justice*, p. 5.

[6] Ibid., pp. 6–10.

[7] Walzer's criticisms of "existentialists" as those "committed to an invented morality" apply much more to Sartre than to Merleau-Ponty. See *Interpretation and Social Criticism*, pp. 10, 57–59.

[8] Walzer, "Political Action: The Problem of Dirty Hands," in *War and Moral Responsibility*, eds. Cohen et al., p. 76.

If Walzer's writings are genuinely existential and also avoid assumptions that misdirect Merleau-Ponty's early politics, one might be tempted simply to read Walzer in lieu of the French existentialist. Yet Merleau-Ponty supplies a needed complement to Walzer's project and suggests an essential corrective to it. Merleau-Ponty's work completes Walzer's insofar as it discusses the *foundation* of an existential politics. Walzer writes about the "meaning" of social goods and insists that we attend to how particular communities create and distribute them. But he never lingers over the conception of consciousness that would be required to explain how this approach to theory is possible. He is silent about the ground of meaning, the conditions for understanding the intentions of others, the cumulative nature of meaning. He presupposes a phenomenology of politics but never writes at that metatheoretical level. At the very least, Merleau-Ponty remains valuable for such a contribution to political theory.

Yet more is at stake in developing a metaphysics of meaning than a theory's completeness. Merleau-Ponty's criticisms of Communists, liberals, and Sartre suggest that when political commentators have no consistent theory of meaning, they often lapse into habits of reasoning at odds with their stated objectives. Foundational misconceptions, he learned, distort political thinking. Such distortions are not entirely absent from Walzer's notion of spheres of justice. Lacking a general theory of the transformation of meaning and of the consciousness of its carriers, Walzer makes unnecessary concessions to political rationalism. That is, he comes closer than he is willing to admit to composing a work of abstractly reasoned political principles.

To support this assertion, we might begin by observing that "meaning" in Walzer's theory is not exactly equivalent to "sens" in Merleau-Ponty's. Sens always implies directedness; meaning has a diachronic dimension. That is why Merleau-Ponty always sees questions of social meaning in the context of a philosophy of historical evolution. Walzer's readings of social goods are more synchronic. "Internal" theorists restrict their arguments to ones available in a given community at a given moment in time. In spite of Walzer's emphasis on the historicity of values, a synchronic orientation is evident in the way he uses a public's current understandings of goods to *disqualify* theoretical arguments that seem too "external," too distant from the popular will. He dismisses, for example, André Gorz's complaints against the private automobile with the observation that "the car is also the symbol of individual freedom; and I doubt that any democratic public within living memory would have voted against it."[9] Presumably therefore internal theorists should not avail themselves of Gorz's argument.

Merleau-Ponty, on the other hand, would have theorists scan the historical horizon for imminent transformations of group sensibilities, for cultural instabilities, and for politically productive collisions of interests. His philosopher proceeds not just from what people currently believe, but from what they might or probably will believe, given the likely course of development of certain tensions in society. From this viewpoint, Walzer's reading of popular attitudes regarding the automobile provides no sufficient reason for theorists to desist from arguing that the private automobile is detrimental to the environment, group activities, and so forth. Theorists may contend against public opinion that cars do more harm than good to our common life and that the problems are worsening. They may reason that their arguments, the development of social problems, and political action will actually alter popular attitudes. If Gorz has grounds for believing that such changes are genuinely possible, he does precisely what prescient political thinkers should do. Foreseeing a coming clash between present trends and the conditions for a freer and more communitarian society, he uses words and action to try to precipitate a change of consciousness in certain powerful groups.

I suspect that Walzer wants to disqualify certain positions because he worries about the tension between democratic government and philosophers who would impose their views of the right on the people. Traditionally, he observes, philosophers have tried to withdraw from their communities by imagining perfect cities and permanent principles of right order. Their stance is in conflict with that of democratic citizens who first "value their own opinions and conventions."[10] But if all values are ultimately local, then philosophers have no special authority. They must enter the fray of democratic political argument, where actual persuasion, not inherent rightness, validates their views.[11]

But as Merleau-Ponty tries to show in his analysis of Communist politics, such tension between philosophers and political thinkers (including democratic citizens) is a product not of philosophy per se, but of thinkers who refuse to conceive truth as a process of

[9] Walzer, *Spheres of Justice*, p. 115.
[10] Walzer, "Philosophy and Democracy," p. 394.
[11] Ibid., pp. 396–397.

correction. He emphasizes that the most astute leaders "read" current trends, propose policies, and pursue them with greater or lesser vigor as the people accept or balk at them. They try to form and educate the popular will at the same time that they correct and limit their own initiatives. There is no unacceptable tension between philosophy and democracy where philosophers understand that their views can be right only to the extent, as Merleau-Ponty would say, that they "find agreement all around" (PP 508, tr. 444).

Perhaps that is what Walzer really meant. Criticized for not giving a sufficiently explicit account of how social meanings can change,[12] he has recently argued that "internal" critics drive cultural evolution by pointing to the unfulfilled principles that any culture generates in defense of its particular distributions.[13] What he may not see, however, is that this account of criticism entails giving up on the claim that the internalist perspective significantly limits the range of political argument. The values incorporated in the practices of modern societies are so multifarious that the social critic can find an "internal" justification for virtually any principle. To return to Gorz's example—true, one meaning of the automobile is personal freedom of travel. But it would not be difficult to show that private transportation is also bound up with other standards like economic freedom, environmental integrity, and artistic creativity. If all of these are available to "internalist" philosophers, then the internalist perspective disqualifies virtually no value. That, I would argue, is an improvement over Walzer's original notion of criticism, which unjustifiably deprived critical discourse of needed perspectives. It also makes a step in the direction that Merleau-Ponty's phenomenology would have advocated from the start.

Yet a problem remains. There is still something *politically* unsatisfactory in wholly unconstrained criticism. Merleau-Ponty objected to political rationalism in part because those who develop principles of justice tend to ignore the close connections between certain preferred meanings and successful action. Thinking, to be properly political, must include an assessment of the social conditions conducive to a particular change and of the strength of the groups whose struggles will be necessary to vindicate hitherto unobserved values. The problem is that not just any meanings find sufficient favor to stir people to act. Merleau-Ponty's phenom-

---

[12] See Galston, rev. of *Spheres of Justice*, by Walzer, p. 332.
[13] Walzer, *Interpretation and Social Criticism*, pp. 40–41.

enological studies led him to believe that the meanings that most powerfully motivate political action are "preconscious." Specific groups are the carriers of background meanings whose evolution is crucial to the fate of specific political projects. This observation has important implications for the content of political theory. If theory is not to generate only abstract and ineffective criticism, it is vital for theorists to orient their writings toward groups whose situation is most likely to impel them to advance necessary social changes.

In this perspective, Walzer falls short on two accounts. First and explicitly, he seems more interested in refining interpretations of principle than in reckoning the prospects for social change. That is, once Walzer finds that a meaning is culturally available, he immediately moves to formulate that meaning and to measure existing practices against it. But the question for one interested in political thinking should be not simply whether a given meaning is present in a culture, but whether a certain interpretation of that meaning stands any chance of motivating people actually to challenge current unjust practices. The thinker's choice of meanings to interpret calls for a political and sociological judgment that Walzer never emphasizes.

Second and implicitly, Walzer does choose an orientation toward particular types of groups and meanings, but his choice is not well grounded. He consistently draws his cultural readings from national communities (Americans, Jews, Chinese). But he never stops to show that national meanings—as opposed to those from economic, linguistic, racial, or other subgroups—are the most powerful ones, or are uniformly accepted, or are subject to transformations especially supportive of his vision of equality. Arguments to such effect would be eminently questionable.[14] Certainly we must also criticize many of Merleau-Ponty's assumptions about the proletariat. But that does not change the general lesson of his existential politics: if political action necessarily aims at success and if success depends upon the evolving, preconscious understandings of specific groups, then critics should not elaborate just any principle available to them in contemporary culture. As political thinkers, they choose their interpretations as a function of their estimated potential for practical effect. The alternative is eth-

[14] Linda Mullenix, "The Limits of 'Complex Equality,' " *Harvard Law Review* 97 (1984), pp. 1806–1807; Andreas Teuber, rev. of *Spheres of Justice*, by Walzer, *Political Theory* 12:1 (February 1984), p. 120.

ical criticism that condemns itself to impotence because it speaks to those least interested or least capable of carrying through social transformations.

Both Merleau-Ponty's insistence that theory should help realize values and Walzer's stress on particularist understandings of justice go wrong, however, in one crucial respect. They confuse a critique of essentialist ethical theory with a claim that general statements of value are out of place in an existential politics. A consideration of the work of John Rawls will show that what is problematic in principled theory is not the statement of principle itself, but the type of information and thinking that goes into its formulation.

Kantian Politics Revisited: John Rawls

Merleau-Ponty has three objections to abstract theories of justice. (1) Every supposedly timeless philosophy of the human good has been discovered by later thinkers to be the product of particular circumstances. (2) People forced to accept "universal" but unfamiliar values experience them as oppression. (3) Allegedly universal values have in fact worked to the benefit of specific groups of people. From such objections Merleau-Ponty concludes that values are "nothing but" components of a social structure (SNS 268, tr. 152). Thus he proposes that doing existential political theory is a matter of perceiving freedom-enhancing trends maturing in the ideas and way of life of particular socioeconomic groups and then planning a course of action that stands the best chance of bringing those trends to fruition. He turns away from Kantian philosophies of precepts and principles to a theory of the progressive transformation of social structures.

That the most widely acclaimed liberal theory of recent decades, Rawls's *A Theory of Justice*, bears a "Kantian interpretation"[15] therefore inevitably revives questions that Merleau-Ponty thought had been laid to rest. It obliges us to ask whether the existential critique of Kantian politics was right and, to the extent that it was, to ask whether Rawls's updated Kantianism remains vulnerable to that critique. I will contend that in spite of some imperfect formulations, Merleau-Ponty's political writings open a provocative, critical perspective on *A Theory of Justice*.

Rawls generates a substantive theory of distributive justice for a

---

[15] Rawls, *A Theory of Justice*, p. 251.

modern democratic society. He argues that the "basic structure" of a just society reflects two serially ordered principles: each person has the most extensive basic liberty compatible with similar liberty for all, and social and economic inequalities work to the advantage of all, under conditions of fair equality of opportunity.[16] More distinctive than these principles, however, is the method by which Rawls reaches them. He asks us to envision them as the outcome of a choice made by parties in an "original position." There people must choose the principles of justice for the society in which they are to live, but they are ignorant of those particularities of condition—income, status, religion, natural assets, historical generation—that so frequently allow them "to be guided by their prejudices."[17] Under these conditions, says Rawls, rational, mutually disinterested persons would seek to ensure that, whatever their eventual position in society, they would not be deprived of primary goods—goods essential to the realization of every life plan. The two principles of justice describe a fair distribution of these goods.

This theory is "Kantian" in the sense that the original position operationalizes Kantian autonomy. Kant required that moral choices be made "autonomously," grounded in a free will, and not "heteronomously," grounded in some desire or contingency external to the will. Similarly Rawls develops principles of justice that if accepted, restrain our pursuit of self-interest for moral reasons. "The veil of ignorance deprives the persons in the original position of the knowledge that would enable them to choose heteronomous principles."[18] As citizens, Rawls concludes, we express our nature as free and equal rational beings when we assess social institutions according to the principles of justice.[19]

Is Rawls's theory open to the existential critique of Kantian politics? Certainly Merleau-Ponty's first complaint, that Kantian theory is grounded in particularity, lacks much critical force. This is because a key lesson of his phenomenology is that we are *inevitably* situated. If this is so, no reasoning frees us from our particularity. The works of Heidegger as much as Sidgwick, of Merleau-Ponty as much as Rawls, bear the marks of their historical moments. Equally true of existentialism and all other philosophies, this ob-

[16] Ibid., p. 60.
[17] Ibid., p. 19.
[18] Ibid., p. 252.
[19] Ibid., p. 253.

jection cannot differentiate among them and therefore cannot be used to condemn any particular form of theory.

But Merleau-Ponty's objection may be not simply that Kantian philosophy is particularist, but that its particularism is unduly and unintentionally subjectivistic. Now Rawls and Merleau-Ponty do share one theoretical commitment. Rawls's critique of utilitarianism and Merleau-Ponty's opposition to ends-means dichotomies alike proscribe theories that view justice as a matter of calculated trade-offs between individual and group welfare. Such theories treat individuals as *objects* of social policy. But where Merleau-Ponty would caution against adopting an equally problematic subjectivism as the alternative to objectivism, Rawls generates his principles of justice by conceiving them as the choice of perfectly rational, ahistorical, disembodied consciousnesses. Merleau-Ponty always warned that theories unaware of their grounding in subjectivism or objectivism miss the true, "situated" nature of "existence" and therefore inadvertently incorporate categories whose logic eventually issues in defective political reasoning.

Such is the case with Rawls. According to him, "a conception of right must impose an ordering on conflicting claims."[20] In order to block trade-offs that may be harmful to some individuals' self-respect, he suggests that we rank our principles serially. "This ordering means that a departure from the institutions of equal liberty required by the first principle cannot be justified by, or compensated for, by greater social and economic advantages."[21] Brian Barry points out what is peculiar about such ordering. Interpreted literally, Rawls's doctrine "can be accepted only if wealth is assigned a value that is literally infinitesimally small in relation to liberty, so that it would be judged worth dropping from general affluence to general poverty, if such a choice were presented to a society."[22] Barry finds such a judgment dubiously rational. Merleau-Ponty would find such a judgment dubiously *political*, and relate its shortcomings to the theorist's view of human consciousness. While explaining his critique of Sartre he once recounted the following anecdote.

> [Sartre once] told me: "Essentially, there is not much difference between a catastrophe where 300 or 3000 die and one where ten or fifteen die. There is a difference in numbers of

[20] Ibid., p. 134.
[21] Ibid., p. 61.
[22] Barry, *The Liberal Theory of Justice*, p. 60.

course, but in a sense, with each person who dies, so also does a world. The scandal is the same. . . ." Retrospectively, I thought: an idea like that shows how far Sartre was, in the prewar years, from a political and historical point of view. . . . From a statistical point of view, which is that of social and political life and of history, there is an enormous difference.[23]

Merleau-Ponty knew that to pose choices from the point of view of the individual consciousness is already to structure the possible outcomes of our deliberations on justice. The consciousness knows only itself intimately. It has privileged access to its own ideas and emotions and at best indirect, inferential access to the ideas of others. From the viewpoint of the consciousness, its extinction is equivalent to destruction of the world. If it is destroyed, the only world-experiencing mind whose certainty is established will be lost. The first priority of the consciousness must be to safeguard itself and its defining characteristic—its "spiritual" freedom. The priority that Rawls assigns to the liberty principle reflects this understanding of consciousness.

A truly "political and historical point of view" is one that never loses sight of the ways that the individual is integrated into a community. It understands that if the community draws its strength and innovative potential from individuals, it is also true that individuals owe their culture and their very survival to the efforts of the community. The dialectical interdependence of individual and community makes absolute principles ill suited to political thinking. For Merleau-Ponty, the number of people interested in and affected by a decision and their prospects for actualizing their values are always relevant to a political thinker. No fixed ordering of principles is acceptable. Because a function of political activity is to protect and advance the values of a collectivity, one who thinks politically cannot afford to adopt a mode of thought that automatically privileges the goals of individuals.

Still, if those who practice political thinking are not to oscillate back into objectivism, they need a concept that, like "existence," never allows them to lose sight of the *relationship* between "subjects" and their "objective" environment. That is why Merleau-Ponty's theory of the situated consciousness is so important. Where individuals are conceived as both creators and carriers of a community's meanings, there can be no question of justice being a matter of either rigid priorities or facile trade-offs. In making

[23] "La philosophie de l'existence," pp. 315–316.

hard choices, political thinkers do not decide by summing up the satisfactions of every affected individual or by constructing a priori principles of distribution. Rather, they consult (and perhaps try to adjust) the allegiances that actual communities have built up in their culture and through their productive activities. No doubt some of Rawls's contemporary critics have gone further than Merleau-Ponty in giving *ethical* reasons for doing political theory in this way.[24] The existentialist's contribution lies in showing how a particular theory of consciousness is necessary to found and secure this perspective.

There is, however, a Rawlsian objection that would get at the most serious normative deficiency of Merleau-Ponty's political theory and would force him to express his objection to Kantian politics more carefully. The objection would begin with the observation that Merleau-Ponty distinguishes progressive from regressive historical trends. But *why* is it progressive for the proletariat to establish socialism and regressive to preserve capitalism? To argue that socialism is superior to free-market liberalism, one must assess them on some common scale—amount of happiness produced, communitarian values fostered, freedoms protected—and somehow rank or compare these values. Moreover, one must explain what freedom and equality are, why they are good, and what other values are affected when they are enlarged. No contention that history is actualizing socialism can substitute for these analyses, since we must decide whether it would be better to support or block that trend. At the same time, it must be conceded that any discussion of ethical measures and definitions necessarily sounds abstract. Precisely because their function is to justify judgments between different, concrete alternatives, such measures cannot simply reproduce the particularistic reasons characteristic of a single ethical system. One can refuse to engage in general ethical reasoning. But as Galston has observed, a refusal merely "replaces explicit, systematic reflection . . . with tacit and ungrounded assumptions."[25] Surely that is not an advance in political thinking. Merleau-Ponty must be faulted for vagueness and for failure to defend his values.

Existentialists evade principled reasoning largely, it seems, out of fear of falling into the errors of essentialism. Assertions that

[24] See, for example, Walzer, *Spheres of Justice*, pp. 6–10; Galston, *Justice and the Human Good*, p. 172; Sandel, "Liberalism and the Limits of Justice," in *Liberalism and Its Critics*, ed. Sandel, pp. 172–173.

[25] Galston, *Justice and the Human Good*, p. 15.

there are specific values or institutions necessary for satisfactory human development seem to contradict the claim that we create all our values historically. The preceding argument was meant to show that apparently atemporal value claims are inevitable in reasoned political discourse. Does this mean then that existentialists must abandon their analysis of the historicity of values? I say "apparently atemporal," however, to emphasize a second point: the existentialists' metaphysical premises actually support rather than forbid their use of general ethical language. For their metaphysics teaches that all discourse is historically and culturally specific. If so, then theorists can quite consistently promote seemingly general statements of value. Historicity, in effect, takes care of itself. That would have been Walzer's lesson had he not tried to block arguments that he judged beyond the cultural pale. Philosophers, without claiming to stand outside history, can try to make their contemporaries see violations of their own ethical understandings. They can try to persuade fellow citizens that certain changes in their societies would enable more people to live more satisfying lives. They might even try to introduce new values into their societies. There is nothing objectionably essentialist in debating over values so long as the debate may include all information relevant to political thinking and so long as all participants realize that they may have to modify their beliefs in the give-and-take of discussion.

The existential objection to political essentialism needs to be reformulated. It needs to build on Merleau-Ponty's recognition of the *political* inadequacy of principled reasoning as it is frequently practiced. He objected to "Kantian politics" not because his contemporaries chose to practice the wrong precepts but because, schooled in Kant's ethical writings, they undervalued consequences, overestimated rationality, ignored social structures, and misunderstood the nature of human motivation. Kantian assumptions crippled their ability to respond appropriately to political dangers and to take advantage of opportunities for progressive change.

The problem with "Kantian politics" is that it develops and promotes principles without attention to the information that is critical to political thinking. The Kantian believes that our thought about justice and our thought about concrete action are analytically separable. Rawls neatly illustrates this tendency. When deciding on the principles of justice themselves, the parties to Rawls's original position are allowed only the most general information. As we design a constitution, legislate, and create policy, however, it is appropriate gradually to lift the veil of ignorance.[26] But concrete political thinking and abstract thinking about justice are not so distinct. Activists pursue what they think is just. They must therefore reproduce in some degree the theoretical reasoning that legitimates their projects. Theorists propose prescriptions for a real world. They must pay attention to constraints on action that are not of theory's devising. In the knowledge that they emphasize as relevant to justice, in the models of the economy they presuppose, in the topics they include and omit, theorists draw maps of the political world that guide those who act politically. Every theory of justice is a primer of political thinking. The only question is, how adequate is a given theory in that perspective?

The answer, for *A Theory of Justice*, is not encouraging. Let us begin with a description of a political situation and draw from it Rawlsian and existential lessons. A liberal proclaims that all citizens have a right to free speech. A critic observes that when radical views are espoused, however, there is police harassment, the courts "discover" stringent time and place restrictions in the law, libel suits are won against the radical press, the media slant their coverage—all in ways that are much less true when more conventional political opinions are expressed. Merleau-Ponty would argue that freedom of speech, because of the way it functions in connection with political and economic institutions in this way of life, has a sens that favors the maintenance of the existing distribution of power and material resources. He might repeat his charge that "values remain nominal . . . unless there is a political and economic infrastructure that makes them enter into existence" (SNS 268, tr. 152).

Merleau-Ponty's point is that standards cannot be meaningfully specified in isolation from the social context that glosses their sens. Absent from the deliberative process that yields Rawls's "reflective equilibrium" are concerns about the class structure of one's society (that will affect the reasonableness of one's expectations that different groups will abide by the principles),[27] about the history of one's principles (that might reveal how attempts to make them effective have worked in practice), about the educative experiences that have formed these dispositions, about anticipated social and

[26] Rawls, *Theory of Justice*, p. 200.

[27] See, for example, Richard Miller's argument that, if Marx's view of society is right, no exploitative, ruling class is likely to accept a commitment to the difference principle. "Rawls and Marxism," in *Reading Rawls*, ed. Daniels, p. 215.

technological transformations that may affect the necessity of having the principles, about how the very words used to express one's principles are understood in different social strata. Merleau-Ponty's phenomenology holds that such matters are *intrinsic* to statements of principle because they are *part of* their meaning. Only awareness of this complexity of meaning will make us adjust our principles in light of the concrete difficulties that they will encounter in the world. Without a structural perspective on our principles, we are likely to see them condemned to ineffectiveness or, worse, appropriated and distorted by the most powerful interests in society. Our passion for justice should leave us dissatisfied with any theory that methodically excludes the information needed to think politically.

A more radical perspective, however, might call into question the concept of justice itself. The Nietzschean sceptic charges that justice is merely fossilized violence. Taking seriously the existentialists' recognition of social violence and their pleas for concrete theory would require destroying all dreams of historical structures that progressively actualize the human good. Such are the claims of Michel Foucault.

Subversive Scepticism: Michel Foucault

Out of Foucault's often elusive oeuvre I have chosen two themes that pose special challenges to Merleau-Ponty's existential politics: the discontinuity of history and the discursive constitution of the subject. In the strongest possible contrast to the Hegelian view that history as a whole might have a sens, Foucault's work highlights ruptures, discontinuities, and irreducible differences in the forms taken by knowing and social practices in the history of consciousness. The argument of *Madness and Civilization*, for instance, is that, in different historical periods, the "insane" were people with different characteristics (sometimes including criminals and the poor, sometimes including those in whom doctors diagnosed previously unknown "illnesses"), subject to different treatments (from awe to vilification, from physical experimentation to confessional therapy), for different reasons (including religious, political, economic). Instead of progress in the theoretical conceptualization of mental illness, there is evidence only for "a consistent tendency to project very general social preconceptions and anxieties into theoretical systems which justified the confinement of whatever social group or personality type appeared to threaten society during a period."[28] Always attentive to the ways that the human sciences have named and excluded different segments of the population, Foucault examines the rules that make it possible to classify objects (e.g., to call certain types of behavior "sane" or "insane"), to label statements as true and false, to ascribe authorship to certain individuals.

He argues that statements and objects of analysis combine in discursive formations that establish systems of possibility for knowledge. Statements have no extradiscursive content; their referents are made possible by the particular discursive formation in which they are enunciated. The convergence of numerous contingent factors—new needs for labor, the emergence of new professions, the invention of new technologies—makes these rules change periodically and empowers different groups to subjugate others with new methods of surveillance and control. No law or logic governs the succession of discursive formations. "Humanity does not gradually progress . . . until it arrives at universal reciprocity . . . ; rather humanity installs each of its violences in a system of rules and thus proceeds from domination to domination."[29]

Foucault profoundly relativizes the notion of subjectivity. If he is right, "nothing in man—not even his body—is sufficiently stable to serve as the basis for this self-recognition or for understanding other men."[30] The self is a discursive product, an artifact formed by power. Disciplinary institutions like workplaces, the military, prisons, and mental institutions enforce standards of "normality" on individuals. The modern subject has been manufactured to fit into categories of research, to respond to surveillance, to expect treatment when it deviates from the norm. Consciousness is nothing but an effect of multiple, arbitrary constraints imposed by various institutional mechanisms. "We are judged, condemned, classified, determined in our undertakings, destined to a certain mode of living or dying, as a function of the true discourses which are the bearers of the specific effects of power."[31]

At one level Foucault can be read as the theorist of a post-Hegelian but still existential politics. Like the existentialists, he emphasizes the irreducible role of meaning in the direction of individual consciousness. He sees meaning as a function of a web of

[28] White, "Foucault Decoded," p. 39.
[29] Foucault, in *The Foucault Reader*, ed. Rabinow, pp. 85–86.
[30] Foucault, *Language, Countermemory, and Practice*, p. 153.
[31] Foucault, *Power/Knowledge*, p. 93.

interreferring social practices and, like Merleau-Ponty, stresses the "anonymity" of the meanings that structure the individual's behavior. He believes that the a priori conditions of knowledge are concrete, humanly created rules and activities. He deploys rhetorical strategies designed to unsettle our conventional understandings of objects and categories.[32] Furthermore, at times Foucault is more penetrating and more existential than the existentialists. He explores previously unrecognized forms of domination—not just the domination of capitalists over workers, but that of prison administrators over inmates, of psychiatrists over patients, of ourselves over ourselves insofar as we internalize advertised norms of sexuality. From the recognition of domination follows commitment: he supports those who resist the subjugating effects of knowledge (the movements of prisoners, antipsychiatry groups, homosexuals, conscripted soldiers).[33]

Most importantly Foucault's "microphysics" of power and his views on historical discontinuity offer the strongest possible corrective to Merleau-Ponty's greatest failing in social theory—his tendency toward undifferentiated holism in the study of social structures. Merleau-Ponty was right to charge that atomistic analyses of perception and deterministic prognoses of political change ignore the ways that phenomena fit into gestalten. These structures influence the subject's understanding of phenomena and condition the subject's reaction to them. But in the 1940s he persistently leapt from this insight to an attempt to embrace *all* the themes of a culture—and finally all the themes of history—in a single perception. "The conception of law, morality, religion, the economic structure intersignify," he wrote, "in the unity of the social event just as the parts of the body imply one another in the unity of the gesture" (PP 202, tr. 173). This means that it is possible to read the economic state of a society in its literature or its theology, but also it suggests that, because of their internal connections, a great variety of social problems might be resolvable through a single, vast structural shift. I call this holism "undifferentiated" because Merleau-Ponty rarely stopped to inspect particular themes to see if they actually had the features that he attributed to them. He believed, for example, that liberalism and Marxism share essentially the same values and yet never took se-

[32] See Philp, "Foucault on Power: A Problem in Radical Translation?" p. 30, and Connolly, "Taylor, Foucault, and Otherness," p. 368.
[33] Foucault, *Language, Countermemory, and Practice*, p. 216.

riously what many regard as inherent incompatibilities between communitarian goals and those of competition and individual achievement. He wagered on the possibility of a world without violence without ever looking at the connections between economic organization and most forms of violence.

Foucault, in contrast, begins with specific applications of power in localized situations. He argues that "manifold relationships of force . . . in the machinery of production, in families, in limited groups and institutions, are the basis for wide ranging effects of cleavage that run through society as a whole."[34] If "power comes from below," theorists must study how oppositions, side effects, and realignments within the microcontexts of power produce the more global effects of domination. Precisely because he carries his genealogies to this level, he uncovers the operation of power in contexts that other theorists ignore. He follows through on the existentialists' unfulfilled demand for concrete, particularist theory. Whatever Foucault's excesses, they do not involve postulating a totalizing movement of history destined to put an end to violence. Merleau-Ponty's problem, to repeat, is not holism per se, nor that he warns theorists to beware of self-sustaining systems of violence. His failing is that he neglects to engage in the concrete investigations that might impel him to identify previously unsuspected structures of constraint, to limit his claims about the extent of structures, and to appreciate the difficulty of reconciling different ethical systems.

A closer look at Foucault reveals, however, that he is something other than an existentialist with evidence. At many points he radicalizes an existential politics beyond recognition. With respect to historical discontinuity, he is not saying merely that historians, in tracing the filiations of ideas through time, have asserted the existence of traditions that further examination discovers to be composed of very dissimilar concepts and practices. He is not initiating a process of correction. Foucault is saying that truth itself "is a thing of this world: it is produced only by virtue of multiple forms of constraint."[35] It follows that different discursive formations are absolutely incommensurable, for commensurability implies the existence of a true measure that could be applied to different epistemic systems. With respect to subjectivity, Foucault is not saying that different social institutions have unduly repressed certain

[34] Foucault, *The History of Sexuality: Vol. 1*, p. 94.
[35] Foucault, *Power/Knowledge*, p. 131.

types of personality or that understanding the role of discourses in subjugating individuals will make it possible finally to liberate them from abuses of power. Unlike the existentialists, he seems to have in mind no picture of a society in which freedom is more perfectly realized.[36] He believes that concepts of repression are "vitiated" by their resonances with notions of sovereignty and normalization.[37] Truth cannot make us free because it is already an effect of discursive practices. Consistency demands that the genealogist eschew reference to "liberation" and "repression." A profound scepticism with regard to both facts and values is at the base of Foucault's studies.

It is not with his disturbing genealogies of modern social norms and practices that an existential politics must take issue. If assertions are made that hitherto unnoticed themes traverse social phenomena or that power is being exercised in ways that diminish individual freedom, existentialists should be committed to examining those claims and to acting to open up new areas of liberty. Foucault's genealogies supplement existentialism by showing how to investigate the structurally dependent character of seemingly independent social phenomena without assuming that everything in a society or, a fortiori in all history, forms a grand unity. It is rather Foucault's theoretical formulations of his genealogies that run counter to the most valuable lessons of Merleau-Ponty's existential politics.

The first lesson is that any mode of thinking that claims to be political must account for something akin to "objectivity." Sartre's theory of consciousness, Merleau-Ponty charged, eroded all attempts to describe the facticity of the situation. When speaking of interpretive freedom, Sartre spoke of something interpreted—a mountain, the way of life of a king. And yet, there was no way in his theory to describe the residuum that underlies individual decisions. If the question of what "the situation" is can always be deferred to another free interpretation, then there is effectively no situation. Even though Foucault uses a much more deterministic language than Sartre, he ends up with a very similar problem. "Interpretation can never be brought to an end," he says, "simply because there is nothing to interpret. There is nothing absolutely primary to be interpreted since, fundamentally, everything is al-

---

[36] He does once allude to (but never elaborates on) an ideal based on "bodies and pleasures." See *The History of Sexuality, Vol. 1*, p. 157. Poster criticizes the vagueness of this allusion in *Foucault, Marxism, and History*, pp. 35–37.

[37] Foucault, *Power/Knowledge*, p. 108.

ready interpretation."[38] He candidly refers to his histories as "fictions," albeit ones that produce "truth-effects."[39]

The problem is that, having lost his grip on the situation, the theorist undermines his own account of factors crucial to his political project. It becomes unclear how he can discuss conditioning circumstances that motivate large numbers of people to behave in similar ways. Why are these circumstances not subject to endless and irreconcilable interpretations by different individuals, such that no generalizations about group behavior are possible? If the answer is that many individuals are subject to the same "forces,"[40] we must ask, what is the nature of that force? Is it not something more than a theorist's fictive interpretation? Political thinkers are interested in "objective" conditions, for those are what cause genuine suffering and motivate social movements.

Merleau-Ponty believes that his analysis of phenomenal structures supplies the objectivity requisite to political reasoning. Structures of social behavior translate into existential terms the sociological concepts of class and culture. The idea of sedimented meanings that motivate behavior captures the conditioning force of the situation on an individual's choices. The orientation of social structures toward an equilibrium identifies a value implicit in the activities of countless individuals. Certainly phenomenal objectivity is not beyond criticism. Foucault's genealogies could be used to make Merleau-Ponty more sensitive, for example, to some of the disciplinary overtones in the Marxist notion of work or to the very limited models of sexuality incorporated in the phenomenological account of the "sexed body." But such criticisms are no argument against trying to get our views on these subjects right. Even if some of Merleau-Ponty's particular claims are wrong, the very fact that he makes them as truth claims challenges others to make them more true and not just to posit rival fictions.

The second lesson of an existential politics is that political thinkers cannot afford to erode all grounds for publicly defensible values. Merleau-Ponty was aware of the contradiction between Sartre's moralistic assessments of the behavior of his contemporaries—implying that he was holding them to some general standards of right and wrong—and his insistence that each individual creates his own values out of nothing but his own will. Foucault's

---

[38] Foucault quoted in Descombes, *Modern French Philosophy*, p. 117.
[39] Foucault quoted in Dreyfus and Rabinow, *Michel Foucault*, p. 204.
[40] Foucault, *The History of Sexuality. Vol. 1*, p. 92.

work is shot through with the same contradiction. His theory of subjectivity relativizes any notion of the good to the discursive formation that makes possible a particular view of the "good" individual. Still, he occasionally offers normative prescriptions and almost always uses terms that are meaningful only in a semantic field of which moral concepts are a part. His notion of "power," Charles Taylor points out, presupposes "truth" and "freedom."[41] "Violence" and "domination" too must coexist with moral concepts of right order (which can be violated) and consent (which dominance suppresses). Foucault's refusal to think systematically about the values that his discourse serves entails a significant political cost. If all we can do is change forms of domination and if no form of domination can be judged less oppressive than another, then there seems to be no ground for demanding change.

In Merleau-Ponty's phenomenology, it is possible to speak of "liberation" because two factors check the relativism implicit in the existential view of man as a self-transcending being. First, knowledge is grounded in the body, and human beings as a species have a common lexicon of originary meanings. There is therefore some foundation for "mutual recognition," for common understandings of responsibility, of the evil of pain, of the capacity for sympathy, of the other as a creator of meaning.[42] Second, human beings have "permanent exigencies." These include a desire for a level of material welfare high enough to allow the flourishing of a variety of capacities and a desire for esteem by others. Of course much remains to be elaborated in these claims. But at least they do not entirely deflect political thinkers from asking whether it is possible to create social conditions that decrease suffering, enable more individuals to develop new capacities, and eliminate avoidable constraints on freedom.

What I am suggesting is that there is something very political at issue in Merleau-Ponty's ideas that "objectivity" and "values" are essential parts of social discourse. At stake is the thinker's standing to have his claims taken seriously by a public. If politics concerns in any sense a *res publica*, a public thing, then a theory that cannot explain how to get from the personal understandings of the interpreter to a public thing is inimical to the very nature of politics. The sceptic who makes all interpretation seem idiosyncratic ends by undermining any sense of the compelling reality of polit-

[41] "Foucault on Freedom and Truth," p. 173.
[42] Connolly concludes similarly in *The Terms of Political Discourse*, pp. 240–241.

ical problems. The genealogist who makes all values seem arbitrary deprives himself of any arguments to enlist others to support the causes that he favors. That Foucault meticulously researched and published his genealogies in spite of his unwillingness to call them "true" and that he supported the resisters of modern culture in spite of his reservations about "liberation" perhaps demonstrates two things. First, as Merleau-Ponty showed in his critique of Aron's scepticism, no one can avoid making truth claims and value statements. They are inherent, existential components of the way we make meaning in political discourse. Our goal is therefore not to suppress them, but to make them explicit and coherent, to overcome the partialities of our current understandings of them, to investigate their connections with social practices that influence their meanings. Second, Foucault's shortcomings suggest that accounting for truths and values requires a more stable conception of self and other than his writings provide. Those seeking a more adequate foundation for Foucault's critical observations could do far worse than to begin with Merleau-Ponty's theory of the historically situated body-subject.

Experience and Dialogue in an Existential Politics

Summarizing Merleau-Ponty's political theory is made difficult both by the vastness of its aspirations and the dispersion of its presentation. If, on the one hand, his views on such topics as the body-subject, structure, lived experience, class, consequentialist ethics, and Marxism are clearly interconnected, it is true, on the other, that the connections are difficult to perceive because his ideas are scattered in academic works, editorials, collections of essays, and lectures. In the preceding chapters I have juxtaposed all available expressions of Merleau-Ponty's thought in an effort to overcome some of the problems of dispersion. My goal has been to understand the inner consistency of his political writings. What those detailed textual analyses may not always have conveyed, however, is the spirit of Merleau-Ponty's enterprise. He often argued that understanding a human work requires not just surveying it, but thinking oneself into the problems and meanings that motivated it. For that reason, I conclude by returning to the situational origin of an existential politics—the eruption of World War II. War exploded in Merleau-Ponty's mind as it did in his country. Its shock wave jarred his thinking, toppling assumptions and compressing old ideas into new compounds. It is that shock that we must try to imagine if we are to appreciate the seriousness and breadth of his political project.

When the army of the Third Reich tore through France, Merleau-Ponty was thirty-two years old. By that time he had been studying philosophy intensively for over fourteen years. He supplemented the Kantianism of the official curriculum with the study of Catholic social thought and, eventually, of Hegel. The disquieting news of the prewar years—the rise of the Nazis, the right-wing leagues in Paris, Guernica, the Moscow trials, Munich—did not escape his attention. But he kept his distance from politics and pursued his primary interests in the areas of psychology and perception. No doubt he felt that he was dealing with the profoundest issues—transcendental subjects, the nature of perception, God— in important ways. No doubt he was confident that, come what may, he possessed the intellectual resources to deal with political as well as philosophical issues.

World War II violently eradicated that confidence. Living in an occupied country, he understood for the first time there is no such thing as political neutrality and withdrawal. He realized that the politically inactive merely take advantage of a split between public and private life that a particular regime temporarily, conditionally, and unequally makes available to its citizens. The circumstances of war demanded that each citizen make an explicit commitment to some regime—to Vichy or, through resistance, to a more just one. And war forced all to confront the inevitability of violence. No philosophy demanding absolute respect for the autonomy of others could possibly guide action in the face of a government that arbitrarily stripped citizens of their freedom and that opposed with deadly force any challenges to its legitimacy.

For anyone morally sensitive to the ugliness of violence, the fact that it is necessary makes its use no easier. In part this is because those who choose violence even in a just cause expose themselves to suffering its blows in return. Merleau-Ponty knew many who died as soldiers or resisters.[43] But they may at least have had the

---

[43] Among Merleau-Ponty's ENS students who died in the war were François Cuzin, Gilles Ferrier du Châtelet, and Raymond Badelle. Archives Nationales 61 AJ 264. Merleau-Ponty's tutor for the agrégation exam, Jean Cavaillès, was captured and executed as a resister. See Gabrielle Ferrières, *Jean Cavaillès. Philosophe et combattant, 1903–1944* (Presses Universitaires de France, 1950), pp. 58, 191. Albert Lautmann, who prepared for the agrégation with him, met a similar fate. Letter from Mme Lautmann, February 1981. And when his student Yvonne Picard was arrested (she was later to die in deportation), Merleau-Ponty took considerable risks to warn

comfort of deciding their own fate. Yet more difficult is the realization that others, including allies and innocents, may be hurt by even the most conscientiously planned decisions of the politically engaged. Their responsibility is to act nonetheless, using violence if necessary to create a less violent political system and keeping violence to a minimum consistent with effectiveness.

With such a sense of responsibility, Merleau-Ponty joined a variety of resistance groups. Most were composed of intellectuals like himself. Encountering the primitiveness of their political instincts must have been sobering. Members of "Socialisme et liberté" carelessly transported evidence of their resistance activity in public.[44] Sartre initially spent time outlining a constitution for a postwar government rather than recruiting and organizing.[45] When their meager efforts were stymied by the Communists' rumor that Sartre was a double agent, Merleau-Ponty appears to have drawn three conclusions. First, their group was too isolated to be politically effective. Second, they had only the barest idea of how to conduct themselves in a world where others used guile and force to achieve their goals. And third, the Communists had exercised a sort of political responsibility.[46] They prevented a group of sincere but naïve bumblers from bringing harm to others and to themselves. In the Communists Merleau-Ponty saw many of the virtues lacking among his confrères—deep roots in a social class, careful organization and discipline, an eye for effective action, and a wiliness controlled by firmness of objective. A purposive, calculative, and critical form of thinking supported all their initiatives.

Observing Communists and other resisters, Merleau-Ponty came to a conclusion for which his academic training did not prepare him: there are nonphilosophical intellectual activities that are nonetheless valid forms of *thinking*. Instead of using clear and distinct ideas, political thinkers trade in words made variable by rhetoric and public interpretation. Instead of taking their bearings by inquiry into principle, they plan action by assessments of power. Nonetheless it is undeniable that they use their intelligence to understand the world and to justify choices. Now if political thinking is at times required to secure every value made possible by

---

his colleagues that they too might be in danger of being turned in to the Vichy authorities. Interview with Simone Debout-Oleszkiewicz, February 28, 1981.

[44] Beauvoir, *Prime of Life*, p. 383.
[45] Sartre, "Merleau-Ponty [1]," p. 140.
[46] Ibid.

human association, the standards of philosophy should not be used to disparage it. It is an intellectual activity that is essential in a world of ambiguous meaning where contingent circumstances often threaten the welfare of others.

This sort of activistic thought makes philosophers uneasy. Political thinking demands that one keep in contact with events in ways that inhabitants of the city of ideas rarely do. Readings of social events appear more fallible than abstract schematizations of values, and taking responsibility for choices that impose sacrifices on others is always painful. Political thinkers also leave behind a trail of concrete decisions, which those who never took comparable risks can later easily mock as wrongheaded.[47] Not surprisingly, reasons to put off political thinking are abundant. There is the moralistic posture that condemns all violence. There is the scientism that denies the very existence of choice. There is the ascent to metatheory that settles the parameters of choice but never deigns to make any. There is a voluntarism that imposes choices, but can give no justification for them. There is a scepticism that refuses to choose by criticizing all conceivable choices. But as soon as one realizes, as Merleau-Ponty did in the war, that political thinking must be done and that it will be done—more or less well, by persons more or less sensitive to the horrors of violence—then all of these intellectualizations begin to ring hollow. If they are used to deny political thinking per se, then they turn into mere abdications of responsibility. Merleau-Ponty set out to do political theory in a way that did not deny the importance and dignity of political thinking.

The fact that the theorist appreciates political thinking does not mean that theory dissolves into practice. Theory retains a variety of distinctive functions. It systematizes the nature of political thinking. If those who are directly engaged in politics use particular meanings available in their culture, it is still up to the theorist to show how those meanings define a whole that can form a critical standard against which practice can be measured. Following Machiavelli's example, moreover, theory explains the underlying consequentialism of political thinking and its relationship to violence. The very idea of making a case in favor of political thinking is left to theorists since activists usually proceed more by conviction than by reasoned justification. Theory also explores the foundations of thought and posts warnings before those that cannot

---

[47] Sichère, *Merleau-Ponty*, p. 128.

support political thinking. More given to reflection than the actor, the theorist repeatedly questions the methods and the goals of political practice. Ultimately he calls even his own thinking into question by seeking out the corporeal and cultural roots of that thought. In all of these respects theory both dwells in the world of action and maintains a certain distance from it; it is receptive to acquisitions from its political environment and yet is often critical of them.[48] Existential theory is an inherently dialogical enterprise.

Dialogue, for Merleau-Ponty, is the process through which we explore, respond to, and improve our grasp of whatever enters our field of perception. Through dialogue we carry forth others' intentions and approximate to the best understanding of objects of common concern. For an embodied being, dialogue is the very condition of truth. But not just any exchange of words counts as dialogue. The profoundest lesson of Merleau-Ponty's existential politics is that many assumptions quickly short-circuit a potentially enlightening political discussion. Idealistic assumptions about rationality lead to a form of theorizing that excludes particularistic values and structural evidence. Objectivistic policy sciences and deterministic schemata of revolution make debate seem unnecessary. The sceptical belief that all claims to value and truth are ultimately forms of unreason deters others in advance from seeing the sceptic's assertions as views worthy of acceptance, correction, or refutation.

Significantly, as Merleau-Ponty would be the first to point out, all of these patterns of thought actually presuppose the sorts of claims that they exclude. The theorist of the universality of reason obliviously reasons in ways peculiar to a particular class and country; the objectivist declares certain tasks impossible or unavoidable, in effect arrogating to himself the right to choose what is valuable for all; the sceptic implies the existence of truths and defensible values by his very efforts to convince others of the importance of his work and by his support of emancipatory movements. Merleau-Ponty's purpose in noting the tensions in his interlocutors' views is not to force them to drop claims that violate their primary theses. It is to remind them all that theory misleads as long as it takes only one-sided views of a world that requires multiple perspectives and dialogical exchange. It is to make them recognize that universality and particularity, determinism and choice, non-sense and sense are all intrinsic to human *existence*.

[48] Jung, *The Crisis of Political Understanding*, pp. 12–13.

The challenge we face is then to devise a political theory of exist-ence that comprehends these dichotomies rather than denies them. At stake in such understanding is not only the inclusiveness of our metaphysics, but the wisdom of our political thought and action.

BIBLIOGRAPHY

Part I: Merleau-Ponty's Published Works

Listed here in order of publication date are only those of Merleau-Ponty's works cited in this study. Those interested in a complete bibliography should consult my article, "The Merleau-Ponty Bibliography," as listed below.

"Discours d'usage prononcé par M. Merleau-Ponty." *Bulletin de l'Association Amicale des Anciens Élèves du Lycée Félix Faure* (Beauvais) (July 13, 1932), pp. 20–28.

"Christianisme et ressentiment." *La Vie Intellectuelle* 7:36 (June 10, 1935), pp. 278–306.

Review of *Être et avoir*, by Gabriel Marcel. *La Vie Intellectuelle* 8:55 (October 10, 1936), pp. 98–109.

Review of *L'imagination*, by J.-P. Sartre. *Journal de Psychologie Normale et Pathologique* 33:9–10 (November–December 1936), pp. 756–761.

"L'agrégation de philosophie" (Comments at the May 7, 1938 meeting of the Société Française de Philosophie). *Bulletin de la Société Française de Philosophie* 38:4 (July–August 1938), pp. 130–133.

La structure du comportement. Paris: Presses Universitaires de France, 1942. Translation: *The Structure of Behavior*. Trans. Alden L. Fisher. Boston: Beacon Press, 1963.

Review of *Les mouches*, by J.-P. Sartre. *Confluences* 3:25 (September–October 1943), pp. 514–516.

La phénoménologie de la perception. Paris: Gallimard, 1945. Translation: *The Phenomenology of Perception*. Trans. Colin Smith. London: Routledge and Kegan Paul, 1962.

"Un entretien avec Maurice Merleau-Ponty: Le mouvement philosophique moderne." *Carrefour*, no. 92, May 23, 1946, p. 6.

"Une enquête d'*action*: Faut-il brûler Kafka?" *action*, July 12, 1946, pp. 14–15.

L'esprit européen, Rencontres internationales de Genève, 1946. Neuchâtel: Les Éditions de la Baconnière, 1947, pp. 74–77, 133, 252–256.

"Les cahiers de la Pléiade, avril 1947" *Les Temps Modernes* 3:27 (December 1947), pp. 1151–1152.

"Indochine S.O.S." *Les Temps Modernes* 2:18 (March 1947), pp. 1039–1052.

"Le primat de la perception et ses conséquences philosophiques." *Bulletin de la Société Française de Philosophie* 41 (1947), pp. 119–135 and discussion, pp. 135–153. Translation: *The Primacy of Perception*. Trans. and ed. James Edie. Evanston, IL: Northwestern University Press, 1964.

"En un combat douteux." *Les Temps Modernes* 3:27 (December 1947), pp. 961–964.

Humanisme et terreur: Essai sur le problème communiste. Paris: Gallimard, 1947. Translation: *Humanism and Terror: An Essay on the Communist Problem*. Trans. John O'Neill. Boston: Beacon Press, 1969.

"Le destin de l'individu dans le monde actuel." *Chemins du Monde* 2 (1948), pp. 30–31.

"Note de la rédaction à 'Kravchenko et le problème de l'URSS' par Claude Lefort." *Les Temps Modernes* 3:29 (February 1948), pp. 15–16.

"Le Manifeste Communiste a cent ans." *Le Figaro Littéraire*, April 3, 1948, pp. 1–2.

"Complicité objective." *Les Temps Modernes* 4:34 (July 1948), pp. 1–11.

Sens et non-sens. Paris: Nagel, 1948. Translation: *Sense and Non-Sense*. Trans. Hubert L. Dreyfus and Patricia Allen Dreyfus. Evanston, IL: Northwestern University Press, 1964.

"Présentation de 'Pages de journal de Victor Serge.'" *Les Temps Modernes* 4:44 (June 1949), pp. 973–974.

"Mort d'Emmanuel Mounier." *Les Temps Modernes* 5:54 (April 1950), p. 1906.

"Réponse à C.L.R. James." *Les Temps Modernes* 5:56 (June 1950), pp. 2292–2294.

"L'adversaire est complice." *Les Temps Modernes* 6:57 (July 1950), pp. 1–11.

"Texte de présentation: Collection Les Temps Modernes." On back cover of Edmund Husserl. *Idées directrices pour une phénoménologie*. Trans. Paul Ricoeur. Paris: Gallimard, 1950.

La connaissance de l'homme au XXe siècle, Rencontres Internationales de Genève, 1951. Neuchâtel: Les Éditions de la Baconnière,

1952, pp. 51–75, 182–183, 186, and scattered comments, pp. 210–296.

Éloge de la philosophie et autres essais. Paris: Gallimard, 1953 and 1960. Translation: *In Praise of Philosophy*. Trans. John Wild and James Edie. Evanston, IL: Northwestern University Press, 1963.

Les aventures de la dialectique. Paris: Gallimard, 1955. Translation: *The Adventures of the Dialectic*. Trans. Joseph Bien. Evanston, IL: Northwestern University Press, 1973.

"A quoi sert l'objectivité?" *L'Express*, no. 88, January 29, 1955, p. 4.

"Où va l'anticommunisme?" *L'Express*, no. 109, June 25, 1955, p. 12.

"Discordia Concors: Rencontre Est-Ouest à Venise." *Comprendre: Revue de Politique et de la Culture* (Société Européenne de Culture près de la Biénnale à Venise), no. 17, September 1956. Comments by Merleau-Ponty, pp. 210–213, 214, 216, 217, 226, 227–228, 229, 237, 252–253, 265, 266, 267, 268, 271, 275–276, 278, 284, 285, 286, 287, 295, 296, 297.

"L'avenir du socialisme" (debate directed by Maurice Merleau-Ponty). *Cahiers de la République* 4:22 (November–December 1959), pp. 27–42.

Signes. Paris: Gallimard, 1960. Translation: *Signs*. Trans. Richard C. McCleary. Evanston, IL: Northwestern University Press, 1964.

"Entretien." In Madelaine Chapsal. *Les écrivains en personne*. Paris: Julliard, 1960, pp. 145–163.

"Un entretien avec Maurice-Merleau-Ponty: La philosophie et la politique sont solidaires" (interview with Jean-Paul Weber). *Le Monde*, no. 4961, December 31, 1960, p. 9.

"Réponse à Olivier Todd." *France-Observateur*, March 2, 1961, pp. 17–18.

"Un inédit de Maurice Merleau-Ponty." *Revue de Metaphysique et de Morale* 67:4 (October–December 1962), pp. 401–409.

Le visible et l'invisible, suivi de notes de travail. Texte établi par Claude Lefort. Paris: Gallimard, 1964. Translation: *The Visible and the Invisible*. Trans. Alphonso Lingis. Evanston, IL: Northwestern University Press, 1964.

Maurice Merleau-Ponty à la Sorbonne. Résumé de ses cours établi par des étudiants et approuvé par lui-même. *Bulletin de Psychologie* (November 1964), pp. 109–336.

L'oeil et l'esprit. Paris: Gallimard, 1964. Translation: "The Eye and the Mind." Trans. Carlton Dallery. In *The Primacy of Perception.* Ed. James Edie. Evanston, IL: Northwestern University Press, 1964.

"La philosophie de l'existence." *Dialogue* 4:3 (December 1966), pp. 307–322.

Résumés de cours: Collège de France, 1952–1960. Paris: Gallimard, 1968. Translation: *Themes from the Lectures.* Trans. John O'Neill. Evanston, IL: Northwestern University Press, 1970.

La prose du monde. Texte établi et présenté par Claude Lefort. Paris: Gallimard, 1969. Translation: *The Prose of the World.* Trans. John O'Neill. Evanston, IL: Northwestern University Press, 1973.

"Projet de travail sur la nature de la perception" and "La nature de la perception." In Theodore Geraets. *Vers une nouvelle philosophie transcendentale.* La Haye: Martinus Nijhoff, 1971, pp. 9–10 and 188–199.

"Philosophie et non-philosophie depuis Hegel," I-II. Notes de cours. Texte établi et présenté par Claude Lefort. *Textures,* nos. 8–9 (1974), pp. 83–129, and nos. 10–11 (1975), pp. 145–173. Translation: "Philosophy and Non-philosophy since Hegel." Trans. Hugh J. Silverman. *Telos* 29 (Fall 1976), pp. 39–105.

Part II: Unpublished Sources by Merleau-Ponty

Inédits: Table of contents (Titles in parentheses attributed by KHW)

RADIO INTERVIEWS AND BROADCASTS

"La politique des 'Temps Modernes.' " Radiodiffusion-Télévision Française (RTF), 1947. Neuf émissions confiées à l'équipe de la revue *Les Temps Modernes*. Les six premières ayant été diffusées du 20.11.1947 au 24.11.1947; les trois dernières n'ayant pas été diffusées (Merleau-Ponty participated only in nos. 1, 2, 4, and 5.):

> (1) Le Gaullisme et le RPF; (2) Communisme et anticommunisme; (3) Réponses à des lettres d'auditeurs; (4) Libéralisme et socialisme; (5) La crise du socialisme; (6) Le mouvement syndicale et les conflits sociaux; (7) David Rousset: Retour de l'Allemagne; (8) Deux appels à l'opinion internationale; (9) Le vrai sens des revendications ouvrières.

"Mélanges: Philosophie, Politique, Littérature." Divers entretiens avec Merleau-Ponty enregistrés par la RTF entre 1948 et 1959:

> (1) La liberté [12.46]; (2) Le surréalisme [7.47]; (3) Le monde de la perception, monde classique, monde moderne [10 et 11.48]; (4) L'homme et l'adversité [9.51]; (5) La philosophie [12.52]; (6) Dans la même émission [12.52] et en parallel, Gaston Bachelard sur la philosophie; (7) Sur *Les aventures de la dialectique* [6.55]; (8) G. Bachelard sur la phénoménologie de E. Husserl [4.59]; (9) En parallel sur ce sujet, Maurice Merleau-Ponty [4.59]; (10) Annexe: Évocation de Maurice Merleau-Ponty, par Jean Wahl.

"Douze entretiens avec Maurice Merleau-Ponty." Entretiens avec Georges Charbonnier, enregistrés pour la RTF entre le 25 mai et le 7 août 1959:

> (1) Vocation du philosophe; (2) L'École Normale Supérieure; (3) La revue: *Les Temps Modernes*; (4) *Humanisme et terreur*; (5) *Les aventures de la dialectique*; (6) Le oui et le non du philosophe; (7) L'existentialisme athée; (8) La crise de la pensée réligieuse; (9) L'homme en porte-à-faux; (10) La pensée bloquée; (11) et (12) Les voyages du philosophe.

"Chutes des entretiens avec Merleau-Ponty." Entretiens avec Georges Charbonnier, enregistrés pour la RTF entre le 25 mai et le 7 août 1959:

> (1) L'acharnement du non-philosophe contre la philosophie; (2) Le Marxisme; (3) Littérature contemporaine; (4) La psychana-

lyse; (5) Difficultés personnelles; (6) Les voyages du philosophe; (7) Éléments.

Part III: Secondary Sources

Adorno, Theodor, and Horkheimer, Max. *The Dialectic of Enlightenment*. New York: Herder and Herder, 1972.

Alquié, Ferdinand. "Humanisme surréaliste et humanisme existentialiste." In *L'homme, le monde, l'histoire* (Cahiers du Collège Philosophique, no. 4). Paris: Arthaud, 1948.

———. "Une philosophie de l'ambiguïté: L'existentialisme de Maurice Merleau-Ponty." *Fontaine* 11:59 (April 1947), pp. 47–70.

Althusser, Louis. *Pour Marx*. Paris: François Maspero, 1974.

L'Arc, no. 46: *Merleau-Ponty*. Aix en Provence, 1971.

Archard, David. *Marxism and Existentialism: The Political Philosophy of Sartre and Merleau-Ponty*. Belfast: Blackstaff Press, 1980.

Aron, Raymond. *L'âge des empires ou l'avenir de la France*. Paris: Éditions Défense de la France, 1946.

———. *The Committed Observer: Interviews with Jean-Louis Missika and Dominique Wolton*. Trans. James and Marie McIntosh. Chicago: Regnery Gateway, 1983.

———. *Introduction à la philosophie de l'histoire: Essai sur les limites de l'objectivité dans l'histoire*. Paris: Gallimard, 1948; orig. 1938.

———. *Marxism and the Existentialists*. New York: Harper and Row, 1969.

———. *Mémoires*. Paris: Julliard, 1983.

———. *L'opium des intellectuels*. Paris: Gallimard, 1955.

———. *Polémiques*. Paris: Gallimard, 1955.

———. *Politics and History: Selected Essays*. Trans. and ed. by Meriam Bernheim Conant. New York: Free Press, 1978.

Audry, Colette. "La vie d'un philosophe." *L'Express*, May 11, 1961, pp. 34–35.

Aviniri, Shlomo. *The Social and Political Thought of Karl Marx*. Cambridge: Cambridge University Press, 1968.

Ayer, A. J. *Philosophy in the Twentieth Century*. New York: Random House, 1982.

Barral, Mary Rose. *Merleau-Ponty: The Role of the Body-Subject in Interpersonal Relations*. Pittsburgh: Duquesne University Press, 1965.

Barrat, R. "Un débat sur le matérialisme." *Cahiers du Monde Nouveau* 7 (August–September 1946), pp. 112–115.

Barry, Brian. *The Liberal Theory of Justice*. Oxford: Clarendon Press, 1973.

Bataillon, M. "Éloge prononcé devant l'Assemblée des Professeurs du Collège de France, le 25 juin 1961." *Annuaire du Collège de France*. Paris: Imprimerie Nationale, 1961.

Beauvoir, Simone de. *L'existentialisme et la sagesse des nations*. Paris: Nagel, 1948.

———. *La force des choses, I*. Paris: Gallimard (Folio), 1963.

———. *La force des choses, II*. Paris: Gallimard (Livre de Poche), 1963.

———. *Mémoires d'une jeune fille rangée*. Paris: Gallimard, 1958.

———. *Pour une morale de l'ambiguïté*. Paris: Gallimard, 1947.

———. *The Prime of Life*. Trans. Peter Green. New York: Harper-Colophon, 1962.

———. *Privilèges*. Paris: Gallimard, 1955.

———. *Pyrrhus et Cinéas*. Paris: Gallimard, 1945.

Berl, Emmanuel. *À contretemps*. Paris: Gallimard, 1969.

———. *La fin de la IIIe République*. Paris: Gallimard, 1968.

———. *De l'innocence*. Paris: Julliard, 1947.

———. "L'innocent et le fantôme." *Revue de Paris* 2 (February 1947), pp. 125–131.

Bernstein, Richard. *The Restructuring of Social and Political Theory*. Philadelphia: University of Pennsylvania Press, 1976.

Bien, Joseph. "Man and the Economic in Merleau-Ponty's Interpretation of Historical Materialism." *Southwestern Journal of Philosophy* 3 (1972), pp. 121–127.

Boschetti, Anna. *Sartre et "Les Temps Modernes": Une enterprise intellectuelle*. Paris: Les Éditions de Minuit, 1985.

Bréhier, Émile. (Listed as "Anon.") Rev. of *Humanisme et terreur*, by Merleau-Ponty. *Revue Philosophique de la France et de l'Étranger* 74 (1949), pp. 490–491.

———. *Transformation de la philosophie française*. Paris: Flammarion, 1950.

Brena, Gian Luigi. *Alla ricerca del Marxismo: Maurice Merleau-Ponty*. Bari: Dedalo Libri, 1977.

Brockelman, P. T. "Sibling Rivalry: The Early Marx and Some Existentialists." *Philosophy Today* 13 (1969), pp. 250–262.

Brunschvicg, Léon. "Entre savants et philosophes." *Annales de l'Université de Paris* 5:4 (July–August 1930), pp. 313–327.

———. "Les fonctions de la raison." *Bulletin de la Société Française de Philosophie* 10–11 (1910), pp. 123–128.

———. "Histoire et philosophie." *Annales de l'Université de Paris* (1953), pp. 203–211.

———. *Le progrès de la conscience dans la philosophie occidentale*. Paris: Félix Alcan, 1927.

Burnier, Michel-Antoine. *Choice of Action: The French Existentialists on the Political Front Line*. Trans. B. Murchland. New York: Random House, 1968.

Caillois, Roland. "L'ambiguïté de l'histoire et la certitude de la philosophie." *Critique* 77 (1953), pp. 867–874.

———. "Destin de l'humanisme Marxiste." *Critique* 28 (1948), pp. 243–251.

———. "De la perception à l'histoire: La philosophie de Maurice Merleau-Ponty." *Deucalion* 2 (1947), pp. 57–85.

———. Rev. of *Une philosophie de l'ambiguïté*, by A. Waelhens. *Critique* 8:58 (March 1952), pp. 284–286.

Campbell, Robert. "De l'ambiguïté à l'héroisme chez Merleau-Ponty." *Cahiers de Sud* 62:390–391 (October–December 1966), pp. 273–284.

———. "M. Merleau-Ponty et ses lecteurs." *Paru* 37 (December 1947), pp. 49–51.

Capalbo, Creusa. "L'historicité chez Merleau-Ponty." *Revue Philosophique de Louvain* 73 (August 1975), pp. 511–535.

Carr, David. *Phenomenology and the Problem of History: A Study of Husserl's Transcendental Philosophy*. Evanston, IL: Northwestern University Press, 1974.

Caute, David. *Communism and the French Intellectuals, 1914–1960*. London: André Deutsch, 1964.

Centineo, Ettore. *Una fenomenologia della storia: L'esistenzialismo di M. Merleau-Ponty*. Palermo: Capucci e Figli, 1959.

Chapsal, Madelaine. *Les écrivains en personne*. Paris: Julliard, 1960.

Chenu, Joseph. "Une philosophie humaine." *Le Monde Français* 14 (November 1946), pp. 499–510.

Christianus. "Saint Antigone." *La Vie Intellectuelle* 15:1 (January 1947), pp. 1–4.

Clark, Simon. *The Foundations of Structuralism: A Critique of Lévi-Strauss and the Structuralist Movement*. Totowa, NJ: Barnes and Noble, 1981.

Cohen, G. A. *Karl Marx's Theory of History: A Defence*. Princeton: Princeton University Press, 1978.

Cohen, Stephen. *Bukharin and the Bolshevik Revolution*. New York: A. A. Knopf, 1973.

Cohen-Solal, Annie. *Sartre*. Paris: Gallimard, 1985.

Connolly, William. "Taylor, Foucault, and Otherness." *Political Theory* 13:3 (August 1985), pp. 377–385.

———. *The Terms of Political Discourse*. Princeton: Princeton University Press, 1983.

Contat, Michel, and Rybalka, Michel. *Les écrits de Sartre: Chronologie, bibliographie commentée*. Paris: Gallimard, 1970.

Cooper, Barry. "Hegelian Elements in Merleau-Ponty's *La structure du comportement*." *International Philosophical Quarterly* 15 (December 1975), pp. 411–423.

———. *Merleau-Ponty and Marxism: From Terror to Reform*. Toronto: University of Toronto Press, 1979.

Cotta, Sergio. *Why Violence? A Philosophical Interpretation*. Trans. G. Gallace. Gainesville: University of Florida Press, 1985.

Curtis, Michael. *Three Against the Third Republic*. Princeton: Princeton University Press, 1959.

Cuzin, François. Rev. of *La structure du comportement*, by Merleau-Ponty. *Confluences* 3:19 (April–May 1943), pp. 460–463.

Dallmayr, Fred R. *Beyond Dogma and Despair: Toward a Critical Phenomenology of Politics*. Notre Dame: Notre Dame University Press, 1981.

Daniels, Norman, ed. *Reading Rawls*. New York: Basic Books, 1976.

Dauenhauer, Bernard. "One Central Link between Merleau-Ponty's Philosophy of Language and His Political Thought." *Tulane Studies in Philosophy* 29 (1980), pp. 57–80.

Desanti, Dominique. *Les Staliniens (1944–1956): Une expérience politique*. Paris: Fayard, 1975.

Desanti, Jean-Toussaint. "Hegel, est-il le père de l'existentialisme?" *La Nouvelle Critique* 56 (June 1954), pp. 91–109.

———. "Merleau-Ponty et la décomposition de l'idéalisme." *La Nouvelle Critique* 4:37 (June 1952), pp. 63–82.

———. "Le philosophe et le prolétaire." *La Nouvelle Critique* 1:1 (1948), pp. 26–36.

———. *Le philosophe et les pouvoirs*. Paris: Calmann-Lévy, 1976.

———. "Sur les intellectuels et le communisme." *La Nouvelle Critique* 76 (June 1956), pp. 92–102, and 77 (July–August 1956), pp. 90–101.

Descartes, René. *Oeuvres philosophiques*. Ed. F. Alquié. Paris: Éditions Garnier, 1963.

Deschoux, M. *La philosophie de Léon Brunschvicg*. Paris: Presses Universitaires de France, 1949.

Descombes, Vincent. *Modern French Philosophy*. Trans. L. Scott-Fox and J. M. Harding. Cambridge: Cambridge University Press, 1980.

Desgraupes, Pierre. "À propos du 'phénomène Koestler.' " *Fontaine* 60 (May 1947), pp. 112–130.

Dreyfus, Hubert, and Rabinow, Paul. *Michel Foucault: Beyond Structuralism and Hermeneutics*, 2d. ed. Chicago: University of Chicago Press, 1983.

Dufrenne, Mikel. "Comment voir l'histoire?" *Esprit* 6 (June 1982), pp. 45–52.

———. *Jalons*. The Hague: Martinus Nijhoff, 1966.

———. "Maurice Merleau-Ponty." *Les Études Philosophiques* 36:1 (January–March 1962), pp. 81–92.

Dufrenne, Mikel, and Ricoeur, Paul. *Karl Jaspers et la philosophie de l'existence*. Paris: Seuil, 1947.

Duvignaud, Jean. "Merleau-Ponty: Une méditation interrompue." *Tendances* 11–12 (June–August 1961), pp. 433–440.

———. Rev. of *La Revue Internationale*. *La Pensée* 13 (July–August 1947), pp. 114–116.

Edie, James. Rev. of *Humanism and Terror*, by Merleau-Ponty, trans. John O'Neill. *Journal of Value Inquiry* 4:4 (Winter 1970), pp. 314–320.

Embree, Lester E., ed. *Life-World and Consciousness: Essays for Aron Gurwitsch*. Evanston, IL: Northwestern University Press, 1972.

Eslin, J.-C. "Critique de l'humanisme vertueux." *Esprit* 6 (June 1982), pp. 7–20.

Farber, Marvin, ed. *Philosophic Thought in France and the United States*. Albany: State University of New York Press, 1950.

Fessard, Gaston. "Deux interprètes de Hegel: Jean Hyppolite et Alexandre Kojève." *Études* (December 1947), pp. 369–371.

———. "Existentialisme et Marxisme au Collège Philosophique." *Études* 252 (1947), pp. 399–401.

Fetscher, Iring. "Der Marxismus im Spiegel der französischen Philosophie." *Marxismus-Studien* 1 (1954), pp. 173–213.

Forest, André. "Études critiques: Philosophie." *Revue Thomiste* 46:2 (May–August 1946), pp. 403–406.

Foucault, Michel. *The Foucault Reader*. Ed. Paul Rabinow. Trans. D.F. Bouchard and S. Simon. New York: Pantheon, 1984.

———. *The History of Sexuality: Vol. 1, An Introduction*. Trans. Robert Hurley. New York: Pantheon Books, 1978.

———. *Language, Countermemory, and Practice*. Ed. D. F. Bouchard. Oxford: Basil Blackwell, 1977.

Foucault, Michel. *Power/Knowledge*. Ed. Colin Gordon. New York: Pantheon, 1980.

Freund, Julian. *The Sociology of Max Weber*. Trans. Mary Ilford. New York: Pantheon Books, 1968.

Galston, William. *Justice and the Human Good*. Chicago: University of Chicago Press, 1980.

———. Rev. of *Spheres of Justice*, by M. Walzer. *Ethics* 94:2 (January 1984), pp. 329–333.

Gandillac, Maurice de. "In Memoriam: Maurice Merleau-Ponty." *Revue Philosophique de la France et de l'Étranger* 152:1 (January–March 1962), pp. 103–106.

Geraets, Theodore. "Le retour à l'expérience perceptive et le sens du *Primat de la perception*." *Dialogue* 15 (December 1976), pp. 595–607.

———. *Vers une nouvelle philosophie transcendentale: La genèse de la philosophie de Maurice Merleau-Ponty jusqu'à La phénoménologie de la perception*. The Hague: Martinus Nijhoff, 1971.

Geuss, Raymond. *The Idea of a Critical Theory*. Cambridge: Cambridge University Press, 1981.

Gilbert, Alan. "Historical Theory and the Structure of Moral Argument in Marx." *Political Theory* 9:2 (May 1981), pp. 173–206.

Goyard-Fabre, Simone. "Merleau-Ponty et la politique." *Revue de Métaphysique et de Morale* 85:2 (April–June 1980), pp. 240–262.

Grathoff, Richard, and Sprondel, Walter, eds. *Maurice Merleau-Ponty und das Problem der Struktur in den Sozialwissenschaften*. Stuttgart: Enke, 1976.

Green, Michael. "Marx, Utility, and Right." *Political Theory* 11:3 (August 1983), pp. 433–446.

Gurvitch, Georges. *Les tendances actuelles de la philosophie allemande*. Paris: J. Vrin, 1930.

Gurwitsch, Aron. "Quelques aspects et quelques développements de la psychologie de la forme." *Journal de Psychologie Normale et Pathologique* (May–June 1936), pp. 413–471.

———. Rev. of *La phénoménologie de la perception*, by Merleau-Ponty, *Philosophy and Phenomenological Research* 10 (1949–1950), pp. 442–445.

———. *Studies in Phenomenology and Psychology*. Evanston, IL: Northwestern University Press, 1966.

Hamrick, William. "Whitehead and Merleau-Ponty: Some Moral Implications." *Process Studies* 4:4 (Winter 1974), pp. 235–251.

Hanly, C.M.T. "Phenomenology, Consciousness, and Freedom." *Dialogue* 5:3 (1966), pp. 323–345.

Hayman, Ronald. *Sartre: A Biography*. New York: Simon and Schuster, 1987.

Heckman, John. "Hyppolite and the Hegel Revival in France." *Telos* 16 (Summer 1973), pp. 128–145.

Hegel, G.W.F. *The Phenomenology of Mind*. Trans. J. B. Baillie. New York: Harper and Row, 1967.

Heidsieck, François. *L'ontologie de Merleau-Ponty*. Paris: Presses Universitaires de France, 1971.

Hervé, Pierre. "Conscience et connaissance." *Cahiers d'action* 1 (May 1946), pp. 1–9.

———. "Doubles jeux." *action*, March 30, 1945, p. 3.

———. "Sommes-nous tous des coquins?" *action*, February 15, 1946, p. 3.

Howard, Dick. *The Marxian Legacy*. New York: Urizen Books, 1977.

Hughes, H. Stuart. *The Obstructed Path: French Social Thought in the Years of Desperation, 1930–1960*. New York: Harper and Row, 1967.

Hyppolite, Jean. "Existence et dialectique dans la philosophie de Merleau-Ponty." *Les Temps Modernes* 184–185 (October 1961), pp. 228–244.

———. *Figures de la pensée philosophique*. Paris: Presses Universitaires de France, 1971.

———. *Genèse et structure de la Phénoménologie de l'esprit de Hegel*. Paris: Éditions Montaigne, 1946.

———. "Notices: Maurice Merleau-Ponty." *Association Amicale des Anciens Élèves de l'École Normale Supérieure* (1962), pp. 54–55.

Invitto, Giovanni. *Merleau-Ponty politico: L'eresia programmatica*. Rome: Lacaita, 1971.

Jeanson, Francis. *Le problème morale et la pensée de Sartre*. Paris: Éditions du Myrte, 1947.

Jung, Hwa Yol. *The Crisis of Political Understanding: A Phenomenological Perspective in the Conduct of Political Inquiry*. Pittsburgh: Duquesne University Press, 1979.

Kant, Immanuel. *Foundations of the Metaphysics of Morals*. Trans. L. W. Beck. New York: Bobbs-Merrill Co., 1959.

King, Jonathan. "Philosophy and Experience: French Intellectuals in the Second World War." *Journal of European Studies* 1:3 (September 1971), pp. 198–212.

Koestler, Arthur. "Arthur Koestler s'explique: Interview avec Jean Duché." *Le Littéraire*, October 26, 1946, p. 2.

———. *Darkness at Noon*. New York: Bantam Modern Classic Edition, 1968.

Koestler, Arthur. "Darkness at Noon Again: An Interview." *Survey* 48 (July 1963), pp. 173–174.

———. *The Invisible Writing*. London: Hamish Hamilton, 1954.

———. *The Yogi and the Commissar*. New York: Macmillan Co., 1945.

Kojève, Alexandre. "Hegel, Marx, et le Christianisme." *Critique* 3–4 (August–September 1946), pp. 339–366.

———. *Introduction à la lecture de Hegel*. Paris: Gallimard, 1948.

Kolakowski, L. "Obsolete Therefore Instructive: Review of *Humanism and Terror*, trans. John O'Neill." *New York Review of Books* 15:23 (3 September 1970), pp. 23–25.

Kovaly, Pavel. "Merleau-Ponty and the Problem of Self-Accusations." *Studies in Soviet Thought* 17 (October 1977), pp. 225–241.

Koyré, Alexandre. *Études d'histoire de la pensée philosophique*. Paris: A. Colin, 1961.

———. "Rapport sur l'état des études hégéliennes en France." *Revue d'histoire de la philosophie* 5:2 (April–June 1931), pp. 147–171.

Kruks, Sonia. *The Political Philosophy of Merleau-Ponty*. Sussex: Harvester Press, 1981.

Kuhn, Helmut. "Existenzialismus und Marxismus: Zu Merleau-Pontys Philosophie der Zweideutigkeit." *Philosophisches Jahrbuch* 62 (1953), pp. 327–346.

Kwant, Remigius C. *The Phenomenological Philosophy of Merleau-Ponty*. Pittsburgh: Duquesne University Press, 1963.

Lablénie, Edmond. *Aspect de la Résistance*. Bordeaux: Taffard, 1969.

Lacouture, Jean. *André Malraux: Une vie dans le siècle*. Paris: Seuil, 1973.

Lagueux, Maurice. "Merleau-Ponty et la linguistique de Saussure." *Dialogue* 4:3 (December 1965), pp. 351–365.

———. "Y a-t-il une philosophie de l'histoire chez Merleau-Ponty?" *Dialogue* 5 (1966), pp. 404–417.

Langan, Thomas. *Merleau-Ponty's Critique of Reason*. New Haven: Yale University Press, 1966.

Lauth, Reinhard. "Versuche einer existentialistischen Wertlehre in der französischen Philosophie der Gegenwart." *Zeitschrift für philosophische Forschung* 10:2 (1956), pp. 245–286.

Lavelle, Louis. *La philosophie française entre les deux guerres*. Paris: Aubier, 1942.

Leenhardt, Roger. *Les yeux ouverts: Entretiens avec Jean Lacouture*. Paris: Seuil, 1979.

Lefebvre, Henri. "Existentialisme et Marxisme: Réponse à une mise au point." *action*, June 8, 1945, p. 8.

Lefort, Claude. Editor's Preface. In *The Prose of the World*, by Maurice Merleau-Ponty. Trans. John O'Neill. Evanston, IL: Northwestern University Press, 1973.

———. Introduction. In *Humanisme et terreur*, by Maurice Merleau-Ponty. Paris: Gallimard, 1980.

———. "Le Marxisme et Sartre." *Les Temps Modernes*. 8:89 (March 1953), pp. 1541–1570.

———. "Maurice Merleau-Ponty." *Le Figaro Littéraire*, May 13, 1961, p. 13.

———. "Penser les rapports de l'homme avec l'Être." *Le Monde*, May 2, 1981 , p. 20.

———. *Sur une colonne absente: Écrits autour de Merleau-Ponty*. Paris: Gallimard, 1978.

Lenin, V. I. *State and Revolution*. New York: International Publishers, 1974.

Lichtheim, George. *Marxism in Modern France*. New York: Columbia University Press, 1966.

Lukacs, Georges. *Existentialisme ou Marxisme?* Paris: Nagel, 1948.

Lukacs, Georges; Cogniot, Georges; Garaudy, Roger; Lefebvre, Henri; Desanti, J.-T.; Caeving, Maurice; Leduc, Victor. *Mésaventures de l'antimarxisme: Les malheurs de Merleau-Ponty*. Paris: Éditions Sociales, 1956.

Lukes, Steven. *Marxism and Morality*. Oxford: Clarendon Press, 1985.

Macquarrie, John. *Existentialism*. Philadelphia: Westminster Press, 1972.

Madison, Gary. *The Phenomenology of Merleau-Ponty: A Search for the Limits of Consciousness*. Athens, OH: Ohio University Press, 1981.

Mallin, Samuel B. *Merleau-Ponty's Philosophy*. New Haven: Yale University Press, 1979.

Marcel, Gabriel. *Being and Having*. Trans. K. Farrer. New York: Harper, 1965.

Maritain, Jacques. *Carnet de notes*. Paris: Desclée de Brouwer, 1965.

Marković, Mihailo. "Marxism as Political Philosophy." In *Political Theory and Political Commentary*, ed. Melvin Richter. Princeton: Princeton University Press, 1980.

Marx, Karl, and Engels, Friedrich. *The Marx-Engels Reader*, 2d edition. Ed. Robert C. Tucker. New York: W. W. Norton and Co., 1978.

Mauriac, François. "Le philosophe et l'Indochine." *Le Figaro*, February 4, 1947, p. 1.

McBride, William, and Schrag, Calvin, eds. *Phenomenology in a Pluralist Context*. Albany: State University of New York Press, 1983.

Meyer, Rudolf. "Merleau-Ponty und das Schicksal des französischen Existentialismus." *Philosophische Rundschau* 5:3–4 (1955), pp. 129–165.

Miller, James. *History and Human Existence: From Marx to Merleau-Ponty*. Berkeley: University of California Press, 1979.

———. "Merleau-Ponty's Marxism: Between Phenomenology and the Hegelian Absolute." *History and Theory* 15:2 (1976), p. 109–132.

Monnerot, Jules. "Liquidation et justification." *La Nef* 4 (February 27, 1947), pp. 8–19.

Mounier, Emmanuel. *Introduction aux existentialismes*. Paris: Gallimard, 1962.

———. "Le message des 'Temps Modernes' et le néo-stoïcisme." *Esprit* 13 (December 1, 1945), pp. 957–963.

———. *Le personnalisme*. Paris: Presses Universitaires de France, 1949.

Mounin, Georges. "Position de l'existentialisme." *Cahiers d'action* 1 (May 1946), pp. 32–37.

Muniz de Rezende, Antonio. "Le point de départ chez Merleau-Ponty." *Revue Philosophique de Louvain* 73 (August 1975), pp. 451–480.

Nadeau, Maurice. "MM. Aron, Merleau-Ponty, et les intellectuels." *Les Lettres Nouvelles* 3:78 (June 1955), pp. 892–903.

Naville, Pierre. *Les conditions de la liberté*. Paris: Saggitaire, 1947.

Olafson, Frederick A. "Existentialism, Marxism, and Historical Justification." *Ethics* 65 (January 1955), pp. 126–134.

O'Neill, John. *Perception, Expression, and History: The Social Phenomenology of Maurice Merleau-Ponty*. Evanston, IL: Northwestern University Press, 1970.

Panaccio, Claude. "Structure et signification dans l'oeuvre de Merleau-Ponty." *Dialogue* 9:3 (1970), pp. 374–380.

Parain, Brice. "Querelle de Khâgneux." *Monde Nouveau-Paru* 11:92 (September 1955), pp. 44–51.

Pariente, J.-C. "Lecture de Merleau-Ponty." *Critique* 186 (November 1962), pp. 957–974 and 197 (December 1962), pp. 1067–1078.

Parkin, Frank. *Marxism and Class Theory: A Bourgeois Critique*. New York: Columbia University Press, 1979.

Patri, Aimé. Rev. of *Humanisme et terreur*, by Merleau-Ponty. *Paru* 42 (May 1948), pp. 61–62.

Patri, Aimé. "Vue d'ensemble sur l'existentialisme." *Paru* 26 (January 1947), pp. 60–66.

Pax, Clyde. "Merleau-Ponty and the Truth of History." *Man and World* 6 (September 1973), pp. 270–279.

Philp, Mark. "Foucault on Power: A Problem in Radical Translation?" *Political Theory* 11:1 (February 1983), pp. 29–52.

Piccone, Paul. "Phenomenological Marxism." *Telos* 9 (1971), pp. 3–31.

Pierce, Roy. *Contemporary French Political Thought*. New York: Oxford University Press, 1966.

Pompeo-Faracovi, Ornella. *Il Marxisme francese contemporaneo fra dialettica et struttura, 1945–1968*. Milano: Feltrinelli, 1972.

Poster, Mark. *Existential Marxism in Postwar France: From Sartre to Althusser*. Princeton: Princeton University Press, 1975.

———. *Foucault, Marxism, and History: Mode of Production versus Mode of Information*. Cambridge: Polity Press, 1984.

Poulantzas, Nicos. *Political Power and Social Classes*. London: New Left Books, 1973.

Rabil, Albert, Jr. *Merleau-Ponty: Existentialist of the Social World*. New York: Columbia University Press, 1967.

Rauch, R. William, Jr. *Politics and Belief in Contemporary France: Emmanuel Mounier and Christian Democracy, 1932–1950*. The Hague: Martinus Nijhoff, 1972.

Rawls, John. *A Theory of Justice*. Cambridge, MA: Harvard University Press, 1971.

Regnier, Marcel. "Existentialisme et personnalisme." *Études* 250 (July–August 1946), pp. 134–146.

Rémond, René. *Les catholiques dans la France des années trente*. Paris: Éditions Cana, 1979.

Ricoeur, Paul. *History and Truth*. Trans. C. A. Kelbley. Evanston, IL: Northwestern University Press, 1965.

———. "Hommage à Merleau-Ponty." *Esprit* 29 (June 1961), pp. 1115–1120.

———. "Husserl et le sens de l'histoire." *Revue de Métaphysique et de Morale* 3–4 (July–October 1949), pp. 280–316.

———. "La pensée engagée: Merleau-Ponty." *Esprit* 16 (December 1948), pp. 911–916.

Robinet, André. *Merleau-Ponty: Sa vie, son oeuvre, avec un exposé de sa philosophie*. Paris: Presses Universitaires de France, 1970.

Rorty, Richard. *Philosophy and the Mirror of Nature*. Princeton: Princeton University Press, 1979.

Sallis, John C. "Time, Subjectivity, and *The Phenomenology of Perception*." *Modern Schoolman* 48 (May 1971), pp. 343–358.

——— ed. *Merleau-Ponty: Perception, Structure, Language*. Atlantic Highlands, NJ: Humanities Press, 1981.

Sandel, Michael, ed. *Liberalism and Its Critics*. New York: New York University Press, 1984.

Sartre, Jean-Paul. *The Communists and Peace, with a Reply to Lefort*. Trans. M. Fletcher and P. Berk. New York: Georges Braziller, 1968.

———. *The Emotions: Outline of a Theory*. Trans. Bernard Frechtman. New York: Philosophical Library, 1948.

———. *L'être et le néant*. Paris: Gallimard, 1943.

———. *L'existentialisme est un humanisme*. Paris: Nagel, 1946.

———. *Huis clos, suivi de Les mouches*. Paris: Gallimard, 1947.

———. "Merleau-Ponty [1]." Trans. William Hamrick. *Journal of the British Society for Phenomenology* 15:2 (May 1984), pp. 128–154.

———. "Merleau-Ponty vivant." *Les Temps Modernes* 17:184–185 (October 1961), pp. 304–376.

———. *La nausée*. Paris: Gallimard, 1938.

———. "Présentation." *Les Temps Modernes* 1:1 (October 1945), pp. 1–21.

———. "À propos de l'existentialisme: Mise au point." *action*, December 29, 1944, p. 11.

———. *Qu'est-ce que la littérature?* Paris: Gallimard, 1948.

———. *Situations III*. Paris: Gallimard, 1949.

Saussure, Ferdinand de. *Cours de linguistique générale*. Paris: Payot, 1964.

Schalk, David A. *The Spectrum of Political Engagement: Mounier, Benda, Nizan, Brassillach, Sartre*. Princeton: Princeton University Press, 1979.

Scheler, Max. *Man's Place in Nature*. Trans. Hans Meyerhoff. Boston: Beacon Press, 1961.

Schilpp, Paul, and Lewis, Hahn, eds. *The Philosophy of Gabriel Marcel*. LaSalle, IL: Open Court, 1964.

Schmidt, James. "Lordship and Bondage in Merleau-Ponty and Sartre." *Political Theory* 7:2 (May 1979), pp. 201–227.

————. *Maurice Merleau-Ponty: Between Phenomenology and Structuralism*. New York: St. Martin's Press, 1985.

————. "Maurice Merleau-Ponty: Politics, Phenomenology, and Ontology." *Human Studies* 6:3 (1983), pp. 295–308.

————. Rev. of *The Adventures of the Dialectic*, by Merleau-Ponty, trans. Joseph Bien. *Philosophy of the Social Sciences* 5 (December 1975), pp. 463–478.

Schorske, Carl. *Fin de Siècle Vienna*. New York: Vintage Books, 1981.

Schrader, George. "The Philosophy of Existence." In *The Philosophy of Kant and Our Modern World*, ed. C. W. Hendel. New York: Liberal Arts Press, 1957.

Scop, Cecilia. "Paris Letter." *Partisan Review* 14:3 (June 1947), pp. 278–284.

Shapiro, Eleanor M. "Perception and Dialectic." *Human Studies* 1 (July 1978), pp. 245–267.

Sheridan, James F. "On Ontology and Politics: A Polemic." *Dialogue* 7 (December 1968), pp. 449–460.

Shklar, Judith. *Freedom and Independence: A Study of the Political Ideas of Hegel's Phenomenology of Mind*. Cambridge: Cambridge University Press, 1976.

————. *Legalism*. Cambridge, MA: Harvard University Press, 1964.

Sichère, Bernard. *Merleau-Ponty ou le corps de la philosophie*. Paris: Bernard Grasset, 1982.

Silverman, Hugh; Sallis, John; and Seebohm, Thomas, eds. *Continental Philosophy in America*. Pittsburgh: Duquesne University Press, 1983.

Silverman, Hugh J. "Re-reading Merleau-Ponty." *Telos* 29 (Fall 1976), pp. 106–129.

Siritzky, Serge, and Roth, Françoise. *Le roman de L'Express*. Paris: Atelier Marcel Jullian, 1979.

Somerville, John. "Violence, Politics, and Morality." *Philosophy and Phenomenological Research* 32 (December 1971), pp. 241–249.

Spiegelberg, Herbert. *The Phenomenological Movement: A Historical Introduction*. The Hague: Martinus Nijhoff, 1960.

Spurling, Laurie. *Phenomenology and the Social World: The Philosophy of Merleau-Ponty and Its Relation to the Social Sciences*. London: Routledge and Kegan Paul, 1972.

Stojanovic, Svetozar. "An Ideology of 'Objective Meaning' and 'Objective Responsibility.' " In *From Contract to Community: Political Theory at the Crossroads*, ed. Fred. R. Dallmayr. New York: M. Dekker, 1978.

Suffert, Georges. "Chronique: Maurice Merleau-Ponty." *Les Cahiers de la République* 33 (June 1961), pp. 81–82.

Taylor, Charles. "Foucault on Freedom and Truth." *Political Theory* 12:2 (May 1984), pp. 152–183.

Tilliette, Xavier. "Une philosophie sans absolu: Maurice Merleau-Ponty, 1908–1961." *Études* (1961), pp. 215–219.

Todd, Olivier. "Nizan et ses croque-morts." *France-Observateur*, February 23, 1961, pp. 15–16.

Trotsky, Leon. *Their Morals and Ours*. New York: Pioneer Publishers, 1942.

Tucker, Robert C., and Cohen, Stephen, eds. *The Great Purge Trial*. New York: Grosset and Dunlap, 1965.

Van Breda, H. L. "Maurice Merleau-Ponty et les Archives-Husserl à Louvain." *Revue de Métaphysique et de Morale* 67:4 (October–December 1962), pp. 410–430.

Viano, Carlo. "Esistenzialismo ed umanesimo in Maurice Merleau-Ponty." *Rivista di filosofia* 64:1 (January 1953), pp. 39–60.

Waelhens, Alphonse de. "De la phénoménologie à l'existentialisme." In *Le choix, le monde, l'existence* (Cahiers du Collège Philosophique). Paris: Artaud, 1947.

———. *Une philosophie de l'ambiguïté: L'existentialisme de Maurice Merleau-Ponty*. Louvain: Publications Universitaires de Louvain, 1951.

Wahl, Jean. "À propos d'une conférence de Maurice Merleau-Ponty sur les aspects politiques et sociaux de l'existentialisme." *Fontaine* 9:51 (April 1946), pp. 678–679.

Walzer, Michael. *Interpretation and Social Criticism*. Cambridge, MA: Harvard University Press, 1987.

———. "Philosophy and Democracy." *Political Theory* 9:3 (August, 1981), pp. 379–400.

———. "Political Action: The Problem of Dirty Hands." In *War and Moral Responsibility*. Eds. M. Cohen, T. Nagel, and T. Scanlon. Princeton: Princeton University Press, 1974.

———. *Spheres of Justice*. New York: Basic Books, 1983.

Warren, Scott. *The Emergence of Dialectical Theory*. Chicago: University of Chicago Press, 1984.

Weber, Max. *The Protestant Ethic and the Spirit of Capitalism*. Trans. Talcott Parsons. New York: Charles Scribner's Sons, 1958.

Weyembergh, Maurice. "Merleau-Ponty et Camus: *Humanisme et terreur* et 'Ni victimes, ni bourreaux.'" *Annales de l'Institut de Philosophie* (1971), pp. 53–99.

White, Hayden. "Foucault Decoded: Notes from Underground." *History and Theory* 12:1 (1973), pp. 23–54.

Whiteside, Kerry. "The Merleau-Ponty Bibiliography: Additions and Corrections." *Journal of the History of Philosophy* 21:2 (April 1983), pp. 195–201.

——. "Perspectivism and Historical Objectivity: Merleau-Ponty's Covert Debate with Raymond Aron." *History and Theory* 25:2 (1986), pp. 132–151.

Whitford, Margaret. *Merleau-Ponty's Critique of Sartre's Philosophy.* Lexington, KY: French Forum Monographs, no. 33, 1982.

Wiggins, Osborne P. "Political Responsibility in Merleau-Ponty's *Humanism and Terror.*" *Man and World* 19 (1986), pp. 275–291.

Wilkinson, James D. *The Intellectual Resistance in Europe.* Cambridge, MA: Harvard University Press, 1981.

Williams, Phillip. *Crisis and Compromise.* New York: Anchor Books, 1966.

Winock, Michael. *Histoire politique de la revue "Esprit," 1930–1950.* Paris: Seuil, 1975.

Wolin, Sheldon. "Max Weber: Legitimation, Method, and the Politics of Theory." *Political Theory* 9:3 (1981), pp. 401–424.

Wolin, Sheldon. "Political Theory and Political Commentary." In *Political Theory and Political Education*, ed. Melvin Richter. Princeton: Princeton University Press, 1980.

INDEX

Taylor, Charles, 301
temporality, 39
Temps Modernes, Les (journal), 3, 33, 35, 39, 163–68, 171–73, 182, 194–95, 205, 207, 209, 217–20, 228–30, 238
terror, 135, 138, 142n
Teuber, Andreas, 287n
Third World, 229, 232, 240, 246
Tilliette, Xavier, 229n
Todd, Olivier, 233–34
transcendental method, 23, 24, 43–44, 60, 151–53, 192
Trotsky, Leon and Trotskyism, 31–32, 34, 35, 103n, 122, 125–26, 141–42, 149, 207–10, 219–20, 242
truth: and dialogue, 81, 89, 306; non-phenomenological conceptions of, 30, 216, 245, 263; and praxis, 11, 64, 236, 239, 263; as process of correction, 81, 123–24, 127, 300; public character of, 89, 300–302, 306; structural dependency of, 53, 109, 126, 252
Tucker, Robert C., 180n

understanding, phenomenological, 59, 125, 174–75, 238
utilitarianism, 108, 170, 173, 176, 290

values: creation of, 39, 112, 263; as "incarnated" facts, 25–26, 114–15, 133, 138–39, 262; objectivity of, 129–30, 141, 300–302; perception of, 26–27; structural dependency of, 107, 288, 294. *See also* ethics
Van Breda, H. L., 24n
Vian, Boris, 35
Viano, Carlo, 134n
Vichy regime, 34, 40, 92, 164, 181–86, 190, 303
Vie Intellectuelle, La (journal), 164, 188
violence: and class, 41, 87, 148–49; in

colonialism, 90, 109; defects in Merleau-Ponty's analysis of, 91, 206, 267–68, 298; defined, 87, 90–91; elimination of, 8, 88, 137, 140, 141, 153, 190–91, 201, 267; in Foucault, 296, 301; idealists' failure to conceive of, 77, 83; in liberalism, 107, 109, 250; Merleau-Ponty's early rejection of, 26; as a necessary political means, 116, 139, 141–42, 184, 194, 207, 222, 248, 303–4; as objectification, 7, 28, 83, 87, 90, 134, 204, 222, 267; relation between freedom and, 39, 244; sens of, 136, 138–39, 142, 206, 222. *See also* master and slave dialectic; other people, perception of
Viollis, Andrée, 103n

Wahl, Jean, 21, 83
Walzer, Michael, 8, 206n, 281–88, 292n, 293
war, importance for Merleau-Ponty's theory, 3, 8, 33–35, 39–42, 106, 164, 177, 183, 191, 225, 302–3. *See also* Algerian war; Indochinese war; Korean War; Munich conference; Spanish civil war
Warren, Scott, 7n, 280n
Watson, Stephen, 254, 256n
Weber, Max, 8, 231, 238, 248, 258–59, 261–63, 266, 267
Weyembergh, Maurice, 189n
White, Hayden, 296n
Whitford, Margaret, 11n, 243n
Wiggins, Osborne P., 177n
Wilkinson, James D., 185n
Williams, Phillip, 270n
Winock, Michel, 218n
Wolin, Sheldon, 9–10
work, 29, 74, 86, 95, 145, 161

Zhdanov, Andrei, 196